THE BLUE DEVILS

THE BLUE DEVILS

US NAVY & MARINE CORPS ACES OF WORLD WAR II

MARK STYLING &
BARRETT TILLMAN

First published in Great Britain in 2003 by Osprey Publishing,
Elms Court, Chapel Way, Botley, Oxford OX2 9LP, United Kingdom.
Email: info@ospreypublishing.com

Previously published as Aircraft of the Aces 3: *Wildcat Aces of World War 2,*
Aircraft of the Aces 8: *Corsair Aces of World War 2,* Aircraft of the Aces 10: *Hellcat Aces of World War 2*

A CIP catalogue record for this book is available from the British Library

ISBN 1 84176 735 2

SERIES EDITOR: Tony Holmes
EDITOR: Sally Rawlings
Design by Tony and Stiart Truscott
Index by Alan Thatcher
Scale drawings by Mark Styling
Figure artwork by Mike Chappell
Aircraft profiles by Mark Styling, John Weal, Chris Davey and Keith Fretwell
Additional text by Tony Holmes and Jon Lake
Printed in China through Bookbuilders

03 04 05 06 07 10 9 8 7 6 5 4 3 2 1

FOR A CATALOGUE OF ALL BOOKS PUBLISHED BY OSPREY MILITARY AND AVIATION PLEASE CONTACT:

Osprey Direct UK, P.O. Box 140, Wellingborough, Northants, NN8 2FA, UK
E-mail: info@ospreydirect.co.uk

Osprey Direct USA, c/o MBI Publishing, P.O. Box 1, 729 Prospect Ave, Osceola, WI 54020, USA
E-mail: info@ospreydirectusa.com

www.ospreypublishing.com

FRONT COVER IMAGE: V-16 pilots head out onto the deck in November 1943. Each had an alloted aircraft according to 6-kill ace Ralph Hanks (his was 'white 37' BuNo 08926), and pilots inspected 'their' F6F once a week. Despite this personal attention, he admits that due to deck spotting, pilots rarely flew their own F6Fs, and were not allowed to apply their names to airframes until late in their combat tour. (© Official US Navy Photograph, courtesy of the National Museum of Naval Aviation)

BACK COVER IMAGE: The Okinawan campaign also saw land-based Hellcats in the form of Marine F6F-5Ns taking a toll on Japaneses nocturnal raiders, with two of the pilots in this group shot attaining ace status over the beleaguered island – Maj Bruce Porter, in the middle in the front row, and Capt Walt Sigler, to the former's left. Both pilots were flying with the VMF(N)-542, and both had earlier scored the bulk of their kills in F4U-1s over the Solomons in 1943.

CONTENTS

WILDCAT ACES OF WORLD WAR 2

CORSAIR ACES OF WORLD WAR 2

HELLCAT ACES OF WORLD WAR 2

PRE-WAR NAVAL AVIATION AND EARLY CAMPAIGNS

When the United States Navy went to general quarters in December 1941, its aviation branch was a weapon in transition. The last carrier-based biplanes had barely disappeared, as USS *Yorktown's* (CV-5) fighter squadron had only recently transitioned from Grumman F3F-3s to monoplane F4F-3 Wildcats.

The father of all Wildcats, Grumman's prototype XF4F BuNo 0383 was progressively modified over a period of two years from the date of its first flight on 2 September 1937 until it appeared in a configuration close to that adopted by production F4F-3s in late 1939. This particular shot shows the aircraft in its transitional phase in early 1939 *(via Phil Jarrett)*

The Wildcat was a leading-edge aircraft in its day. Powered by a Pratt & Whitney R-1830-76 radial engine, the F4F-3 was only the third monoplane to enter fleet service in the US Navy. The -3A model, produced in smaller numbers, had the R-1830-90 engine with a single-stage, two-speed, supercharger. Both engines were rated at 1200 horsepower and both aircraft models had 'stiff' (non-folding) wings bearing four Browning .50 cal machine guns.

At the time of Pearl Harbor the Navy had seven carriers in commission, three of which were assigned to the Pacific Fleet in Hawaii. In fact, on 7 December USS *Lexington* (CV-2) was ferrying Marine Corps scout-bombers to Midway while *Enterprise* (CV-6) had just delivered a Marine fighter squadron to Wake Island. *Saratoga* (CV-3), meanwhile, was embarking her air group in San Diego, California, while also loading another Marine fighter unit.

On the East Coast *Yorktown* faced a minor crisis. Her assigned fighter squadron, VF-5, was temporarily on neutrality patrol, so she hastily embarked a *Ranger* (CV-4) squadron – VF-42 – then steamed for the Pacific. *Ranger* herself was the first US carrier laid down as such from the word go, and was unsuited for the vast Pacific Ocean theatre – she spent most of the war with the Atlantic Fleet. Two newer carriers, *Wasp* (CV-7) and *Hornet* (CV-8), were also based on the East Coast, but would eventually fall victim to the Imperial Japanese Navy.

Despite somewhat different aircraft types (*Lexington* still flew Brewster Buffalos rather than Wild-

Newly-received F4F-3s of *Ranger*'s VF-42 taxy for take-off from NAS Norfolk, Virginia, in the spring of 1941. The nearest aircraft is 42-F-8, featuring an aluminum fuselage, green tail and chrome-yellow wings. The BuNo on the vertical stabilizer is 2527, which makes this F4F only the 67th production Wildcat ever built *(via Robert L Lawson)*

cats), each US Navy carrier embarked a well-balanced air group of four squadrons. With the exception of *Ranger* and *Wasp*, which boasted two VF units apiece, each ship carried two squadrons of Douglas SBD-2/3 Dauntlesses, a Douglas TBD-1 Devastator torpedo squadron and an F4F-3/3A 'FitRon' (Fighter Squadron). Nominal strength of each unit was 18 aircraft, plus an SBD for the air group commander, or CAG. Contrary to some accounts, each prewar air group was identified by its ship rather than the carrier's hull number. *Lexington*, for instance, was CV-2; she flew the Lexington Air Group, rather than Air Group Two, but all her squadrons bore that numeral (VB-2, VF-2, VS-2 and VT-2). The first numbered air groups that were not originally affiliated with a particular carrier only appeared in mid-1942.

Bearing early-war markings, VF-72's 'Fox 14' is salvaged after a landing incident at Pungo Airfield, North Carolina. The two-tone grey colour scheme is evident, as is the unusual rendering of the side number – 72F14 – without the usual hyphens separating the squadron number, type and individual aircraft. VF-72 flew from its parent carrier, USS *Wasp*, until she was sunk in September 1942, then fought much of the Solomons campaign from *Hornet*, and ashore on Guadalcanal – the unit's tally for 1942 was 38 kills. Six aces flew with VF-72, but only Ens G L Wrenn scored five victories whilst assigned to the unit *(via Robert L Lawson)*

The Wildcat was still relatively new in fleet service. Barely a year before, in November 1940, Fighting Squadron Four had received the initial batch of production F4F-3s from Grumman's Bethpage, New York, factory. However, by this stage the Royal Navy's Fleet Air Arm (FAA) was already operating its first truly modern fighters – Grumman G-36A export models originally ordered by the French *Aéronavale*. When Germany invaded France in the summer of 1940, the G-36s were delivered to Britain instead, where they were redesignated Martlet Is.

In December 1941 the US Navy possessed nine fighting squadrons ('fighter' was a postwar term) and the Marine Corps four. Of these, one Navy and one Marine unit flew Brewster F2A-3 Buffalos; the rest were either operational with F4F-3s and -3As, or re-equipping with them.

At the time of Pearl Harbor the Navy counted 131 Wildcats in operational squadrons: 103 in the Atlantic Fleet and 29 with the Pacific. Two Marine Corps squadrons in Virginia and one in Hawaii numbered 61 F4Fs, while another two-dozen or so resided in fleet pools and miscellaneous commands. However, the Navy F4F squadrons faced a serious deficit, with only 48 per cent of their authorised aircraft on strength – Grumman production was struggling to catch up with allotments. Ironically, the Marines (long accustomed to taking a back seat) actually showed a surplus, with 112 per cent of authorised strength.

Following an effort of extreme manual dexterity, the lead pilot of this anonymous quartet of F4F-3s has managed to twist both himself and his camera around to record 'his' section proudly stacked up in echelon port formation. Photographed just months prior to the outbreak of war in August 1941, all three Wildcats wear an unusual red cross alongside their national insignia, both on the fuselage and the wings. This marking was applied for joint-service war games staged in Louisiana *(via Phil Jarrett)*

Organization among F4F units was no different from other carrier squadrons. Wildcats were divided into three or four divisions, usually led by the commanding officer, executive officer and flight (operations) officer, respectively. However, by late 1941 a doctrinal shift was gaining momentum in naval fighter circles. Dating from the biplane era, three-aircraft sections and six-aircraft divisions were still employed in most Wildcat and Buffalo squadrons. But combat experience from Europe showed a trend toward two-fighter sections and four-fighter divisions (respectively termed 'elements' and 'flights' in the Army Air Force). The advantage derived from this tactical change was greater flexibility and a net increase in combat effectiveness, for two pair of leaders and wingmen held greater initiative than two trios. In the dynamic, high-speed, world

Directed by a chief petty officer, four 'whitehats' prepare to install the port wing on a VF-3 aircraft. Note the 'Felix the Cat' emblem below the windscreen – employed by various units since 1941, it has remained one of the most enduring insignia in naval aviation. Additional aircraft are stored overhead, attached to the hangar deck roof, above the SBD-2s of VS-3 and TBD-1s of VT-3. Originally based aboard *Saratoga*, these units (with VB-3) also saw combat from other carriers during 1942 *(via Robert L Lawson)*

of aerial combat, section integrity frequently broke down, and a loner caught by a competent pair was likely to be doomed. Eventually, combat would sort out the difference, with the Japanese only following the global trend in mid-1943.

By January 1942 the US Navy and Marine Corps fighting squadrons were very much a mixture of old and new aviators. Most squadron COs and XOs were Naval Academy graduates, career officers of lieutenant or lieutenant commander rank. As a rule, they were at least 3000-hour pilots, usually with experience in a variety of aircraft types. For instance, since 1930 Lt Cdr John S Thach, who led VF-3 within the Saratoga Air Group, had served in patrol squadrons as well as fighters.

Middle-level aviators were generally lieutenants (junior grade) whose collateral duties involved supervising engineering, gunnery, navigation and other departments. However, by far the largest group of pilots within any unit held the rank of ensign. The most junior were recent graduates of NAS Pensacola, but several had as much as three years fleet experience.

Finally, the Navy (and, to a lesser extent, the Marines) possessed a cadre of non-commissioned aviators. Designated naval aviation pilots, or NAPs, the enlisted fliers were already known for a high level of competence and experience. Nearly all were commissioned in the year after Pearl Harbor, and many rose to leadership positions. However, some Annapolis-bred officers never truly adjusted to the situation and failed to make full use of their NAPs' professional skills. The programme expired upon retirement of the last serving NAPs, circa 1970.

Marine Corps F4F squadrons were virtually identical to their Navy counterparts, with one difference. While nearly all Marine aviators were carrier-qualified, no Marine squadrons regularly operated from carriers until late 1944. In part the reason was a scarcity of carriers, which became increasingly scarcer during 1942. But Marine Corps aviation was doctrinally a supporting arm of the infantry – as much as the artillery. Consequently, though several units launched off carrier decks for Guadalcanal and other climes, they flew combat from airfields in direct support of the 'mud Marines'.

A plane captain rides 3-F-19 by elevator up to *Saratoga*'s flight deck in 1941. Other 'Fighting Three' Wildcats are already secured with wheel chocks and tie-downs. At this time the standard complement for carrier fighter squadrons was 18 aircraft and 19 or 20 pilots. However, early combat experience quickly demonstrated a need for more F4Fs, and by the Battle of Midway the number had grown to 27 F4Fs *(via Robert L Lawson)*

Campaigns

The little Grumman's US debut on the wartime stage was inauspicious. Though FAA Martlets had shot down German aircraft as early as Christmas Day 1940, the F4F's first loss in a combat theatre with the US Navy came at friendly hands. *Enterprise* diverted six F4F-3s to Ford Island, Pearl Harbor, on the evening of 7 December, and mixed signals resulted in tragedy. Frightened and shell-shocked anti-aircraft gunners, unaware that friendly aircraft were landing, opened fire on VF-6. In the darkness and confusion, two F4Fs were shot down, and pilots bailed out of two more. Three well-trained aviators died in the shambles. Thus began the

Wildcat's status as a 'first-to-last warrior' in the Pacific arena.

This unusual photograph shows an anonymous F4F-3 taxying into a hidden dispersal somewhere in the Pacific in early 1942. Judging by the vegetation, this shot may have been taken on one of the Hawaiian islands, although exactly where and when remains a mystery. Carved out of the undergrowth, the dirt taxyways lead to individual one-aircraft revetments. The Wildcat in the distance has had camouflage netting hung over it to further hide its position from the air *(via Aeroplane)*

Meanwhile, across the International Date Line on Wake Island, VMF-211 was bleeding the enemy in an action that remains legendary to this day. *Enterprise* had delivered Maj Paul Putnam's squadron only days before, and Wake's garrison 'air force' had hardly settled in when enemy bombers struck. Seven Wildcats were destroyed on the ground, leaving just five to confront the enemy's entire 24th Air Flotilla in the Marshall Islands. Owing to parts shortages, there were never more than four operational F4Fs, and then only briefly. In the next four days the Marine aviators claimed six enemy aircraft – four Mitsubishi G3Ms, later called 'Nells' by Allied intelligence, and a Kawanishi H6K 'Mavis'. Lt David Kliewer and Tech Sgt W J Hamilton shared the first bomber on 9 December, followed by two each on the 10th and 11th for Capt Henry Elrod and Lt C P Davidson, respectively. On that date Lt J F Kinney hit another G3M, which made off trailing smoke. The next day Capt F C Tharin splashed a flying boat

Over the next two weeks VMF-211 worked minor miracles under the direction of Lt Kinney. Cut off from all help, the Marines fought on despite severe shortages of bombs, ammunition and spare parts – even tools. By cannibalising parts from the wrecks, and by constantly improvising, VMF-211 maintained a small, but effective, resistance against enemy air and sea power. Despite dwindling resources – only two F4Fs were flyable at the end – Putnam's squadron sank two ships and claimed eight aircraft. The last aerial combat occurred on the 22nd when Japanese carrier aircraft raided Wake, and Capt H C Freuler led the interception. That mission cost one pilot and both remaining F4Fs. When the enemy seized the island on their second attempt the following morning, aviators and mechanics fought on as infantry.

By then the US Pacific Fleet had regrouped and was able to plan its first tentative steps: a series of hit-and-run raids against enemy bases. On 1 February 'The Big E' launched strikes against Kwajalein Atoll in the Marshalls. After dropping light bombs, VF-6 engaged Mitsubishi A5M 'Claudes' and Lt(jg) W E Rawie shot one down in a head-on pass. It was the first aerial victory for a carrier-based F4F, and was followed by another that afternoon as land-based bombers harried Vice Adm W F Halsey's task force.

This February 1942 action shot shows a VF-3 F4F-3 being given the signal to launch by the deck officer, who is gesturing with his arms outstretched in the foreground. All this is taking place aboard USS *Lexington*, which was steaming 400 miles off Rabaul, New Britain, at the time. 'Fighting Three', capably led by Lt Cdr John S Thach, were about to make naval history by repelling a formation of 17 Mitsubishi G4M 'Betty' bombers sent to sink their temporary home. Two months after this action, 'Lex' lost both her weighty, but near useless, eight in turrets (seen here in the background) during a quick refit, and received 1.1 in quad anti-aircraft guns in their place *(via Aeroplane)*

Simultaneously, the newly-arrived *Yorktown* attempted strikes against bases in the Gilberts. Adverse weather spoiled the effort, but VF-42 nevertheless destroyed a Kawanishi flying boat near the task force that afternoon. However, these early successes were offset by heavy operational losses attributed both to poor weather and aircrew inexperience.

The next operation was also aborted, but, ironically, it produced naval aviation's first hero of the war. *Lexington* was detected by Japanese recce aircraft some 400 miles off Rabaul, New Britain, on 20 February and prepared to 'repel boarders'. A force of 17 Mitsubishi G4M 'Betty' bombers attacked, and were intercepted by Lt Cdr Thach's unit. VF-3's carrier, *Saratoga*, had received torpedo damage and was laid up for repairs, so it had replaced 'Lex's' VF-2, which was converting to F4Fs.

In a drawn-out action that afternoon, 'Fighting Three' splashed all but two of the raiders in exchange for one pilot and two Wildcats. Lt(jg) E H O'Hare found himself positioned to intercept with a wingman whose guns malfunctioned, but he dived in nonetheless. In three gunnery passes he expertly shot three bombers into the sea, mortally damaged another which crashed on its return flight to base, and set another on fire. Credited with five victories in his first combat, he was hailed as the Navy's first ace of the war. Awarded the Medal of Honor, he was immediately promoted two ranks to lieutenant commander and became a unit CO. He would return to combat flying F6F-3 Hellcats in late 1943, and eventually perish soon after in circumstances still not clear to this day.

Described as naval aviation's first hero of the war (he was also its first ace), Lt(jg) Edward 'Butch' O'Hare made headline news following his quick-fire destruction of five 'Betty' bombers out of the 17 sent to attack *Lexington* on 20 February 1942. He only made three passes at the formation, but his aim was well up to the mark, and he was duly awarded the Medal of Honor soon after his return to the carrier

There followed more *Enterprise* raids on Wake (24 February) and Marcus Islands (4 March), capped by a joint *Lexington*-*Yorktown* operation against Lae, New Guinea, on 10 March. Japanese shipping was sunk and damaged, and aerial resistance was marginal. However, the next operation in the same area would provoke an historic clash.

In early May Task Force 17 (*Lexington* and *Yorktown*) entered the Coral Sea, which washed the shores of Australia to the southwest and New Guinea to the northwest. The object was Japanese bases in the Solomon Islands, followed by the interception of an enemy troop convoy bound for Port Moresby, New Guinea. Thus was set into motion the first aircraft carrier duel in history.

On the 4th, Yorktown Air Group struck the naval air base at Tulagi, north of Guadalcanal. Some 14 ships were claimed sunk (actually three were destroyed) against meagre aerial opposition. A VF-42 section heard calls for help from VT-5 and engaged a trio of Mitsubishi F1M 'Pete' floatplanes, claiming all three.

'Butch' O'Hare is congratulated by his skipper, Lt Cdr 'Jimmy' Thach (right). Taken well after the former's Medal of Honor mission off Rabaul, New Britain, this photo was one of many circulated by the Navy at the time. Thach and O'Hare were widely recognised as two of the finest aerial gunners in the Navy before the war, and both men proved their reputations in combat. Thach later became a F4F ace in the Battle of Midway, running his tally to six victories *(via Robert L Lawson)*

The two-day Battle of the Coral Sea began on 7 May, and Task Force 17 had things all its own way. Despite confused scouting reports, a 93-plane strike group from both US carriers found the Japanese covering group built around the light carrier *Shoho*. In a set-piece attack reminiscent of a prewar drill, the carrier was smothered under a rain of bombs and torpedoes as her fighters tried to defend her. The Japanese launched a futile mixture of A5Ms and A6M2s – the first combat between Zeros and Navy F4Fs. The 'Yorktowners' had the best of it, VF-42's Lt Cdr James H Flatley splashing an A5M while Ens Walter A Haas bagged the first A6M kill by a Navy Wildcat pilot. He then added an A5M as well. The F4Fs got away clean, with VF-2 adding a floatplane en route to the target.

However, that same afternoon the Americans came under attack. The enemy covering force, composed of Pearl Harbor veterans *Shokaku* and *Zuikaku*, launched 27 aircraft which went after TF-17 as dusk settled. Thirty F4Fs hunted through the gloom, aided by ship-based radar controllers who gave VF-2's Lt Cdr Paul Ramsey initial contact. The two units destroyed or damaged 11 raiders, losing a Wildcat and a pilot each.

The battle continued the next day as both forces exchanged air strikes. Again *Lexington* and *Yorktown* units strove for a co-ordinated attack, but weather favoured the Japanese, whose carriers steamed under lowering clouds. VF-42 flew close escort on VT-5, keeping up their airspeed by weaving above the sluggish TBDs. Though intercepted by Zeros, *Yorktown's* F4Fs did a good job, fighting at a disadvantage but allowing all the Devestators to escape. Two SBDs were lost, however.

One of the most famous of all F4F photos was taken in Hawaiian waters on 10 April 1942. Flying 'Fox One' is John S Thach, while 'Butch' O'Hare flies formation in F-13. Thach's aircraft bears three rising-sun victory flags and O'Hare's five. On 20 February, when he was credited with downing five 'Bettys', O'Hare flew BuNo 4031, side number F-15 *(via Robert L Lawson)*

Lexington Air Group did not fare as well. Widely dispersed in clouds, tactical cohesion also suffered from the low airspeed flown by the escort leader. With Lt Noel Gayler's F4Fs deprived of any initiative, Zeros shot down three in exchange for one A6M, while the air group commander and another SBD crew were lost. Though *Shokaku* took bomb damage, she survived the day. *Lexington* would not.

Sixty-nine Japanese aircraft found TF-17 under clear skies, opposed by 17 Wildcats and 23 Dauntlesses on low-level anti-torpedo-plane patrol. The F4Fs, fighting by sections and divisions, engaged in a series of interceptions covering miles of ocean and thousands of feet in altitude. Despite optimistic Japanese claims, the F4Fs suffered four losses while the outclassed SBDs lost five. However, US aviators and shipboard gunners accounted for 19 attackers, and probably saved *Yorktown* from additional bomb hits. But *Lexington* was mortally wounded by aerial torpedoes and sank that evening, taking 33 aircraft to the bottom of the Coral Sea.

Both sides learned much from this first battle, especially the fighter units. The F4F's performance disparity with the A6M came as a surprise – the latter was faster, climbed better and turned tighter. Lessons had to be learnt quickly as an even greater battle was just 30 days away.

VF-42 pilots aboard *Yorktown*, 6 February 1942. Front, left to right: B T Macomber, A J Brassfield, R M Plott, W N Leonard, C F Fenton (XO), O Pederson (CO), V F McCormack, W S Woolen, L L Knox. Rear: E D Mattson, R L Wright, H B Gibbs, W W Barnes, J D Baker, E S McCuskey, R G Crommelin, J P Adams, W A Haas. Before Coral Sea, Pederson was 'fleeted up' to air group commander and was succeeded by Fenton as CO *(via Robert L Lawson)*

MIDWAY

The last week in May was a frenetic period for the Pacific Fleet fighting squadrons. Not only were they still absorbing the latest Wildcat model, but they had to prepare for a hasty departure from Pearl Harbor. It was hard enough for *Enterprise's* VF-6 and *Hornet's* untried VF-8 to get to grips with their myriad problems, but *Yorktown's* entire air group had the further strain of a total structural reorganisation while 'Old Yorky' entered dry dock for repairs to her battle damage.

Owing to heavy losses at Coral Sea, most of *Yorktown's* prewar air group was put ashore, replaced by *Saratoga* squadrons. Lt Cdr Thach came aboard with a cadre from VF-3, but the majority of fighter pilots remained from VF-42. They had minimum time to both 'shake out' as a new unit, and learn their new aircraft.

The F4F-4 differed in two respects from the 'dash three': it possessed folding wings, allowing fighter strength to increase to 27 Wildcats per carrier, and its armament was raised from four guns to six. With no increase in power, the new Grumman was slower than its predecessor, with less ammunition. The increase in armament was attributed to a request by the Royal Navy, who wanted greater firepower in the Martlet to allow it to cope with its German and Italian foes. US fighter pilots, accustomed to dealing with less well-armed Japanese aircraft, were not pleased.

'Fighting Six' Wildcats with SBD-3 Dauntlesses ranged on *Enterprise's* flight deck in May 1942. The obvious marking difference from the immediate post-Pearl Harbor period is the return of the national insignia to six positions (top and bottom of both wings), but without the red 'meatball' centre. VF-6 entered the Battle of Midway in June with 27 F4F-4s, the first combat for the six-gun, folding-wing, variant of the Grumman fighter. Naval aviators were widely disappointed in the new version, which proved both heavier and slower, and was equipped with less ammunition than the F4F-3 *(via Robert L Lawson)*

Jimmy Thach spoke for most naval aviators when he said, 'A pilot who cannot hit with four guns will miss with eight'. Therefore, he relied on superior tactics to equalise the Zero's better performance. In the few days available, he trained the squadron in his 'beam defense' method of mutual support. It would shortly become famous as the 'Thach Weave'.

Behind the scenes at CinCPacFleet, one of the most significant intelligence intercepts of the war was being evaluated – American cryptanalysts had detected Adm Isoruko Yamamoto's plan for the capture of Midway Atoll, 1100 miles northwest of Oahu. Thus, Rear Adm Raymond Spruance departed with *Enterprise* and *Hornet* in Task Force 16, while Rear Adm Frank Jack Fletcher remained aboard *Yorktown* with Task Force 17. Three US carriers were committed against four of Vice Adm Chuichi Nagumo's veteran flattops. The greatest battle of the Pacific War to date would determine the fate of Hawaii.

Midway itself was jam packed with Army, Navy and Marine Corps aircraft, including VMF-221. Primarily equipped with the Brewster F2A-3 Buffalo, Maj Floyd Parks' squadron also possessed seven ex-Navy F4F-3s.

The Wildcats were assigned to the squadron's fifth division under Capt John F Carey, as some of his pilots had at least prevuiously flown the type in San Diego. However, there was precious little time to sort out the newly-arrived Grummans before Nagumo launched his first strike at dawn on 4 June.

VMF-221 entered the Battle of Midway with 20 Brewster F2A Buffaloes and seven Wildcats. However, the unit sustained severe losses during the morning of 4 June, with 15 pilots killed and several more wounded. This F4F-3 was shot up by Zeros and barely made it back to Midway, where it was crash-landed by wounded pilot, Capt John F Carey. Ironically, despite the F2A's miserable reputation after Midway, many pilots preferred the Buffalo to the F4F due to it being more responsive, although it was a less stable gun platform *(via Robert L Lawson)*

Alerted by radar, Midway scrambled 25 fighters barely in time to intercept 107 enemy carrier bombers and fighters. In a lopsided 15-minute battle, VMF-221 was cut to pieces, with 15 fighters being lost, including two F4Fs – the Wildcats had got off easier than they might have. Carey's fifth division was denied the chance to fight as a unit, owing to confusion generated by the inbound air raid. Up on CAP at dawn, six of the seven F4Fs patrolled until ordered to land, though two Wildcats did not hear the recall. When the scramble came, another F4F became bogged down in the sand and could not take-off with Carey. Though all six operational F4Fs did engage the enemy, they attacked piecemeal.

The Marine pilots were credited with 10 shootdowns (five by the Wildcats), which seemed to track with the 10 Japanese combat losses. However, Midway's AA gunners apparently did most of the damage, and historian John B Lundstrom has since determined that the fighters got three kills at most. Regardless of the actual score, VMF-221 was now effectively out of the battle.

Northeast of Midway, the two US task forces awaited word of Nagumo's appearance. Once his presence was confirmed, Spruance and Fletcher independently launched deckload strikes from each carrier. However, the F4F's contribution to this phase of the battle was severely limited both by circumstance and fate.

Having seen the capabilities of Japanese air groups a month before, Vice Adm Fletcher's staff retained most of *Yorktown's* fighters for task-force defense. Thach, and five of his pilots, flew close escort to VT-3, while Bombing Three climbed to altitude, hunting Nagumo. The F4Fs were stretching their fuel and their luck almost to breaking point – Thach, for instance, offered to push the escort out to 175 miles.

Meanwhile, *Enterprise* and *Hornet* launched larger escorts for their respective bombers and 'torpeckers', but to little avail. Lt J S Gray, skipper of VF-6, unknowingly tacked onto *Hornet's* TBDs. Unable to communicate with Torpedo Eight, he remained overhead with ten Wildcats, reporting to *Enterprise*, while VT-8 attacked the enemy carriers unescorted and was destroyed. Soon after, VT-6 also

VF-6's 'Fox Seven' takes off from *Enterprise* on 18 May 1942, shortly before the carrier sailed for Midway. One variation on standard markings is the black numeral 'seven' well forward on the fuselage, minus the usual F prefix. Commanded by Lt James S Gray during the battle, VF-6 claimed nine aircraft shot down and two damaged. Only one of 'The Big E's' F4Fs was lost in return – a water landing with the pilot recovered *(via Robert L Lawson)*

went in alone and suffered severe losses. At the same time VF-8's ten Grummans were lost when their CO ran them out of fuel while trying to remain with the longer-ranged SBDs. Two pilots died in water landings.

Only the 'Yorktowners' reached the target intact, Thach's six F4Fs fighting a desperate battle against the odds in order to protect VT-3 from the Japanese interceptors. In the first combat test of the 'Thach Weave', the VF-3 pilots constantly brought guns to bear on Zeros dogging one anothers' tails. Thus negating the opposition's superior performance, the Wildcats tied up part of the Japanese CAP while claiming five kills and two probables for one loss. But the 130-knot TBDs had little chance, and none returned to *Yorktown*.

However, as Thach turned away he witnessed a miracle in the making. Three Japanese carriers were burning themselves to destruction, victims of three SBD squadrons which arrived unhindered at high altitude. Making superb use of a priceless five minutes, the *Enterprise* and *Yorktown* scout-bombers destroyed HIMJS *Akagi, Kaga* and *Soryu*. The battle had completely reversed.

But *Hiryu* remained afloat, with a largely-intact air group. Thanks to reconnaissance by cruiser-based floatplanes, the location of TF-17 was now known to the Japanese, who immediately launched 18 Aichi D3A 'Val' dive bombers, escorted by four Zeros. They were met by a dozen VF-3 Wildcats, which benefited from accurate radar information and a little help from TF-16 fighters. In a frantic few minutes 11 'Vals' went down, including three each credited to Lt(jg)s E S McCuskey and A J Brassfield of VF-3. *Yorktown's* gunners splashed another bomber, but the remainder got through, hitting CV-5 three times. Listing badly, she lost steerageway and went dead in the water.

Hiryu was already preparing another strike: ten Nakajima B5N 'Kate'

Seven F4F-4s of *Hornet's* VF-8 during the Battle of Midway. Individual aircraft numbers appear on the fuselage and in large, non-standard positions high on the engine cowlings. Like most of Hornet Air Group, 'Fighting Eight' put in a disappointing performance during the crucial engagement, claiming just five victories in exchange for 12 aircraft and three pilots lost to all causes. Thus, VF-8 inflicted the least damage on the Japanese while sustaining the highest losses of the three carrier fighter squadrons engaged *(via Robert L Lawson)*

The top-scoring fighter pilot in the Battle of Midway was VF-3's Lt(jg) E Scott McCuskey, a VF-42 veteran. On 4 June 'Doc' McCuskey flew two intercepts, claiming three 'Val' dive bombers and two Zero fighters in defense of *Yorktown*. He thus became the top Navy ace of the first six months of the Pacific War with 6.50 victories. He later added eight more kills flying F6F Hellcats with the new VF-8 from the Essex-class carrier *Bunker Hill* in 1944 *(via Robert L Lawson)*

torpedo planes with six escorts. Zeros were scarce by then, as three had been shot down over *Yorktown*.

The US carriers had also respotted their decks, reinforcing the CAP. Airborne VF-3 pilots recovered aboard *Enterprise*, refuelled and rearmed, and were ready when the second enemy attack arrived. Superb damage control had got *Yorktown* back up to 19 knots in less than three hours, allowing the resumption of air operations. However, some of Thach's pilots were still cranking up their wheels when the 'Kates' descended in high-speed approaches. At a cost of two F4Fs lost to Zeros, VF-3 splashed five 'Kates' and two Zeros, with McCuskey running his one-day total to five. But tragically VF-8's misfortune continued as a *Hornet* pilot was killed by 'friendly' AA fire as well.

Despite a spirited defense, some of the Nakajimas penetrated the CAP and shipboard flak to put two torpedoes into *Yorktown*. It was too much for the carrier to withstand, and Capt Buckmaster ordered 'abandon ship'. Therefore, Vice Adm Fletcher, the senior officer afloat, was effectively out of the battle. He turned over conduct of the battle to Rear Adm Raymond Spruance in TF-16.

Late that afternoon SBDs from *Enterprise* and *Yorktown* found the remains of the Japanese force and quickly sunk *Hiryu*. However, owing to the uncertainty about other enemy carriers in the area, all available F4Fs were retained for CAP. The Wildcat's role in the crucial Battle of Midway was essentially over. When *Yorktown* succumbed to a Japanese submarine at dawn on 7 June 1942, the naval engagement was finally over.

Three new aces were crowned at Midway – Thach (6), McCuskey (6.5) and Brassfield (6.33), joining O'Hare and Lt N A Gayler (5 each). Additionally, VF-3/-42 produced Lt(jg)s W A Haas with 4.83 victories and W N Leonard with four. Therefore, after six months of war the top seven fighter pilots in the US Navy had flown wholly or partly with 'Fighting Three'. During the same period, the five carrier fighter squadrons had claimed 113.5 victories, split the following way:

VF-3	*Lexington, Yorktown*	50.5
VF-42	*Yorktown*	25
VF-2	*Lexington*	17
VF-6	*Enterprise*	16
VF-8	*Hornet*	5

Sadly, when VF-42 was disestablished after Midway, the Navy's most experienced fighter squadron passed into history. However, by this stage the Mitsubishi Zero had been proven beatable. At the end of this first phase of the war, the F4F's exchange rate against the A6M stood at 1.5 to 1. It would remain the high figure for the rest of the year.

GUADALCANAL

Despite the institutional experience gained at Coral Sea and Midway, some F4F squadrons still knew little about the opposition. For example, Lt L H Bauer, the new CO of *Enterprise's* VF-6, later stated that the Zero was an unknown quantity to most of his pilots. In fact, after initial combat in the Solomons, 'Fighting Six' considered removing the outboard machine gun in each wing in order to 'lighten ship' and improve manoeuvrability. This ignorance of the enemy's capabilities saw the carrier fighters begin the first American offensive of the war totally ill-prepared – they paid a high price in men and machines as a result.

Operation *Watchtower* began at dawn on 7 August 1942. Supporting the invasion of Guadalcanal were three PacFleet carriers: *Saratoga, Enterprise* and *Wasp*. They entered combat with 98 fighters, as the nominal complement now was 36 per squadron. *Wasp* had no combat experience, but she had twice delivered RAF Spitfires to Malta earlier in the year, and her air group was night qualified – a rare advantage at the time.

The Japanese command at Rabaul, New Britain, launched 27 'Bettys' and 17 Zeros, plus nine 'Vals' which were to be sacrificed beyond their tactical radius. Of the 18 Wildcats that intercepted from VF-5 and -6, no less than nine were shot down. Five 'Bettys' and two A6Ms went down, plus all the 'Vals', the latter either from combat or fuel exhaustion. Beyond that, however, the VF squadrons lost another six aircraft to various causes, and, in total, six pilots – it remained the F4F's worst ever one-day loss to enemy aircraft. A *Wasp* SBD was also shot down.

In retrospect, the interceptions started poorly and disintegrated rapidly. Too few F4Fs were airborne at the outset – one division was misdirected away from the battle, and others were caught at a tactical disadvantage. Attacked from above, they were defeated in detail. Beyond that, the Americans faced high-quality opponents. The Tainan Air Group boasted most of Japan's top fighter aces at the time – veterans like Petty Officers Saburo Sakai and Horiyoshi Nishizawa, both with many victories to their credit. The fact that the Zero pilots optimistically claimed some 40 kills did nothing to reduce their impact on the American aviators.

Among the most successful F4F pilots during the landings was a warrant officer – Machinist Donald E Runyon of VF-6. Formerly a NAP, the soft-spoken Runyon was widely regarded as one of the finest fighter pilots in the US Navy. He lived up to his reputation with credits for two

The Navy's top F4F ace was Machinist Donald E Runyon, formerly an enlisted pilot, who scored eight aerial victories in three combats during August 1942. On the 7th, the day of the initial Guadalcanal landings, the VF-6 flier claimed two Aichi D3A dive bombers, followed the next day by a Mitsubishi bomber and a Zero. On the 24th, during the Battle of the Eastern Solomons, he destroyed three more Aichis and a Zero. Later commissioned, Runyon returned to combat in 1943-44 and added three more victories flying F6Fs with VF-18 from *Bunker Hill* *(via Robert L Lawson)*

bombers on the 7th and a 'Betty' and a Zero on the 8th. He would shortly become the Navy's leading F4F ace, a distinction he would retain for the remainder of the war.

When Vice Adm Fletcher withdrew his three carriers from the landing area, the Marines ashore were left without air cover. To make matters worse, a strong Japanese surface force pummelled Allied warships that night in the lopsided Battle of Savo Island. Bereft of all support, the transports departed with most of their cargo still aboard. Thus, the 1st Marine Division was left entirely on its own. However, two squadrons were quickly dispatched aboard the escort carrier *Long Island* (CVE-1), which reached a launch position on 20 August. Nineteen Wildcats and a dozen Dauntlesses of VMF-223 and VMSB-232 respectively, landed at Henderson Field, Guadalcanal, that evening. They became the original 'plankowners' of the 'Cactus Air Force'.

Newly-promoted Maj John L Smith had no combat, and little leadership, experience, but he built a winning team in VMF-223. Over the next few days he, and his largely-untried lieutenants, took the measure of their opponents. Smith and his engineering officer, Capt Marion E Carl (a Midway survivor), would become the first major American aces of World War 2. Combined with Lt Col Richard C Mangrum's scout-bombers, they soon began making their presence felt among Japanese units in the Solomon Islands.

The war's third aircraft carrier duel occurred on 24 August, but the land-based Marines also had a role to play. Supported by part of an Army Air Force P-39/P-400 squadron, Smith's pilots fought their first major engagement that afternoon. They intercepted six 'Kate' level bombers, escorted by 15 Zeros, off HIMJS *Ryujo* and, in a frantic, confusing, tussle, shot down seven raiders for the loss of three Wildcats and two pilots. It was an important victory, proving that Marine fighters could more than hold their own. Additionally, in this combat Marion Carl became the first fighter ace of the US Marine Corps – a further 120 others would follow in his slipstream over the next three years.

At sea, Fletcher had detached *Wasp* for refuelling, but retained *Enterprise* and *Saratoga* to meet the first Japanese attempt to reinforce Guadalcanal. The battle turned upon communications, which, if anything favoured Vice Adm Nagumo's force with Coral Sea veterans *Shokaku* and *Zuikaku*. Poor-quality radios conspired with atmospheric conditions to allow an unescorted *Saratoga* strike to sink *Ryujo*, but to miss the greater threat.

Meanwhile, the two Japanese air groups had little difficulty finding their target. Late that afternoon 27 'Vals' and ten Zeros attacked 'The Big E,' fighting their way through no fewer than 53 airborne Wildcats of VF-5 and -6. Initial radar contact was made at some 90 miles – an excellent performance for the equipment – so the Americans had adequate warning. In the race to meet the incoming raid, one division of VF-5 made a record 'pit

Maj John L Smith led VMF-223, the first fighter squadron ashore on Guadalcanal. From 20 August to 16 October, he was credited with 19 kills, while his unit claimed a total of 110. Upon returning to America, Smith was awarded the Medal of Honor as the nation's then top ace. At war's end he remained the second-ranked Wildcat pilot behind Maj Joe Foss. Tough, aggressive and wholly mission-oriented, Smith was regarded as one of the premier unit commanders ever produced by the 'Corps *(via Robert L Lawson)*

Reportedly a VMF-223 aircraft, this F4F-4 remains something of a mystery. It has been described as one of John L Smith's Wildcats, but the significance of the 19 victory flags remains unknown. Even more questionable is the odd rendering of the numeral two, which appears to have been modified from another figure. The early Wildcat squadrons at 'Cactus' usually assigned specific aircraft to individual pilots, but the practise eventually broke down as maintenance and losses dictated otherwise *(via Robert L Lawson)*

stop', refuelling and taking off again in just 11 minutes.

Perhaps the most distinctive form of victory markings applied to Wildcats were VF-6's 'tombstones', which appeared towards the end of their eventful Pacific deployment in September 1942. Each F4F-4 aboard *Enterprise* sported the emblem, with 41 Japanese suns representing the squadron's claims from the Guadalcanal campaign – in truth, records reveal 43 victories from 7 to 24 August. Rather appropriately, the pilot who contributed more than his fair share to this tally, Machinist Donald Runyon, is seen here posing alongside the marking applied to his Wildcat. Three other aces spent time with VF-6 at some point or another during this historic cruise – Lt(jg) F R Register (6.50 kills, also flew with VF-5), AP1/c L P Mankin (5 kills, and also spent time with VF-5) and Lt A O Vorse, Jr, (5 kills, and flew with VF-2 and -3) *(via Robert L Lawson)*

But the situation was compounded early on, largely owing to communications problems. In 1942 the US Navy still lacked enough radio frequencies to handle search, strike and fighter direction tasks independently of one another. Consequently, available channels became crowded, and vital information never reached airborne pilots.

Morever, not all the F4Fs were able to engage, and despite heavy losses, the Japanese aviators exhibited a high degree of professionalism. They hit *Enterprise* three times, inflicting serious damage, and forcing many of her aircraft to recover aboard 'Sara', or to land ashore. Incredibly, a follow-up Japanese strike group came within 50 miles of the US task force and might have finished 'The Big E' off, but inexplicably turned back instead.

The Wildcat pilots submitted claims of 45 'bandits' splashed, while the SBDs and TBFs claimed eight more. Although the actual Japanese losses were nowwhere near as dramatic (Nagumo only launched 37 aircraft in total!), the Americans actually shot down, or mortally damaged, 25 machines – two-thirds of those launched against Fletcher. *Zuikaku*'s entire nine-plane bomber squadron was lost on this mission.

One of the American aviators responsible for the Japanese losses was Donald Runyon, the VF-6 pilot being credited with four victories on 7-8 August. He matched that total again on the 24th, claiming three 'Vals' and a Zero for a total of eight credited victories in just three combats during the month. No carrier pilot would surpass his record for a year-and-a-half. Like many veterans of the 1942 battles, Runyon returned to combat in 1944, adding three more victories to his logbook while flying Hellcats.

The Battle of the Eastern Solomons confirmed many of the lessons first learned at Coral Sea and Midway. The crucial importance of scouting and communications was reinforced, but carrier fighter doctrine had largely matured to its full potential with the F4F. Fighter direction continued improving throughout the year as well, ultimately evolving into the superb system in place by 1944. Additionally, *Enterprise* and *Saratoga* demonstrated flexibility in operating one anothers' Wildcats smoothly and efficiently.

Fighter operations ashore were also functioning with greater efficiency. Thanks to the coastwatchers – Australian or British military and political officers, planters and missionaries – advance warning of Japanese air raids gave land-based Wildcats the 45 minutes they needed to get to altitude. However, the coastwatcher network was hampered in poor weather, when high-flying aircraft could not be seen. The situation improved somewhat in early September with arrival of the Third Defense Battalion's radar set at Henderson Field. This combination of human and electronic early warning was crucial to intercepting inbound raids. And there was seldom a shortage of enemy aircraft: in the three weeks beginning 21

August Japanese land- and carrier-based squadrons attacked the US beach-head ten times, averaging more than 30 aircraft per raid.

With repeated opportunities, Smith and his engineering officer, Capt Marion Carl, quickly became the first triple aces of the US armed forces in World War 2. Despite VMF-223 being reinforced by Maj Robert E Galer's VMF-224 on 30 August, the F4Fs were nearly always outnumbered, even with the addition of the Bell P-39 *Airacobras* of the USAAF's 67th Fighter Squadron. However, the lopsided odds ensured frequent combat for the Marines. For instance, on 26 August Carl was jumped in the landing pattern, cranked up his wheels and engaged the audacious Zero over the beach – his quarry exploded before hundreds of witnesses. His victim was quite possibly Lt Junichi Sasai, a well-regarded leader of the Tainan Kokutai, who had claimed four victories on 7 August alone.

Despite near-constant combat, improvements were steadily made at 'Cactus'. One of the most important was begun in late August when a grassy expanse east of Henderson Field was prepared for operation. Officially designated the 'Fighter Strip' (and later 'Fighter One'), it was commonly called the 'cow pasture' due to its rural nature. Aside from relieving some of the congestion at Henderson, it allowed Wildcat squadrons to operate more independently.

During this same period, 'Cactus' became the unexpected recipient of yet another fighter squadron. On 31 August – a week after the Eastern Solomons carrier duel – *Saratoga* was torpedoed by a Japanese submarine for the second time in eight months. The damage was not severe, but most of the air group went ashore while the big flat-top received repairs. Consequently, Lt Cdr Leroy Simpler's VF-5 rounded out a three-service contingent to 'Cactus Fighter Command'. On 11 September 'Fighting Five' arrived with 24 Wildcats. Five weeks later only four of those aircraft remained. The unit's aces were Mark K Bright, Hayden M Jensen, Carlton B Starkes and John M Wesolowski, who scored their kills whilst mostly flying from Guadalcanal. The Navy's only enlisted ace also emerged from the campaign – Aviation Pilot 1st Class Lee P Mankin, who flew with VF-5 from *Saratoga* and VF-6 from *Enterprise*.

Marine aviators also were also scoring heavily at the same time – VMF-224's CO, Maj Bob Galer, ran his tally into double figures, as did Lt Col Harold 'Indian Joe' Bauer of VMF-212. Bauer, possibly the finest fighter pilot in the Marine Corps, managed several 'guest appearance' missions with -223 prior to his own squadron arriving at Guadalcanal in force. It was an ironic situation, as Carl and Bauer had first encountered one another while flying F3Fs in VMF-1 three years before. A rivalry had soon developed between the two, but was resolved when, in VMF-221 at San Diego in 1941, they had squared off in Brewster F2As and, in Carl's words, 'went at it man to man'. The mock dogfight ended in a draw, with neither pilot gaining an advantage. From that beginning a warm, respectful, friendship emerged.

Bauer's best day came on 3 October when, leading a division in Marion Carl's flight, 'the coach' claimed four Zeros confirmed, with another probably destroyed. Carl, who scored one victory in the same combat, was almost as pleased with his friend's success as Bauer himself.

The next fighter reinforcement took the form of Maj Leonard K 'Duke' Davis' VMF-121, which arrived on 9 October. Launched from the escort carrier *Copahee* (CVE-12), the fresh squadron added 24 much-needed F4Fs to the 'Cactus Air Force'. Davis's executive officer was to become the leading ace not only of the campaign, but of the Marine Corps. Capt Joseph J Foss had connived his way out of a photo squadron into fighters, and immediately began setting records. He claimed his first victory just four days after landing on Guadalcanal, and became an ace five days after that! On 25 October he became the Marines' first ace in a day, credited with five Zeros in two missions.

However, by early October VMF-223 and -224 were largely a spent force, the unrelenting pace of operations resulting in their removal from the theatre, despite there being few replacements to 'step into the breech'. On 12 October Smith left 'The Canal' with 19 victories, and Carl was close behind with 16.5. Four days later Joe Bauer again made his presence felt. USS *McFarland*, an old destroyer that had been converted into a fast transport, arrived at 'Cactus' with much-needed aviation fuel and ordnance. As gasoline was being barged ashore, nine 'Val' dive bombers evaded the F4F CAP, arrived overhead, and immediately attacked. One enemy pilot bombed the barge, which exploded in a geyser of flame – the explosion also inflicted fatal damage on *McFarland*.

At that moment, Bauer was leading VMF-212 into the 'Fighter Strip' following a long ferry flight from Espiritu Santo. Low on fuel, but with full ammunition, 'The Coach' again showed his team how 'the game was played'. He dived into the 'Vals', and working his way from back to front, flamed three in succession. Only a shortage of fuel prevented him from splashing more.

Widely acknowledged as one of the finest aviators of all time, Marion E Carl first gained attention as a fighter pilot. Flying with VMF-221 at Midway and -223 at Guadalcanal, he claimed 16.5 victories in F4Fs and finished as the third-ranking Wildcat ace. He led -223 on its second combat tour, adding two more kills in F4U-1 Corsairs during 1943-44. Following the war, as a lieutenant colonel, Carl established world altitude and speed records, conducted early jet tests aboard carriers, and pioneered Marine Corps helicopters. While a flag officer he flew jet and helicopter missions in Vietnam, retiring as a major general in 1973 *(via Robert L Lawson)*

SANTA CRUZ

The Santa Cruz Islands, which lent their name to the fourth aircraft carrier battle, had no geographic impact upon the Guadalcanal campaign. Lying some 300 miles east of the Solomons, they were so remote from 'Cactus' that they might as well have never pushed up from the ocean floor as far as the hard-pressed USMC pilots were concerned. However, the fleet engagement of 26 October 1942 *was* an integral part of the see-saw contest for control of Henderson Field. The naval-air duel off Santa Cruz was intended by the Japanese to cover a major reinforcement attempt of Guadalcanal. Several postponements by the Japanese 17th Army delayed the overall effort until 25 October. Thus, the stage was set for a new Wildcat squadron's debut in the war's largest theatre.

'Fighting Ten' was part of Air Group Ten, the first such organization committed to combat under a numerical designation instead of a ship's name. However, its home – the *Enterprise*, patched up from her Eastern Solomons damage of late August – was far from new to combat. The skipper of VF-10 was Lt Cdr J H Flatley, who had fought Zeros as a *Yorktown* pilot at Coral Sea. His 'Grim Reapers' boasted 34 Wildcats going into the battle, which finally commenced following preliminary manoeuvring and a false alarm air strike on the evening of the 25th.

Enterprise was teamed with *Hornet*, still flying a hodge-podge air group which included only two of her own squadrons. Her fighter strength comprised 38 F4Fs of VF-72, led by Lt Cdr H G Sanchez. Though both carriers operated independently, overall command rested with Rear Adm T C Kinkaid, riding in 'The Big E'.

Opposing Task Force 61 were four Japanese carriers, again led by Vice Adm Chuichi Nagumo. Santa Cruz would mark his final appearance as a carrier leader; like Kinkaid, he was not an aviator. However, Nagumo was vastly more experienced.

The Santa Cruz odds of four carriers to two represented the greatest disparity that American carrier men would face during the war. The highly-experienced *Shokaku* and *Zuikaku* were joined by the CVLs *Zuiho* and *Junyo*, with the latter operating in the advance force. Nagumo's Zero *hikotais* thus outnumbered the US Navy fighter force, the former boasting 82 Zeros compared with 72 F4F-4s. Unlike the recent Eastern Solomons battle, no land-based fighters were involved, even peripherally.

Each force knew the other's location and launched air strikes almost simultaneously. The Japanese were first off the mark with a co-ordinated 64-machine strike from *Shokaku, Zuikaku* and *Zuiho. Hornet's* first launch included two VF-72 divisions escorting 15 scout-bombers and six torpedo aircraft. A half-hour behind was a smaller *Enterprise* contingent: 11 strike aircraft screened by eight VF-10 Wildcats. About the same time *Hornet's* final contribution departed the task force, again with two VF-72 divisions (short one F4F for a total of seven) escorting 18 bombers.

Still climbing outbound, the Air Group 10 formation was caught low and slow barely 60 miles from TF-61. Nine *Junyo* Zeros, escorting their own strike aircraft, could not resist the temptation. They initiated a surprise attack from above and behind the *Enterprise* group, and played merry hell. One Avenger fell immediately, with two more forced down with heavy damage. Lt John Leppla's division, responsible for protecting the TBFs, was shredded to pieces. Leppla, a *Lexington* Coral Sea veteran, was soon killed, while two of his wingmen were shot down and captured. The sole surviving pilot of the division nursed his battle-damaged fighter for more than three hours before returning to *Enterprise.*

The other F4F division was led by Lt Cdr Flatley, skipper of 'Fighting Ten'. Shrugging off the initial Zero avalanche, his pilots dropped their external tanks, turned into the threat and fought back. Flatley splashed a persistent Japanese fighter then regrouped.

The 'Grim Reapers' of VF-10 pose in front of their impressively decorated scoreboard alongside the island on *Enterprise* at the end of their first tour in February 1943. Entering combat in October 1942, 'The Big E' squadron was instrumental in the carrier battle of Santa Cruz and the later defense of Guadalcanal. Under the gifted leadership of Lt Cdr James H Flatley (front, fifth from left), the first-tour 'Reapers' claimed 43 shootdowns and eventually produced ten aces. One of the few carrier fighter squadrons with three combat tours, VF-10 logged cruises in F6F Hellcats during 1944, again in 'The Big E', and F4U Corsairs from *Intrepid* in 1945 *(via Robert L Lawson)*

This confused shootout resulted in five US losses against four Zeros. A surviving TBF aborted with engine problems before the three remaining Avengers attacked a cruiser, without result. After a Dauntless trio independently near-missed another cruiser, the main *Enterprise* strike had exhausted its weapons, achieving little for their efforts. There was no option but to turn for home.

However, unknown to aviators on either side, two *Enterprise* SBDs had managed to ambush Nagumo by inflicting bomb damage on *Zuiho*. One-quarter of the Japanese flight decks were now out of commission.

Hornet's first strike then came across the same surface force that attracted the *Enterprise* survivors. Both the VB- and VS-8 aircrews had been deprived of a shot at enemy carriers at Midway, and they were determined to tackle the surviving flat-tops. Consequently, the SBDs flew on past the crippled *Zuiho* and pressed on northward, where they were rewarded with a chance of bombing *Shokaku*. VF-72 lost three F4Fs and pilots while protecting the dive bombers from the persistent Japanese CAP, but the Wildcats' sacrifice proved not to be in vain – *Hornet's* Dauntlesses tipped into their 70-degree dives and hit *Shokaku* with three or more bombs, knocking her out of the battle. Additionally, the cruiser *Chikuma* had also been hit, and Sanchez's Wildcats, along with the SBD gunners, splashed at least five Zeros during the running gunfight. The odds against the Americans were rapidly diminishing.

Almost simultaneously 138 Japanese aircraft then began attacking Task Force 61. In addition to his initial strike of 64 aircraft, Nagumo had put up a second group composed of 19 dive bombers, 17 'Kates' and nine Zeros, as well as a third batch of 17 more 'Vals', with a dozen Zero escorts. These strikes would subject *Enterprise* and *Hornet* to the longest sustained air attack experienced by US carriers during the first two years of the war.

Though most of the Japanese squadrons were two hours flying time from TF-16, their staggered launch compressed the effect of their attacks. For almost three hours the US carriers were under actual, or impending, attack from five separate or co-ordinated formations which comprised 57 'Vals', 39 'Kates', 42 Zeros and three reconnaissance aircraft.

Zuikaku's 'Vals' preceded *Shokaku's* 'Kates' in a 20-minute attack that started just before 0900. The 38 airborne Wildcats were too few to deal effectively with 40 attackers, let alone their Zero escorts, and the problem was compounded by poor communications and weather. The first interception was made only 20 miles out when eight VF-72 pilots contacted the 'Vals'. However, the F4Fs were too low to do much good, and they lost three of their number in exchange for a trio of 'Vals'.

Meanwhile, seven 'Vals' got a shot at *Hornet*. Though three splashed, the others made three hits, badly damaging the year-old carrier. Then the torpedo planes arrived. Only one *Hornet* pilot got among the raiders long enough to make a difference. His name was Ens George L Wrenn.

Separated from his leader, Wrenn duelled briefly with the 'Vals' and Zeros, then came across the speedy Nakajima torpedo planes. Joined by two other F4Fs, he shot two 'Kates' into the water. Then, alone, he engaged another pair and claimed their destruction. Finally, low on fuel and ammunition near the task force, he shot the wing off another Nakajima. During the mission Wrenn had tangled with eight hostiles and claimed five, thus becoming *Hornet's* only ace.

Between F4Fs and AA guns, half the 'Kate' assault had been broken up. However, 11 more split to starboard, closing on the damaged carrier. Zeros kept the few available F4Fs off the Nakajimas, which pressed on through the screen's thick flak, and although *Hornet*'s gunners 'splashed' five 'Kates', two got close enough to put torpedoes into her hull. The carrier rapidly lost power and, listing to starboard, stopped dead in the water.

Japanese pressure was unrelenting. Next on the scene were *Shokaku's* dive bombers, which attacked at 1015. It seemed as if a month's production from the Aichi plant had arrived overhead TF-61 all at once as *Enterprise*'s pilots fought D3As from both Japanese large carriers. Noting the abundance of targets, some pilots switched off two or even four of their six guns in order to conserve ammunition. Other problems also arose as drop tanks refused to release, further hindering the F4F-4's performance by gravely restricting the aircraft's manoeuvrability.

VF-10's 'Red Seven' division was led by Lt S W Vejtasa, better known as 'Swede'. A former *Yorktown* SBD pilot, he had joined the 'Grim Reapers' at Flatley's invitation, and immediately went to work. Orbiting the task force, he latched onto a string of 'Vals' headed for *Hornet.* He quickly shot two into the water, while one of his wingmen took care of a third dive-bomber.

Lt Stanley W Vejtasa set a record for Wildcat pilots with seven victories during one mission. On 26 October 1942, during the Santa Cruz engagement, the VF-10 aviator claimed five 'Vals' and two 'Kates', possibly saving *Enterprise* from destruction. Originally a *Yorktown* SBD pilot and a Coral Sea veteran, Vejtasa had been recruited into fighters by Lt Cdr Flatley, then of VF-42. Vejtasa received a well-deserved Navy Cross for his flying and gunnery at Santa Cruz. The significance of the victory flags on this F4F, side number 79, is unknown *(via Robert L Lawson)*

By then *Zuikaku's* 'Kates' had arrived, and Vejtasa tied into them, too. Detaching his second section, he led his wingman to intercept 11 of the speedy torpedo planes as they descended onto *Enterprise.* Chasing the green-painted Nakajimas in and out of clouds was hard enough, without the added danger of having to dodge 'friendly' flak, but Vejtasa persisted. In the next several minutes he rode up close to five B5Ns and sent them burning into the choppy grey waves. Then, out of ammunition, he could only watch in frustration as 'The Big E' was struck by two bombs. The task force then managed to evade *Junyo*'s 'Vals' for 20 minutes in the forenoon hour, low clouds preventing the raiders from concentrating their attacks – most bombs fell amongst *Enterprise*, the battleship *South Dakota* (BB-57) and the light cruiser *San Juan* (CL-54). Between combat, battle damage and fuel loss, 11 of the 17 bombers failed to return to *Junyo.*

However, the prolonged attack had worked against *Hornet*'s returning strike escort. After a long flight out and back, which had seen them lose three of their eight F4Fs, VF-72 pilots now had to shoot their way back home, only to find their ship unable to recover them. Heavily engaged was the division of Lt John S Sutherland, which claimed five kills, including two by Sutherland himself. Whatever the actual results of the Wildcats' attacks, VF-72's third division certainly helped disrupt *Junyo*'s bombing strikes on TF-61.

The last of the Japanese strikes took the form of *Junyo*'s six 'Kates'. Their appearance forced the cruiser *Northampton* (CA-26) to part *Hornet*'s tow line, and her escorting destroyers promptly stood clear. The Japanese leader put his torpedo into the carrier's starboard beam, but was then killed in a barrage of AA fire, along with one of his other crews. But the damage was done. With a 14-degree list, *Hornet* was abandoned, to be finished off by Japanese destroyers patrolling in the area that night.

By the time the surviving fighter pilots got aboard *Enterprise*, it was obvious that the Japanese had won the battle. That evening anxious aviators speculated on the fate of missing squadron-mates. In combat, or on operations, VF-10 and -72 had lost a staggering total of 23 Wildcats and 14 pilots, two of whom were prisoners. Another 10 F4Fs sank with *Hornet*, raising total American losses to 80 aircraft.

In all, TF-61 claimed 115 shootdowns – 67 by the two air groups (56 by F4Fs) and 48 by shipboard gunners. In fact, only 67 Japanese aircraft were actually shot down, John B Lundstrom's analysis concluding that near the US task force, enemy losses were almost evenly divided between fighter action and AA fire. However, another 28 Japanese aircraft ditched, or crashed with battle damage, and four more were lost aboard *Shokaku* and *Zuikaku* – making a total of 99.

In overall fighter comparison, the F4F edged out the Zero 15 to 13, though the figure approached parity if post-combat attrition is counted. The extent of battle damage leading to aircraft losses can never be known precisely, but this rough comparison demonstrates that properly-flown Wildcats were holding their own against the opposition.

Although tactically a Japanese victory, the Battle of Santa Cruz proved futile in the long run. The tenuous American grasp on Guadalcanal remained unchanged, and *Hornet* was the last US carrier sunk by an attack from the air for two years. Furthermore, the Imperial Navy had lost 145 skilled aircrew, including 23 experienced leaders. They were never replaced in kind.

'Cactus' Climax

After the failure of Japan's late-October effort to seize Guadalcanal, American strength gradually increased. Among fighter squadrons, individual replacement pilots trickled in to fill the gaps within battle-weary frontline units like VMF-121 and -223. Meanwhile, Maj Paul J Fontana's newly-arrived VMF-112 observed Armistice Day by claiming three bombers and two Zeros. They added nine more the next day, as the last crisis loomed at Guadalcanal.

Overlooked in most histories of the 'Cactus Air Force' is the contribution of VMO-251. Ostensibly an observation squadron, Maj John Hart's unit flew F4F-4s, as well as the 'dash seven' photo-recce variants. On 11 November the squadron's pilots, on detached duty to 'Cactus', began shooting down enemy aircraft, the first two being a Zero and a bomber credited to Maj W R Campbell and 1st Lt H A Peters.

Beginning 12 November, the Japanese launched a four-day effort to reinforce the island. Nineteen torpedo-armed 'Bettys' went for US shipping which was unloading off Kukum Point, and the attack was broken up by 15 Wildcats, plus some Army Air Force fighters. Seventeen of the land-attack bombers, plus five Zeros, fell to fighters and flak, mostly accountable to VMF-112 and -121. The low-level combat cost three F4Fs, but the transports continued disembarking troops.

Bearing a black number 29, this VMF-121 F4F-4 taxies on Guadalcanal's pierced-steel matting in November 1942. By that time the squadron had been at 'Cactus' for almost a month. The facility is probably Henderson Field, owing to the SBD and B-17 barely visible in the background. However, F4F operations had previously been moved to an auxiliary field east of Henderson, variously called the 'fighter strip', or more often the 'cow pasture'. The South Pacific climate quickly bleached out aircraft colours, leaving a paler shade than was originally applied. Guadalcanal's alternately muddy and dusty environment, coupled with minimal maintenance facilities, left aircraft with a decidedly 'hang-dog' appearance. Then-Maj Donald K Yost, commanding VMF-121 in early 1943, described it in the following terms;
'The insignia and bright markings designating position in the squadron with which our planes were decorated previously gave way to white or black numbers on the fuselages. Even these numbers were not distinguishing, and usually did not run in sequence. As a result, planes failed to gain an identity. Adding to the anonymity of the F4F-4s which I flew from Guadalcanal were the white airplane-fabric patches glued over numerous bullet holes. Many planes were composites of wings or control surfaces scavenged from wrecked planes, and the whole covered with the mud and dust which seemed ever-present on the fighter strips we flew from in those days'
(via Robert L Lawson)

A VMF-121 aircraft lands at Camp Kearney, later site of Miramar Naval Air Station. Under Capt Leonard K Davis, the squadron operated in the San Diego area from March to August 1942. However, retaining full strength proved almost impossible owing to near-constant transfers of pilots and aircraft to new units. The squadron barely reached operating strength before embarking for the Southwest Pacific. Normal practise on Guadalcanal seldom allowed for individually-assigned aircraft after the early period of the campaign. The usual situation was described by Maj Don Yost;
'The one dereliction from security regulations tactitly permitted was the custom of painting a small Japanese flag on the fuselage below the cockpit for each enemy aircraft destroyed in the air. However, since no plane was regularly assigned to an individual, the plane rather than the pilot was honoured. Because of the limited availability of aircraft, pilots flew any plane that was flyable and loaded for the mission. As a result, a new pilot on his first combat mission might be flying a plane that was well covered with flags'
(via Robert L Lawson)

Two future Medal of Honor winners scored in this fight: Capt Joe Foss, with three kills, and 2nd Lt Jeff DeBlanc, with two, among the total 23 claims. Theirs was a fitting contribution to the Marine Corps' heaviest day of aerial combat in the first year of the war.

The battle continued in Ironbottom Sound that night. An outnumbered American cruiser-destroyer force locked horns with Japanese battleships and other warships, preventing bombardment of Henderson Field. Five US Navy vessels were sunk, as were two Japanese destroyers, while one battleship was crippled.

A misty dawn on the 13th revealed IJNS *Hiei* immobilised and within easy reach of Henderson, which launched SBDs and TBFs to finish her off. Eight defending Zeros were dispersed between 0630 and 0830, elements of three Wildcat squadrons splashing three for the loss of a single F4F, although its pilot was saved.

Meanwhile, *Enterprise* had returned to the area and launched reinforcements for 'Cactus'. Six 'Grim Reapers' arrived with nine VT-10 Avengers in time to celebrate *Hiei's* demise, and to intercept the Japanese troop transports and bombardment group that was steaming rapidly towards Guadalcanal.

'Cactus' was shelled that night, but most rounds fell on the 'Fighter Strip'. Two F4Fs were destroyed and 15 damaged, but by dawn on the 14th there were still 14 operational Wildcats, plus 10 Army fighters. They were all needed as a strong Zero CAP was maintained over 11 troop transports bearing down 'The Slot' toward Guadalcanal's northern coast. The Americans simply could not let additional enemy troops ashore.

While land-based Marine and VF-10 Wildcats fought Zeros and floatplanes over the convoy, *Enterprise* launched additional aircraft. After sinking the cruiser *Kinugasa*, the carrier-based SBDs and F4Fs landed ashore. 'The Big E' retained 18 Wildcats for her own protection – the balance of Air Group 10, however, was now fully committed to 'Cactus'.

Lt Col Joe Bauer, by now working at Fighter Command HQ, stood the inactivity as long as he could. Perhaps nowhere else in the Pacific did so many gifted fighter leaders work so closely as on that day. Flying alongside Bauer were Duke Davis and Joe Foss of VMF-121, plus Jim Flatley of VF-10. After supervising near-constant missions taking off to defeat the Japanese transports, Bauer decided to take a look for himself. That evening he was lost on a strafing mission and eventually received a posthumous Medal of Honor. His citation said in part, 'His intrepid fighting spirit and distinctive ability as a leader and an airman, exemplified in his splendid record of combat achievement, were vital factors in the successful operations in the South Pacific Area.'

Seven of Rear Adm Tanaka's transports were sunk or turned back in the dash for Guadalcanal. In the heaviest day of aerial activity to date, 'Cactus' had launched 86 Navy, Marine and Army bomber sorties, plus 42 Wildcats. Of the latter, VMF-112 was most heavily engaged. However, *Enterprise* fighter pilots were also heard from, including the redoubtable team of Lt Jock Sutherland and Lt(jg) Henry Carey, both veterans of Midway and Santa Cruz.

In exchange for 30 enemy aircraft claimed shot down, the 'CAF' lost two F4Fs and five SBDs. Japanese claims matched the US total, while their own casualties were 12 Zeros and three floatplanes.

When the four surviving transports beached themselves on the morning of the 15th, the Guadalcanal campaign had peaked. Aerial combat quickly abated, as that day involved only two combats with a combined eight claims by VF-10 and VMF-121. In fact, no further Navy victory claims would be made until the end of January.

1942 IN REVIEW

The Pacific Theatre – by far the largest in World War 2 – produced its own band of 'few' fighter pilots. However, the Pacific 'Few' were even fewer than those in RAF Fighter Command in 1940! In fact, their numbers were directly inverse to the time and area involved. From December 1941 through June 1942, the five Navy fighter squadrons' frontline strength totalled only 138 aircrew. For the remainder of the year, 50 of those veterans, and 136 others, bore the burden of the Guadalcanal battles. Thus, the US Navy fought the first 12 months of the Pacific War with 224 combat fighter pilots.

Of these, 27 were killed in action or accidents through to July, with another 31 lost through to November, plus two captured. The total of 60 casualties among frontline Navy fighter pilots equated to a 27 per cent loss rate. Obviously, the Guadalcanal campaign inflicted greater attrition – one out of three pilots engaged were killed. This was to be expected from the grinding, sustained, pace of operations, compared to the sporadic, tentative, nature of the carrier war over the first six months since the Pearl Harbor raid.

Two Marine squadrons committed about 40 pilots at Wake and Midway. The 'Cactus' contingent added approximately 130 more, with a small degree of duplication among Midway survivors. In whole, or in part, six VMF units flew from Guadalcanal through to November, sustaining some 25 pilots killed. Throughout the six-month campaign, 'Cactus' fighter pilots sustained a 20 per cent loss rate. Battling disease, climate and tenuous supplies, the F4F squadrons were short of everything but targets.

Typical of Guadalcanal's mixed-service operations is this scene, which captures Marine Corps F4F-4s with Army Air Forces P-38Fs, circa November 1942. The Lockheed Lightnings afforded 'Cactus Fighter Command' a much-needed high-altitude capability, but P-38 maintenance remained complicated, leading to a relatively low in-commission rate. The Wildcat's simplicity endeared it to mechanics and pilots alike, while a single underwing drop tank helped offset the type's inherently short range ***(via Robert L Lawson)***

VMF-224 was the second Wildcat unit despatched to Guadalcanal, and they arrived on 30 August 1942. Leading the unit into battle was the highly talented Maj Robert E Galer, who soon proved both his ability as a leader and as a fighter pilot of some note. Over the next two months – the hardest fought of the Guadalcanal campaign – Galer's squadron accounted for 61.5 Japanese aircraft, with the major himself downing 14 of this total. He finished fourth in the rankings for the Corps in 1942, and was awarded the Medal of Honor upon his return to the US

Pacific F4F Squadron Scores (from July to December 1942)

VMF-223	134.5	'Cactus'; includes 22.5 by TAD* pilots
VMF-121	119	'Cactus'
VMF-224	61.5	'Cactus'; includes 6.5 by TAD* pilots
VMF-212	57	'Cactus'
VF-5	45	*Saratoga* and 'Cactus'
VF-6	44	*Enterprise*
VF-72	38	*Hornet*
VMF-112	36.5	'Cactus'
VF-10	31	*Enterprise* and 'Cactus'
VMO-251	13	'Cactus'
VF-71	7	*Wasp*
VMF-122	5	'Cactus'

*TAD – temporary attached duty from other squadrons

By the end of 1942 the Navy had at least 16 Wildcat aces, who are listed below:

Mach D E Runyon	VF-6	*Enterprise*	8
Lt S W Vejtasa	VF-10	*Enterprise*	7.25
Ens H M Jensen	VF-5	*Saratoga*, Guadalcanal	7
Lt(jg) F R Register	VF-6, -5	*Enterprise*, Guadalcanal	7
Lt(jg) E S McCuskey	VF-42, -3	*Yorktown*	6.50
Lt(jg) A J Brassfield	VF-42, -3	*Yorktown*	6.33
Lt. Cdr J S Thach	VF-3	*Lexington, Yorktown*	6
Ens G L Wrenn	VF-72	*Hornet*	5.25
Ens M K Bright	VF-5	*Saratoga*, Guadalcanal	5
Lt N A M Gayler	VF-3, -2	*Lexington*	5
AP1/c L P Mankin	VF-5, -6	*Saratoga, Enterprise*	5
Lt(jg) E H O'Hare (KIA)	VF-3	*Lexington*	5
Lt(jg) C B Starkes	VF-5	*Saratoga*, Guadalcanal	5
Lt J F Sutherland	VF-72, -10	*Hornet, Enterprise*	5
Lt A O Vorse, Jr	VF-3, -2, -6	*Lexington, Enterprise*	5
Lt(jg) J M Wesolowski	VF-5	*Saratoga*, Guadalcanal	5

Two other F4F pilots deserve a mention; Lt Cdr J H Flatley scored at least four kills while serving as executive officer of VF-42 at Coral Sea and as skipper of VF-10 at Santa Cruz. He may well deserve another victory, but the indefinite phrase 'assist' clouds the matter. Additionally, Lt(jg) W A Haas, of the hard-working VF-42, has a decimal total of 4.83 from the contemporary wartime figure of six victories.

By the end of 1942 the United States Marine Corps had produced 30 aces, all of which are listed below:

Capt J J Foss	VMF-121	23 +3*
Maj J L Smith	VMF-223	19
Capt M E Carl	VMF-221, -223	16.5
Maj R E Galer	VMF-224	14
2Lt K D Frazier	VMF-223	12
Lt Col H W Bauer (KIA)	VMF-223, -224, -212	10
1Lt J E Conger	VMF-223, -212	10
Capt L D Everton	VMF-223, -212	10
1Lt W P Marontate (KIA)	VMF-121	10 +3*
2Lt T H Mann	VMF-224, -121	9
2Lt G L Hollowell	VMF-224	8
Maj J F Dobbin	VMF-224	7.5
M G H B Hamilton (KIA)	VMF-223, -212	7
2Lt R A Haberman	VMF-121	6.5
2Lt C M Kunz	VMF-224	6
1Lt G K Loesch	VMF-121	6 +2.5*
2Lt J L Narr	VMF-121	6
2Lt Z A Pond	VMF-223	6
1Lt R F Stout	VMF-224, -212	6
2Lt E Trowbridge	VMF-223	6
Capt D K Yost	VMF-121	6
Maj F R Payne	VMF-223, -212	5.5
Maj L K Davis	VMF-121	5
2Lt C J Doyle (KIA)	VMF-121	5
1Lt F C Drury	VMF-223, -212	5
Maj P J Fontana	VMF-112	5
2Lt C Kendrick (KIA)	VMF-223	5
2Lt H Phillips	VMF-223	5
2Lt W B Freeman	VMF-121	5 +1*
2Lt O H Ramlo	VMF-223	5

*Note – +3, +2.5 or +1 indicates further F4F victories in 1943

ONE MAN'S WAR – A PILOT PROFILE OF JOSEPH FOSS

Capt Joseph J Foss at the end of his Guadalcanal tour in early 1943. Credited with 26 Japanese aircraft, he was then the leading fighter ace of the United States, and was shortly to be awarded the Medal of Honor – a distinction he shared with seven other F4F pilots. Despite his exceptional combat success as executive officer of VMF-121, Foss suffered from recurring malaria, which would plague him until after the war. Indeed, he was forced to return to the US after embarking on his second combat tour as CO of the F4U-equipped VMF-115 in September 1943 because of illness. Due to a bureaucratic error, Foss was denied a regular commission postwar, so he helped form the South Dakota Air National Guard, logging 1500 happy hours in P-51Ds prior to transitioning to jets. He subsequently attained the rank of brigadier general in the Air Force Reserve, serving a spell as national president of the Air Force Association. Enjoying successful careers in politics, professional sports and commercial aviation, Foss also helped form the American Fighter Aces Association, and recently became president of the National Rifle Association of America *(via Robert L Lawson)*

Joseph Jacob Foss was destined to become a hunter. Born to a Norwegian-Scots farming family in South Dakota in 1915, he learned early in life the principles of stalking and marksmanship. Combined with a childhood passion for aviation, perhaps it was inevitable that he would become a fighter pilot. The same Scandinavian heritage and rural upbringing led to similar success among others of his generation: Richard Bong, Marion Carl and Stanley Vejtasa, to name but a few.

Like millions of his generation, 11-year-old Joe was inspired by Charles Lindbergh's transatlantic flight in 1927. The future ace's first flight occurred with his father as paying customers in a barnstorming Ford Trimotor. Though Frank Foss died while Joe was in high school, the youngster persisted in his dream of flying. And his ambition became focused when a squadron of Marine Corps biplanes passed through Sioux Falls in 1930. The excitement and glamour of fighters capable of landing on aircraft carriers planted a seed in Joe Foss that would germinate in years to come. Leader of the formation was Capt Clayton C Jerome, later wartime Director of Marine Corps Aviation.

Foss realised that any hope of a career in the military depended upon a college education. It was a major challenge for a financially-strapped farm family during the depression of the 1930s. As a part-time college student he accumulated enough credits to enter the University of South Dakota in 1939. While there he scraped up enough money to complete a private-pilot's course. Then, eternally optimistic, Foss hitch-hiked 300 miles to Minneapolis, Minnesota, to apply for the naval aviation cadet programme. Of 28 applicants, he was one of two chosen. Upon graduation in June 1940 he reported to Chamberlain Field in Minneapolis for elimination flight training.

Foss' prior experience apparently helped, as he survived the 12-hour 'E base' curriculum. He then proceeded to NAS Pensacola, and following seven months further training, was commissioned as a second lieutenant in the 'Corps. However, he had barely pinned on his coveted wings of gold when he learned that he would become a 'plowback' instructor, remaining at Pensacola for the next nine months. He was not pleased.

Foss was officer of the day on 7 December 1941. The base commander, a Navy captain, pointed at the 26-year-old lieutenant and, in so many words, said, 'You're in charge'. Foss admits that he swallowed hard, replied, 'Yes, sir!' and prepared to defend NAS Pensacola from Japanese commandos. He spent the first day of the war on a bicycle, arranging for security of the perimeter!

New Year's Day 1942 brought cheerier prospects, but only barely. Delighted to be heading closer to the war – NAS San Diego, California – he was distressed at his orders to report to VMO-1, a photo-reconnaissance squadron. At that point Foss demonstrated early signs of the initiative that would take him to the top of the list of Marine Corps aces. Determined to get into fighters, he began a calculated campaign to overcome the anti-Marine bias of the commanding officer of Aircraft Carrier Training Group (ACTG). At first progress was slow, which is to say non-existent. Though new Marine Corps squadrons were forming at nearby

Kearney Field (now NAS Miramar), there was little need for aspiring F4F pilots in ACTG. Like a patient hunter, Foss bided his time.

Then he hit upon a plan. Overhearing some Navy pilots complaining about the mortality rate in carrier training, Foss decided to take advantage of the situation. He told the CO that he would volunteer for the funeral detail in exchange for a cockpit seat in ACTG. His earnestness won out, and Foss began a cram course on the Wildcat, aerial gunnery and carrier procedures. He still credits the instruction he received at ACTG for much of his later success, especially the patient tutelage of Lt Edward Pawka, who would finish the war as an air group commander.

However, Foss was a more than willing pupil. In seven weeks during June and July, he logged 156 flight hours – an incredible average of more than three hours per day for 47 days. With that kind of experience, Foss was noticed, and on 1 August he was assigned to VMF-121, becoming executive officer to Capt Leonard K Davis – a product of the Annapolis class of 1935.

Over the next two weeks it became obvious that the unit would shortly be sent to a combat zone. Therefore, while time allowed, Foss married a former Sioux Falls schoolmate, but there was no opportunity for a honeymoon. Promoted to captain, he barely had time to pin on his new bars before VMF-121 embarked in the liner *Matsonia*, destination unknown.

The destination did not remain a secret for long. Arriving in the Southwest Pacific, VMF-121 was loaded aboard the escort carrier *Copahee.* Twenty Wildcats were catapulted off the morning of 9 October. It would be Foss' only combat mission from a carrier deck, but his arduous work at ACTG back in San Diego had paid off. Landing at Henderson Field, the newcomers were told that their fighters were now based at the nearby 'cow pasture', one mile east. Another fighter strip was under construction to the west, near Kukum Point.

Looking around, Foss was impressed with the make-do nature of the 'Cactus Air Force'. Henderson was riddled with bomb craters, and wrecked aircraft were strewn about, awaiting collection. However, there were also two radar stations and three batteries of big 90 mm anti-aircraft guns in the vicinity. VMF-121 had arrived just in time, as the remnants of John L Smith's -223 flew their last 'Cactus' mission the next day.

As 'exec', Foss led a flight of two four-fighter divisions whenever eight Wildcats were available to him. His pilots included six second lieutenants and a flying sergeant, who all averaged out at 23 years of age. Foss, at 27, was the old man of the flight. Collectively known as 'Foss' Flying Circus', the flight would be credited with 61.5 victories, and four others besides Foss would become aces. Two of them would be lost in action, however.

Foss flew several F4F-4s at Guadalcanal, without one permanently assigned. Most of VMF-121's aircraft used white numbers on wings and fuselage, and Foss arrived in number 13. This was quickly changed to 53 to avoid duplication with another F4F, but he has also been identified with numbers 50 and 84.

At noon on 13 October, VMF-121 scored its first victories as an independent squadron. Second Lts William B Freeman and Joseph L Narr, both future aces, claimed a bomber and a Zero, respectively. Later that afternoon Foss led a dozen F4Fs to intercept 14 twin-engined bombers escorted by 18 Zeros. In his first combat, Foss was jumped by a Zero which overshot his F4F and pulled up ahead of him. He got in a good burst at the enemy fighter and claimed it destroyed. In moments, however, he was beset by three more, which shot out his oil cooler. When his engine seized, Foss poked the Grumman's nose down and screeched into a rough, bumpy, landing at 'Fighter One'. He said that he learned a vital lesson from this first sortie, vowing that from then on, 'The boys could call me "Swivel-Neck Joe" '.

Foss' first dogfight established a pattern. He became a rough-and-tumble fighter along the lines of Joe Bauer. Though he seldom returned from combat without bullet holes in his F4F, he still believed in getting in close – so close, in fact, that another pilot joked that the 'exec' left powder burns on his targets.

Foss got his next chance the following afternoon. Composition of the Japanese formation was similar to the day before: 12 bombers with 15 fighters. As the Mitsubishis split to bomb both airfields, VF-5 waded into them from a better altitude. However, Foss' F4F lagged behind the others and he had to be satisfied with picking off a Zero which dived after a Marine Wildcat. Another of his flight, Master Sgt J J Palko, claimed a twin-engined reconnaissance plane. VMF-121 lost an F4F and its pilot.

Though air defence was the Wildcats' primary role, other missions arose. When ammunition supply permitted, fighters often strafed Japanese positions, rather than take a full .50-cal load back to the 'Fighter Strip'. On other occasions the F4Fs ranged farther afield. At dawn on the 16th Foss led a strafing mission, shooting up landing craft near Kokumbona. Diving through AA fire, the Wildcats inflicted heavy losses on Japanese infantry, but one pilot failed to return.

Though holding their own in the air, the fighter pilots spent long, arduous, nights on the ground. During mid-October enemy warships bombarded Henderson Field and the surrounding area three nights running. Some fliers resorted to the desperate method of trying to sleep near the frontlines, south of the field.

After his first few combats, Foss grew more appreciative of the fighter doctrine handed down from the Navy. He held that, 'Looking around doesn't cost anything and is a healthy habit for pilots to develop'. He also found the 'Thach-Flatley' weave (the name was a misnomer) a near-perfect method of countering the Zero's superior performance because, as he said many times, 'It allowed us to point eyes and guns in every direction'.

Following a large interception on the morning of 18 October, Foss was leading another flight outbound when the Zero top cover descended. Though a trailing F4F went down, Foss' flight turned the tables and caught three Zeros from above. He flamed the nearest, hit another which made off trailing smoke, and then fought a short battle with the third. Finally, gaining an angle, he drew lead and fired, setting the engine alight.

Next, Foss latched onto a group of bombers already under attack by VF-71. Though identified as twin-tailed types, they were familiar 'Bettys' from the Misawa Naval Air Group. Foss hit one, then dived below the formation and pulled up steeply. Firing almost vertically, he saw his bullets destroy one engine. The Mitsubishi dropped out of formation and later crashed in 'The Slot'. Nine days after landing at Guadalcanal, Joe Foss was an ace.

On the morning of the 20th Lt Col Joe Bauer, running 'Cactus Fighter

Command', sent Foss off with seven F4Fs to intercept 15 Zeros, the latter being ably supported by Maj Davis and his section of eight Wildcats. In a close, manoeuvring, combat, Foss claimed two kills. Then another Zero put 7.7 mm rounds into his engine. As he had done on his first mission, Foss force-landed back on his airfield, though this time in a more controlled fashion than before. One Marine pilot was lost to Zeros.

With advance knowledge of a Japanese build-up, 'Fighter Command' kept as many Wildcats available as maintenance allowed. On the 23rd VMF-121 was up in strength as Davis and Foss each had their flights airborne. With Zeros and bombers overhead, there was no shortage of targets. Both flights engaged. Foss' first opportunity was a Zero tearing after an F4F, firing with all guns. Foss closed in, clamped down on the trigger and the Zero exploded. Next, he tagged onto another which attempted to evade in a loop. Foss had never been taught to shoot while inverted, but he followed and caught the Japanese pulling over the top. He described it as a lucky shot, but flamed his victim nonetheless.

Nosing down to regain airspeed, Foss spotted an exuberant Zero pilot performing a slow roll. It was a quick set-up, but Foss put his gunsight on the fighter as its wings rolled through the vertical and fired. He gazed in amazement at the spectacle of the enemy aviator blown out of his cockpit, minus his parachute. Without time to reorient himself, the lone Marine was aware of other aircraft falling around him – Duke Davis' flight was obviously doing its job overhead. However, a brace of Zeros then sandwiched Foss between them. Trusting in the Grumman Iron Works, he pressed home his run on the frontmost Zero. Both pilots fired and both scored, but Foss' superior armament made the difference. Passing off his port wingtip, the Zero came apart in flames.

He emptied his guns at another bandit, then realized that the fourth Japanese had hit him. With smoke streaming from his abused Pratt & Whitney, Foss followed previous procedure and began a long glide toward home. When he landed the battered Wildcat he had raised his tally to 11 victories, but reminded himself that this was the fourth F4F he had returned too damaged to fly again. Nevertheless, VMF-121 had claimed 11 of the day's 22 kills credited to 'Corps pilots – the balance going to VMF-212.

On 25 October Japanese naval, air and ground forces expected to occupy Henderson Field, and the F4F pilots were beneficiaries of the action. Presaging the carrier battle off Santa Cruz the next day, Zero fighter sweeps capped 'Cactus' throughout the morning. Their orders: circle for upwards of four hours, then land when it was clear the Imperial Army owned the place.

Joe Foss had other ideas. Before 1000 he led six Wildcats off the 'Fighter Strip' and tangled with the first wave of nine Zeros. Fighting their way upward from only 1500 ft, the Marines claimed three victories for one F4F lost. Foss was credited with two of the kills but later berated himself for wasting ammunition in long-range shooting. After a few missions he learned the value of getting close and firing short bursts. Later, whilst touring training bases he told aviation cadets that he lost four certain kills because of poor fire discipline.

Subsequently, a VMF-212 division tangled with intrusive Zeros, then Foss was up again. He led an eclectic bunch – his wingman, Oscar Bate, plus three VF-71 pilots, putting their skills to use after *Wasp* was torpedoed and sunk on 15 September. They tangled with a potent *chutai*: six fighters of the Tainan Air Group flown by experienced pilots, including two aces. For once the F4Fs had the altitude advantage, allowing Foss to start the fight by gunning one Zero from astern. Then the other five A6Ms bounced the diving Grummans.

Foss was attacked by a Zero which fired at him and missed. Reversing hard to starboard, the Marine was now on the A6M's tail and shooting before the Japanese could evade. The enemy pilot bailed out seconds before the Zero exploded. Low on ammunition, Foss turned for home. However, he noticed two Zeros stalking another F4F and shouted a warning. His radio call saved the Wildcat, but both A6Ms then turned on him. Foss ducked into a cloud, reversed course and emerged to find one of the stalkers under his guns. Closing in to be sure, he destroyed the Zero with his remaining ammunition.

With five victories in two take-offs, Foss had become the first Marine Corps ace in a day. Proud of his accomplishment, he boasted to Lt Doyle, 'That was one hop I didn't get any bullet holes in my plane'. Doyle, seizing an opportunity, pointed to the dimpled armour plate behind Foss' headrest. 'What do you call those?', he retorted.

The Navy-Marine F4Fs claimed four victories from this fight, and in fact got three. Moreover, Foss had made 14 claims in 13 days. He was running at a rate that was even in advance of Smith and Carl – the latter had actually been one of Foss' instructors at Pensacola.

Despite almost daily flights with frequent combat and perennial bombing and shelling, Foss retained his stamina and enthusiasm. Not content with playing the fighter pilot role, he and some other VMF-121 stalwarts occasionally borrowed rifles and went prowling in the jungle – however, Lt Col Joe Bauer promptly put an end to that sport, as trained fighter pilots were virtually irreplaceable.

Though very crude, living facilities on Guadalcanal had improved from the early days of the late summer. Pilots slept in six-man tents and ate dehydrated eggs for breakfast under a tarp. Somebody had a scratchy old gramophone which played worn-out records of popular songs, and outdated magazines were available. Bathing facilites were basic, but effective – the nearby Lunga River. Many pilots grew short beards, as it was more convenient than shaving in cold water. However, they learned to keep the beards trimmed because facial hair could interfere with the proper fit of an oxygen mask.

'Washing Machine Charlie' and 'Millimeter Mike' were the generic names which Marines assigned to harassing enemy night fliers and hidden artillery pieces which shelled the airfields. Therefore, some pilots tried sleeping during the day. However, since two patrols a day were common, to say nothing of unexpected scrambles, a 'combat nap' was a catch-as-catch-can affair.

After 11 days of relative inactivity, Foss was shooting again on 7 November. Late that afternoon he led seven F4Fs against Japanese warships steaming down 'The Slot'. In one of the largest reinforcement efforts yet, a cruiser and nine destroyers were covered by six Zero floatplanes ('Rufes') which had attacked a formation of VMF-112 Wildcats. As Foss related later, 'Somebody was going to get left out'. He downed one A6M2N, pulled around for a shot at another and saw his wingman, 2nd Lt 'Boot' Furlow, flame the last one. When Foss looked around for another target, he observed the eerie spectacle of five empty parachutes.

Preparing to strafe the ships, Foss threw a cautionary glance over his shoulder. There was at least one other floatplane among the clouds, so he climbed into position and initiated a high-side run. Only as he closed did he discern it was a biplane – undoubtedly an F1M2 'Pete'. With excessive speed, Foss passed close aboard when the sharpshooting rear-seat man opened fire. Several bullets struck Foss' airframe, with one 7.7 mm round starring the portside glass of his windscreen.

Foss decided to respect the enemy's ability. Approaching for a pass from below, he put a telling burst into the starboard wingroot. The 'Pete' dropped away as Foss noticed another Mitsubishi. He repeated the successful low astern approach and ignited the floatplane in one pass.

En route home, Foss encountered a series of line squalls. He diverted around some of the clouds, but when he broke into the clear he realised he was off course. Then his engine began cutting out. Apparently the Japanese gunner had inflicted serious damage, as the R1830 began trailing smoke, then cut out completely.

He mothered the doomed Wildcat, stretching his glide as much as he dared. He had sight of land ahead and steered for it. It proved to be Malaita, the long, thin, island east of Guadalcanal. The ensuing water landing was rough and bumpy, being performed more than two miles offshore. As the F4F rapidly sank nose first, Foss struggled with his parachute harness. Then, with one foot caught under the seat, he went down with his aircraft. As it sank, Foss struggled for air. In desperation, he gulped in saltwater. He realised that he was close to drowning.

Fighting panic, Foss forced himself to concentrate. He talked himself through the escape and, once loose in the cockpit, he inflated his Mae West. From approximately 30 ft he was carried upward, inhaling more water in the process. Upon breaking the surface, Foss was exhausted. The tide was against him and he knew it was useless to try swimming to shore. Therefore, he kicked off his shoes and tried to float on his back. He wanted to rest and regain his strength before trying anything else. However, future plans were chillingly interrupted when one or two shark fins sliced through the water nearby. He spread his chlorine capsule around him and that seemed to help.

By dark, Foss was no closer to land. However, some canoes came out from shore, obviously looking for him. Foss lay still in the water, half convinced they were Japanese, when he heard someone say, 'Let's look over here'. The searchers turned out to be planters and mill workers. They hauled him aboard with his waterlogged parachute and took him home.

'Home' proved to be a large mission, complete with two bishops. Additionally, there were Australians, Europeans and even two Americans. One of the nuns had been on Malaita 40 years and had never seen an automobile. The first aeroplanes she had seen were Japanese. That night Foss dined on steak and eggs. His hosts invited him to stay for two weeks, but the errant ace explained how he had a pressing previous commitment. He accepted their hospitality overnight, being buzzed by a VMF-121 Wildcat in the process.

On the eighth, a PBY Catalina landed and taxied up to shore. Foss,

Colour Plates

This 14-page section profiles many of the aircraft flown by the elite pilots of the US Navy and Marine Corps, plus the more notable Martlet naval aviators of the Fleet Air Arm. All the artwork has been specially commissioned for this volume, and profile artists Chris Davey, Keith Fretwell and John Weal, plus figure artist Mike Chappell, have gone to great pains to illustrate the aircraft and their pilots as accurately as possible following in-depth research. Aces' machines that have never previously been illustrated in colour are featured alongside accurate renditions of the more famous Wildcats from World War 2.

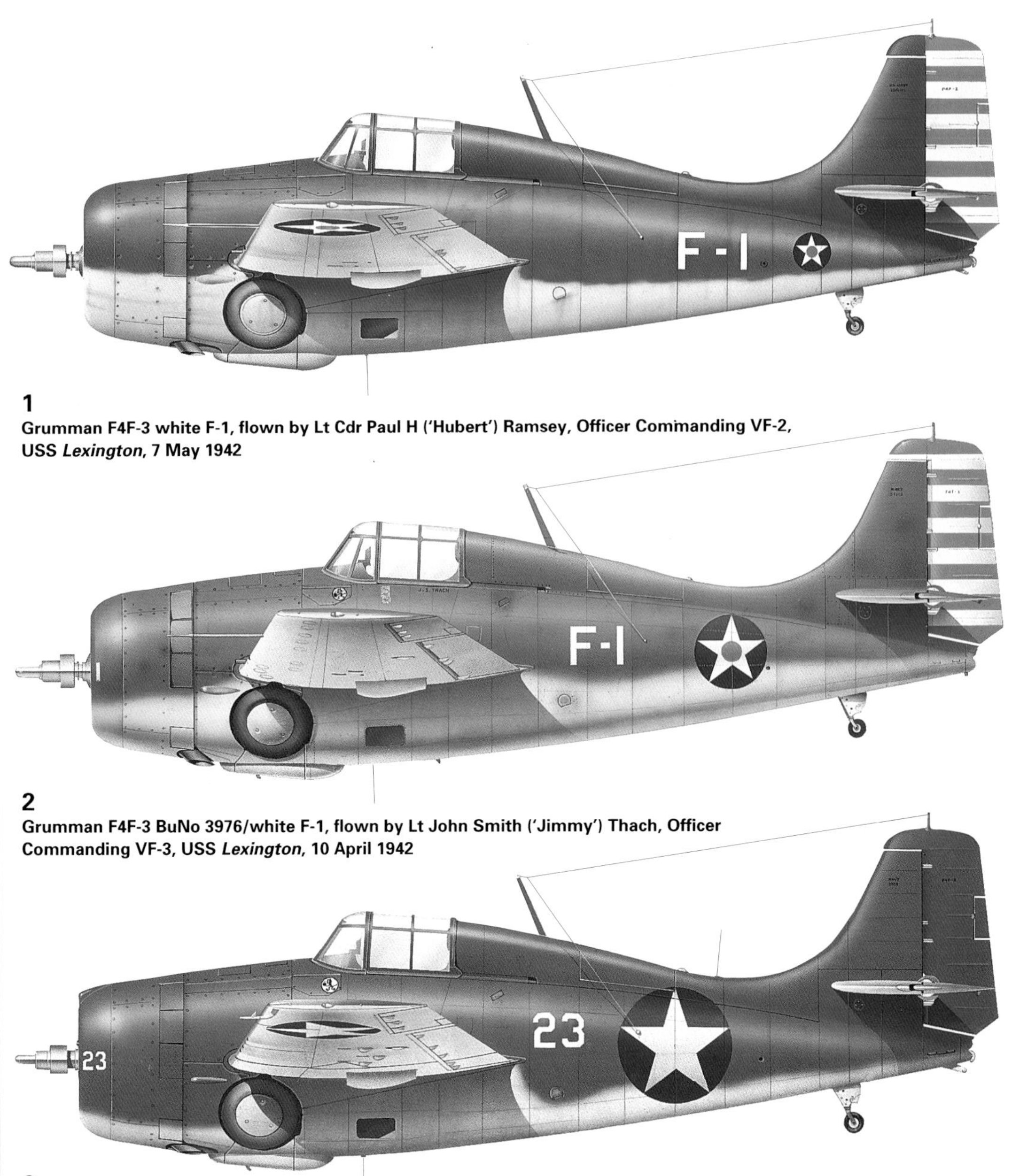

1

Grumman F4F-3 white F-1, flown by Lt Cdr Paul H ('Hubert') Ramsey, Officer Commanding VF-2, USS *Lexington*, 7 May 1942

2

Grumman F4F-3 BuNo 3976/white F-1, flown by Lt John Smith ('Jimmy') Thach, Officer Commanding VF-3, USS *Lexington*, 10 April 1942

3

Grumman F4F-4 BuNo 5093/white 23, flown by Lt Cdr John S Thach, Officer Commanding VF-3, USS *Yorktown*, Midway, 4 June 1942

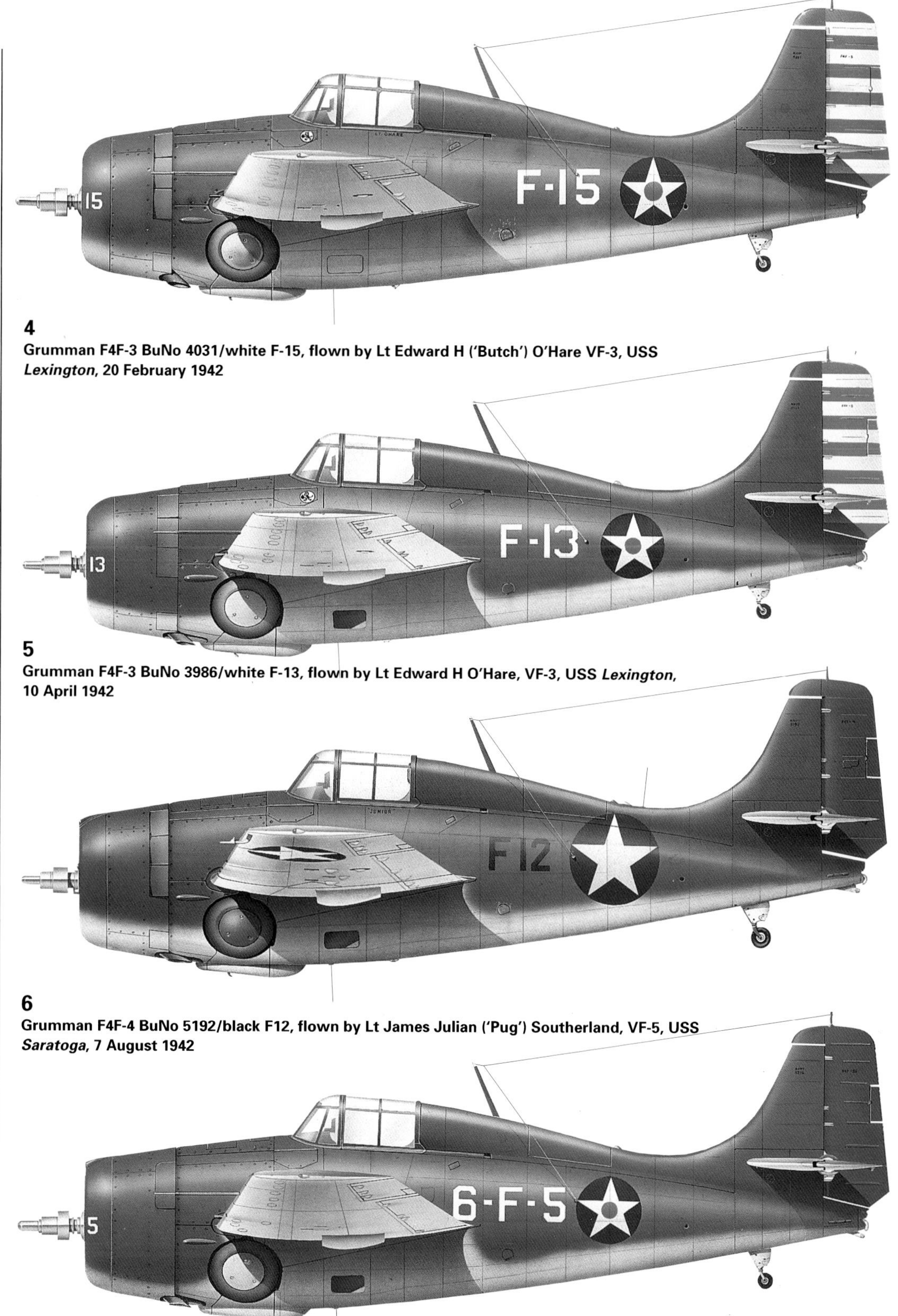

4
Grumman F4F-3 BuNo 4031/white F-15, flown by Lt Edward H ('Butch') O'Hare VF-3, USS *Lexington*, 20 February 1942

5
Grumman F4F-3 BuNo 3986/white F-13, flown by Lt Edward H O'Hare, VF-3, USS *Lexington*, 10 April 1942

6
Grumman F4F-4 BuNo 5192/black F12, flown by Lt James Julian ('Pug') Southerland, VF-5, USS *Saratoga*, 7 August 1942

7
Grumman F4F-3A BuNo 3916/white 6-F-5, flown by Ensign James G Daniels, VF-6, USS *Enterprise*, 7 December 1941

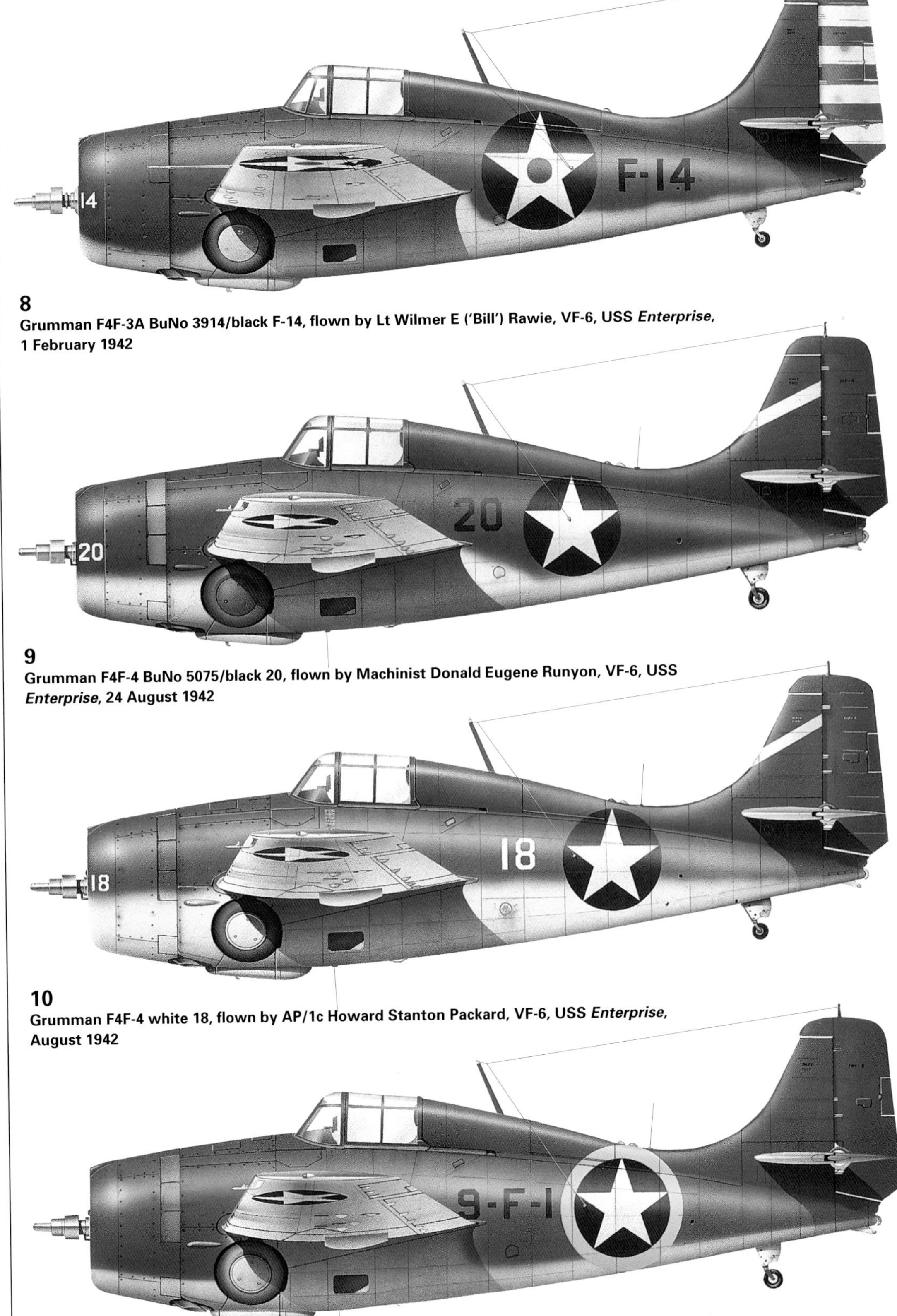

8
Grumman F4F-3A BuNo 3914/black F-14, flown by Lt Wilmer E ('Bill') Rawie, VF-6, USS *Enterprise*, 1 February 1942

9
Grumman F4F-4 BuNo 5075/black 20, flown by Machinist Donald Eugene Runyon, VF-6, USS *Enterprise*, 24 August 1942

10
Grumman F4F-4 white 18, flown by AP/1c Howard Stanton Packard, VF-6, USS *Enterprise*, August 1942

11
Grumman F4F-4 black 9-F-1, flown by Lt Cdr John Raby, VF-9, USS *Ranger*, *Operation Torch*, November 1942

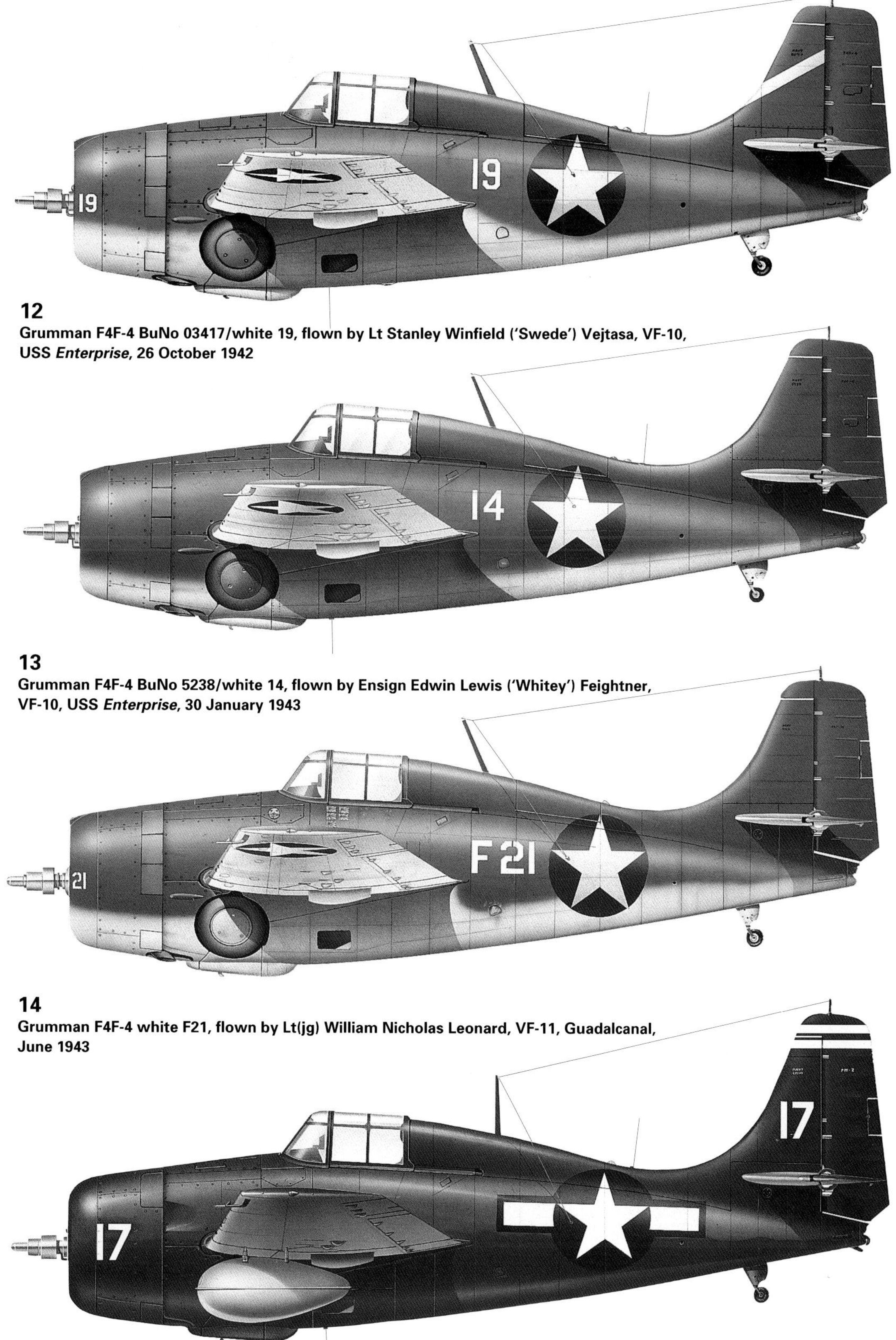

12
Grumman F4F-4 BuNo 03417/white 19, flown by Lt Stanley Winfield ('Swede') Vejtasa, VF-10, USS *Enterprise*, 26 October 1942

13
Grumman F4F-4 BuNo 5238/white 14, flown by Ensign Edwin Lewis ('Whitey') Feightner, VF-10, USS *Enterprise*, 30 January 1943

14
Grumman F4F-4 white F21, flown by Lt(jg) William Nicholas Leonard, VF-11, Guadalcanal, June 1943

15
General Motors FM-2 white 17 of VF-26, USS *Santee*, October 1944

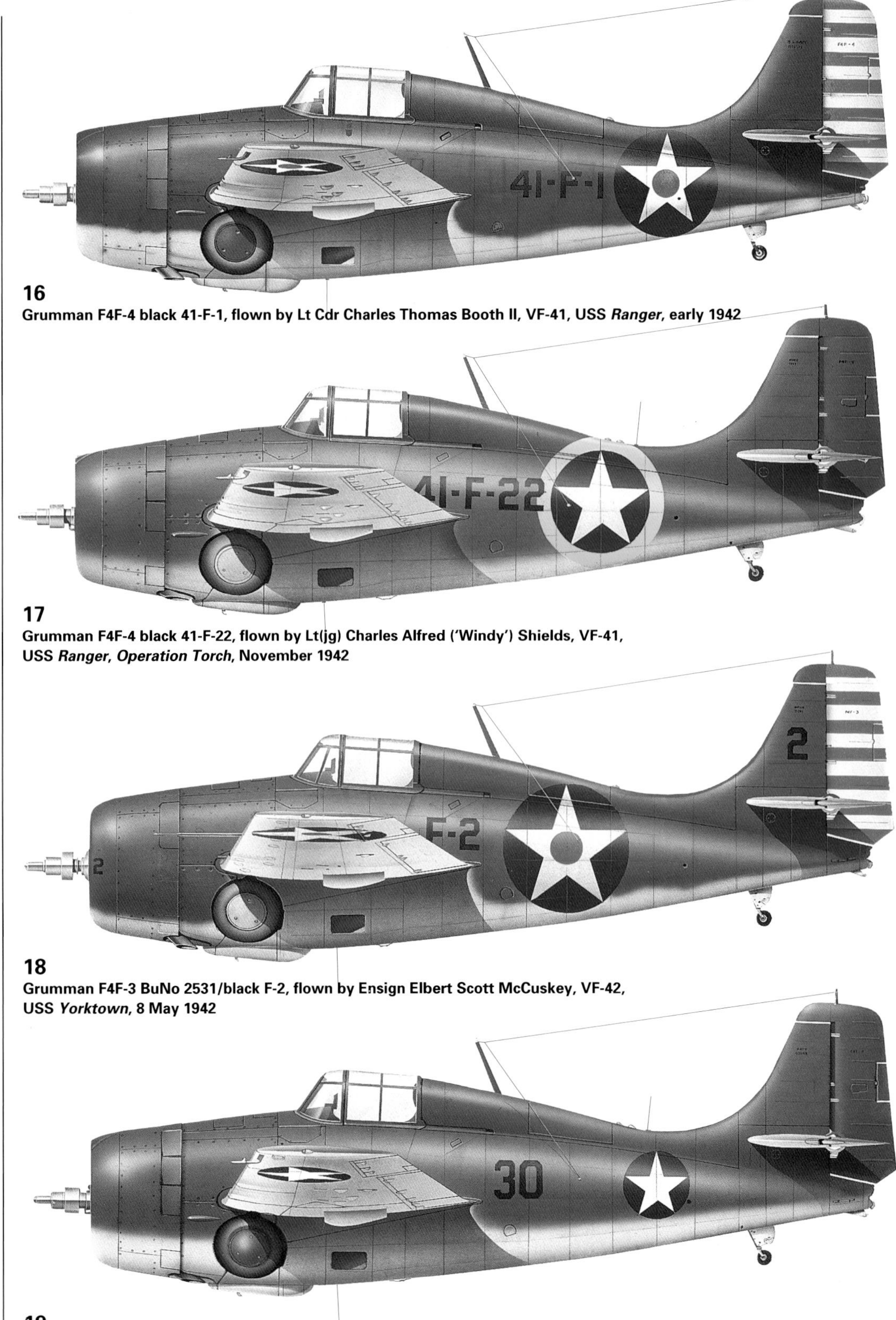

16

Grumman F4F-4 black 41-F-1, flown by Lt Cdr Charles Thomas Booth II, VF-41, USS *Ranger*, early 1942

17

Grumman F4F-4 black 41-F-22, flown by Lt(jg) Charles Alfred ('Windy') Shields, VF-41, USS *Ranger*, *Operation Torch*, November 1942

18

Grumman F4F-3 BuNo 2531/black F-2, flown by Ensign Elbert Scott McCuskey, VF-42, USS *Yorktown*, 8 May 1942

19

Grumman F4F-4 BuNo 02148/black 30, flown by Lt Cdr Courtney Shands, VF-71, USS *Wasp*, August 1942

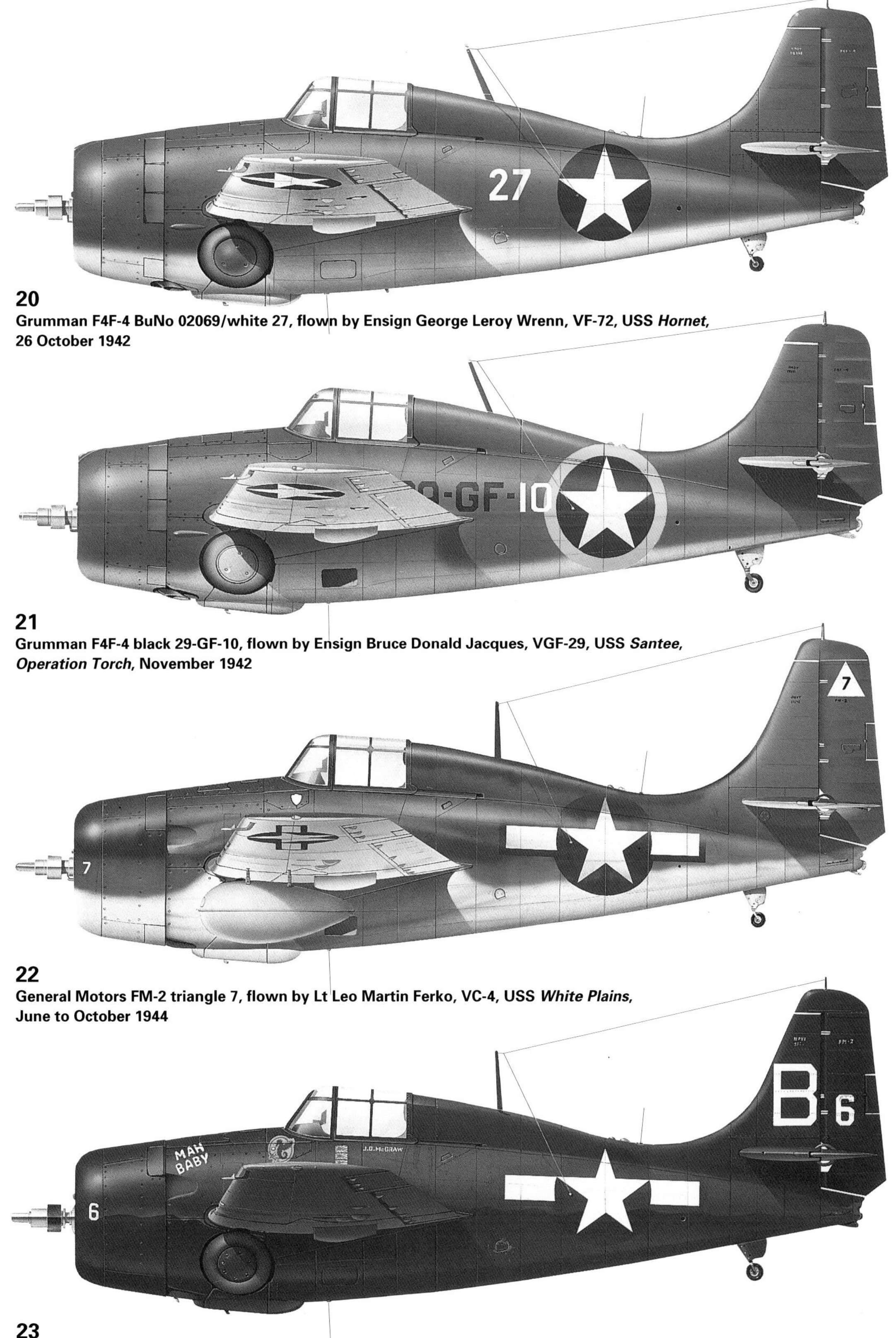

20

Grumman F4F-4 BuNo 02069/white 27, flown by Ensign George Leroy Wrenn, VF-72, USS *Hornet*, 26 October 1942

21

Grumman F4F-4 black 29-GF-10, flown by Ensign Bruce Donald Jacques, VGF-29, USS *Santee*, *Operation Torch*, November 1942

22

General Motors FM-2 triangle 7, flown by Lt Leo Martin Ferko, VC-4, USS *White Plains*, June to October 1944

23

General Motors FM-2 white B6 *MAH BABY*, flown by Ens Joseph D McGraw, VC-10, USS *Gambier Bay*, 24 October 1944

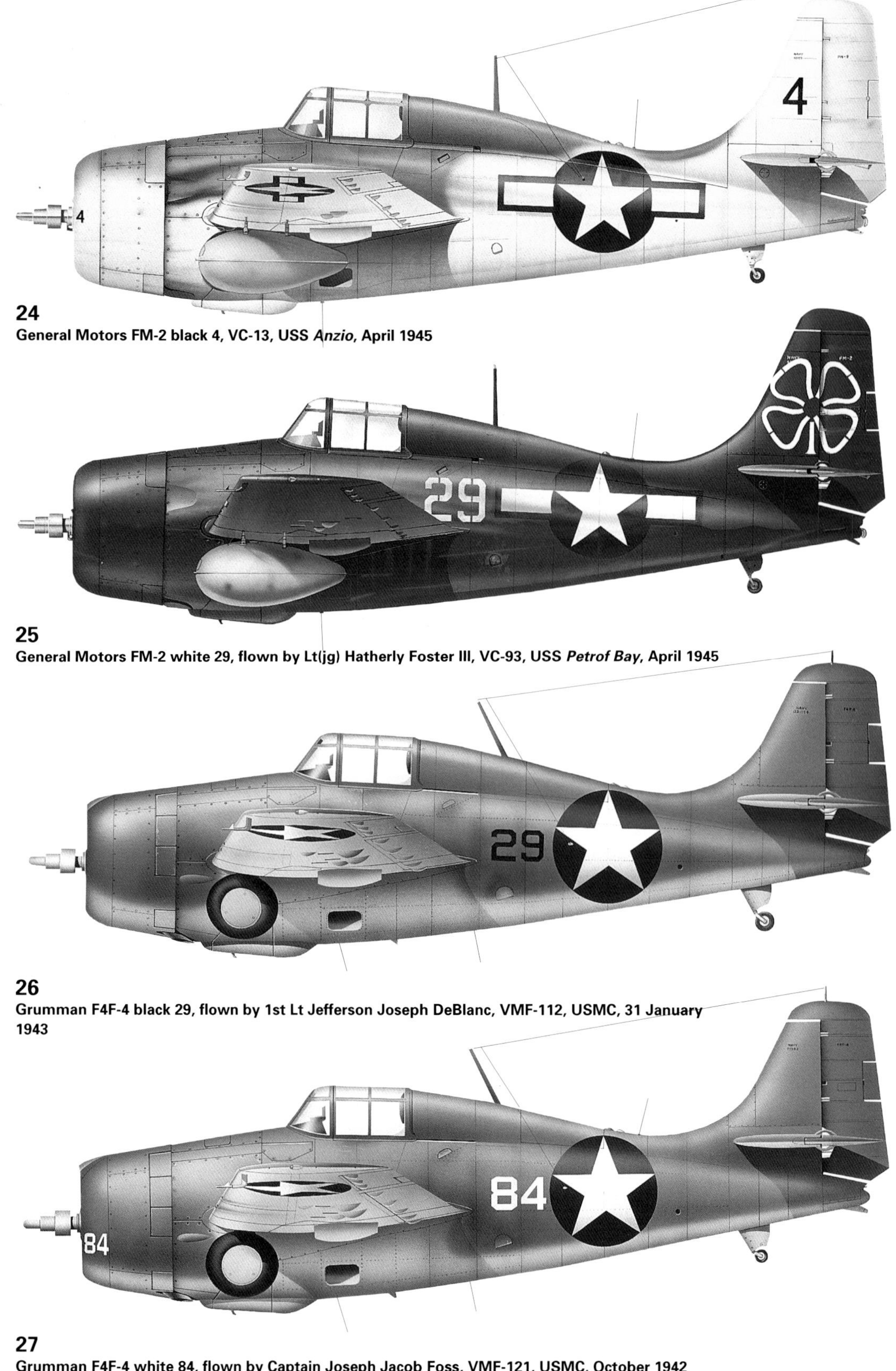

24
General Motors FM-2 black 4, VC-13, USS *Anzio*, April 1945

25
General Motors FM-2 white 29, flown by Lt(jg) Hatherly Foster III, VC-93, USS *Petrof Bay*, April 1945

26
Grumman F4F-4 black 29, flown by 1st Lt Jefferson Joseph DeBlanc, VMF-112, USMC, 31 January 1943

27
Grumman F4F-4 white 84, flown by Captain Joseph Jacob Foss, VMF-121, USMC, October 1942

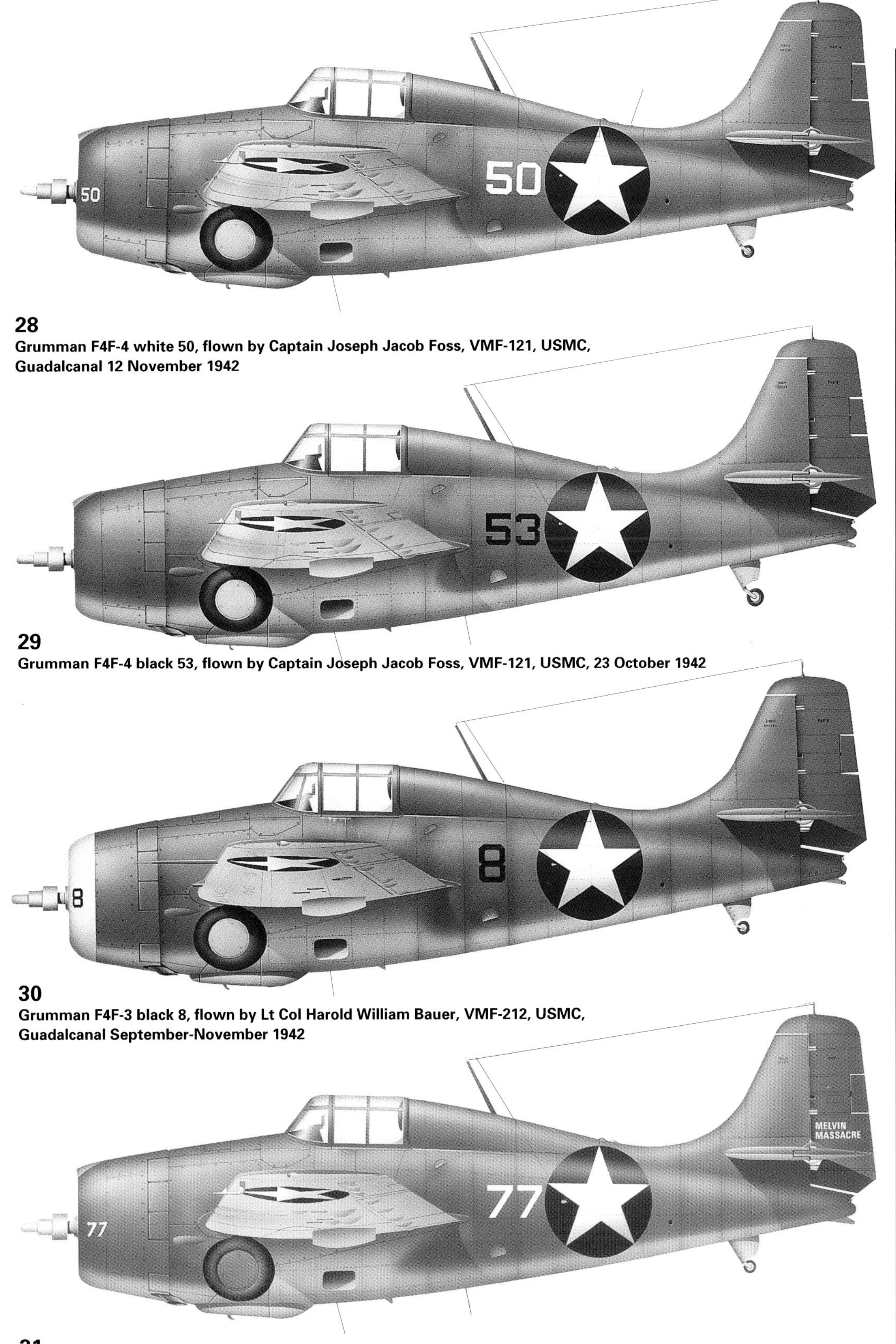

28
Grumman F4F-4 white 50, flown by Captain Joseph Jacob Foss, VMF-121, USMC, Guadalcanal 12 November 1942

29
Grumman F4F-4 black 53, flown by Captain Joseph Jacob Foss, VMF-121, USMC, 23 October 1942

30
Grumman F4F-3 black 8, flown by Lt Col Harold William Bauer, VMF-212, USMC, Guadalcanal September-November 1942

31
Grumman F4F-4 02124/white 77, flown by Lt James Elms Swett, VMF-221, USMC, 7 April 1943

32
Grumman F4F-4 BuNo 02100/black 13, flown by Captain Marion E Carl, VMF-223, USMC, Guadalcanal August 1942

33
Grumman F4F-4 BuNo 03508/black 13, flown by Captain Marion E Carl, VMF-223, USMC, Guadalcanal September 1942

35
Grumman F4F-3 white MF-1, flown by Major R E Galer, VMF-224, USMC, Guadalcanal September-October 1942

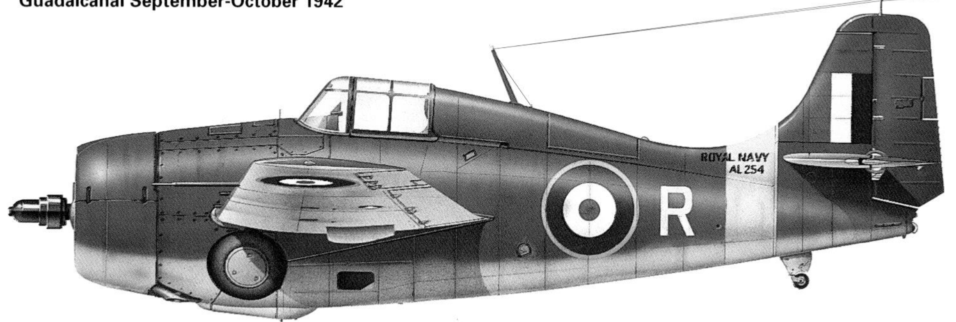

36
Grumman Martlet I AL254/R, flown by Sub-Lt Eric Brown, No 802 Sqn, Fleet Air Arm, HMS *Audacity*, 8 November 1941

34
Grumman F4F-4 white 2, unit and pilot unknown, USMC, Guadalcanal September 1942

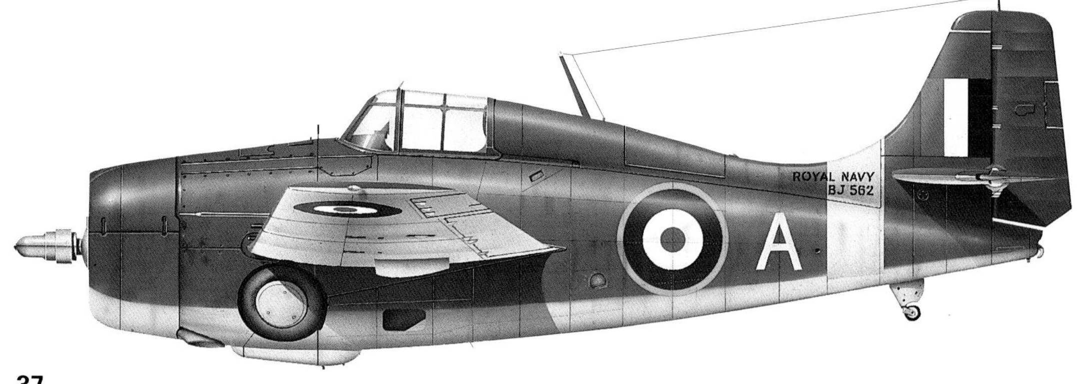

37

Grumman Martlet I BJ562/A, flown by Sub-Lt Parke, RNVR, No 804 Sqn, Fleet Air Arm, Skeabrae, Orkney, 24 December 1940

38

Grumman Martlet III AX733/K, flown by Sub-Lt W M Walsh RN, No 805 Sqn, Fleet Air Arm, Western Desert, 28 September 1941

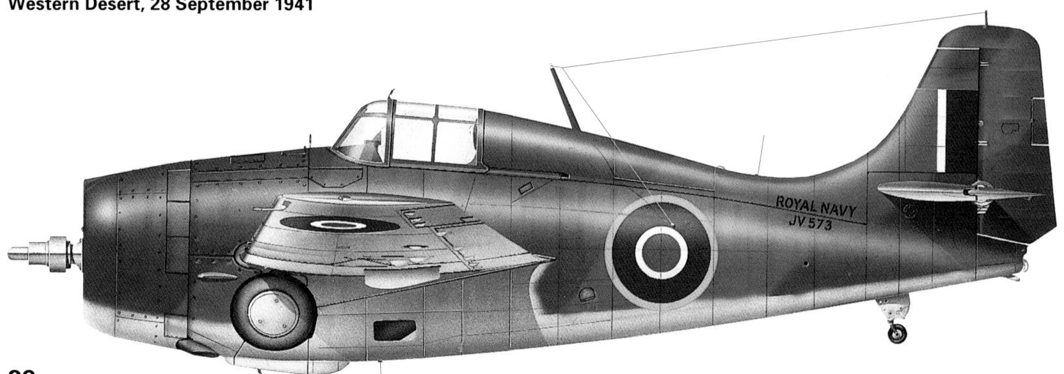

39

Grumman Wildcat V JV573, flown by Sub-Lt R A Fleischman-Allen RN, No 813 Sqn, Fleet Air Arm, HMS *Vindex*, February 1945

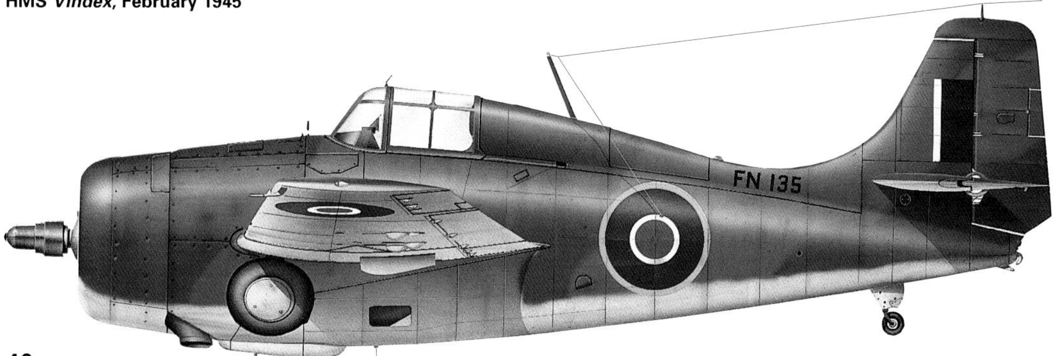

40

Grumman Wildcat (Martlet) IV FN135, Sub-Lt R K L Yeo RN, No 819 Sqn, Fleet Air Arm, HMS *Activity*, 30 March 1944

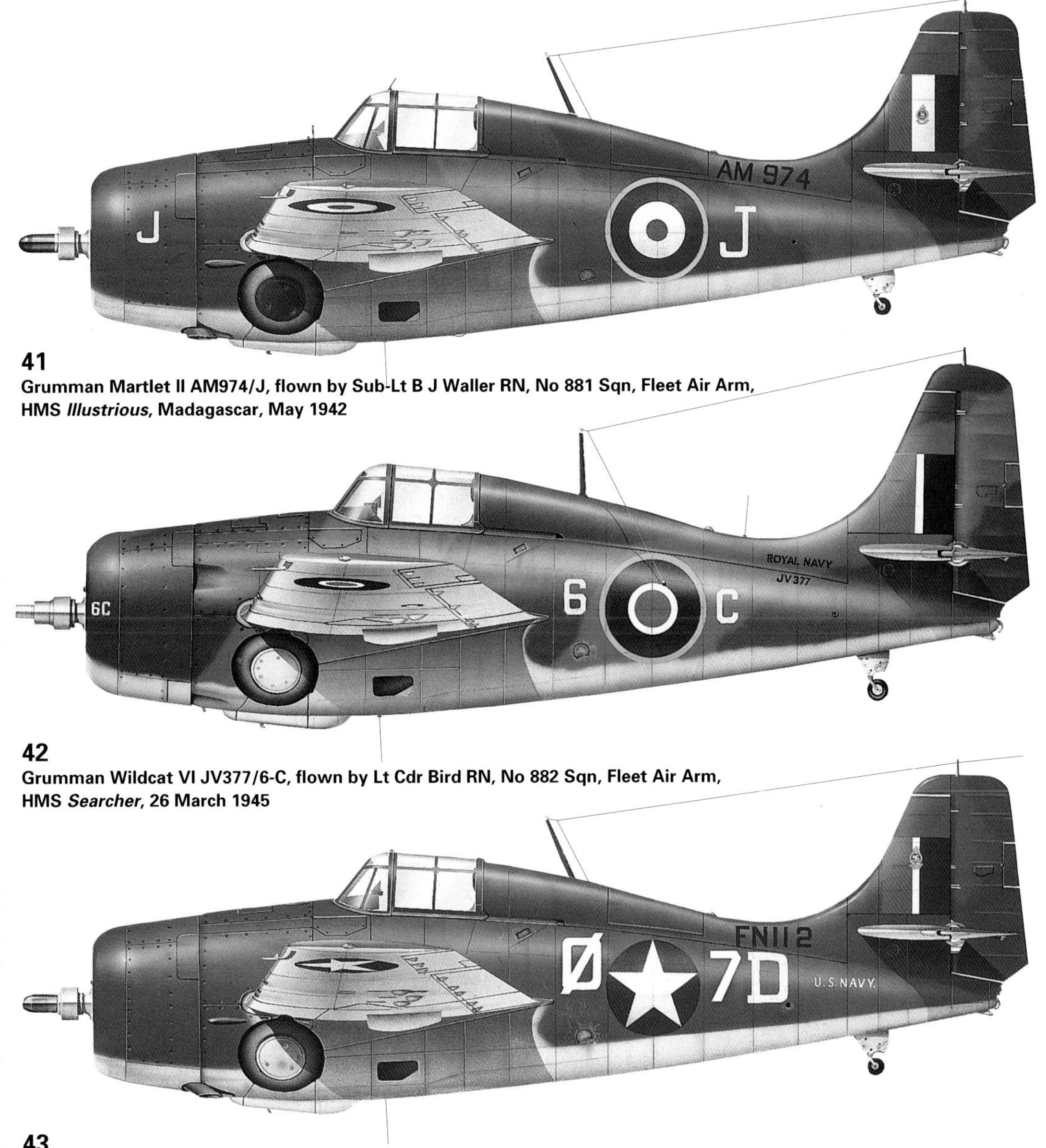

41
Grumman Martlet II AM974/J, flown by Sub-Lt B J Waller RN, No 881 Sqn, Fleet Air Arm, HMS *Illustrious*, Madagascar, May 1942

42
Grumman Wildcat VI JV377/6-C, flown by Lt Cdr Bird RN, No 882 Sqn, Fleet Air Arm, HMS *Searcher*, 26 March 1945

43
Grumman Martlet II FN112/0-7D, flown by Lt Dennis Mayvore Jeram RN, No 888 Sqn, Fleet Air Arm, HMS *Formidable*, *Operation Torch*, 9 November 1942

1. Major Robert E Galer was CO of VMF-224 during its tour on Guadalcanal in late 1942

2. Leading ace at Guadalcanal was Captain Joe Foss of VMF-121. His flying attire is typical of the campaign

3. Martlet I pilot Sub-Lieutenant Eric 'Winkle' Brown of the Fleet Air Arm's No 802 Sqn in November 1941

4. Leading FM-2 ace Lieutenant Ralph Elliot was CO of VC-27 aboard USS *Savo Island* in 1944/45

5. Lieutenant of VF-21 in the Solomon Islands in late summer 1943

6. Lieutenant(jg) 'Butch' O'Hare of VF-3 in his green/grey service uniform in the New Year of 1942

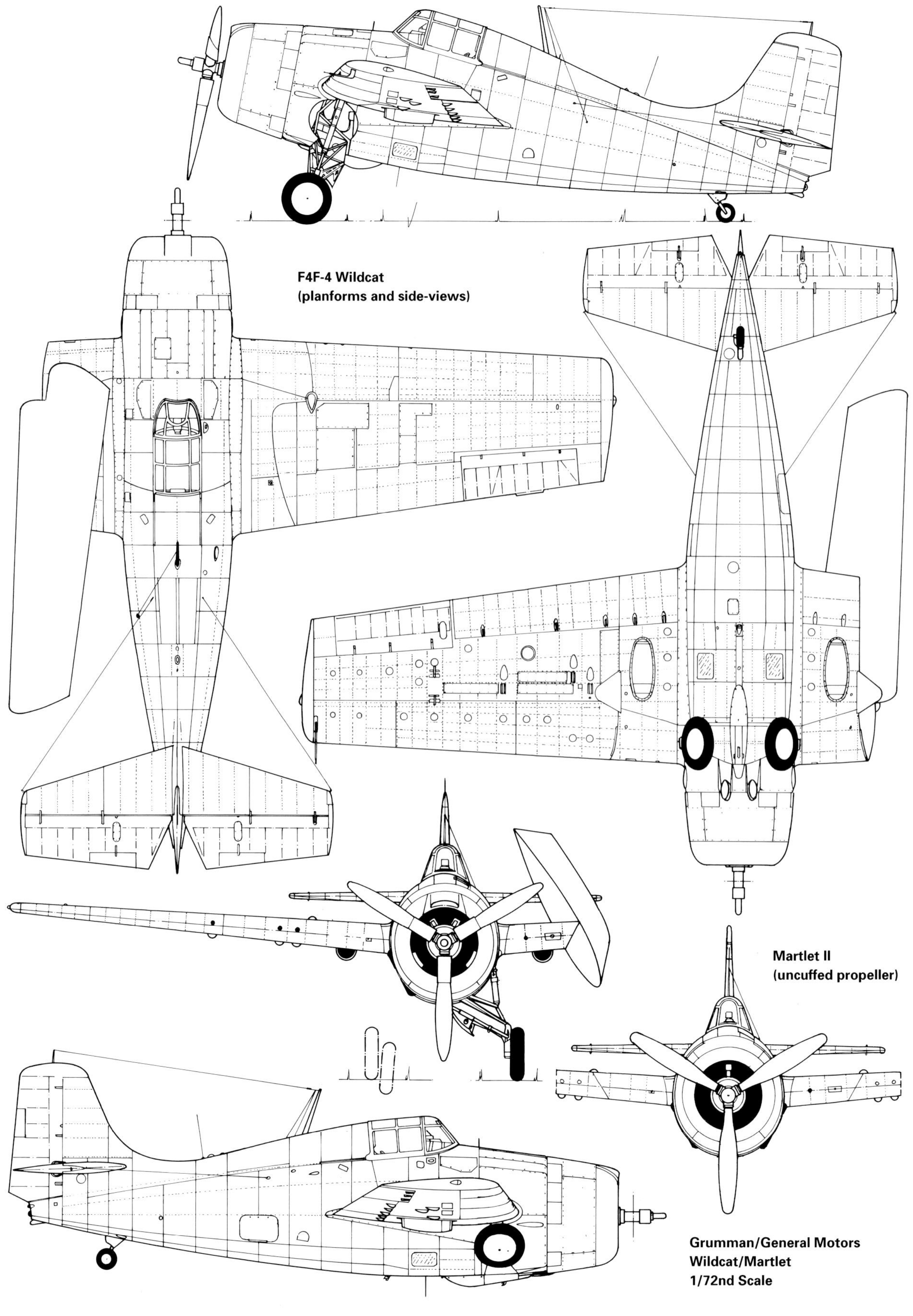
F4F-4 Wildcat
(planforms and side-views)
Martlet II
(uncuffed propeller)
Grumman/General Motors
Wildcat/Martlet
1/72nd Scale

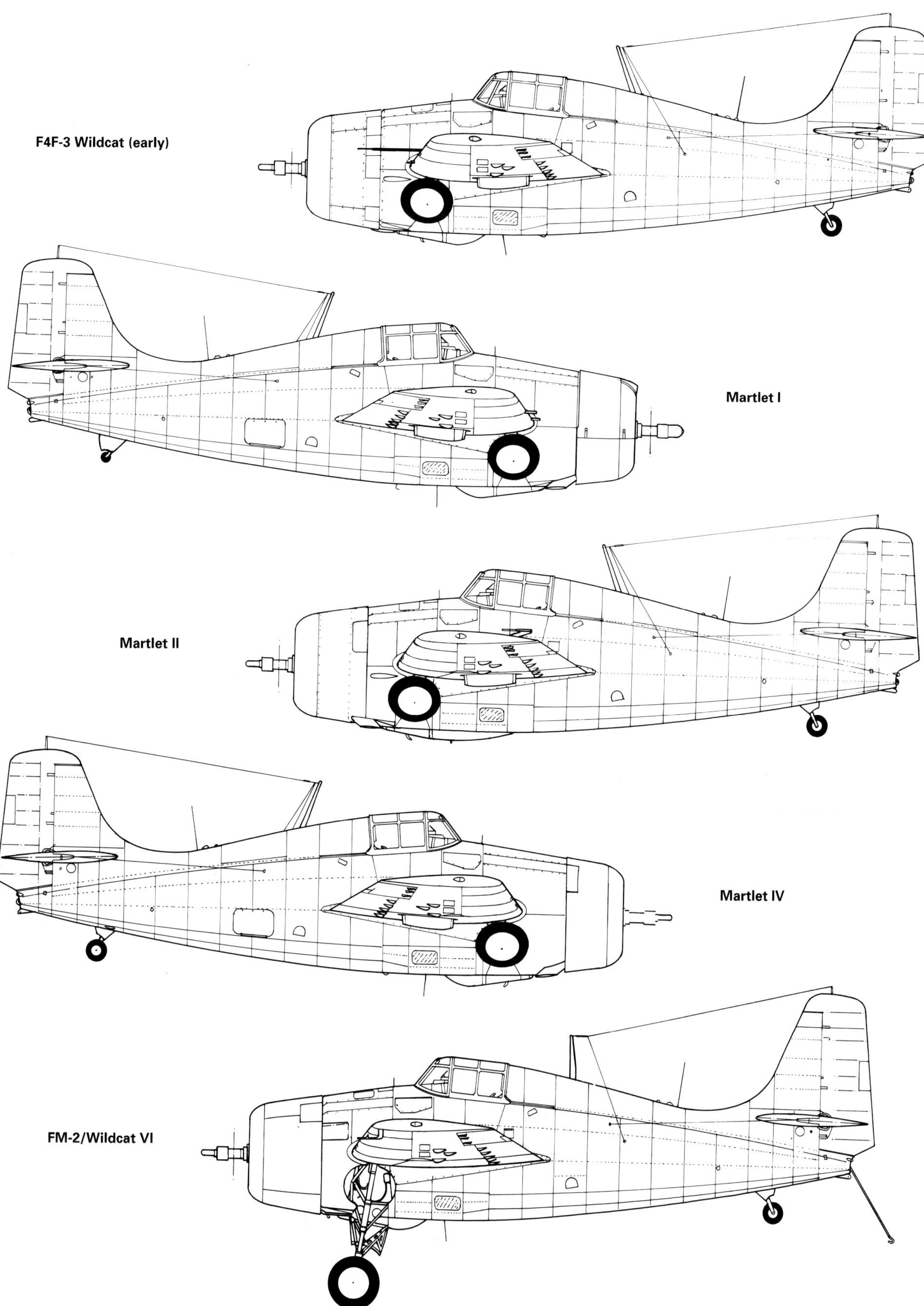
F4F-3 Wildcat (early)
Martlet I
Martlet II
Martlet IV
FM-2/Wildcat VI

THE APPENDICES

COLOUR PLATES

1

F4F-3 white F-1, flown by Lt Cdr Paul H ('Hubert') Ramsey, Officer Commanding VF-2, USS *Lexington*, 7 May 1942

This aircraft was used by Ramsey to achieve his first two kills – two Zeros downed on 7 May 1942 (he claimed a third as a probable). It is unusual in retaining the tiny national insignia well back on the rear fuselage, a larger design by then being in widespread use. Ramsey claimed a Bf 109 (actually a Zero) on 8 May, with another as a probable. He later became the CO of Carrier Replacement Group 11. VF-2 scored 17 kills, all on 7/8 May 1942. Like most aircraft operating in the combat zone, this F4F-3 has had its fuselage code abbreviated from 2-F-1 (indicating the second-fighter unit's-first aircraft) to remove the squadron identifier.

2

F4F-3 BuNo 3976/white F-1, flown by Lt John Smith ('Jimmy') Thach, Officer Commanding VF-3, USS *Lexington*, 10 April 1942

On the outbreak of war, VF-3 had only ten F4F-3s (plus one borrowed from NAS San Diego) of an intended establishment of 18, having converted from the Brewster F2A-2 during August 1941. A 1927 graduate of the Naval Academy, Jimmy Thach had joined VF-3 as gunnery officer in June 1939, leading the successful team which won the Fleet gunnery trophy for VF-3, before becoming XO and finally squadron commander in December 1940. This aircraft was flown by Thach on 20 February 1942 when he and his wingman shot down a Kawanishi flying boat shadowing the carrier task force, and by Lt Noel A M Gayler when he shot down a G4M later the same day. Thach shot down a G4M himself while flying F-13 and damaged another on 20 February. This aircraft was decorated with three Japanese flags and the distinctive 'Felix the Cat' insignia of VF-3. It also has the high camouflage demarcation common on early non-specular blue grey/light grey aircraft, and the code number repeated on each side of the cowling, as per standard US Navy regulations. This combat veteran was finally lost while serving with VF-2 during the Battle of Coral Sea.

3

F4F-4 BuNo 5093/white 23, flown by Lt Cdr John S Thach, Officer Commanding VF-3, USS *Yorktown*, Midway, 4 June 1942

VF-3 re-equipped with F4F-4s at Kaneohe Bay in Hawaii in May 1942, passing its F4F-3s to VMF-212. It then embarked aboard the USS *Yorktown* for the Battle of Midway. Thach had, however, lost his pilots to VF-2 aboard the ill-fated *Lexington* and had to basically reform the unit from largely new and inexperienced ensigns, to which was added a core of experienced pilots from VF-42. In direct contrast to Jimmy Flatley's retention of the six-aircraft division (with three two-fighter sections), Thach preferred a four aircraft division as the primary tactical unit. In developing tactics for his squadron, and the Navy as a whole, Thach emphasised defensive tactics, advising against initiating attacks unless you held an altitude advantage. His leadership of 'Fighting Three' earned him a DSM. Thach used this aircraft to down three Zeros, and a new F-1 to destroy a torpedo bomber (and claim another as a probable) later the same day, bringing his tally to six confirmed kills and a probable. This aircraft was pushed over the side of the crippled *Yorktown* on 6 June to reduce top weight in an effort to prevent her from keeling over and sinking.

4

F4F-3 BuNo 4031/white F-15, flown by Lt Edward H ('Butch') O'Hare VF-3, USS *Lexington*, 20 February 1942

'Butch' O'Hare claimed five Mitsubishi G4M1 Model 11 'Bettys' of the 4th Air Group Air Striking Force during the Battle of Bougainville, all in a single mission and while flying this aircraft, with a sixth claimed as a probable. O'Hare gained two more kills in F6Fs but was killed in action in November 1943. VF-3 scored some 36 kills with the Wildcat at Bougainville and Midway. This historic aircraft had initially served with VMF-211 and survived the devastating attack on Oahu. After service with VF-3, it was passed to VF-2 and was one of only six F4Fs from VF-2 to survive the Coral Sea battle, taking refuge on the *Yorktown*. It was then passed to VF-42 and ended its days on 29 July 1944 when a pilot from MAG-23 wrote it off.

5

F4F-3 BuNo 3986/white F-13, flown by Lt Edward H O'Hare, VF-3, USS *Lexington*, 10 April 1942

Flown by O'Hare for the historic photo mission with Thach on 10 April 1942, F-13 had seen extensive action during the Bougaineville campaign. On 20 February, for example, it was flown by both Thach and Lts Noel Gayler and Lee Haynes, with Thach scoring 1.5 kills. The F4F wears standard markings for the period, with red and white rudder stripes aft of the main hinge line only, and with medium sized national insignia. The red rudder stripes and central 'dot' were removed from 15 May 1942, while white codes were more slowly replaced by black from late 1941. It was lost while serving with VF-2 at Coral Sea.

6

F4F-4 BuNo 5192/black F12, flown by Lt James Julian ('Pug') Southerland, VF-5, USS *Saratoga*, 7 August 1942

Southerland used this aircraft to shoot down the first two Japanese aircraft of the Guadalcanal campaign, launching from the USS *Saratoga*. After downing a pair of enemy bombers, he was himself shot down by PO1C Sakai Saburo of the Tainan Air Group. The aircraft was formally stricken on 30 September, more than a month after it was lost! Southerland had to wait until 1945 when he (by now a Commander) downed a pair of 'Tonys' and a Zeke. VF-5's Wildcats were unusual in retaining the F code designator for longer than other squadrons, and in applying nicknames in black below the canopy rail. F-12 actually belonged to Ensign Mortimer C ('Junior') Kleinmann.

7

F4F-3A BuNo 3916/white 6-F-5, flown by Ensign James G Daniels, VF-6, USS *Enterprise*, 7 December 1941

This aircraft displays the markings worn by Fleet Wildcats on the outbreak of war, with a small star, full white squadron-role-aircraft code and no rudder stripes. Daniels escaped being shot down by US AAA on the first day of war, a fate which befell five other VF-6 F4Fs! He never made ace, but did share in the destruction of one aircraft (being officially credited with 0.33) and was credited with the probable destruction of 0.33 of another machine. His unit – VF-6 – was more successful, however, counting among its members two Wildcat aces – Lt(jg) Lee Mankin with five kills and Ensign Donald E Runyon, who later added three F6F kills to his tally of eight scored while flying F4Fs.

8

F4F-3A BuNo 3914/black F-14, flown by Lt Wilmer E ('Bill') Rawie, VF-6, USS *Enterprise*, 1 February 1942

In this F4F Bill Rawie scored the Navy's first kill of the Pacific War, downing a Mitsubishi A5M4 flown by Lt Kurakane Akira of the Chitose Air Group over the island of Taroa in the Marshall chain – he gained a further 0.33 of a kill on 4 June 1942.

9

F4F-4 BuNo 5075/black 20, flown by Machinist Donald Eugene Runyon, VF-6, USS *Enterprise*, 24 August 1942

One of the US Navy's top-scoring enlisted Naval Aviation Pilots (NAPs), and originally one of the 16 'Fighting Chiefs' of VF-2, Don Runyon scored eight kills with VF-6. He added three more to this tally after his promotion to Lt(jg) and service with VF-18. This aircraft was built at Long Island and delivered to the Navy on 10 February 1942, being assigned to VF-6 on 1 April. It participated in the Tokyo Raid and the Battle of Midway, and was transferred to VF-5 on 25 August, with whom it became black 38. It was destroyed by enemy bombing at Henderson Field on 15 October. The aircraft carries the LSO stripe on the port side of the fin, intended to allow Landing Signal Officers to determine the F4F's attitude on approach.

10

F4F-4 white 18, flown by AP/1c Howard Stanton Packard, VF-6, USS *Enterprise*, August 1942

Aviation Pilot First Class Howard Packard scored two damaged, one probable and one kill with VF-6 during June-August 1942. One of ten NAPs transferred to 'Fighting Six' from VF-2 in March 1942, he later won a DFC. Packard's aircraft was unusual in VF-6 in having white codes and in being decorated with victory symbols in the shape of small Japanese flags.

11

F4F-4 black 9-F-1, flown by Lt Cdr John Raby, VF-9, USS *Ranger*, *Operation Torch*, November 1942

Aside from the distinctive yellow ring around the national insignia applied for *Operation Torch*, this F4F-4 otherwise wears standard markings. Most of Raby's pilots were extremely inexperienced, many having less than 25 carrier landings. Unfortunately for them, they came up against some highly experienced French fighter pilots, some of whom had even been aces during the Battle of France. Moreover, the Curtiss Hawk 75 was more agile than the F4F-4, and the Vichy French had the advantage of flying over their own territory. Nevertheless, *Torch* proved a relatively inexpensive training ground for the F4F pilots. Raby himself downed a Leo 45 and a Curtiss Hawk, claiming a second Hawk as a probable.

12

F4F-4 BuNo 03417/white 19, flown by Lt Stanley Winfield ('Swede') Vejtasa, VF-10, USS *Enterprise*, 26 October 1942

Vejtasa scored three kills while serving with VS-5 during May 1942, and added 7.25 more (plus a probable) during his time with VF-10, seven of the latter score being downed in a single mission on 26 October!

13

F4F-4 BuNo 5238/white 14, flown by Ensign Edwin Lewis ('Whitey') Feightner, VF-10, USS *Enterprise*, 30 January 1943

'Whitey' Feightner amassed four confirmed kills and a probable during his service with VF-10, downing three 'Bettys' in this aircraft on 30 January 1943. During a second tour of duty with VF-8 in 1944 (flying the F6F) he added five more kills and a probable. Unusually for an *Enterprise*-based F4F, this aircraft lacks an LSO stripe.

14

F4F-4 white F21, flown by Lt(jg) William Nicholas Leonard, VF-11, Guadalcanal, June 1943

During earlier service Leonard had found the performance of the F4F-4 marginal with the new 58 gallon underwing tanks, describing the aircraft as a 'Dog' when flown in this configuration. He scored two kills with VF-42, two more with VF-3 and added a pair of Zeros on 12 June 1943 with the VF-11. His F4F is seen as it appeared on that day, with five victory flags and a tiny 'Sundowners' badge below the cockpit. Retention of the F role designator in the code was extremely unusual as late as June 1943.

15

FM-2 white 17 of VF-26, USS *Santee*, October 1944

Non-specular blue grey topsides and light grey undersides gave way to overall dark gloss sea blue from March 1944, with markings in insignia white. This FM-2 has silver underwing tanks, which seem to have remained more common than blue until the end of the war. VF-26 used a pair of narrow white bands across the fin tip as its unit marking, applied in white. Lt Cdr Harold Funk scored a single victory while flying with VF-23 on 8 September 1943, and added six more on 24 October 1944 whilst with VF-26, bringing him ace status.

16

F4F-4 black 41-F-1, flown by Lt Cdr Charles Thomas Booth II, VF-41, USS *Ranger*, early 1942

Charles Booth's F4F-4 wearing the full red and white rudder trim used until May 1942, with full codes in black and outsize national insignia. Unusually the aircraft does not wear the Boar's head insignia of the 'Red Rippers' which was applied beneath the windscreen of many squadron aircraft. Booth commanded VF-41 during *Operation Torch*, claiming one Dewoitine D.520 of the unit's total tally of 14 kills. Wildcat successes were marred, however, by the destruction of two RAF aircraft – a PRU Spitfire (identified as a black Bf 109) and a Hudson (claimed as a LeO 45).

17

F4F-4 black 41-F-22, flown by Lt(jg) Charles Alfred ('Windy') Shields, VF-41, USS *Ranger*, *Operation Torch*, November 1942

Although his Silver Star citation and official kill listings record the destruction of only two aircraft by Shields during *Torch*, other sources indicate that his score may have been as high as four. After shooting down a D.520 he attacked a pair of Hawks that were threatening a wingman, downing one and leaving the intended victim to polish off the other. He then destroyed a further Hawk, and shot down a Douglas DB-7 as it took off, before being shot down and forced to bail out. A further kill (of a 'Tony') scored with VF-4 in November 1944 may have brought Shields up to full ace status.

18

F4F-3 BuNo 2531/black F-2, flown by Ensign Elbert Scott McCuskey, VF-42, USS *Yorktown*, 8 May 1942

This Wildcat was used by Scott McCuskey (who had earlier shared in the destruction of a four-engined patrol aircraft) to gain his first full victory – a Zero from the carrier *Shokaku* during the Battle of the Coral Sea. Low on fuel, McCuskey landed aboard the damaged *Lexington*, where his aircraft remained as the ship burned, exploded and sank. McCuskey himself enjoyed a longer career, moving to 'Fighting Three' and reaching a total of 6.5 Wildcat victories, plus a further seven kills while flying Hellcats with VF-8. His F4F score included three 'Vals' destroyed when 12 Wildcats tackled 18 dive-bombers hell bent on sinking *Yorktown*. Despite splashing 11 Aichis, CV-5 was hit three times, causing mortal damage. The carrier was later sunk by a Japanese submarine.

19

F4F-4 BuNo 02148/black 30, flown by Lt Cdr Courtney Shands, VF-71, USS *Wasp*, August 1942

Shands destroyed five enemy aircraft in this machine, strafing them in a predawn strike against Tulagi on 7 August 1942. He added another ground kill to his tally, but was unable to open his scoring against aerial targets.

20

F4F-4 BuNo 02069/white 27, flown by Ensign George Leroy Wrenn, VF-72, USS *Hornet*, 26 October 1942

Wrenn used this aircraft to destroy five torpedo bombers on 26 October, landing back on the damaged *Enterprise* after the *Hornet* was itself crippled. His eventual tally was 5.5, and he never repeated his success of 26 October. Wrenn's F4F went on to VF-10 and was then returned to the USA for overhaul in May 1943. It ended its days with operational training command.

21

F4F-4 black 29-GF-10, flown by Ensign Bruce Donald Jacques, VGF-29, USS *Santee*, *Operation Torch*, November 1942

The CO of VGF-29 at *Torch* was Lt John Thomas 'Tommy' Blackburn, who was later to win fame as the leader of the F4U-equipped VF-17 – he was already an experienced carrier aviator at this early stage in the war. However, during *Torch* his leadership proved insufficient for his unit to gain more than a single kill, gained by the lowly Ensign Jacques over what he took to be a 'Bloch 174', but which was, in fact, a Potez 63.

22

FM-2 triangle 7, flown by Lt Leo Martin Ferko, VC-4, USS *White Plains*, June to October 1944

Martin Ferko accounted for four of VC-4's twelve kills, downing a pair of Zeros on 24 October and a pair of 'Jills' the following day. This FM-2 wears an unusual finish, more common in the Atlantic (where VF-4 scored the USN Wildcat's only two victories against German aircraft) with non-specular blue topsides and white undersides.

23

FM-2 white B6 *MAH BABY*, flown by Ensign Joseph D McGraw, VC-10, USS *Gambier Bay*, 24 October 1944

Wearing the snorting seahorse insignia and 'B' identity code of VC-10, McGraw's FM-2, with his name below the cockpit and the name *MAH BABY* on the cowling, also wears three Japanese flags representing his first three kills. The two kills which brought him to ace status were scored while he was attached to VC-80 following the sinking of the *Gambier Bay*.

24

FM-2 black 4, VC-13, USS *Anzio*, April 1945

April 1945 saw a brief period of success for VC-13, whose pilots accounted for eight enemy aircraft, with two probables and a damaged. A Zero and a 'Val' fell to Lt(jg) Doug Hagood on 6 April whilst serving with this unit – he also claimed a 'Val' as damaged. This FM-2 may have been an emergency replacement rushed out to the Pacific theatre, since it still wears North Atlantic colours.

25

FM-2 white 29, flown by Lt(jg) Hatherly Foster III, VC-93, USS *Petrof Bay*, April 1945

Several VC squadrons operated aircraft with distinctive unit identification markings, and those of VC-93 were among the most attractive, with an outline shamrock repeated on the fuselage and upper surface of the starboard wing. VC-93 enjoyed a six-day period of success, downing 17 aircraft, four of which fell to the guns of Hatherly Foster.

26

F4F-4 black 29, flown by 1st Lt Jefferson Joseph DeBlanc, VMF-112, USMC, 31 January 1943

With a total score of nine victories (plus a single probable), one of which was scored while flying the F4U, DeBlanc was the Marines' 11th highest Wildcat ace. He completed his F4F tally by downing five aircraft in a single day – 31 January 1943. Low on fuel, and with his F4F badly damaged, DeBlanc was forced to abandon his aircraft at little more than treetop height, but was spotted bailing out close to a Japanese-held island by coast watchers on a nearby (friendly) island and was rescued. His aircraft is typical of 'Corps F4Fs at the time, with non-specular blue and grey camouflage, large national insignia and a two-digit code in black, with no unit identification whatsoever.

27

F4F-4 white 84, flown by Captain Joseph Jacob Foss, VMF-121, USMC, October 1942

Joe Foss may have been the top scoring Marine pilot of World War 2. 'Pappy' Boyington scored 22 victories with the USMC, and claimed to have scored another six with the 'Flying Tigers'. The latter kills include 1.5 confirmed ground kills, and two confirmed aerial victories (for which he was paid), but records researched by Frank Olynyk (the expert on US aces) cannot confirm the other 2.5. Olynyk is punctilious in pointing out that this does not mean that Boyington didn't score them, only that they can't be confirmed. This would seem to put Foss, with 26 confirmed kills, at the top of the USMC aces list. This aircraft was used by Foss to down several of the 19 Zeros he destroyed during his Guadalcanal tour.

28

F4F-4 white 50, flown by Captain Joseph Jacob Foss, VMF-121, USMC, Guadalcanal 12 November 1942

Executive Officer to Major Leonard K 'Duke' Davis, Foss scored his first kill on 13 October 1942. Judged 'too old' for fighters, he was a natural 'shot', and this eventually led to the last of his many requests for transfer from a recce unit to be approved. Foss flew white 50 for several of his victories. On 12 November 1942, for instance, he downed two 'Bettys' and a single Zero to notch up numbers 20, 21 and 22. White 50 was entirely representative of Cactus Air Force F4Fs, with no personal or unit markings.

29

F4F-4 black 53, flown by Captain Joseph Jacob Foss, VMF-121, USMC, 23 October 1942

Foss used this anonymous-looking aircraft to shoot an attacking Zero off the tail of a member of his division on 23 October 1942, thus claiming his eighth victory. He had a great respect for the enemy, and is quoted as saying 'If you're alone and you meet a Zero, run like hell. You're outnumbered'. Foss' score of 26 confirmed kills made him the most successful pilot of the Guadalcanal campaign

30

F4F-3 black 8, flown by Lt Col Harold William Bauer, VMF-212, USMC, Guadalcanal September-November 1942

Bauer amassed a total of ten kills (plus a probable kill of a Zero) during the bitter fighting for Guadalcanal – one of them while attached to VMF-224, and four (plus the probable) while flying with VMF-223. The official USMC listing gives Bauer ten kills, including the probable which he himself refused to claim! He was appointed commander of all fighters on Guadalcanal on 23 October 1942, issuing the advice 'When you see Zeros, dogfight 'em!' The optimistic and aggressive Bauer, often known as 'the Coach' or 'Indian Joe', went missing in action on 14 November 1942, over Guadalcanal, and received his Medal of Honour posthumously. His F4F is unusual in having a white cowling lip.

31

F4F-4 BuNo 02124/white 77, flown by Lt James Elms Swett, VMF-221, USMC, 7 April 1943

On 7 March 1943, 67 Aichi 'Val' dive bombers, escorted by 110 Zeros, attacked US shipping around Guadalcanal. Seventy-six 'Cactus' interceptors were scrambled to deal with this massive raid, including a four-aircraft division led by Swett, a 22 year old who had yet to fire his guns in anger! Swett led his formation into a squadron of 15 'Vals' as they tipped into their attack dive from 15,000 ft, having to ignore concentrated friendly AAA aimed at the dive-bombers. Swett accounted for two 'Vals' in the dive, and nailed another as it pulled out. Four more fell as they attempted to egress the target area, the gunner of the eighth smashing Swett's cockpit canopy and hitting his engine. His damaged aircraft (already holed in the port wing by a friendly 40-mm AAA shell) didn't make it home, the pilot having to ditch after his oil-starved engine seized. Swett scored a further 8.5 kills (with three probables, and a quarter share in a damaged 'Judy') while flying F4Us.

32

F4F-4 BuNo 02100/black 13, flown by Captain Marion E Carl, VMF-223, USMC, Guadalcanal August 1942

Like many of the top-scoring Guadalcanal pilots, Carl enjoyed a generous slice of luck. Of 38 Marine pilots killed or wounded, eight were shot down during their first two days, and another nine were lost during their first week of operations. But it was not just the tyros who were shot down. Foss, Galer, Smith, DeBlanc and Swett were all shot down but survived to fight again, while Bauer, arguably the most talented Marine fighter pilot at Guadalcanal, was lost in action. Marion Carl was no exception, and was shot down in this aircraft on 9 September 1942, but quickly replaced it with another 'lucky 13'.

33

F4F-4 BuNo 03508/black 13, flown by Captain Marion E Carl, VMF-223, USMC, Guadalcanal September 1942

With little escort work to be done, and with frequent appearances by Japanese carrier-based fighters virtually over their home airfield, the Cactus Air Force enjoyed all the traditional advantages of the defender and had a target rich environment, allowing big scores to be built up. Marine pilots claimed 395 kills between 20 August and 15 November, with VFs-5 and -10 adding 45 more, for the loss of 101 F4Fs. In reality the Japanese lost about 260 aircraft, but even this represented a kill:loss ratio better than 2.5:1, and ensured eventual victory. Only a handful of US pilots were productive, but those who did built up large tallies. Carl, for instance, scored 16.5, to which he later added two while flying F4Us.

34

F4F-4 white 2,unit and pilot unknown, USMC, Guadalcanal September 1942

Kill tallies were rarely painted on Marine F4F, it being felt that such decorations would generate unwelcome attention from the enemy. There were exceptions, especially during the brief periods when photographers from *Stars and Stripes*, or other propaganda sheets, were touring the frontline – this machine was duly decorated and photographed during one such visit.

35

F4F-3 white MF-1, flown by Major R E Galer, VMF-224, USMC, Guadalcanal September-October 1942

Robert Galer's F4F-3 is unusually colourful, with its red cowling lip and fuselage stripe. Thirteen flags appear below the cockpit rail, representing Galer's total official USMC tally, although individual unit records show a total of 14 kills. At least one of his aircraft wore the name *'Barbara Jane'* on the nose. During September and October 1942, Galer amassed 14 kills and three probables, including seven confirmed victories over the Zero, and this total, achieved only on the F4F, made him the fourth top-scoring Wildcat ace.

36

Martlet I AL254/R, flown by Sub-Lt Eric Brown, No 802 Sqn, FAA, HMS *Audacity*, 8 November 1941

Eric Brown, later famous as a test pilot (flying an unparalleled number of different types, including most captured enemy aircraft) and as the leading carrier aviator (with 2400 carrier landings) in the Fleet Air Arm, first encountered Grumman's latest fighter when Martlet Is were 'acquired' by No 802 Sqn at Donibristle in early 1941. He scored a victory in the type on 8 November that same year, claiming the destruction of a KG 40 Fw 200. The Martlet I was an unusual aircraft, intended for French *Aéronavale* service, but with no provision for carrier operation, and with metric instruments. It also had a 'pull to accelerate/push to decelerate' throttle, which was soon modified by the British to operate in the 'right' sense. The aircraft were diverted to the RN after the fall of France, and were fitted with four wing-mounted 0.50 cal guns in place of the 7.62 mm Darne weapons originally specified. They were powered by a Wright R-1820-G205A Cyclone engine, driving a Hamilton Standard propeller, because the F4F-3's Pratt & Whitney R-1830 was not then cleared for export.

37

Martlet I BJ562/A, flown by Sub-Lt Parke, RNVR, No 804 Sqn, FAA, Skeabrae, Orkney, 24 December 1940

On Christmas Eve 1940, Lt Carver and Sub-Lt Parke sighted a Ju 88 over Scapa Flow shortly after taking off after a suitably festive, lunch. They gave chase and eventually put an engine out of action, thus forcing the bomber to crash land in a field. The aircraft wears standard FAA fighter camouflage and national insignia, with a sky blue recognition band around the fuselage similar to those applied to all British fighters during the period.

38

Martlet III AX733/K, flown by Sub-Lt W M Walsh RN, No 805 Sqn, FAA, Western Desert, 28 September 1941

No 805 Sqn was a constituent part of the RN Fighter Unit which operated alongside RAF squadrons in the Western Desert during 1941 and 1942, operating with the Hurricane-equipped Nos 803 and 806 Sqns. The Martlets scored victories against three Savoia Marchetti SM.79s, a single Ju 88 and a Fiat G.50. The latter was downed by Sub-Lt W M Walsh, flying this Martlet III. Originally painted azure blue overall, the unit's Martlets soon picked up stone upper surfaces to camouflage them against the desert. The Martlet III was also used by No 806 Sqn, which claimed four kills when it escorted the *Operation Pedestal* convoy to Malta during August 1942, flying from HMS *Indomitable*.

39

Wildcat V JV573, flown by Sub-Lt R A Fleischman-Allen RN, No 813 Sqn, FAA, HMS *Vindex*, February 1945

Formerly F Flight of No 1832 Sqn, which formed flights of four Wildcat Vs for service on escort carriers, No 813 Sqn's Flight augmented units equipped with the Swordfish and Fulmar aboard HMS *Campania*, and then HMS *Vindex*. During early 1945 the unit's pilots shot down three Ju 88s, one of these falling to Fleischman-Allen, who had also shared in the destruction of an Fw 200 in December 1943, whilst serving with No 842 Sqn. The Martlet (later Wildcat) V was identical to the FM-1, and was likewise built by General Motors, although the FAA continued to refer to the aircraft as a 'Grumman'. This aircraft is by no means unusual in lacking identification codes.

40

Wildcat (Martlet) IV FN135, Sub-Lt R K L Yeo RN, No 819 Sqn, FAA, HMS *Activity*, 30 March 1944

Another composite squadron was No 819, operating a mix of Wildcats and Swordfish from

HMS *Activity*. While escorting convoy JW58, on 30 March 1944 Yeo shared a Ju 88 with Lt J G Large, while unit pilots accounted for two Fw 200s and a Bv 138 over the next three days. Yeo moved to No 816 Sqn aboard HMS *Chaser*, with whom he downed a Bv 138 on the last day of May 1944.

41

Martlet II AM974/J, flown by Sub-Lt B J Waller RN, No 881 Sqn, FAA, HMS *Illustrious*, Madagascar, May 1942

One of the most successful Martlet pilots, having a hand in the destruction of three enemy aircraft, Waller opened his scoring with a Potez 63 on 6 May 1942, shared with Lt Bird. The next day he downed two Morane MS.406 fighters, sharing one with Sub-Lt J A Lyon and the other with Lt C C Tomkinson, who downed a third single-handedly.

42

Wildcat VI JV377/6-C, flown by Lt Cdr Bird RN, No 882 Sqn, FAA, HMS *Searcher*, 26 March 1945

Lt Cdr Bird, who had earlier helped Waller down a Potez 63 while serving with No 881 Sqn in May 1942, led his unit in the last productive FAA Wildcat operation of the war – he claimed one of the four III./JG 5 Bf 109Gs downed by his formation during a sweep off Norway on 26 March 1945. A mix of numerals and letters were common in FAA Wildcat/Martlet codes, sometimes with three digits, sometimes with only two. The last digit was always a letter, and was the individual aircraft identity.

43

Martlet II FN112/0-7D, flown by Lt Dennis Mayvore Jeram RN, No 888 Sqn, FAA, HMS *Formidable*, *Operation Torch*, 9 November 1942

Although not the top-scoring Martlet pilot, Jeram was the only FAA ace to fly the aircraft, adding his two Wildcat victories to a probable and four kills scored while seconded to the RAF's No 213 Sqn – equipped with Hurricane Mk Is – during the Battle of Britain. Flying during *Operation Torch*, over and off Algeria, Jeram claimed a 'Potez 63' (actually a Bloch MB.174 of GRII/52, Vichy Air Force) on 6 November, and shared in the destruction of a German-flown Ju 88 on 9 November with Sub-Lt Astin. His aircraft wears a US-style star painted over its roundels, and has even had the legend 'U.S.NAVY' applied to the rear fuselage. It does, however, retain the traditional crest of No 888 Sqn superimposed on the fin flash.

FIGURE PLATES

1

VMF-224 boss Maj Robert E Galer is shown in his standard issue USMC summer service uniform in late 1942. He has a set of gold navy wings pinned to the left breast of his tunic, above two rows of ribbons that include the Medal of Honour.

2

In marked contrast to Galer, Capt Joseph J Foss is depicted in January 1943 on Guadalcanal wearing 'fighting garb'. This consists of a 'suit/summer/flying', utility cap, adorned with the 'Corps globe and anchor badge, and Marine 'boondocker' boots. The leather patch on Foss' suit has been embossed in gold with Navy wings, rank and 'USMC' titling. He is carrying an AN-H-15 helmet, goggles and a life vest. His pistol belt supports a M1911A1 .45 cal pistol, first aid kit, ammo pouch and canteen.

3

Wearing a dark blue Royal Navy service uniform, with a matching heavy wool turtle neck jumper and standard issue Mae West, Sub-Lt Eric 'Winkle' Brown of No 802 Sqn was dressed for comfort and warmth aboard HMS *Audacity* in late 1941. His headgear is also RAF standard issue, with the addition of smaller, but wider, US headphones.

4

Top-scoring FM-2 ace Lt Ralph Elliot of VC-27 aboard USS *Savo Island* in late 1944. He is wearing full flying gear including an AN-H-15 tropical helmet, goggles, US Navy 'suit/summer/flying', inflatable life vest, seat-type parachute with life raft, naval aviator's gloves and a Smith and Wesson .38 cal revolver and survival knife.

5

This Navy Lieutenant was attached to VF-21 in the Solomons in mid-1943, and he is wearing summer 'khakis', an A-2 flying jacket and khaki service cap

6

Lt(jg) E H 'Butch' O'Hare in January 1942, wearing the naval aviator's pre-war green/grey service uniform. Note the rank badges worn on the cuffs and collar, and the 'bullion wings' on the left breast.

dressed only in worn-out trousers and stockings, scrambled aboard. All the way back he chatted with the pilot, longtime friend Maj J R 'Mad Jack' Cram, who updated Foss on 'Cactus' gossip.

Upon returning to Guadalcanal, Foss was told that Fighter Command had claimed 15 enemy aircraft on the seventh. His own three victories raised his tally to 19, tying him with Maj Smith of VMF-223. However, there was also grim news – five-kill ace 2nd Lt Danny Doyle was missing in action. He was last seen chasing an enemy aircraft on the day Foss went down. No trace of him was ever found.

Back only one day, Foss received the Distinguished Flying Cross from Vice Adm William F Halsey, the theatre commander, on 9 November 1942. Also decorated were 2nd Lts W B 'Whiskey Bill' Freeman and Wallace G Wethe, also of VMF-121. Two days later, Foss was back in action. However, he missed both interceptions on 11 November when VMF-121 lost four pilots, plus Maj Davis and one other slightly wounded. Foss had much better luck on the 12th.

That morning Rabaul launched a major effort against four US transports unloading Army troops at Lunga Roads. Sixteen 'Bettys' and 30 Zeros strobed on 'Cactus' radar early in the afternoon, and the ships withdrew to the channel where they could maneouvre. Meanwhile, Foss was airborne with eight Wildcats, supported by an equal number of P-39 Airacobras. Taking advantage of low clouds, the attackers got in beneath the CAP, but were immediately beset by VMF-112. Foss' top-cover flight then screamed to wavetop level to help. This descent was performed at as fast a velocity as Foss ever achieved in a F4F. Whatever the actual speed, his full-power dive was so rapid that his windscreen iced up in the warmer, lower, air, and his canopy burst from the increasing pressure. Other Wildcats lost inspection panels in the headlong plunge.

Foss and his pilots chased the speedy Mitsubishis into a cloud of American flak, descending to 50 ft or less. Ignoring the peril, Foss hauled into within 100 yards of the nearest bomber and aimed at the starboard engine, which spouted flame. The G4M tried a water landing, caught a wingtip and tumbled into oblivion. Foss set his sight on another 'Betty' when a Zero intervened. The F4F nosed up briefly and fired a beautifully-aimed snapshot which sent the A6M spearing into the water. He then resumed the chase.

Setting up to starboard, Foss tracked the next 'Betty' in line and fired, but missed. Still low, he was concerned about being trapped by other Zeros. However, he passed to port and made a deflection shot which connected with the 'Betty's' wingroot. Flames spread along the wing and the bomber made a controlled water landing. As he passed over the sinking bomber, Foss noted that the enemy tail gunner hosed off an angry burst as a parting shot. Overhauling another 'Betty', the Marine fired and saw strikes, but inflicted no significant damage. At that point two more Zeros joined the fight, forcing Foss to break off. He steered his F4F in the direction of Savo Island, where a P-39 crossed his flight path, intent on yet another bomber.

Out of ammunition and low on fuel, Foss turned for home. However, other Japanese fighters remained in the area, and he dodged one persistent Zero before eluding it in the clouds.

Through a combination of US fighters and flak, the American warships escaped serious damage, and none of the aerial torpedoes found their intended targets. Total F4F credits amounted to 16 bombers and seven Zeros. In fact five of the 16 'Bettys' that returned to base never flew again. Though only one Zero was known to be lost, US fighters had clearly mastered the situation. Rabaul's A6Ms could no longer protect the bombers. From this combat Foss' tally rose to 22, the first time an American pilot had achieved such a score in World War 2.

That night, Foss sat out the surface engagement raging in Ironbottom Sound. From their living area under the palm trees, aviators heard gunfire and occasionally saw muzzle flashes or exploding shells. An outgunned Allied cruiser-destroyer force prevented yet another Japanese bombardment, but at a high cost – two destroyers sunk on the spot and three more dead in the water. Two cruisers had received serious damage while the task-force commanders, Rear Adms Callaghan and Scott, had both been killed in the clash.

Foss was airborne soon after dawn on the 13th, scouting the area for an expected Japanese landing. However, the naval 'slugfest' had prevented enemy troopships from continuing southward. Beyond Savo Island, Foss was treated to the unexpected sight of a crippled enemy battleship, unable to steam clear of danger. Later in the day Foss and company covered Navy and Marine bombers and torpedo planes which were sent out to destroy HIJMS *Hiei* – she duly became the first Japanese battleship sunk in World War 2.

More Japanese shipping was on the way. Search aircraft on the morning of 14 November brought word of a major reinforcement convoy: 11 troop ships and 12 escorts. Bearing 7000 fresh infantry, the convoy had to be stopped. The 'Cactus Air Force' began a day-long series of flights aimed at sinking Rear Adm Raizo Tanaka's command.

After co-ordinating fighter escorts all day, Lt Col Bauer decided to take a look for himself. Attached to Foss and Lt Furlow that evening, he participated in a strafing mission against the convoy, which was passing the Russell Islands. They pressed their attacks almost to wavetop level, strafing packed decks full of enemy soldiers. Pulling away, Foss and Bauer were alerted of danger by tracers flashing past. Looking back, Foss saw two Zeros descending and, with Bauer, turned into the threat. Bauer took one head-on and shot it into the water – his tenth confirmed kill.

Foss and Furlow went after the other, which eluded them in the criss-crossing tracers over the convoy. The two Marines reversed course, looking to rejoin Bauer but could not find his aircraft. Then Foss noticed an oil slick near the Zero's crash site. Circling low, he saw Joe Bauer afloat in his Mae West, waving animatedly toward Henderson Field. It was not clear whether the doomed Zero had hit Bauer's engine or whether 'The Coach' had been knocked down by AA gunners. In any event, Foss tried to radio for help but could not get through. With a dip of his wing, he rolled out on a return course and sped for home in the gathering dusk.

Foss' main concern was daylight, which was fast fading. Knowing he stood little chance of finding Bauer after dark, he landed, scrambled out of his F4F and found another operations officer, Maj Joe Renner. Immediately he led Foss to a Grumman J2F amphibian and hopped into the cockpit. With Foss in the passenger's seat, Bauer's friends raced back to 'The Slot' as fast as the Duck would take them. They were escorted by two

Capt Joe Foss pensively stares off into the middle distance, his weary fatigues perhaps best illustrating the strain that he, and every other 'Corps pilot in-theatre, had been subjected to for the previous six months. This photograph was just one of dozens taken by the Marine Corps for publicity purposes in the weeks after Foss had beaten Eddie Rickenbacker's 26-kill record from World War 1

'Joe's Flying Circus' in February 1943. Foss, on the far left, poses on a specially-marked Wildcat with the seven other members of his flight. The name *Marine Special* on the cowling appears to be painted in white block letters. Such non-regulation adornments were unusual on Guadalcanal during the campaign, but became somewhat more common after the island was declared secure *(via Robert L Lawson)*

rapidly-drafted Wildcat escorts from VMF-112 and -121.

In full darkness, little was visible other than five burning ships. Renner flew low, criss-crossing the combat area, but neither he nor Foss could see anyone in the water. Deeply concerned, Renner considered a water landing to wait out the night, but Foss realised that with more enemy fleet units approaching, 'The Slot' was no place for an ungainly biplane. With growing apprehension they reluctantly turned for home, determined to return at first light.

They made the right decision. Another surface engagement flared up that night, costing the Japanese another battleship and several destroyers while the US Navy lost three destroyers. At dawn on the 15th, Tanaka's three surviving transports ran themselves aground on Guadalcanal's northern coast. Only one of the remaining destroyers managed to put any troops ashore.

The tireless Joe Renner was back in his Duck, protected by Foss with eight Wildcats. Ordinarily, Foss would have grounded himself – he was running a 103-degree temperature – but everyone at 'Cactus' wanted to retrieve 'The Coach'. Determined to pick up Bauer, or any other American flier they could find, the rescuers ran into like-minded enemy aviators. While Renner tried to stay out of the way, Foss and Lt Oscar Bate each splashed a 'Jake' floatplane. The gunner in Foss' Aichi fired all the way down, leaving the fighter ace with an abiding respect for Japanese aircrews. No trace of Lt Col Harold Bauer was ever found .

Back on the ground, Foss was diagnosed with advanced malaria. His flight was taken over by 2nd Lt Bill Marontate, already credited with ten victories. Foss hardly noticed the passage of time. Despite quinine medication, he lapsed in and out of awareness.

With the destruction of the Japanese convoy, the worst was over for 'Cactus'. On 19 November Foss felt well enough to join several other VMF-121 pilots in New Caledonia. Still groggy and achy, he had lost 37 lbs on Guadalcanal. On the 30th Davis' veterans proceeded to Sydney, Australia, and revelled in the near-forgotten luxury of civilisation.

Whilst there, Foss met the leading Australian fighter aces, Wg Cdr Clive R Caldwell and Sqn Ldr Keith W Truscott. Foss judged 'Killer' and 'Bluey' as 'good blokes', but he noticed a disturbing attitude among some veterans of the European and North African campaigns, who seemed to regard the Japanese as second-rate opponents. Despite Foss' record of 23 credited victories, when he expressed the opinion that a lone F4F was outclassed by a single Zero, some of his hosts openly scoffed. A few weeks later, trying to fight a turning battle in their Spitfires, they belatedly learned that the brash American knew whereof he spoke.

Headed back to combat in mid-December, Foss was waylaid at New Caledonia with a relapse of malaria. He spent Christmas dinner with a hospitable French family who spoke no English, but enjoyed the sumptuous meal just the same. Then, flying overnight, he landed on Guadalcanal early on New Year's Day 1943.

Foss quickly settled back into the routine of bombings and shellings, though improvements had been made in his six-week absence. The 'Fighter Strip' now boasted steel planking, and the operations office was run by Lt Col Sam Jack, VMF-121's original commanding officer.

However, the pace of operations was such that Jack needed some help.

Therefore, Foss filled the morning of 15 January by arranging for fighter escort of strikes against Japanese ships near the Russells. However, he was airborne that same afternoon with seven F4Fs as top cover for SBDs. Bill Marontate saw some square-winged Zeros (later called 'Hamps') and took his division down to engage. Four kills were scored, including one by Marontate – his 13th. However, he then apparently collided with a 'Hamp', as he was seen falling minus one wing. Though somebody reported seeing a pilot successfully bail out of a stricken Wildcat, Marontate never returned. He remained VMF-121's second-ranking ace.

The 'backbone' of VMF-121 pose for an informal group shot in late October 1942. From left to right, the pilots are 2nd Lt Roger A Haberman (6.5 kills), 2nd Lt Cecil J 'Danny' Doyle (5 kills), Capt Joe Foss (26 kills), 1st Lt W P Marontate (13 kills) and 2nd Lt Roy M Ruddell (3 kills) – their individually tailored attire emphasises the 'make do' nature of the campaign. 'Danny' Doyle was killed on 7 November 1942, and Bill Marontate was lost following a collision with a 'Hamp' on 15 January 1943, his F4F being seen to plunge seaward minus one wing

In the ensuing combat, Foss tried a snapshot at one A6M and missed. Another dived in front of him, but this time his aim was dead on: the 'Hamp' exploded. Almost immediately an F4F crossed his nose with a Mitsubishi in tow. Foss fired almost reflexively, not expecting results, but when he looked back the fighter was falling in flames.

Next, Foss jumped a Zero dogging Oscar Bate's tail. Realising its peril, the A6M reversed into the threat. Both pilots fired from close range, but apparently neither scored. Foss could see the Japanese aviator in the cockpit, even noting the anti-glare panel in front of the windscreen.

Twice more the Mitsubishi and Grumman passed one another, firing repeatedly. Foss recognized his opponent as skilled and aggressive, describing this combat as 'one of the most nerve-wracking situations I was ever in'. Following the third set of scissors, Foss was ready to disengage owing to other Zeros in the area. As he glanced back, he saw his antagonist circling below and beginning to trail flames. Foss then ducked into a cloud, happy to be alone. When he emerged, Foss rejoined on Bate and returned to base. Dodging fresh craters in the runway, they landed with bombs falling all around them.

Foss' last mission at Guadalcanal was flown 10 days later. He led his flight, and four P-38s, to intercept a large Japanese force of Zeros and 'Vals' estimated to number more than 60 aircraft. Rather than be drawn into combat by some tempting Zeros which he recognised as bait, Foss elected to maintain altitude and position. Prolonged sparring with the A6Ms allowed 'Cactus' to scramble additional fighters which dealt with the raiders. In one of the war's ironies, during Joe Foss' most satisfying mission he fired not one round.

On 26 January Foss, and most of the other VMF-121 veterans, left Guadalcanal, bound for home. He arrived by ship on 19 April, still showing the effects of malaria. By the time he was reunited with his wife in Washington, DC, Foss realised that he was about to begin 'the dancing bear act'. He learned that he was the first American fighter pilot to equal the Great War record of Capt Eddie Rickenbacker – that feat was to act as a springboard to the rest of his life.

This portrait of Foss, taken on 20 March 1943 (almost two months after his final mission over Guadalcanal), shows him in his dress uniform en route to the US. It was taken during VMF-121's brief period of R&R in Hawaii

A Wartime History of VMF-121

Marine Fighting Squadron 121 (VMF-121) was established at Quantico, Virginia on 24 June 1941. The unit was still absorbing 21 F4F-3s on 7 December when Maj Samuel J Jack hastily recalled his command from various outlying fields and, four days later, arrived in San Diego, California. Following expansion and transition to F4F-4s at Camp Kearney (now NAS Miramar), Jack turned the unit over to Capt Leonard K Davis in March 1942. Embarking for the South Pacific with other elements of Marine Air Group 14, VMF-121 arrived at New Caledonia in August – just in time to prepare for events at Guadalcanal.

On 26 September Davis – now a major – sent five pilots to 'Cactus', where they were temporarily attached to VMF-223 or -224. Whilst on Guadalcanal, two of the detached pilots scored four-and-a-half victories. They were soon reinforced as the rest of the pilots arrived on 9 October, followed by the ground echelon four days later. Operating from 'Fighter Strip One', VMF-121 immediately began taking a toll of the enemy.

The squadron's best day in combat occurred on 25 October, with 18 shootdowns credited. Capt Foss claimed five Zeros in two missions, while Davis became an ace with victories over a Zero and a 'Val'. Probably the hardest day of battle was 11 November when VMF-121 lost six aircraft and four pilots against 10 victories during enemy attacks on US shipping.

Davis remained in command until 16 December, well after the crisis had passed at Guadalcanal. He was relieved by Maj Donald K Yost on New Year's Day, who was in turn succeed by Maj Joseph N Renner and Ray L Vroome.

VMF-121 continued flying F4F-4s until the spring of 1943. At that time, after 161.5 victory claims in Wildcats, the squadron transitioned to F4U-1 Corsairs. Not only was that figure the highest in the Marine Corps to date, but it also remained tops for all Navy and USMC Wildcat squadrons as well. The squadron's first combat in Corsairs occurred on the morning of 12 June when, in a dogfight over the Russells, five pilots claimed six confirmed and four probable Zeros.

The squadron's best day in F4Us occurred on 30 June 1943 in a series of combats over, and around, Rendova. Throughout the morning and afternoon constant CAPs were flown in the area, resulting in claims for 16 Zeros and three probables, plus three 'Bettys' destroyed. From these combats emerged VMF-121's first F4U ace, Capt Kenneth M Ford. Two days later, again over Rendova, VMF-121 confirmed its last Corsair aces: Capts Robert M Baker and Perry L Shuman. In all, 40+ shootdowns were credited through July, with a dozen VMF-121 aces having been placed on the roster since October 1942.

After three combat tours in the Solomons the veteran unit returned to the US, settling at MCAS Mojave, California, in October. At that time Capt Quintus B Nelson began 'turn-around' training in preparation for another overseas deployment.

By October 1941 three of the Marine Corps' four fighting squadrons operated F4Fs – VMF-111 and -121 (pictured) with Marine Air Group One at Quantico, Virginia, and VMF-211 at Ewa, Hawaii. The fourth unit, VMF-221, flew Brewster F2A Buffaloes at San Diego, California. This pale-grey Wildcat carries white side markings showing 121-MF-?, the individual aircraft number unfortunately being obscured by the wing. The squadron emerged from World War 2 as the Marine Corps' top-scoring fighter unit *(via Robert L Lawson)*

VMF-121's 'ready room' at Guadalcanal. Between scrambles and scheduled patrols, the open-air environment lent itself to cards and checkers, as seen here. Sitting at the table, left to right, are Lts J L Narr and F C Drury, Maj L K Davis, and Lts G K Loesch and J A Stubb. Kibbitzers are Maj P J Fontana (CO VMF-112) and Lt Finney, an intelligence officer. Narr, Drury, Davis, Loesch and Fontana all became fighter aces *(via Robert L Lawson)*

Maj Walter J Meyer became the tenth CO on 1 December, and remained in command until May 1945, far longer than any of VMF-121's other wartime leaders. By July 1944 the squadron was headed back into combat, returning to Espiritu Santo in early August. Preceded by the ground echelon to Peleliu Atoll in the Palaus, the Corsairs landed on 25 October – the second anniversary of Joe Foss' five-kill day. Once established at Peleliu, VMF-121 began a lengthy series of fighter-bomber strikes against Yap Atoll in the Carolines. While the unit was based at Ulithi Atoll, 1st Lts H H Hill and G C Huntington teamed up to shoot down a 'Myrt' recce-aircraft on 28 April. It was -121's first victory in 21 months, and it proved to be their last of the war.

From May through to July the squadron was led by Majs Claude H Welch and Robert Tucker, before 1st Lt R M Loughery took over on 1 August. Two weeks later Japan agreed to surrender and, on 1 September, -121 embarked for America. At war's end VMF-121 was easily the top-scoring fighter squadron in the Marine Corps. Though aerial opposition was virtually non-existent on its second tour, the 1942-43 era in the Solomons brought the squadron 208 credited victories – well ahead of second-place VMF-221 with 185 shootdowns.

VMF-121 received two decorations during the war: the Presidential Unit Citation for Guadalcanal from August to December 1942, and the Navy Unit Commendation for Peleliu and the Western Carolines from September 1944 to January 1945. The 14 fighter aces produced by the unit remained the record for the Marine Corps.

VMF-121 Aces

Maj Joseph J Foss	26	Medal of Honor
1Lt William P Marontate	13	KIA 15 January 1943
Capt Gregory K Loesch	8.5	KIA September 1943
2Lt Joseph L Narr	7	
2Lt Roger A Haberman	6.5	
2Lt William B Freeman	6	
Capt Francis E Pierce, Jr	6	
Capt Perry L Shuman	6	F4U ace
Maj Donald K Yost	6	
2Lt Thomas H Mann, Jr	5.5	+3.5 with VMF-224
Capt Robert M Baker	5	F4U ace
Maj Leonard K Davis	5	
2Lt Cecil J Doyle	5	KIA 7 November 1942
Capt Kenneth M Ford	5	F4U ace

Six pilots scored at least one victory with the unit en route to wartime totals of five or more – 1Lt O M Bate, 1Lt H H Long, 1Lt H A McCartney, Capt D C Owen, Maj R B Porter and Capt J H Reinburg. Porter and Reinburg also eventually gained commands of their own.

ON THE OFFENSIVE

Between the convoy battle of mid-November 1942 and early February 1943, when the island was declared secure, the nature of the Guadalcanal campaign changed. In December 1942 four Marine Corps Wildcat squadrons were operating from the two fighter fields: VMF-112 (still under Maj Fontana), -121 (temporarily under 1st Lt W F Wilson), -122 (Capt E E Brackett) and VMO-251 (now under Maj J N Renner). In fact, by year-end VMO-251 pilots had claimed 11 more confirmed kills, the top scorers being 1st Lts M R Yunck and K J Kirk, Jr, with three each. Yunck finished the war an ace, adding two more victories while flying Corsairs over Okinawa in 1945.

Most of VMF-121's original pilots enjoyed leave in Australia over the Christmas period, returning to complete their combat tours in January. These included Capt Joe Foss, who ran his wartime total to 26 with three 'Rufe' floatplanes on 15 January. Ranging as far north as New Georgia, VMF-121 claimed 40 kills during the month, ending the most successful squadron tour in the 'Cactus Air Force'.

January ended with a flourish. On the 30th two divisions of VF-10 (now back aboard *Enterprise*) intercepted 12 'Betty' torpedo bombers intent on sinking the cruiser *Chicago* (CA-29). Already slowed by battle damage, she was vulnerable to attack near Rennell Island.

'The Big E's' lead division splashed three bombers, then 'Reaper Leader' himself – Jim Flatley – arrived. Only two 'Bettys' survived, but four lasted long enough to torpedo the crippled warship, which quickly capsized and sank. Ens E L Feightner, better known as 'Whitey', was credited with three kills in this, one of the last combats by carrier-based F4Fs. Like many other Wildcat pilots, he would become an ace in F6Fs during the Central Pacific offensive of 1944.

A land-based pilot got in plenty of shooting the next day. Newly-promoted 1st Lt Jefferson J DeBlanc of VMF-112 already had three confirmed kills when he led his division on an escort mission on 31 January. Covering bombers which attacked shipping at Vella Lavella, DeBlanc met a swarm of Japanese fighters at 14,000 ft. As the SBDs and TBFs withdrew, they were intercepted and called for help. Diving to 1000 ft, DeBlanc remained to fight, despite dwindling fuel, and in a low-level dogfight, claimed three 'Rufes' and two Zekes. 1st Lt J P Lynch and 2nd Lt J B Maas each destroyed a Zero as well. However, DeBlanc and Tech Sgt James Feliton were forced to bail out over Kolombangara Island. Both aviators were retrieved by the coastwatcher, who kept them away from the Japanese, before being rescued two weeks later. DeBlanc's successful fight against the odds would earn him a Medal of Honor.

During the first week of February, two old-line carrier squadrons made their last victory claims with F4Fs. Now based at New Caledonia, 'Fighting Six' splashed four patrol aircraft in three days to end the 'Shooting Stars'' F4F combat. VF-72, flying from Guadalcanal, claimed six Zeros during strikes against New Georgia on the fourth. The old *Wasp* squadron then passed into history.

Medal of Honor winner 1st Lt Jefferson J DeBlanc was VMF-112 most successful pilot with eight kills. Five of these came on the last day of January when he led his division on a bomber escort mission against shipping at Vella Lavella. His charges were intercepted by a mixed formation of Zekes and 'Rufes', and he proceeded to shoot down two of the former and three of the latter, before he himself was forced to bail out. He then spent two weeks in hiding with coastwatcher forces, before being 'traded back' to the Marines for a sack of rice!

The 'Wolf Pack' of VMF-112 gather around their heavily decorated scoreboard in February 1943. Led by ace, Maj Paul J Fontana, this unit scored 61.5 kills during its tour at Henderson Field, which commenced in late October 1942. Three aces were produced by the squadron at 'Cactus' – the CO (5 kills, all of which were scored in 1942), 1st Lt J J DeBlanc (8 kills) and 1st Lt J G Percy (5 kills). This photograph was taken shortly before the squadron returned to the US, and shows 58 victories on the scoreboard

The same day that VF-72 closed out its combat log, another era opened in F4F history. A half-dozen escort fighting squadrons (VGF) were deployed in the Southwest Pacific early in 1943, but few of them flew from their parent carriers. *Sangamon* (CVE-26), *Suwannee* (CVE-27) and *Chenango* (CVE-28) largely operated their squadrons ashore, and nearly all the combat missions were flown from Solomons airfields.

Most successful of these was VF-21. Originally established as VGF-11, Lt Cdr C H Ostrom's squadron became VC-11 in March 1943, but was redesignated 'Fighting 21' soon after. Meanwhile, on 4 February Ostrom's Wildcats escorted two joint-service strikes on shipping at Munda. The day netted claims of 10 kills for three VGF-11 F4Fs.

The new order began to change in February, with the arrival of Maj W E Gise's VMF-124. As the first Corsair squadron in combat, 'Fighting 124' received much attention. Aside from superior performance, the F4U possessed greater range than the Wildcat, and immediately began fighter sweeps and escorts well up into the Solomons chain. Meanwhile, there was still ample work for F4Fs.

That work, however, was largely limited to the Marines. Few Navy fighters found combat from March through May, the exception being two scuffles by VF-27 and -28 around Cape Esperance and the Russells on 1 April. That deficit would soon be made up.

On 7 April the Japanese launched an awesome mission against Guadalcanal: 67 'Vals' under a cloud of 110 Zekes. They were intercepted by elements of three Marine and four Army squadrons flying F4Fs, F4Us, P-38s, -39s and -40s. Of the two F4F squadrons intercepting that afternoon, VMF-214 drew first blood. Capt George Britt's pilots claimed six Zeros and four Vals between Cape Esperance and Koli Point. Two were

This 'atmospheric' line-up shot was taken on 13 May 1943, during a month-long lull in the seemingly endless struggle to secure Guadalcanal. This temporary reprieve allowed both the Japanese to re-group for one final assault (which took place exactly a month from the date this shot was taken), and the USMC to begin phasing in the F4U Corsair in place of the Wildcat. The squadron featured in this view has previously been misidentified as VMF-223, who returned to the US after an exhaustive combat tour in late October 1942. These weary machines actually belong to VF-11 'Sundowners', who finished with 55 kills in-theatre, a score which made them the most successful Navy/Marine fighter squadron at Henderson Field in 1943. Note the pilots' salubrious 'tent city' erected in amongst the palms, which was easily within sprinting distance of the makeshift flightline *(via Aeroplane)*

credited to Tech Sgt Alvin J Jensen, one of the last enlisted pilots flying fighters. Shortly commissioned a lieutenant, Jensen would finish the war with seven confirmed kills. It was the squadron's only combat in F4Fs.

Next up was VMF-221 under Capt Robert Burns. While the Zero escort tied up most interceptors, a running battle drifted eastward from Esperance toward the anchorages. By that time, F4Fs and Army fighters had cut nearly 30 Zekes out of the pack, but the 'Vals' remained nearly intact. Therefore, the Aichis went for US shipping off Tulagi, leaving only one Wildcat division to handle the bombers.

The VMF-221 division leader was 1st Lt J E 'Zeke' Swett, entering his first combat. As 15 'Vals' rolled into their dives from 15,000 ft, Swett tagged onto the hindmost and flamed two. Then, entering the US flak zone, he pressed home his attack and caught another as it pulled out above the water. However, his F4F was then struck by a US anti-aircraft shell. He circled briefly over a nearby island, assessing the damage, then rejoined the fight.

Spotting five Aichis retiring northward, Swett bent his throttle to overtake them. Again working from back to front, he splashed two in passes from low astern. That made five. He then overtook another string of 'Vals' a mile-and-a-half ahead. Conscious of his dwindling ammunition, he bored in close and triggered economical bursts; two more went down.

At that point Zeke Swett might have disengaged. Instead, he overhauled the last visible 'Val' and traded machine-gun fire with the rear gunner. Both scored hits. The 'Val' trailed off, dragging a smoky plume, while Swett ditched his battered Wildcat. After nearly drowning he was retrieved by a PT boat, and was destined to receive the Medal of Honor. Staff Sgt Jack Pittman also claimed a 'Val', the 12th credited that day. It exactly matched the Japanese recorded loss of Aichis. However, the enemy only admitted nine of the claimed 27 Zeros, compared to seven F4Fs lost (with all Wildcat pilots safe).

The 'Vals', largely unmolested, sank a tanker and two destroyers. Overall, American fighters were credited with 40 shootdowns versus 29 acknowledged in Japanese records. Only one Corsair pilot got a shot in, and though Army fighters claimed 11 Zeros, the major killing was done by F4Fs.

The events of 7 April marked the last Marine Corps combat involving Wildcats in the Solomons. By 19 May VMF-221 had converted to Corsairs, as did -214 in June. Later that summer whilst flying Corsairs, -214 would become better known as the 'Black Sheep'.

Guadalcanal and environs were reasonably quiet for the rest of April and most of May. June was another matter. On the 12th VF-11's Lt W N Leonard intercepted more than 30 Zeros 10 miles northwest of Russell Island. Though low on fuel, the 16 'Sundowners' piled in and emerged with 14 kills. Five went to Lt(jg) Vernon E Graham, who became the Navy's only land-based ace in a day, and the last to 'turn the trick' in a Wildcat. Out of fuel, he crashed attempting a dead-stick landing, but recovered to fly again. Marine F4Us claimed six more victories.

Japan's displaced carrier air groups again struck Guadalcanal on the 16th. The attack involved 94 aircraft, the biggest raid since 7 April. It was also a big day for the defenders, 'AirSols' fighters claiming 76 kills from the 94 attackers. Forty-two were credited to Army fliers, including five Zeros by P-38 pilot 1st Lt Murray J Shubin. But again the top squadron was VF-11, led by the CO, Lt Cdr Charles M White. Several 'Sundowners' got among the bombers, with Lt(jg)s Charles R Stimpson and James S Swope claiming four and three, respectively. Six US fighters were lost, including three F4Fs and a P-40 in collisions. The Corsairs only managed fleeting shots at three Zeros.

Another full day of battle occurred on 30 June. Covering the Rendova landings, adjoining New Georgia, US fighters claimed 112 shootdowns – 67 by Corsairs, 34 by the Navy and 11 floatplanes picked off by Army fighters. It was an all-day event, lasting from mid-morning into late afternoon, ranging all over the Munda area. Controlled by ship-based fighter directors, VF-21 had 32 Wildcats airborne on dawn CAP, orbiting with drop tanks nearly 200 miles from Guadalcanal. Lt Cdr Ostrom's pilots anticipated plenty of shooting, and they were not disappointed. During the day they claimed 32 victories against four losses. Lt(jg) W C Smith tagged two Zeros and a 'Betty', as did Lt(jg) G F Boyle. Lt Ross Torkelson got two 'Bettys' and a probable,

In 1943 the highest scoring F4F fighter units in the US Navy were shore-based, VF-21 and -11 sharing over 120 kills in an eight-month period. One of the latter unit's most successful pilots at this time was Lt(jg) Vernon E Graham, who became the sole land-based naval 'ace in a day' when he destroyed five A6Ms on 12 June out of a force of 30 intercepted by 16 VF-11 F4F-4s northwest of the Russell Islands. The unit claimed a further nine Zeros, and despite returning to 'Cactus' without fuel, Graham still managed a dead-stick crash landing

This 'Sundowners' ' F4F-4 Wildcat sustained battle damage in July 1943, near the end of the squadron's tour. The aircraft displays typical markings of the period – two-tone blue/grey basic scheme with four-position stars. White stenciled 'F27' on the fuselage and '27' on the wings and cowing are augmented by VF-11's distinctive 'Sundowner' insignia below the windscreen *(via Robert L Lawson)*

while two other future aces, John Symmes and Tom Roach, both scored doubles.

The Rendova landing presented F4F pilots with their last major combat of the war. By August all South Pacific Marine fighter squadrons had re-equipped with F4Us, and the little Grumman's tenure finally expired. That same month the last Navy squadrons flying F4Fs in the Southwest Pacific were withdrawn from combat: VF-26, -27 and -28, based in the Russells. Each listed 10 to 12 victories in the April to July period. The last recorded kills by Navy F4Fs in the Pacific occurred on 25 July when VF-21 claimed eight Zekes near Munda. Ens N W Hutchings got three while Lt(jg) T H Moore splashed two. When the smoke finally cleared, an era in US naval aviation had ended.

Solomons Summary

From February through to July, VF-21 (by whatever designation) claimed 69 aerial victories – tops for 1943 F4F squadrons. In fact, VF-21 was surpassed only by the Corsairs of VMF-213 as the top 'AirSols' fighter squadron in the period ending in August, when F4Fs finally disappeared from combat. During the first eight months of 1943, F4Fs still claimed 44 per cent of all aerial victories credited to Navy and Marine fighting squadrons in the Pacific Theatre.

Overall, 'Cactus' and carrier-based F4F squadrons produced about 30 aces by the time the Japanese evacuated in early February 1943. Another five Navy and four Marine aces had emerged from Guadalcanal and environs by that summer, when the air war moved toward Rabaul. All were land-based aviators, who helped 'use up' the remaining Navy F4F-4s in the theatre.

Two VF-11 'Sundowners' made the list, Lt(jg)s Charles R Stimpson and Vernon E Graham claiming six and five kills respectively, while James S Swope came painfully close with 4.67 (Stimpson and Swope both became Hellcat aces during 1944). 'Fighting 21' produced three aces in 1943: Lt Ross E Torkelson, killed on 22 July, plus Lt(jg)s John Symmes and Thomas D Roach. Lt(jg) Cecil E Harris of VF-27 opened his victory log in the Solomons before going on to greater success with *Intrepid's* (CV-11) VF-18 in late 1944. Another future ace who scored his first success in VF-27 F4Fs was Lt Sam L Silber who, as a lieutenant commander, led Hellcats from *Bunker Hill* (CV-17) during VF-18's 1943-44 deployment.

Among the top Marines, Smith, Bauer, Galer and Foss received the Medal of Honor (MoH) for their 1942 combat, as did Lts Jeff DeBlanc of VMF-112 and Jim Swett of -221 for their exploits early in the New Year. In all, seven F4F pilots received their nation's highest

While the Solomons campaign progressed into early 1943, new F4F squadrons were engaged in training in the United States. Here, six Wildcats of VF-24 slide into echelon over Floyd Bennett Field, New York, during April. The squadron eventually deployed with the far more capable F6F-3 Hellcats in the light carrier *Belleau Wood* *(via Robert L Lawson)*

decoration, including Capt Elrod of Wake Island and Lt(jg) O'Hare of the Navy – nearly half of all MoH fighter pilots in the Pacific War.

However, that conflict was not quite over for the Wildcat. As part of the Fourth Wing in the Ellice Islands, 1100 nautical miles east of Guadalcanal, VMF-111 and -441 were the last Marine combat squadrons flying Wildcats. Though the war along the International Dateline was tedious by Solomons standards, it could turn violent on occasion. VMF-441 had the distinction of scoring the last F4F victories in US service: two bombers were destroyed and one damaged by Capt W P Boland, Jr, during raids against Funafuti on 27 March and 8 August 1943. However, -441 received some FM-1s in December and began converting to Corsairs in January 1944. After that, the only Marine Corps Wildcats remaining in the Pacific Theatre were a few F4F-4 'hacks' and photo F4F-7s attached to headquarters and service squadrons.

The class of 1943

Combat from January to July 1943 produced the last F4F aces, which are listed as follows:

1Lt J E Swett	VMF-221	7	+8.5*
Lt(jg) C R Stimpson	VF-11	6	+10*
Lt R E Torkelson (KIA)	VF-21	6	
Lt(jg) T D Roach	VF-21	5.5	
Lt(jg) J C C Symmes	VF-21	5.5	+5.5*
1Lt J J DeBlanc	VMF-112	5	+3†
Lt(jg) V E Graham	VF-11	5	
Capt F E Pierce, Jr	VMF-121	5	+1†
1Lt J G Percy	VMF-112	5	+1†

Note – † indicates prior F4F victories in 1942

* indicates later victories in F4Us or F6Fs

Pacific F4F Squadron Scores (from January to August 1943)

VF-21	69	Solomons (includes 10 kills as VGF-11)
VF-11	55	Guadalcanal
VMF-121	40	Guadalcanal
VMF-112	25	Guadalcanal
VMF-221	25	Guadalcanal
VMO-251	20	Guadalcanal
VF-10	13	*Enterprise* and Guadalcanal
VF-27	12	Solomons and Russells
VF-28	12	Solomons and Russells
VF-26	11	Solomons and Russells
VMF-214	10	Guadalcanal
VF-72	6	Guadalcanal
VF-6	4	New Hebrides
VMF-441	2	Ellis Islands
Total	**304***	

*F4U score during the same period was 386

TORCH AND LEADER

In comparison to the Pacific war, the F4F's contribution to the European Theatre was almost minuscule. Aside from anti-submarine composite squadrons embarked in escort carriers (CVEs), US Navy Wildcats participated in only two significant actions against the European Axis powers. The first of these was also the largest – Operation *Torch*, the invasion of French Morocco in November 1942.

Four American carriers were committed to *Torch* – *Ranger* and *Suwannee* (CVE-27) supporting the main landing force at Casablanca, with *Sangamon* (CVE-26) and *Santee* (CVE-29) off the northern and southern beaches, respectively. In all, they embarked some 109 F4F-4s, plus SBD-3s and TBF-1s.

Opposing the US landings were naval, air and land forces of the Vichy government of France. The prospect of combat against a traditional American ally – even one now aligned with Nazi Germany – seemed extremely ironic to many carrier pilots. And the irony only increased as one of the French units based in Morocco traced its genealogy to the *Escadrille Lafayette* of 1916.

US Army troops went ashore on 8 November against erratic opposition. However, the French Air Force put up a fight. During three days of almost constant flying, the largely-untried F4F pilots gave far better than they got from the more experienced French, who were mounted on Dewoitine 520s and Curtiss Hawk 75s. The major aerial combat occurred on 8 November when carrier pilots claimed 18 victories. Thirteen kills fell to Lt Cdr C T Booth's VF-41 in a dogfight north of Cazes Airfield. The CO of their *Ranger* team-mates, VF-9's Lt Cdr John Raby, added one more. The remaining four were claimed by pilots of VGF-26 aboard the escort carrier *Sangamon*.

The second day's operation brought far less combat, with honours going exclusively to *Ranger* Wildcats. 'Fighting Nine' claimed five kills and VF-41 a solitary victory during missions around Fedala. The CVE-based units were in action again on the 10th as a VGF-29 pilot off *Santee* shot down a Potez 63 inland.

Throughout Operation *Torch*, 25 French air force and naval aircraft were claimed shot down by F4Fs, though two British machines were also probably destroyed in error. The top scores were as follows:

Lt(jg) C V August	VF-41	*Ranger*	2
Lt M M Furney	VF-41	*Ranger*	2
Lt(jg) B N Mayhew	VF-41	*Ranger*	2
Lt Cdr J Raby	VF-9	*Ranger*	2
Lt(jg) C A Shields	VF-41	*Ranger*	2
Lt E W Wood, Jr	VF-41	*Ranger*	2

Whilst its West Coast brethren were slugging it out over the vast Pacific battle front, F4F-4-equipped VF-41 on the East Coast were forced to bide their time flying mundane patrols over the mid-Atlantic from their parent carrier USS *Ranger*. BuNo 4084 exhibits all the standard markings worn by US Navy fighters in the first six months of the war. The squadron's chance of glory would eventually come at the end of 1942, however, when the Ranger Air Group flew support missions for the Allied *Torch* invasion force that landed in Vichy French territory in North Africa in November. By that stage all red in the national insignia had been deleted, with VF-41's Wildcats having had a thin yellow ring added to the edge of the roundel specially for this operation *(via Phil Jarrett)*

A VF-41 F4F-4 is waved on its way from *Ranger*'s wooden decks as a pair of US Army Piper L-4 Cubs cruise incongrously overhead – a handful of these spotter aircraft were ferried out to North Africa for the army aboard *Ranger*. To the right of the Wildcat is fresh ordnance for the ship's 18 SBD-3 Dauntlesses of VS-41, which were heavily involved attacking Vichy French naval and air force installations. *Ranger* boasted no less than 54 F4F-4s, split evenly between VF-9 and -41, going into *Torch*, but suffered considerable losses to enemy air and ground fire – 12 Wildcats destroyed in total, with four pilots killed and three cpatured. However, these losses were somewhat overshadowed by VGF-29's experience aboard the escort carrier USS *Santee* (CVE-29). In barely three days of combat, the unit lost no less than 10 of its 12 Wildcats. Four of these were written off in landing accidents at the short and muddy emergency airstrip at Safi – fortunately, only a single pilot, Lt(jg) G N Trumpter, was killed in amongst all this carnage, his F4F-4 crashing in the Atlantic due to a loss of oil pressure whilst on a dawn patrol with VGF-29 on the morning of the invasion. He was never found *(via Jerry Scutts)*

Despite their successes, overall US attrition was serious. By 11 November, in addition to five air-to-air losses, another six F4Fs had fallen to flak, and 14 more were lost operationally. The heaviest burden was carried by *Ranger*'s two fighter squadrons, as VF-9 and -41 lost a dozen Wildcats between them. Still, *Torch* proved valuable to dozens of young fighter pilots who tested their tactics and their skills over Morocco before moving on to the Empire of Japan. One of Lt Cdr John Raby's VF-9 pilots was Ens Marvin J Franger, who shot down a Curtiss H-75 over Morocco. By war's end Franger was the only Navy ace with confirmed victories on each of his three combat tours, flying from the decks of four different carriers.

Atlantic F4F Squadron Scores in 1942-43

VF-41	14	*Ranger*	Operation *Torch*
VF-9	6	*Ranger*	Operation *Torch*
VGF-26	4	*Sangamon*	Operation *Torch*
VF-4	2	*Ranger*	Operation *Leader*
VGF-29	1	*Santee*	Operation *Torch*

Almost a year after *Torch* the British Home Fleet supported a strike against German shipping in Bodø, Norway. The muscle behind Operation *Leader* was *Ranger* with Air Group Four. Because the Pacific Theatre had priority for F6F-3 Hellcat production, VF-4 still flew F4F-4s. However, Lt Cdr Charles L Moore had no less than 27 Wildcats both for strike escort and Force CAP when *Ranger* launched her air group north of the Arctic Circle on 4 October 1943.

Two strikes were launched during the morning, both escorted by Wildcats. The F4Fs' primary role was flak suppression, as no German aircraft opposed the mission. Lt Cdr Moore's aircraft sustained hits, and though two SBDs and a TBF were lost, seven Axis-controlled ships were successfully sunk.

That afternoon the task force retired westward, still within range of

Adorned with the distinctive yellow-ringed national insignia applied specially for *Torch*, a small section of *Ranger*'s burgeoning Wildcat force lets fly with a 36-gun broadside of .50 cal ammunition. All 54 F4F-4s systematically had the 'cobwebs' blown out of their Brownings in the days leading up to the invasion, the weapons also being calibrated and aligned. Squadron armourers can be seen on the wings of each aircraft, checking that the belt-fed ammunition passes smoothly through the gun breeches. No doubt making an unheavenly din below decks, a fair proportion of the crew – including a handful of interested, and somewhat anxious, fighter pilots – have ventured out to watch the spectacle *(via Jerry Scutts)*

land-based aircraft. *Ranger's* fighter director controlled two divisions of F4Fs, and put Lt B N Mayhew's section onto a radar contact. Mayhew and Ens D S Laird made short work of the Junkers Ju 88 'snooper', which crashed 22 miles from the carrier. Minutes later a Heinkel He 115 got somewhat closer before falling afoul of Lt E F Craig's division, again including Mayhew and Laird – the floatplane splashed 13 miles from *Ranger*. One Wildcat crashed on landing and went over the side, but the pilot was saved.

This combat was the US Navy's first success against the Luftwaffe. Moreover, 'Diz' Laird, later credited with five Japanese aircraft, became the only Navy ace to score against both major Axis powers. The F4F's final air-to-air claim against Germany was a Dornier Do 217D bomber, damaged by a VC-6 aircraft off *Core* (CVE-13) nearly 500 miles west-southwest of Brest on 22 December.

By that time the Wildcat was well established in its primary role against Germany – supporting anti-submarine operations. In early 1943 the US Navy began to close the dreadful mid-Atlantic gap – the ' black hole' – wherein merchant convoys were beyond the range of land-based patrol aircraft. The 8300-ton *Bogue* (CVE-9) class carriers were based on merchant ship hulls, with 442 x 81-ft flight decks – tiny by any standard, but adequate to the challenge. Escort carriers operating composite squadrons of TBF-1 Avengers and F4F-4 Wildcats were specially trained in 'hunter-killer' tactics to locate and destroy U-boats. *Bogue's* VC-9 scored the first

The pilot gently eases open the throttle of his F4F-4 in anticipation of the signal to launch midway through the opening day of hostilities on 8 November 1942. The aircraft is fitted with a pair of 58-gal drop tanks, which significantly improved the Wildcat's modest combat radius, without comprimising its exemplary 'deck manners'. This machine was part of the Ranger Air Group *(via Aerospace Publishing)*

A year after its bitter baptism of fire over French Morocco, the redesignated VF-29 was still operating in the Atlantic aboard the cramped decks of *Santee*, although the enemy was now German U-boats. The unit's dozen F4F-4 had also adopted a distinctive three-tone colour scheme unique to this theatre by the time this shot was taken in November 1943. The 'Atlantic' scheme consisted of Non-Specular Dark Gull Grey upper surfaces, NS Insignia White fuselage sides and Gloss White under-surfaces. VF-29 eventually transferred to USS *Cabot* (CVL-28) in the Pacific in early 1944 after recieving FM-2s *(via Jerry Scutts)*

hunter-killer success on 22 May, their result being dramatically out of proportion with their numbers. By summer's end, the Battle of the Atlantic had swung in favour of the Allies.

It would be unfair to attribute conquest of the U-boats solely to CVEs, as other factors were significant. Increasing numbers, and effectiveness, of escort vessels, as well as signals intelligence, were important. But the hunter-killers produced disproportionate results merely by their presence. Nobody will ever know how many U-boat commanders had their attacks thwarted simply because carrier aircraft were airborne near a convoy.

Nor would it be accurate to assign major importance to the F4F's ASW role. Wildcats contributed by spotting U-boats and suppressing anti-aircraft fire from surfaced submarines, allowing Avengers to press for the kill. But not even six-gun fighters were immune from the volume of flak that U-boats could put up after Adm Doenitz promulgated his famous 'fight back' order of mid-1943.

German submarines sprouted a forest of AA guns – single- and multiple-mount 20 and 37 mm. And they were effective. Throughout the Battle of the Atlantic, U-boats shot down at least seven US Navy aircraft. The first occurred on 13 July 1943 when a *Core* search team found *U-487* on the surface, 700 miles south of the Azores. Lt(jg) E H Steiger led the attack in his Wildcat, strafing ahead of Lt R P Williams' Avenger. The TBF straddled the submarine with four depth charges, then pulled off to evaluate the situation.

Calling for reinforcements, Williams needed to slow the submarine lest it escape. He requested another strafing run and, though the F4F had only one gun firing, Steiger attacked. But this time the AA gunners were fully alert, filling the sky with flak. The Wildcat nosed down and crashed near the U-boat. However, two more F4Fs and a pair of TBFs shortly arrived, led by VC-13's skipper, Lt Cdr C W Brewer. Four more depth charges finally put paid to *U-487*'s brief, but bloody, career.

In February 1944 FM-2s began replacing F4F-4s and FM-1s in East Coast composite squadrons. By VE-Day the late-model Wildcats equipped all 13 East Coast VC units, which averaged nine FM-2s and a dozen TBM-1Cs or -1Ds.

At war's end the US hunter-killer groups had sunk 54 U-boats, including 30 by air action alone. The Battle of the Atlantic never generated the individual acclaim common to aerial combat in the Pacific, but the strategic effect proved incalculable.

THE EASTERN WILDCAT

In addition to the 54 aces in F4Fs, four other fighter pilots scored five or more victories in 'the wilder Wildcat'. The FM-2 flew from escort carriers throughout 1944 and 1945, supporting amphibious and anti-submarine operations. However, the versatile aircraft also served admirably in close air support, spotting naval gunfire, and – when the occasion arose – aerial combat.

Grumman stopped building Wildcats and Avengers in 1943 to concentrate on the F6F Hellcat. Therefore, the Eastern Aircraft Division of General Motors Corporation took up F4F and TBF production so both types could remain in fleet service. The FM-1 was merely an Eastern-built F4F-4, but the follow-on fighter was 'a cat of a different colour'.

The FM-2 actually began life as the XF4F-8. Powered by a Wright R-1820, and distinguished by its taller vertical stabiliser and rudder, the lighter, more powerful, Wildcat first flew in late 1942. After Eastern learned the methods of large-scale production, FM-2s began rolling off the Linden, New Jersey, assembly line in September 1943.

Eastern Aircraft Division of General Motors Corp began delivering FM-2s to the fleet in early 1944. Bearing the striking 'Atlantic' scheme, this Wildcat of Composite Squadron (VC) 13 was based on the escort carrier *Tripoli* in March of that year. Lighter, yet more powerful, than the F4F-4, the FM-2 redressed the performance disadvantage which the Grumman fighter had ceded to Japanese opponents for two years. However, aerial combat in the European Theatre was limited to a one-day strike launched from *Ranger* against Bodø, Norway, in October 1943. On that occasion VF-4 F4Fs shot down two German 'snooper' aircraft *(via Robert L Lawson)*

The organisation of most CVE units contrasted with their big-deck counterparts. Composite squadrons contained both bombers and fighters in a single command, typically with 12 FM-2s and nine or more TBM-3s. Generally, the squadron commander flew Avengers while a senior fighter pilot led the FM contingent. There were, however, a few CVE 'air groups' organised along the lines of *Independence*-class CVLs, with separate fighter and torpedo squadrons.

As deliveries increased, FM-2s began appearing in deployed squadrons early in 1944. The new fighter's first aerial victory probably occurred on 20 March 1944 while USS *Midway* (CVE-63) sailed north of New Ireland in the Bismarck Archipelago. In a brief scuffle Lt(jg) J H Dinneen and Ens R P Kirk of VC-63 claimed the destruction of a 'Tony', a Japanese Army fighter, for the squadron's only victory of the war.

The next score occurred a fortnight later during a task group operation near the Marianas. On 6 April Lt(jg) R N Glasgow of *Coral Sea*'s (CVE-57) VC-33 splashed a 'Betty' bomber off Saipan. This area became a major venue for Wildcat operations when, in mid-June, the Fifth Fleet approached the Marianas in force. During operations leading up to the invasion of Saipan, seven more composite units scored their first kills.

The most successful FM-2 unit was VC-27, which flew from *Savo Island* from late 1944 to early 1945. Credited with 62 aerial victories, the composite squadron produced five of the nine top-scoring FM pilots. This aircraft, BuNo 56805, bears the late-war gloss blue colour scheme, with *Savo Island*'s distinctive arrow emblem on the vertical stabilizer. Here, a rough arrested landing has resulted in a collapsed port landing gear on 10 January 1945, the squadron having commenced operations the previous day in support of an invading force landing in the Lingayen Gulf on the northern island of the Pilippines *(via Robert L Lawson)*

The Battle of Leyte Gulf (or Second Philippine Sea) was a two-day 'slugfest' fought over 24-25 October 1944. Because the CVEs were so heavily engaged, it became the most intense period of aerial combat for FM-2s during the entire war. On the 24th carrier pilots were credited with 270 aerial victories, including 65 by 11 of the composite squadrons engaged. The most active were VC-3 and -27, each with 14 kills, and VF-26 with 11.

The last two Wildcat aces in a day were crowned on 24 October. Lt Kenneth G Hippe of VC-3 returned to *Kalinin Bay* (CVE-68) with a score of five 'Lillys' in 20 minutes, while other VC-3 pilots claimed nine more kills. Lt Cdr Harold N Funk flew two sorties from *Santee* (CVE-29), claiming four bombers and a Zeke in the morning, then an 'Irving' that evening – this was more than half of VF-26's total on the 24th.

Aerial combat abated the next day, with 37 FM-2 successes among the 71 total by naval aviators. However, it was an entirely different matter on the surface. At dawn on the 25th a large enemy force emerged from the eastern end of San Bernardino Strait between Leyte and Samar. Taken by surprise, and vastly outgunned, the CVE force of Rear Adm Clifton Sprague fought for its life.

Among the six carriers of 'Taffy Three' was *Gambier Bay* (CVE-73), embarking Composite Squadron 10. With almost no warning, pilots scrambled into their aircraft and frantically started engines as battleship and cruiser shells exploded close aboard. One of the FM-2 pilots was 20-year-old Ens Joseph D McGraw, who had three kills to his credit, including a pair of 'Lillys' from the day before. He recalls:

'I just beat my wingman, Leo Zeola, to the last fighter on the port

Perhaps the most widely-travelled Wildcat unit was VF-26. Flying F4Fs, the escort-carrier squadron participated in the North African invasion in November 1942 while flying from *Chenango*. Then, in early 1943, the escort carrier sailed to the Solomon Islands where VF-26 alternately operated from shipboard and ashore. After conversion to FM-2s, the squadron returned to combat aboard *Santee* from April to October 1944. In all, 'Fighting 26' claimed 46 victories during the war and produced one of only four FM aces: Lt Cdr Harold N Funk, who splashed six Japanese aircraft on 24 October during the Battle of Leyte Gulf *(via Robert L Lawson)*

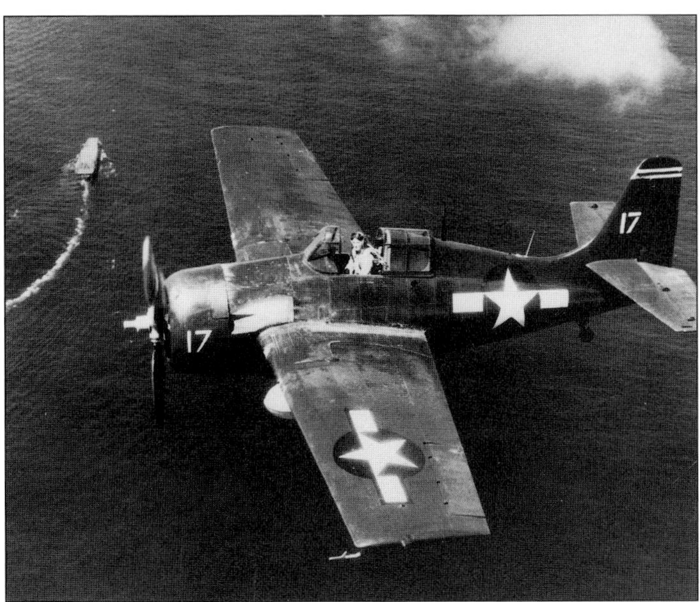

side aft corner of the flight deck. In fact, it was my airplane, "Baker Six". I got it started and then had to wait for all the aircraft ahead of me to take-off, so I sat there counting shell splashes and getting in some quality prayer time!

'I got off as the last fighter, I think, as I had to dodge a big hole on the forward port corner of the deck just as Capt Viewig was throwing the ship into a turn. I seem to remember that the flight deck officer tried to get me to taxy all the way up to an area he had chosen as the proper take-off spot, but I poured on the coals, waved him out of the way and took off as soon as I saw the deck clear in front of me. That gave me a better chance to avoid the holes forward.'

In October 1944 20-year-old Ens Joseph D McGraw downed three aircraft whilst with VC-10, then bagged two more as part of VC-80

Unlike many other displaced CVE pilots, McGraw avoided the crowded landing strip at Tacloban, on Samar, and sought a friendly flight deck. He landed aboard *Manila Bay* (CVE-61) and volunteered for a strike against retreating Japanese cruisers. His third flight of 25 October was a CAP, leading the second section in a VC-80 division. An accurate radar vector put the four Wildcats directly onto some 18 'Vals' and 12 Zekes. The ensuing combat illustrates the FM-2's ability against a well-flown A6M5 Zero. After flaming four 'Vals' in their first pass, the Wildcats pulled up to confront the top-cover Zekes. McGraw recalls:

'The leader of the Zeros was good and he hit our division leader in the engine, putting him in the water (he was later picked up). As I had pulled up so hard and steep, I lost my wingman, but avoided the Zeros as they dove by. So I rolled left out of my climb and saw the lead Zero and his wingman pulling up from downing our leader. I was in a great position above and to the right of his wingman, so I shot him in the engine and wingroot with a burst long enough to cause him to flame and explode.

'That either surprised or made the Zero lead really mad, because he did the tightest turn I've ever seen to try to get on me. But I also pulled up into a tight climbing left turn into him, and he missed his shot behind me. The FM-2's tight turn must have surprised him because I got around quickly on him into a head-on, and put a fast burst into his engine. That really made him mad, because he quickly pulled hard up into me in what I thought was an attempt to ram. I had also pulled up hard to avoid him; it was a close thing.

'As I looked over my shoulder, in another tight turn, I saw he was smoking heavily and already diving for the clouds. I also saw three more Zeros turning into me to cut me off from their smoking leader. I took a long-range shot at the nearest one as I turned and dove for the water, but only sieved his tail. Luckily I got away, enjoying the satisfaction of seeing them also turn back to where they had come from.

'The Zero leader was flying a dark-green aircraft with no white circles around the "red meatballs", and he had large white letters and numbers on his tail, with what looked like a white streak of light-

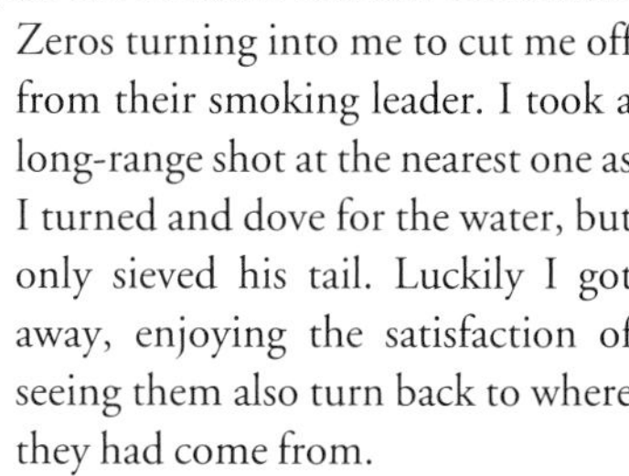

VC-80 FM-2s in late 1944 display differing colour schemes. The lead Wildcat, number 11, wears the tri-colour pattern, while its wingman bears the late-war gloss blue overall. From October 1944 to January 1945 the squadron shot down 16 Japanese aircraft in the Philippine Islands: four 'Oscars', three 'Vals', two Zekes, two 'Tojos', and one 'Jake', 'Jill', 'Irving', 'Sally' and 'Tony'. Top scorer was Ens Charles Guthrie with 2.5 victories, closely followed by Lt J L Morrissey and Ens J D McGraw with two each. McGraw, displaced from VC-10 when *Gambier Bay* was sunk, became an ace as a result of victories with both squadrons *(via Robert L Lawson)*

ning or slash marking across his tail below the letters and numbers. I had the feeling he was an old hand and had expected the old Wildcats to be easy prey, so he was surprised and let his temper get the better of him – he probably didn't know about the much-improved FM-2 version. I don't know what happened to him, but with his engine shot up I don't suppose he made it back to his base.'

Upon landing aboard *Manila Bay* after dark, McGraw had logged 11 hours in three missions. In all, VC-10 Wildcats scored eight victories during the day, including those initially claimed after having been displaced from their baby flat-top, which was sunk by enemy shellfire.

By far the most successful air-to-air composite squadron was VC-27. Between October 1944 and January 1945 *Savo Island*'s Wildcats splashed 61.5 enemy aircraft, including 17 bombers of various types. The CO, Lt Ralph Elliott, was credited with nine victories in that period – the highest score not only in FM-2s, but for all Navy Wildcat pilots. His VC-10 colleague, Joe McGraw, recalls Elliott as being 'a tough fighter pilot even before he got into combat'.

Another Wildcat ace was Lt(jg) George H Davidson, also of VC-27. He entered combat with VF-21 in the Solomons, scoring his first victory in 1943. However, he tallied three solo and three shared victories aboard *Savo Island* for a total of 4.5, and thus became the only 'composite' ace as a result of both F4F and FM service. Incredibly, three other VC-27 aviators each claimed 4.5 victories, giving *Savo Island* five of the top nine places among CVE fighter pilots.

VC-27 had 26 scoring fighter pilots within its total of 61.5 victories; a TBM gunner also scored a kill. The top five pilots claimed 27 shootdowns, or nearly half the total. Timing and opportunity proved decisive, as only four other CVE units (VF-26, VC-81 and -84, plus VOC-1) tallied 20 or more victories. VC-27's startling five-day performance in late October netted 28 shootdowns, followed by nine in mid-December and 24 more during four days in early January 1945.

During the Philippines, Iwo Jima and Okinawa campaigns, two FM-2 units provided crucial support as observation-composite squadrons. Specially trained to 'spot' naval gunfire, VOC-1 and -2 flew almost continuously during daylight, providing battleships and cruisers with accurate target information ashore. Flying from *Wake Island* (CVE-65) and

This Wildcat pilot collided with one of VC-80's TBM-1C Avengers upon landing aboard *Manila Bay*. CVEs were the smallest of all aircraft carriers, requiring precision flying even beyond that of the 'large' *Essex*-class ships. The flight deck of a *Casablanca*-class escort carrier measured 477 ft long, though the deck of an *Independence*-class CVL was two feet narrower. The fact that naval aviators routinely flew off these tiny ships in most weather, and often at night, speaks volumes for their highly-developed skills *(via Robert L Lawson)*

Ranking FM-2 ace Lt Ralph Elliot of VC-27 climbs aboard 'his' Wildcat, parked on the deck of *Savo Island* in late 1944. 'Baldy' was the name of his brother's German Shepherd!

Although not photographed 50 years ago like the remaining aircraft in this volume, the Confederate Air Force's beautifully restored FM-2 is worthy of inclusion nonetheless as it wears authentic markings for little-publicised unit, VOC-1, who flew from the decks of USS *Wake Island* (CVE-65) and USS *Marcus Island* (CVE-77) in 1945. Heavily involved in the Iwo Jima and Okinawa invasions, this unit served as naval gunfire spotters, flying almost continually over the islands relaying information on the fall of shells back to the Navy's battleships and cruisers. Although fully occupied performing this specialised role, pilots from VOC-1 nevertheless managed to shoot down 20 Japanese aircraft, placing the unit fourth in the overall FM-2 kill rankings

Marcus Island (CVE-77), VOC-1 probably logged more hours per pilot than any other fighter squadron in the Pacific Fleet. The pilots also found opportunity for aerial combat, claiming 20 kills. Meanwhile, VOC-2 in *Fanshaw Bay* (CVE-70) splashed five bandits at Okinawa. But, undeniably, their greatest contribution was calling in gunfire for Marines fighting ashore.

One of the greatest coincidences in Naval Aviation history occurred on 12 January 1945. While TF-38 launched strikes against Japanese and Vichy French forces in Saigon and elsewhere, escort carriers maintained CAPs which turned up a few contacts. One of those was a 'Jake', intercepted about 350 nautical miles off the Indochina coast by two Wildcats off *Nehenta Bay* (CVE-74). The VC-11 section attacked and destroyed the floatplane – nothing unusual in that, except that the successful pilots were Lt(jg)s Alton S and Grant L Donnelly. It was the only occasion in US Navy history when two brothers shared an aerial victory. Furthermore, it was VC-11's only shootdown of the war!

By VJ-Day, FMs of 38 composite squadrons had been credited with some 432 aerial victories. The leading units were as follows:

The Top-Scoring FM-2 Squadrons

VC-27	*Savo Island*	61.5	+1 by TBM
VF-26	*Santee*	31	
VC-81	*Natoma Bay*	21	+1 by TBM
VOC-1	*Wake Island* and *Marcus Island*	20	
VC-84	*Makin Island*	19	+1 by TBM
VC-21	*Nassau* and *Marcus Island*	18	
VC-3	*Kalinin Bay*	17	
VC-75	*Ommaney Bay*	17	
VC-93	*Shamrock Bay*	17	
VC-5	*Kitkun Bay*	16	
VC-10	*Gambier Bay* and Tacloban Field	16	+1 by TBM
VC-80	*Manila Bay*	16	

Of the 432 aircraft shot down 12 per cent of the kills were claimed by nine pilots

The Top-Scoring FM-2 Pilots

Lt R E Elliott	VC-27	*Savo Island*	9
Lt Cdr H N Funk	VF-26	*Santee*	6 +.50
Lt K G Hippe	VC-3	*Kalinin Bay*	5
Ens J D McGraw	VC-10, -80	*Gambier Bay, Manila Bay*	5
Lt L M Ferko	VC-4, -20	*White Plains, Kadashan Bay*	5
Lt T S Sedaker	VC-84	*Makin Island*	4.83
Lt(jg) G H Davidson	VC-27	*Savo Island*	4.50 +1 in F4Fs
Ens T S Mackie	VC-27	*Savo Island*	4.50
Ens R E Pfeifer	VC-27	*Savo Island*	4.50

Lt Kenneth G Hippe of VC-3 downed five 'Lilly' bombers in a 20-minute spell on the first day of the Battle of Leyte Gulf (24 October 1944), thus becoming the last Wildcat 'ace in a day'. Lt Cdr Harold N Funk of VF-26 had also bagged five aircraft earlier that same morning, before going on to destroy a sixth latter in the day

FLEET AIR ARM

The Royal Navy's effect upon the F4F was considerable. The Fleet Air Arm (FAA) introduced the type to combat a year before Pearl Harbor, and exerted influence in its armament fit which ran contrary to opinion in US Navy squadrons. But for all that, the Wildcat was the first truly modern fighter flown from British carriers, and represented an enormous leap forward in Royal Naval aviation.

One of the last survivors of the 85-strong batch of Martlet Is originally 'acquired' by the FAA is swung around into position on a recently defrosted ramp in Scotland in early 1942. Many of the ex-French G-36As had either been written off or retired from service by this stage, a handful lingering on with training squadrons around the UK. This weary example belonged to No 795 Sqn, one of several operational training units tasked with churning out qualified Martlet pilots. The more numerous Martlet Mk II was the favoured instructional tool by this stage in the war, although a handful of rare, fixed-wing, Mk IIIs (ex-Greek Navy) were also employed in tuitional roles
(via Aeroplane)

Until the verge of war in 1939, the Royal Air Force retained widespread control of naval aviation. Then, at nearly the last minute, the senior service recognised the importance of an integrated air component and moved to correct matters. The resulting 'dark blue versus light blue' arrangement was not wholly agreeable to all parties, as RAF Coastal Command retained control of maritime search and patrol. However, British carrier aviation was able to proceed apace, no longer fighting for RAF funds.

In September 1939, FAA strength was merely 231 aircraft, including 142 Swordfish and 46 Walrus. HMS *Glorious* embarked 12 Sea Gladiators, but clearly there was urgent need for a fast, modern, carrier fighter. Though navalised versions of the Hawker Hurricane and Supermarine Spitfire were eventually produced, neither was wholly satisfactory. The Seafire, especially, was susceptible to damage in ordinary deck landings, and the two-seat Fairey Fulmar – although built as a carrier fighter – lacked performance. Fulmars, which entered service with No 806 Sqn in September 1940, were followed by No 802's Martlets the next month. Some 25 kts faster than the Fulmar at sea level, the Grumman extended that advantage to 85 kts at altitude.

Ironically, France's *Aéronavale* became the source of Britain's original Wildcats. The G-36A export version was essentially an F4F-3 with Wright's R-1820 engine in place of the Pratt & Whitney. Eighty had been ordered but none could be delivered before France fell in June 1940. Consequently, the Royal Navy took over the original batch and soon ordered a further 100 G-36Bs with folding wings and the original R-1830 engines. These F4Fs were christened Martlet Mk Is and IIs, respectively.

Despite their advanced design, the Mk Is had limited utility. Hampered by French instrumentation, equipment and armament, they remained land-based with No 804 Sqn at Hatston. Difficulties with tailwheels and impromptu .50 cal mounts caused problems, but the Martlets served well enough. On Christmas Day 1940 a section from No 804 intercepted a Ju 88 reconnaissance bomber over the Home Fleet base at Scapa Flow. Lt L V Carter and Sub-Lt Parke shot out one engine, and the Junkers crash-landed in a bog near Loch Skail. The Martlet had drawn

A trio of fixed-wing Martlet Is formate for the camera during an official photo-shoot staged for a Navy photographer in September 1941. One machine wears an individual letter code, whilst the lead fighter has the number '57' painted behind the roundel. A pale blue European theatre band has been applied at the base of the fin on each Martlet, this marking being more commonly seen on RAF fighters – FAA machines wore it for a very brief period in 1941/42 only. Although no distinguishing unit markings are visible, it is likely that these machines belong to either No 778 or 795 Sqns, both of which provided Martlet training at the time *(via Aeroplane)*

first blood – that same month VF-4 accepted the US Navy's first F4F-3s.

The first Martlet squadron to make a carrier deployment was Lt Cdr John Wintour's No 802. Armed with six Mk IIs, the tiny unit boarded HMS *Empire Audacity* in September 1941, bound for the North Atlantic convoy routes to Gibraltar. *Audacity* was a captured German steamer – the 5500-ton *Hannover* – and although capable of only 14 kts, her quick conversion to an escort carrier over-rode her limited operational capability.

Wintour's Martlets were primarily intended to defend slow convoys from scouting and attack by long-range Luftwaffe bombers. However, the Grummans also proved useful in anti-submarine work by providing advance warning of enemy vessels. Two sightings were made during the first week out, forcing the U-boats to submerge. Then, on 21 September, Sub-Lts N H Patterson and G R P Fletcher got their chance. They bounced a Focke-Wulf Fw 200 Kondor which was bombing some torpedoed ships and, between them, fired 320 rounds of .50 cal to shoot off the aircraft's tail – interestingly, they identified it as a Kurier, the civil airliner from which the bomber had originated. That afternoon another Martlet section chased away a Ju 88 snooper. No 802 Sqn had been proven effective, but the outbound leg cost Convoy OG-74 five ships. The return to Britain in October met little opposition.

However, *Audacity* was back at sea before month's end, fighting worsening weather more than the Germans. High winds and heaving seas rendered flight operations difficult to impossible, with the CVE's deck pitching as much as 65 ft. One Martlet was lost overboard during the storms whilst attempting to land, but the pilot was recovered.

On 8 November Lt Cdr Wintour was vectored onto a radar contact, resulting in an interception. The CO made two passes, setting the Focke-Wulf alight, although it maintained level flight. However, one of the gunners got a clear shot at the Martlet and sent the Grumman down, before Sub-Lt Hutchinson finished off the Kondor. Later that day Sub-Lt Eric Brown's 'Red Section' flushed two Kondors and pursued them independently. 'Winkle' Brown fought a prolonged duel in heavy clouds, finally ending up nose-to-nose with the Fw 200. He splashed the bomber, but morale suffered – two shootdowns for loss of the popular CO was considered a poor exchange.

However, by now *Audacity* was proving her worth. Convoy OG-76 reached Gibraltar completely intact – a rare achievement in late 1941. No 802 did a quick turnaround in Britain and, under Lt Cdr Donald Gibson, returned to sea with only four Martlets to escort 32 merchantmen in mid-December.

When this photo was released in September 1941, it was captioned, 'A Yankee fighter in the Royal Navy'! Now flying line abreast, the trio of Martlets featured in the previous shot hold an impeccable formation for the camera, which leads one to assume that these fighters aren't being flown by student pilots! *(via Phil Jarrett)*

The cruise began poorly and only worsened. On only the third day out Sub-Lt Fletcher attacked a surfaced U-boat which, rather than dive, chose to fight. Accurate 37 mm fire struck the Martlet, which crashed near *U-131*. Escorts finally sank the submarine that had killed Fletcher.

Two days later, on 19 December, 'Red Section' was again engaged. Eric Brown repeated his head-on tactics with similar results as before, becoming the first fighter pilot to destroy two Kondors. His wingman damaged another which escaped into cloud cover. That afternoon Lt Cdr James Sleigh's 'Yellow Section' found another bomber and he duplicated Brown's approach. Firing down to minimum range, he pulled up at the last second and just collided with the Fw 200. Back on deck he found part of the bomber's aileron lodged in his tailwheel.

The three remaining fighters were airborne almost constantly during daylight, reporting multiple contacts. But there was no aerial protection at night, the favoured hunting time of U-boat skippers. On the night of the 20th/21st *U-751* accomplished Adm Doenitz's orders to sink the troublesome carrier, a task it duly performed with three torpedoes. Loss of life was heavy, and only five pilots survived.

During its three-month combat career No 802 Sqn had shown the way to the future. By destroying five Fw 200s and diverting at least ten U-boats from their mission, the Martlets had proven the worth of escort-carrier fighters. More squadrons and more CVEs would follow.

During the period of *Audacity*'s North Atlantic convoys, another Martlet squadron was making itself known in warmer climes. No 805, previously of HMS *Formidable*, operated under RAF control at Sidi Haneish, Egypt, with eight Martlet IIIs (ex-Greek Navy F4F-3As diverted to the RN). Following inconclusive combats with Bf 109s and Me 110s, the unit finally scored on 28 September 1941. Flying a coastal patrol along the Libyan border, Sub-Lt W M Walsh engaged three Italian Fiat G.50s and emerged with the first Martlet victory over the second major Axis power in Europe.

Moving to Tobruk, No 805 found more combat along the coastal convoy routes. Sub-Lt A R Griffin broke up a *Regia Aeronautica* torpedo attack on 28 December, shooting down one SM.79 and dispersing the others. However, one of the Italian gunners had the range and shot the Martlet into the water. By July 1942 the squadron had accounted for two more Savoias and a Ju 88, then moved to East Africa for patrols over the Indian Ocean.

Carrier-based Martlets were also active in the region. Embarked in HMS *Illustrious*, Nos 881 and 882 Sqns participated in the occupation of Diego Suarez, Madagascar, in May 1942. From the 5th to the 7th the Mk IIs provided ground support and protected the task force

The Martlet II boasted two extra .50 cal Brownings and, most importantly, folding wings, as shown here in this superb Charles E Brown photograph. Like the Martlet I, it was built in small numbers, only 100 being delivered to the FAA from October 1940 onwards – the first ten Mk IIs were fitted with the old fixed wing, and were immediately relegated to training duties once in the UK. Of the remaining 90 aircraft, 36 were shared amongst a handful of squadrons operating from Home Fleet carriers, this particular machine belonging to No 881 Sqn aboard HMS *Illustrious*, for example. Along with sister-squadron No 882, this unit first saw action during the British occupation of the Vichy French naval base at Diego Suarez, on the island of Madagascar, in May 1942. Both strafing and combat patrols were flown by the units, although No 881 was the only squadron to shoot down enemy aircraft – two Potez 63-11 light bombers and a three Morane MS.406 fighters. In return, a single Martlet was shot down by the Vichy pilots. The FAA's highest scoring Martlet pilot of the war, Lt C C Tomkinson, claimed all 2.5 of his kills during this operation *(via Phil Jarrett)*

from Vichy French aircraft. During that time No 881 shot down three MS.406 fighters and two Potez 63 fast reconnaissance bombers, in exchange for one Martlet that crash-landed. That left only one Axis enemy not yet represented among victims of the FAA's Grummans – an oversight about to be redressed.

Vichy French forces swept from the sky, a No 881 Sqn Martlet II is manhandled back to its spot on *Illustrious*' salty deck following a patrol on 7 May 1942. Note the aircraft's wheel-chocks perched atop the port wing *(via Aeroplane)*

Sailing the Bay of Bengal in early August, *Illustrious* and *Formidable* drew the attention of Japanese maritime patrols. On the 7th the British force was sighted by two Kawanishi H6K flying boats, one of which eluded interception. However, Sub-Lts J E Scott and C Ballard of 'Triple Eight' Squadron destroyed the second 'Mavis', rounding out an Axis grand slam for the Martlet.

Later that same month, Martlets were concerned with German and Italian opponents in the Mediterranean. Operation *Pedestal* involved three carriers – *Eagle, Victorious* and *Indomitable* – escorting a Malta-bound convoy with No 806 Sqn embarked in the latter. Though the bulk of the air defense was handled by 48 Sea Hurricanes and Fulmars, 806's half-dozen Grummans were heavily involved during repeated air raids on the 12th. Upwards of 100 bomber and torpedo aircraft were engaged, with Martlets accounting for four of the 30 claimed kills – two SM.79s, a Reggianne Re.2000 and a Ju 88. One Martlet was lost, as were a dozen other British fighters. Nor was such damage limited to FAA aircraft. By the time *Pedestal* was completed, *Eagle* had succumbed to a U-boat and only five of the 14 merchantmen reached Malta. However, these sacrifices were enough to sustain the island until the aerial siege finally ended.

'Don't forget to put this on, sir!' By January 1943 No 882 Sqn had re-equipped with the ultimate Grumman Martlet, the Mk IV, and had switched carriers to HMS *Victorious (via Aeroplane)*

The year's combat ended off Algeria during Operation *Torch* in November. Aside from the US Navy phase against French Morocco, two Royal Navy carriers with Martlets supported the eastern part of the plan. *Formidable*, now returned from the Indian Ocean, embarked No 888 and 893 Sqns with Mk IIs and IVs, respectively. No 882 Sqn aboard *Victorious* also flew Mk IVs, bringing the Grumman total aboard both ships to 42. The newer mark was, in fact, the F4F-4B, with the six-gun armament favoured by the Royal Navy.

Combat began on 6 November when Lt D M Jeram led a 'Triple Eight' section in chasing down a Bloch 174. Two days later a flight of No 882 Sqn 'captured' Blida Airfield near Algiers. This unprecedented accomplishment was consumated when the flight leader landed after observing white flags on the ground. While his wingmen circled overhead, Lt B H C Nation received the surrender of the pro-Allied base commander. After turning over his prize to

A considerable chunk of No 893 Sqn is spotted along the centreline of HMS *Formidable* prior to launching on patrol over the Mediterranean in February 1943. A sailor is positioned at each wing tip to prevent the Martlets from 'dinging' their flying surfaces when the carrier heels over into wind. Further crewmen await the signal below the fuselages that will see them whip the wheel chocks away. No 893 Sqn's next period of combat occured in July 1943 when they supported Operation *Husky*, which saw the Italian island of Sicily invaded by the Allies *(via Aeroplane)*

Illustrating just how 'mushy' the Martlet/Wildcat undercarriage really was, a No 878 Sqn Mk IV lists to port as the starboard wing is elevated by the stiff breeze blowing over *Illustrious*' bows. The pilot is gingerly taxying forward under the direction of the sailor in sandals(!), and once in position he will open the throttle and start his take-off run when he sees lieutenant(flying) drop his flag. This shot was taken in early 1944 whilst the carrier was sailing in the Mediterranean *(via Aeroplane)*

startled American troops, Nation returned to *Formidable* with a story to dine out on for a very long time!

The tentative Anglo-Franco truce was shattered on the 9th as Luftwaffe bombers interceded. Consequently, No 882 Sqn claimed a He 111 destroyed and a Ju 88 damaged, while No 888's Jeram bagged another Junkers, which he shared with his wingman.

Thus far in *Torch* the only Martlet squadron deprived of air combat was *Formidable*'s No 893. However, on the 11th a four-plane flight intercepted and shotdown a twin-engined aircraft identified as an Italian SM.84. Tragedy ensued when the FAA pilots later learned that they had actually destroyed an RAF Hudson based at Gibraltar.

The first half of 1943 was relatively uneventful for Martlet pilots. *Furious*' two fighter squadrons, Nos 881 and 890, plied the North Sea on generally fruitless patrols, but did turn up occasional business. Three Bv 138s were shot down during July before the venue shifted back to the Atlantic. The tri-motor Blohm und Voss seaplane would become the Martlet's most frequent victim, with 12 entries in the victory log.

At this same time in the Pacific, US Wildcats and British Martlets were co-mingling in the same ship. USS *Saratoga* and HMS *Victorious* had arranged a cross-deck evolution for a short period, combining all the fighters of both air groups in the latter carrier. There was some maintenance adjustment to be made, as Nos 882, 896 and 898 Sqns' Martlet IVs had Wright engines compared to the F4F-4's Pratt & Whitneys.

However, the Anglo-American force co-operated during Operation *Toenail* – seizure of New Georgia Island during late June and early July. 'Fighting Three', under Lt Cdr L H Bauer, experienced no problems operating with the FAA, despite different landing-signal procedures. In fact, the Americans rather favoured the arrangement, as they benefited from the Royal Navy custom of serving liquor aboard ship. At least one exuberant F4F-4 pilot reminded his shipmates of that fact by dropping a message on 'Sara's' flightdeck in a beer can – an *empty* beer can! *Victorious* departed the Pacific in August without having engaged Japanese aircraft.

On 1 December 1943 – two years after *Audacity's* loss – another Fw 200 fell afoul of Martlets. The escort carrier *Fencer* flew a composite squadron, No 842, consisting of Martlet Mk IVs and Swordfish, and two fighters tackled the lone Fw 200 with expected results. It was the sixth destroyed by British Martlets.

A new variant began arriving in late 1943 as Eastern FM-1s were delivered as Martlet Mk Vs. The

Not all Wildcat squadrons enjoyed the luxury of a large flight deck from which to operate, Nos 882 and 898 Sqns, for example, calling the modest confines of HMS *Searcher* home. This flypast was performed specially for photographer Charles E Brown in mid-April 1944, the carrier and her air wing having just come off of flak suppression missions flown in support of FAA aircraft attacking the pocket battleship *Tirpitz* in the Norwegian fjords *(via Aeroplane)*

first combat for the new model occurred on 12 February 1944 when *Pursuer* launched elements of Nos 881 and 896 Sqns to defend against four-engined bomber attack. Armed with radio-controlled glide bombs, Fw 200s and He 177s tried to disrupt a Gibraltar convoy, but were intercepted by four Mk Vs. In a rare nocturnal combat, Martlets claimed one of each without loss. The carrier pilots reported that German gunners seemed to use the Martlet's glowing exhaust stubs as aiming points.

Four days later, and nearly 200 miles west of Ireland, *Biter's* Mk IVs claimed a Ju 290, adding yet another multi-engine bomber to the Grumman's growing list. Two New Zealanders, Lt W C Dimes and E S Erickson, fired 1460 rounds into the huge aircraft to ensure its destruction. However, the Junkers was the last victim of the Martlet. In March British names for American aircraft were standardised along US lines, so Royal Navy F4F and FMs also became Wildcats. So too did the Tarpon become the Avenger in British service.

Though Grumman fighters had long flown the appalling Arctic convoy routes, as yet they had found no conclusive combats. All that changed during March and April 1944. *Activity* and *Tracker*, with Nos 819 and 846 Sqns, escorted convoy JW-58, which was subjected to a near-constant enemy presence. Between 30 March and 1 April the Wildcat Mk IVs claimed six bombers, including three Kondors on the 31st – this raised the tally to ten Fw 200s destroyed by Martlets since September 1941.

Meanwhile, Operation *Tungsten* went ahead on 3 April as six Royal Navy carriers attacked the German battleship *Tirpitz* in a Norwegian fjord. CVEs *Pursuer* and *Searcher* contributed Wildcat Mk Vs, but no aerial opposition developed.

No 819 continued on its winning ways on 1 May while flying in

Caught in mid-air by its 'sting' hook, a No 898 Sqn Wildcat IV comes back aboard *Searcher* to complete another successful strafing mission against German flak batteries in Norway *(via Aeroplane)*

northern climes. 'Yellow Section' surprised a Bv 138 which had been stalking one of *Activity's* Swordfish and splashed the snooper 26 minutes after launch. Lt Large and Sub-Lt Yeo credited the 'Stringbag' crew with radioing the enemy's position during the hunt. Nos 898 and 896 added three more Bv 138s in May and June.

Few Wildcats wore D-Day invasion strips as most aircraft were involved elsewhere on Russian convoy patrols, Norwegian coastal strikes or Mediterranean and Far East deployments. However, one unit that was very much in the thick of things over Normandy was No 846 Sqn, embarked on HMS *Tracker*. The unit primarily flew in support of Avengers, also from No 846 Sqn, in anti-shipping strikes up and down the Channel. This machine, an Eastern-built Mk V, bears the legend, 'That Old Thing', in yellow above the wing, and is seen cruising along the English south coast in late June 1944 *(via Aeroplane)*

Pursuer and *Searcher* appeared off Southern France in August with Nos 881 and 882 Sqns flying Mk VIs and Mk Vs, respectively. Operation *Anvil-Dragoon* thus marked the first major appearance of FM-2s in British service, but the Grummans were limited to strike missions and ground support. During the next three months, more Wildcats were involved in similar operations in the Aegean Sea – again without opportunity for air-to-air combat.

Attention shifted to the far north as *Campania* escorted a two-ship convoy, JW-61A. On 3 November No 813 Sqn's Lt Leamon and Sub-Lt Buxton expended 370 rounds to 'flame' a Bv 138, while ten days later Sub-Lts Machin and Davies dispatched a second. Then, working the next JW/RA convoy, No 835, off *Nairana*, splashed another Blohm und Voss on 12 December. Despite poor visibility and rapidly-fading light, Sub-Lt Gordon made the kill with merely 60 rounds per gun.

JW- and RA-64 in February 1945 provided repeated opportunities, but frustrating results, for Nos 813 and 835 Sqns. Still embarked in *Campania* and *Nairana*, respectively, they were augmented by a solitary Fulmar nightfighter in *Campania*. The Wildcats were vectored onto half-a-dozen bogeys, only two of which were confirmed destroyed. No 813 splashed a Ju 88 on 6 February, but lost a fighter and its pilot in the process, cause unknown. Three more Junkers were intercepted on the 10th, during which the Grummans fired nearly 4000 rounds. However, the Germans' speed and good use of clouds limited claims to a probable, one possible and a damaged. No 835's sharpshooting D G Gordon, who had proven so efficient on 12 December, was back in form on 20 February. He and Sub-Lt P H Blanco required only 260 rounds of .50 cal to destroy a snooping Ju 88. Meanwhile, another section on the opposite side of the convoy probably splashed another.

One of the FAA's first Wildcat Mk VIs is put through its paces in Britain, prior to being issued to a frontline squadron in the autumn of 1944. Equivalent to the US Navy's FM-2, Wildcat VIs served primarily in the Far East, although the first squadron to re-equip with the type was No 881, very much a Home Fleet unit from the Martlet's earliest days *(via Phil Jarrett)*

One of the Wildcat's last battles in Royal Navy service was perhaps the most intriguing of all. On 26 March 1945 *Searcher's* No 882 Sqn escorted an Avenger strike along the Norwegian coast in company with other carrier aircraft. Eight Bf 109Gs attacked beneath an overcast, gaining the initial advantage by damaging one Wildcat Mk VI. The low-level combat was resolved in favour of the Grumman's manoeuvrability, however, with four Messerschmitts being claimed destroyed and one damaged.

Only four days before the war in Europe ended, FAA Wildcats flew their last mission against Germany. Three CVEs – *Queen, Searcher* and *Tracker* – launched 44 sorties against Kilbotn, in Norway, which sank two ships and a U-boat. Wildcat flak suppression limited losses to one fighter and an Avenger on 4 May.

On VJ-Day in September 1945 the FAA boasted 1179 carrier aircraft – five times the number of six years before. Of those, only No 882 Sqn at Cochin was still flying Wildcats – 24 Mk VIs intended for *Searcher*.

The Fleet Air Arm produced some 16 aces, including those seconded to the RAF. However, very few scored five or more victories in any one FAA aircraft type. Lt C C Tomkinson's 2.5 (all Vichy French aircraft shot down over northern Madagascar in May 1942 whilst the pilot was attached to No 881 Sqn) remained the highest score for the Martlet/Wildcat, while No 882 Sqn was the most successful unit with seven kills. For comparison, here are the top scores in other FAA fighters:

Fulmar	Lt Cdr S G Orr	No 806 Sqn	8.50
Sea Hurricane	Lt Cdr R A Brabner,	No 801 Sqn	5
Sea Gladiator	Cdr C L Keighly-Peach,	HMS *Eagle* Flight	3.50
Corsair	Lt D J Sheppard,	No 1836 Sqn	5
Skua	Lt Cdr W P Lucy,	No 803 Sqn	3.33
Hellcat	Sub-Lt E T Wilson,	No 1844 Sqn	4.83
Seafire	Sub-Lt R Reynolds,	No 894 Sqn	3.50

Despite this apparent disparity in individual scores, the Martlet/Wildcat showed very favourably in total victories credited. The 54 attributed to the type was exceeded in the Royal Navy only by the Fulmar. The difference is explained by the exceptional variety of service provided by 1082 Martlets/Wildcats flying with more than 30 squadrons from 1940 to 1945. No other FAA fighter enjoyed so long a wartime career, nor did any other achieve victories over all four major Axis air forces: Germany, Italy, Vichy France and Japan.

PILOT PROFILE - CAPTAIN ERIC 'WINKLE' BROWN, CBE, DSC, AFC, RN

As detailed above, the Fleet Air Arm produced very few aces during World War 2, principally because the 'Senior Service' employed its aerial assets on a mix of convoy protection and ground attack tasks. When enemy aircraft were encountered, dedicated RAF (in Europe) or US Navy (Indian and Pacific Oceans) fighter units would usually neutralise any attacks. Therefore, if the strict rules of 'acedom' – five kills – are to be applied, then the pilot featured in this monograph should not be included, as he finished the war with only two confirmed kills and a probable to his credit. This nevertheless ranked him closely behind the most successful Martlet pilot of the war, Lt C C Tomkinson.

However, statistics often hide as much of the true picture as they reveal, and the combat experience of Capt Eric 'Winkle' Brown is a perfect

A youthful Sub-Lt Eric 'Winkle' Brown clutches onto his gloves and maps as he makes his way to the stern of *Audacity*, where his Martlet II is being prepared for its next patrol over Gibraltar-bound convoy OG-74. This snapshot was taken by a fellow No 802 Sqn pilot in early October 1941 – the squadron had already made their presence felt by this stage in the cruise, having destroyed a Fw 200 a fortnight before. Brown and his fellow pilots never flew in their Irvin jackets, as worn here, due to the fact that they quickly became water-logged in the event of a ditching, and could easily drag the wearer down to a watery grave. However, they proved adept at staving off the inclement weather up on deck prior to launching on patrol *(via Capt E Brown)*

example of this. He was flying Martlet Is and IIs on convoy patrols three months *prior* to the Japanese raid on Pearl Harbor, claiming kills weeks before the US Marine Corps opened their account over Wake Island.

Brown's pre-war flying on Gloster Gauntlet biplane fighters with the Edinburgh University Air Squadron taught him the basics of aerial combat in the relaxed surroundings of a nation at peace, albeit steadily preparing for war. Many of his contemporaries within the FAA were lost early in the first three years of the conflict due to a general lack of experience, principally because time did not then allow pilots to spend many months sharpening their skills prior to entering frontline service.

Upon the outbreak of war, Brown voluntarily switched services to the Navy, and after initially flying Sea Gladiators, he was posted to No 802 Sqn at Donibristle, in Fife, where he flew the less than inspiring Blackburn fighters, the Skua and the Roc. Fortunately, he was never forced to go into combat in either type, and in early 1941 his squadron became the first unit within the FAA to receive Martlets, these machines being ex-French *Aéronavale* G-36As that had been diverted to Britain following the fall of France three months earlier. Thus began his brief association with the Grumman fighter.

The following interview was conducted in August 1994 specially for this volume, and Capt Brown's memories of his Martlet flying provide a uniquely British angle to the Wildcat/Martlet story.

'The first thing that struck us about these Martlet Is, or G-36s, to give them their correct designation, was that the instrumentation within the cockpit was still in metric units! Nevertheless, we were still very impressed for this aircraft, from our point of view, was really the bridge between the biplane and the monoplane.

'Up to that point we had had some real rubbish in the Fleet Air Arm, and you really couldn't call our previous aircraft, the Roc, a fighter at all. We also had plenty of biplanes like the Sea Gladiator and the Swordfish, but both types were by now very outdated. Therefore, we were very happy to see this "creature" arrive on the scene.

'We were being prepared to go aboard the Navy's first escort carrier, HMS *Empire Audacity*, although we didn't know this at the time. This new weapon of war was the child of Churchill's genius – he had the idea that if we could get a suitable merchant ship and literally slice the top off it and put a flight deck on it, we could operate suitable aircraft in the convoy protection role.

'We couldn't spare the bigger carriers for this task as they were needed elsewhere. This first escort carrier was, in fact, an ex-German banana boat (SS *Hannover*) which had been captured in the West Indies. It was brought back to the UK and had had a flight deck of 423 ft in length built over its hull. There was no hangar, so all six (later eight) Martlets had to be ranged on the deck. They took up further usable take-off space for launching aircraft – so much so that the first pilot to launch on a mission had only about 300 ft of deck to take-off from.

'Prior to embarkation we spent

Few photographs of the converted German merchantman HMS *Empress Audacity* were taken prior to her brief career commencing in September 1941. This side-on shot clearly shows her 'islandless' flightdeck and tactical 'dazzle' paint scheme *(via Capt E Brown)*

much of the spring and summer of 1941 flying intensive work-ups with the Martlet Mk Is, and later Mk IIs, in the Fife area. The RAF were also quite interested in the fighter at the time, from both a recognition point of view and also as a dissimilar dogfighting opponent for their Hurricanes (pincipally those from RAF Digby) and Spitfires. It handled itself well against both types, being very comparable overall to the Hawker fighter. If anything, it was perhaps more rugged than the Hurricane, but it didn't share the latter's impressive rate of roll. However, the Martlet had a startling initial rate of climb, although the higher it got the more the Hurricane caught it up. The Martlet was built for medium to low level work, and to emphasise this point none had oxygen fitted to them.

'With this positive dogfighting experience under our belts we felt confident that we could more than hold our own against the Luftwaffe fighters of the day, and were very disappointed that we never got a crack at them. However, in light of the US Navy's experience with the Zero, which proved near impossible to counter in a turning fight, and our post-war evaluation of the Fw 190, it was perhaps just as well that we never encountered these fighters in our Martlet IIs. To help us deal with our known targets – Kondors – we also had a spell of fighter liaison with a Halifax bomber squadron prior to our deployment. The primary aim of this exercise was essentially to teach you how much the slipstream of these big aircraft could toss you around if you attempted a stern attack.

'We eventually got aboard in September 1941, the squadron embarking eight pilots and six aircraft. Once at sea on this historic trip, we found ourselves on the North Atlantic to Gibraltar run, which passed through some of the roughest water in the world. This really wasn't ideal, operationally speaking, for a small ship like ours as you got a lot of heavy flight deck movement.

'To illustrate how bad this was, on one occasion we measured that the ship's stern was rising and falling through a total arc of 65 feet. It also rolled as well as pitched, and we lost an aircraft off the deck on operations during our second patrol, performed in early November 1941, when the ship rolled over eight degrees from neutral – this, of course, was occurring both to port and starboard.

'The stern was heaving heavily on this particular occasion, and after one attempted landing by the unfortunate pilot, he was struck by the deck on the "up swing" as he came over the stern on his second recovery. It hit the aircraft square on, and literally tossed it overboard. Fortunately, the Martlet's inherent floatation characteristics then came into play, the in-built buoyancy bags fitted in the wings inflating as soon as their activating hydrostatic valves came in contact with the water.

'Our task was to carry out constant patrols round the convoy looking out for surfaced U-boats, which performed much of their attack work on the surface until close to the convoy itself. The Focke-Wulf Fw

This truly remarkable photograph, borrowed from Capt Brown's own private scrapbook, shows him leading his section in a rather unorthodox fashion whilst undertaking an interception over the Atlantic in September 1941. The shot itself was taken by the pilot of a Pan American Boeing 314, nicknamed *'Dixie Clipper'*, which was flying a routine passenger run between the Azores and Lisbon, in Portugal. At the time the US was still neutral, and the skipper of the flying boat took serious umbrage to being intercepted at close quarters by the trio of No 802 Sqn fighters. He duly sent his photographic handiwork to the American Embassy in Lisbon, who in turn forwarded it to the London consulate. From there, it finally reached the Admiralty, who instructed a young Sub-Lt Brown's commanding officer to reprimand him. 'Winkle' duly lost three months seniority in rank for, as his boss wryly told him, 'a lapse of concentration in the duty that you were supposed to be fulfilling'. Eric's section mates on this patrol were, to starboard, Sub-Lt Graham 'Fletch' Fletcher and, to port, Sub-Lt Bertie Williams *(via Capt E Brown)*

200 Kondors were very active relaying to the U-boats the positions of convoys, as well as bombing any straggling elements of the flotilla itself.

'We had quite a busy time with the Kondors during this period, and, despite our best efforts, they had their successes against us, not only from the viewpoint of good reconnaissance reporting. On our second convoy patrol (OG-76), a Fw 200 succeeded in shooting down our CO, Lt Cdr John Wintour, who, upon setting the Kondor alight, thought he had inflicted the *coup de grace* on the Focke-Wulf and drew up alongside the aircraft to survey the situation, whereupon the dorsal gunner promptly shot him down.

'I inadvertently chanced upon the best angle of attack against a Kondor during my first encounter with the type on 8 November 1941, although I have to confess to having thought about this approach prior to this engagement. Indeed, we had even discussed the head-on attack in the crew room aboard ship, but dismissed it because we never thought that we would have a sufficient speed advantage to overhaul the Fw 200, unless of course we were vectored in from head on from the start. I had a belief that the forward dorsal turret couldn't depress its guns below a certain angle, and, similarly, the ventral gondola couldn't elevate its guns to cover the "blind spot" either. This blank area ahead could then be exploited providing you came in very flat.

'I only resorted to this form of attack after my frustrated efforts at text-book beam and quarter attacks had failed to make any impression, other than to set the starboard inner engine alight, and I lost him in cloud. This pilot, as with most other Kondor crews that we encountered, also resorted to the favoured tactic of turning into me every time I ran in to attack – when I made the head-on pass he just flew straight on at me, keeping the Kondor straight and level so as to give the gunners a stable platform from which to aim from.

'After several minutes we eventually broke back in to clear skies head-on to each other! I closed on him with the flattest possible trajectory, being careful not to stray into his forward firing zones. We had six .50 cal machine guns in our Martlet Mk IIs, which sprayed out a fair amount of lead, and I could actually see the windscreen of the Kondor disintegrating in front of me as I closed on the bomber. These guns were a revelation to us as they were a far heavier calibre than we had ever previously used.

'Our convoy patrols were usually performed in pairs at 1000 ft at a speed of around 150 kts, and we only "opened up" when we saw the chance of potential action. One had a lot of confidence in the Martlet, which was just as well really as we were flying a single-engined aircraft over water 800 miles from any land bases. To make matters worse, if you did ditch some distance from the carrier, it was unlikely that a vessel could be spared from the convoy to come and pick you up.

'To this end, we tended to do the patrol with the convoy just in sight, one of us going clockwise and the other anti-clockwise. We weren't allowed to talk on the radio at all, unless of course it was an emergency – for example, if we spotted a U-boat running into attack the convoy. It was, therefore, a very peculiar existence just flying around in large circles in complete silence. We were flying the Mk II Martlet by this stage which was powered by the very smooth Twin Wasp radial engine, which gave off a confidence-boosting "purr" when running properly.

'*Audacity* only completed three-and-a-half legs of convoy protection duty before we were "hacked" on the return trip with HG-76 on the night of 20/21 December 1941 by U-751. During this entire period I intercepted three Kondors, destroying two and losing the third in cloud. The weather was always dreadful during our time aboard the carrier, with thick cloud cover usually aiding the Luftwaffe crews on almost all interceptions.

The calm before the storm – a group of recently-embarked No 802 Sqn sub-lieutenants and a pair of armourers pose for the camera just prior to *Audacity* joining up with OG-74. Sitting in the cockpit is Norris 'Pat' Patterson who, along with 'Fletch' Fletcher (no cap in photo), shared the first unit kill of the cruise on 21 September 1941 when they destroyed a Fw 200 of KG 40. Fletcher was killed by a flak battery aboard *U-131* on *Audacity*'s second patrol, whilst the remaining trio ('Sheepy' Lamb, left, and 'Bertie' Williams, right) also died in later combat *(via Capt E Brown)*

'From a No 802 Sqn perspective, we had three sections (two aircraft) on the first convoy patrol we performed, and they all experienced at least one contact, and four sections on the second, which again all crossed swords with the Luftwaffe. On the odd occasion we were also shot at by "friendlies", usually Coastal Command Sunderlands and Liberator Is. We were also scrambled to intercept civilian Boeing Clipper flying boats flying the Lisbon-Azores route, these slow contacts usually being picked up first as blips on *Audacity*'s radar, and unidentifiable as to type.

'Aside from our standing patrol, which would be sent off to investigate any contacts approaching the convoy, we also maintained two Martlets on the deck at immediate readiness, with pilots strapped in. A further pair were then on standby. The squadron had four pairs of crews for its six aircraft, with the final pairing being classed as available at five minutes' notice. This allowed them to get their heads down after having performed a patrol, or a long spell at alert on the pitching deck.

The alert aircraft had their engines kept warm by brief engine runs every half-hour, and as soon as word came through to launch it was simply a matter of actuating the inertia starter switch and flying off the carrier once it had been turned into wind. Occasionally we would even launch when the ship was still steering into wind. We used flap on launch, and as the Martlet had no intermediate flap setting – it was either up or down – we modified the moveable surfaces by inserting small wooden blocks (like wedge door stops) when the flaps were fully open whilst the aircraft was idle on the deck. It was then closed up to the blocks, giving us 20 degrees of flap, which helped our climb out from take-off immensely. As you climbed out you opened the flaps even further and the blocks simply fell away!

Firmly harnessed into his Martlet II, Sub-Lt Brown sits on the rolling deck of *Audacity,* awaiting the call to scramble. Endless hours could be spent sitting in the damp cockpit environment of a lashed down Martlet whilst the standing patrol droned tirelessly about overhead *(via Capt E Brown)*

'Workload was very heavy in the Martlet straight after take-off as the undercarriage had to be hand-cranked shut. This took 29 turns, and you had to be careful not to snag you R/T helmet lead around the handle. One pilot had crashed his aircraft only weeks after the first Martlet Is had arrived in Scotland when he got himself tangled up and wound his head down into the cockpit.

'The maintenance section aboard ship worked miracles with our Martlets as all rectification work had to take place out in the open on the flight deck, usually at night. These chaps struggled just to keep their footing on the invariably wet and heaving deck, and because they weren't allowed to show lights at night so as to avoid detection by U-boats, they operated with hand torches which had had the bulbs covered with blue paper. Even then, they were not allowed to put these on until they were in a compartment or in the cockpit. Despite these harsh conditions, they never complained due to their total dedication to the job, and they were No 802 Sqn's real heroes.

Fortunately, we didn't bend our Martlets too often despite the weather, which kept heavy maintenance for the engineering section down to a minimum. This was due primarily to the aircraft's marvellous landing characteristics, aided by the self-centring arrester wires fitted to the carrier. The undercarriage on the aircraft was also very "mushy", which allowed it to absorb high vertical velocities without producing any rebound reactions. We also enjoyed an excellent forward view of the carrier on approach to landing, and the Martlet's innocuous stall characteristics meant that you could fly it right down to the lower speed limits during a recovery without too many worries. This machine really could not have been bettered for the job at hand in late 1941.

'In all the time I operated the Martlet the only real feedback we got from the US regarding our aircraft concerned Grumman's attempts at Bethpage to solve the take-off swing experienced when operating from land bases. No in-service evaluations or reports from US Navy squadrons ever reached us to my knowledge. The manufacturer let it be known to us they were planning on replacing the solid tail wheel with a longer oleo fitted with a pneumatic type. Conversely, we learnt through the US Embassy in London that their Navy were very interested to hear how the .50 cal machine gun behaved in combat. They wanted to know if we were suffering high stoppage rates, and if so, were we able to clear the guns with the cocking handles. We never saw any engineers or representatives from Grumman up in Scotland!

'We reported back to the Americans that we were impressed with the spread of fire with the guns, and the accuracy we achieved through a combination of the aircraft's remarkable stability – if anything, the Martlet was *too* stable to be a fighter – and its superb gunsight, made our gunnery scores very respectable. We suffered stoppages, but nothing too severe.

'The Martlet really was ideally suited to carrier aviation, and I've yet to meet an ex-F4F/FM-2 pilot who has anything bad to say about the aircraft. One thing often forgotten when discussing aircraft of this type, is the peace of mind derived by the pilot from flying a machine with good deck landing characteristics. In operations you have the stress of the combat, and with land operations once that climax is over all you then have to do is get yourself back to the airfield. In naval aviation, a), you've got to first find your carrier, and directions were rarely given, with most navigation being done by simple dead-reckoning in total radio silence; and b), once you did find it, getting back aboard a vessel that, more often than not, was pitching and rolling about quite heavily. So you really had three distinct periods of extremely high stress to deal with per flight.'

One of the lesser known wartime actions undertaken by the FAA saw two squadrons of Wildcats support a massed Allied force invading the South of France in August 1944 as part of Operation *Anvil-Dragoon*. Although no aerial opposition was encountered, these Wildcat Mk Vis of No 881 Sqn nevertheless made their presence felt by undertaking dozens of ground attack missions equipped with 250 lb bombs. This busy photograph shows squadron machines being readied for the next wave of sorties from HMS *Pursuer*, bombs being fitted to the Wildcats' inner wing pylons. Immediately behind the pilot's head in the middle of this shot is a rare example of FAA wartime nose art, here taking the form of a female rabbit *(via Aeroplane)*

TRAINING

While there has always been an aura of glamour surrounding military flying, the path to pilot's wings has never been easy. Perhaps the sentiment was best expressed in a training manual which stated, 'Naval aviation is not a sport. It is a scientific profession'. The needs of that profession were expanding dramatically in 1941, striving to provide tens of thousands of pilots, aircrew, maintenance and support personnel for the growing threat of war. While concessions to increased need were implemented, a high standard was still maintained and met – one student pilot in three failed to complete flight training.

The syllabus was altered considerably during the war years, but those pilots in fleet squadrons at the time of Pearl Harbor had already survived a gruelling year-long course at NAS Pensacola, Florida. There the cadets advanced through five squadrons, beginning on Naval Aircraft Factory N3N floatplanes and progressing to either the wheeled versions of the N3N or the Boeing-Stearman N2S. Eventually the aviation cadets (AvCads) graduated to North American SNJs, then seaplanes such as Consolidated PBYs, and finally to obsolescent fighters like the Boeing F4B. Upon graduation and commissioning as ensigns or Marine second lieutenants, the new aviators had logged some 300 or more flight hours.

Before establishment of the Carrier Qualification Training Unit (CQTU) at NAS Glenview, Illinois, in 1942, those fliers assigned to fighters learned their trade in their fleet squadrons. Pre-war fighter pilots also conducted individual battle practice (IBP), learning air combat from more experienced fliers.

Occasionally it was necessary to take down an overconfident youngster one or two rungs. Some of the 'old hands' resorted to potentially humiliating tactics – dogfighting while eating an apple, or even 'reading' a newspaper! Then, as now, combat proficiency was an evolutionary experience. So too was learning the fine points of aerial gunnery. The aim of every fledgling fighter pilot was to qualify as an 'expert', thus winning the right to paint the gunnery 'E' on his assigned aeroplane.

Meanwhile, a 'finishing school' had been established at NAS North Island, San Diego. Beginning in the summer of 1941, the Aircraft Carrier

An extremely loose formation of nondescript F4F-4s cruise at medium altitude during a training sortie over California on 26 March 1943. The general appearance of these fighters reflects the far less strenuous existence enjoyed by the Aircraft Carrier Training Group units, whose groundcrews could afford to spend a little more time maintaining their fighters within the luxury of permanent hangars at stations like NAS San Diego and the USMC's Camp Kearney. Virtually all Wildcats used by the training groups were 'war-weary' aircraft shipped back from the Pacific Theatre, and on at least one occasion an F4F-4 that had allegedly been flown by Joe Foss at Guadalcanal was issued to a Mojave, California, based unit. New pilots going through training at the base recall that the battered Wildcat sported 20 or more victory flags. However, it had most likely been successful in the hands of several pilots *(via Phil Jarrett)*

Training Group (ACTG) taught the basics of carrier flying with a cadre of experienced instructors. Despite its name, ACTG was concerned with more than just flying off and landing aboard carriers. For fighter pilots, tactical instruction was also a part of the curriculum, concentrating on aerial gunnery.

By late 1943, the few remaining F4F-4s in Navy service had been relegated to second-line training squadrons in the US. Their they were used and abused by the next generation of Wildcat pilots who would fly the far more potent FM-2 into combat. These aircraft all wear suitably large training codes, as well as the briefly used (from July to October 1943, to be precise) red 'star and bar' surrounds. This fine shot was officially released to the press by the US Navy on 26 October 1943 *(via Aeroplane)*

After Pearl Harbor all big-deck carriers were committed to combat, and few escort carriers were available for training. And since the onset of winter precluded instruction on the Great Lakes, Carrier Qualification Training Unit moved to San Diego until the spring. Eventually, two modified cruise boats were commissioned for carrier training on Lake Michigan: USS *Wolverine* (IX-64) and *Sable* (IX-81) in August 1942 and April 1943, respectively. Fledgling carrier pilots qualified with eight landings, either in SNJ trainers or fleet aircraft such as F4Fs, SBDs or TBFs.

Though autonomous from 1939, the Fleet Air Arm still relied heavily upon the RAF for training through much of the war. The Commonwealth Air Training Plan produced thousands of aircrew, not only in Great Britain, but in Canada, Australia, India and South Africa. Other Royal Navy pilots won their wings at NAS Pensacola. Those who passed through the RAF schools then went to FAA training units for specialised instruction in naval procedures and, of course, carrier operations.

Leadership has always been the crucial element in military affairs, and whatever failings F4F squadrons faced in their equipment was amply compensated for by their commanding officers. The nearly 20 Navy and Marine squadrons which flew Wildcats in Pacific combat during 1942 possessed an almost uniformly high standard of leadership – mostly Annapolis-trained professional officers with considerable aviation experience.

Many of these men are well known to history: John S Thach (VF-3), James H Flatley, Jr (VF-10), John L Smith (VMF-223), Robert E Galer (VMF-224) and Harold W Bauer (VMF-212) being the most familiar. However, others such as Paul H Ramsey (VF-2), Leroy C Simpler (VF-5), Louis H Bauer (VF-6), Charles R Fenton (VF-42) and Leonard K Davis (VMF-121) produced competent and motivated squadrons. Their methods varied widely, from the thorough professionalism of a Flatley to the flint-edged demeanor of a Smith; from the flamboyance of a Ramsey to the quiet competence of a Galer. Most of the highly-successful fighter skippers were born teachers, 'Jimmy' Thach, 'Jim' Flatley and 'Indian Joe' Bauer being prime examples.

But regardless of their personalities or methods, all of these men shared one common trait – they subscribed to the classic military technique of leading from the front. Few of them were the best pilots in their units, but nearly all made efficient use of the human resources available to them. Additionally, the finest leaders shared one other characteristic – they took care of their subordinates, both in the air and on the ground. Fifty years later, intelligent commanders still follow their example.

VICTORY CREDITS AND WILDCAT EVALUATION

When the Pacific War began, the US naval service had no standard method of evaluating or crediting aerial victories. However, the increasing tempo of air combat in early 1942 required that such methods be adopted, and individual air groups produced their own means of reporting combat action. The result generally was a mimeographed sheet of paper with standard questions, and room for amplifying drawings.

Aerial victory credits were generally assessed at unit level, unlike the USAAF tier of evaluation boards. The Navy method was largely dictated by the physical environment in which F4F units operated – from aircraft carriers or remote airfields. Thus, most victory claims were taken at face value, and so noted in a pilot's logbook. However, by the Battle of Midway, apparently some Navy fighting squadrons invoked an internal check upon initial claims. In that battle the three F4F squadrons claimed 45 kills – they actually got 29, or about two-thirds of what they claimed.

That ratio fits the historical average. As a general rule, western air forces tend to overclaim by *at least* a factor of one-third. Thus, for every three kills credited, approximately two enemy aircraft were generally shot down. Examination of individual squadrons' records shows that claims become more accurate with experience. Among F4F squadrons, the trend was most evident with the Marines on Guadalcanal. Their initial claims were usually well off the mark, but with a diminishing error factor as pilots observed genuine kills as a means of comparison. However, conditions on Guadalcanal conspired against accurate records – a scarcity of paper, coupled with increasing fatigue among all hands. Additionally, many unit histories or reports were only compiled after leaving the island.

One aspect of 1942 victory credits remains largely unexplained: the frequent credit of an ' assist'. Apparently the term had different meanings in different units. Sometimes, an assist was considered as a fractional credit wherein two or more pilots contributed to downing a hostile. Other times, 'assist' merely indicated that a fighter pilot contributed in some way to a successful combat. The term seems to have died out in late 1942, replaced by fractional credits.

As inaccurate as American victory claims could be at times, they were almost never as wildly inflated as their opponents'. The Japanese Navy consistently overclaimed by orders of magnitude, to the point that historians have concluded that an institutional optimism pervaded IJN fighter units! If a Zero pilot fired at an Allied aircraft, the target was apparently considered at least probably destroyed.

Perhaps the best-known instance of this involved the 107-aircraft attack on Midway on the morning of 4 June. Zeros engaged 25 F2As and F4Fs, destroying 15 in a quarter of an hour. However, upon returning to their carriers the Zero pilots claimed 40 'destroyed' and numerous 'probables' – all F4Fs. In turn, the Marines were credited with 11 shootdowns against the enemy's 10 actual losses. The fact that AA fire also destroyed several Japanese aircraft makes respective credits difficult to allocate.

In the end, the numerical claims of air combat – 'the score' – mattered less than the aftermath. If enemy losses in destroyed and damaged aircraft prevented him from launching another strike, that was what counted most. During 1942, outright aerial supremacy seldom existed for either side after Coral Sea. But the results attained by Navy and Marine F4F squadrons increasingly swung air superiority in favour of the Americans. The long-range results proved irrevocable for the Empire of Japan.

By VJ-Day, the total Wildcat score stood at 1514.5 aerial victories credited to US units. They broke down by service and type as follows:

US Marine F4Fs	(11 squadrons)	562 victories
US Navy F4Fs	(28 squadrons)	520.5 victories
US Navy FMs	(38 squadrons)	432 victories

Of 76 Wildcat units credited with victories, the top 15 were:

VMF-121	Solomons	160
VMF-223	Solomons	133.5 (22.5 TAD)
VF-5	*Saratoga* and Solomons	79
VGF-11/VF-21	Solomons	69
VC-27	*Savo Island*	61.5
VMF-224	Solomons	61.5 (6.5 TAD)
VMF-112	Solomons	61
VMF-212	Solomons	57
VF-11	Solomons	55
VF-3	*Lexington, Yorktown*	50.5 (some as VF-42)
VGF/VF-26	*Sangamon*, Solomons and *Santee*	46
VF-72	*Hornet* and Solomons	44
VF-10	*Enterprise* and Solomons	43
VMO-251	Solomons	33
VMF-221	Solomons	30

Unique among all Wildcat squadrons was VF-26, which began as VGF-26 aboard *Sangamon* and claimed four Vichy aircraft during Operation *Torch*. Redesignated VF-26 and sent to the Pacific in 1943, the squadron logged a further 11 victories while land-based in the Solomons. Finally, though functioning as a VC unit, VF-26 flew FM-2s aboard *Santee* in 1944. In the latter capacity the squadron ranked second among all CVE units with 31 kills, primarily in the Philippines campaign. No other squadron drew Axis blood while flying Wildcats for three consecutive years.

F4F/FM-2 Evaluated

After the Battle of Midway, Lt Cdr John Thach said that, 'Only fighters can keep our aircraft carriers afloat'. The increasing importance of fighters in the composition of carrier air groups bore out Thach's assessment, as F4F numbers steadily increased. At the time of Pearl Harbor, each carrier fighter unit possessed 18 aircraft. By Midway the number was 27 – a 50 per cent increase in six months. At the start of the Guadalcanal campaign the carriers nominally had 36 F4Fs apiece. The trend would only continue as the war progressed closer to Japan. By 1945 the new-generation *Essex*-class ships embarked a staggering 73 Hellcats or Corsairs, including nightfighter and photo-reconnaissance detachments.

Whatever its performance deficiencies, the F4F possessed one supreme advantage – availability. During the crucial summer of 1942, the F6F was a full year from combat deployment and the F4U was more than six months away from arriving at Guadalcanal. In that respect the Wildcat was the Navy counterpart to the USAAF's Curtiss P-40. However, attrition nearly matched production. From July through November 1942, Pacific Fleet carrier fighter squadrons received 197 Wildcats, including a few recce-F4F-7s. Losses to all causes were 115, or 58 per cent – small wonder then that back on Long Island, Grumman was working no less than three shifts.

In contrast to the Hellcat and Corsair, the Wildcat lacked two endearing characteristics as seen from the command level – range and payload. The former was particularly important in the war's largest arena, as many Navy and Marine Corps strike missions were flown beyond the F4F's radius of action. The fact that most such missions succeeded was a testimony to the skill and dedication of unescorted SBD and TBF crews, who often faced enemy fighters alone.

Wildcats were seldom called upon to perform genuine strike missions, though bombs and rockets were occasionally used. In both large carriers and CVEs, other aircraft (most notably TBF/TBM Avengers) were dedicated to the attack role. Therefore, the F4F's minimal strike potential was seldom a serious drawback, though certainly the type lacked the versatility of later fighters.

Unquestionably, the F4F – and to a lesser extent the FM – was best employed in the air-defense role. Flying both from carriers and from Guadalcanal, Wildcats were most effectively used to deter or minimise the effects of Japanese attack aircraft – horizontal and dive bombers, as well as torpedo planes. Certainly the aces' best missions were flown against enemy bombers – especially Aichi D3A 'Vals'. Of the eight F4F aces in a day, O'Hare, Vejtasa, Wrenn and Swett scored against bombers, as did FM pilots Hippe and Funk.

Despite the service's institutional reluctance to popularise individual fighter pilots, some aviators became well known. The Navy produced 25 F4F/FM aces and the Marines 34, eight of whom were killed during the war. Butch O'Hare remained the only carrier-based F4F pilot awarded the Medal of Honor, but Guadalcanal-based Marines were showered with decorations. Smith,

The FM-2 was the ultimate Wildcat to see service from the wooden decks of the US Navy's burgeoning carrier escort force. As part of its accelerated clearance trials prior to the type being issued to frontline units, this early production airframe was put through its paces by the NAS Patuxent River test establishment – its ownership is detailed in the small stencilled writing beneath the cockpit. The star and bar is outlined in red, dating this shot as having been taken in July 1943, and the hastily scrawled number eight on the nose and tail was added specifically for 'spotting', or parking, purposes whilst the FM-2 was at sea *(via Phil Jarrett)*

Galer, Bauer and Foss all received the Medal of Honor for 1942 combat, while DeBlanc and Swett were recognised for their early 1943 records. Combined with the posthumous postwar award to Major Elrod of Wake Island, eight F4F pilots received America's highest military decoration – more than were presented to pilots of any other single-engine aircraft flown by US armed forces in the war.

The British Admiralty was less concerned with the Grumman's range and strike limitations than the US Navy Bureau of Aeronautics. As noted previously, the Wildcat's greatest selling point to the Royal Navy was its respectable performance and robust construction. With no other single-seat fighter designed as a carrier aircraft from the ground up, the FAA was more than pleased with the Martlet. Flight-deck crews also appreciated the American 'tail-down' means of catapult launch at a time when most British carrier aircraft required a cradle for the 'tail-up' method of shooting machines off the 'booster'.

WEAPONS

It has been said that the guns are the 'soul' of a fighter. In the Wildcat that meant the superb M2 Browning .50 cal, arguably the finest aircraft weapon of the war.

The F4F-3/3A series was armed with four .50 cals, each with 450 rounds per gun, thus making a total of 1800 shells. However, with the advent of the folding-wing F4F-4 in late 1941, the US standard of six M2s was employed. Oddly, the 'improved' armament was instigated by the Royal Navy, which by then had ordered 220 Martlet Mk IVs. Between the wing-fold mechanism and the extra guns, ammunition capacity was reduced to 240 rounds per gun, or 1440 total. To fighter pilots, the difference was substantial: the 'dash four' was heavier and slower than the F4F-3, with only some 18 seconds firing time – barely half the older Wildcat's.

The deficit was eventually redressed in the FM-2, which reverted to the four-gun package which had proven satisfactory in the early 1942 battles. Additionally, the FM's frequent close air support role was enhanced by this additional ammunition, which allowed more time on station before 'firing out'.

Essentially, US Navy fighter squadrons used two methods in aligning their guns. Probably most common was convergence of all six weapons around a point 1000 ft ahead of the fighter. The size of the circle varied from squadron to squadron, but three mils was certainly as small as any one cared to use. In that case, three mils subtended three ft at 1000 ft range, for a pattern one yard in diameter.

However, only an expert aerial gunner could make good use of a three-mil harmonisation. Most pilots were not so proficient, and consequently, a wider dispersion was developed by boresighting each set of guns at different ranges: usually 250, 300 and 350 yards for outboard, middle and inboard guns, respectively. This 'pattern boresight' was attributed to Lt Cdr Gordon Cady, who flew F4Fs with VF-11 at Guadalcanal during 1943. Though inherently less lethal than the tighter cone of fire, its greater dispersion of lead made some hits more likely, which could often have a telling effect in any case due to the fact that Japanese aircraft lacked both airframe armour and self-sealing tanks.

The US Navy was probably the only air arm in the world which regularly practiced full-deflection aerial gunnery. In order to shoot effectively at high target-crossing angles, reflector sights were developed, replacing the tubular variety left over from the biplane era. In F4Fs the most common sights were the N-2 and Mk VIII types, with the latter eventually becoming standard. It featured a centre dot, or 'pipper', subtending one mil, with 50- and 100-mil radii to help calculate deflection. The rule of thumb was called the 'two-thirds rule', in which the correct lead at boresight range (1000 ft) was two-thirds the target speed in knots. Thus, a 300-knot enemy aircraft engaged from broad on the beam required a 200-mil hold-off.

Fleet Air Arm practice largely paralleled American usage – not surprising, considering that identical weapons were employed. The standard Admiralty harmonisation was 250 yards, though evidently without the overlapping pattern boresight favoured by the US Navy. Similarly, Martlets widely employed the standard US Mk VIII optical sight, with centre pipper surrounded by 50- and 100-mil rings.

Where variety existed in FAA use, it seems to have been in the different squadrons' choice of ammunition sequencing. When No 802 Sqn embarked in *Audacity* in 1941 their Mk IIs were loaded with one armour-piercing (AP) round for every four ball. During 1943, No 800 Sqn's Martlet Mk IVs loaded incendiary rounds in the inboard and outboard guns, with AP in the middle weapon. However, during the same period No 881 Sqn's Mk IIs employed five rounds ball to two AP. With the return of the four-gun armament in Mk Vs and VIs, standard loading was incendiary inboard and outboard AP. Some squadrons accomplished the same purpose by by utilising a mix of AP and incendiary rounds in the same belts.

Special-mission considerations occasionally show up in action reports. For instance, in early 1944 No 882's Mk Vs loaded one gun with tracer and AP to aid in sighting while strafing. At the time of the squadron's combat with Bf 109s in March 1945 the belting was 20 incendiary, 20 AP, 20 tracer and 20 ball. Otherwise, FAA fighters apparently did not widely use tracers.

Aside from air-to-air gunnery and strafing, Wildcats seldom employed weapons other than guns. However, both F4Fs and FMs demonstrated an ability to put other ordnance on target – sometimes under dire circumstances. Ironically, the F4F's most successful attack missions were flown with the fewest assets. VMF-211's superb performance at Wake Island was made possible by hard-working, innovative, pilots and ordnancemen who adapted 100-lb Army bombs to Navy racks. Despite almost no training in dive bombing, the 'Leatherneck' aviators sank a Japanese destroyer and damaged a light cruiser before the island garrison was over-run.

Once the FM-2 arrived in numbers, CVE-based Wildcats possessed a significant strike capability with the 3.5-in high-velocity aerial rocket (HVAR). Capable of carrying three under each wing, an FM-2 possessed nearly the equivalent of a destroyer's broadside, effective against bunkers and many warships. However, the HVAR's rapid ballistic drop after rocket burnout posed serious problems in sight alignment, requiring fairly close firing ranges.

GUADALCANAL DEBUT

The Americans began their offensive against the Japanese South West Pacific perimeter in early 1942. Adm King's plan was to advance step-by-step from Efate, in the New Hebrides, to Espiritu Santo further up the chain. From newly constructed bases the offensive could continue onto the Solomons and the Bismarcks. On 4 April the theatre was split between two commands; Gen Douglas MacArthur took the South West Pacific while Adm Chester Nimitz took command of the Central Pacific. The overall US strategy was that Nimitz's forces would advance upwards across the Pacific from island to island, starting in the Gilberts in November 1942, then onto the Marshalls, the Marianas, Iwo Jima and Okinawa. At the same time MacArthur would push north through the Solomons, New Guinea and onto the Philippines.

The key to success in the Solomons campaign was the rapid capture and completion by the Marines of a semi-operational Japanese airfield on Guadalcanal soon after the invasion of 7 August 1942. Ready to accept aircraft by the 12th, it became known as Henderson Field a few days later. Aircraft operating from Henderson and its satellites – 'Fighter Strips One' and 'Two' – were to become known as the 'Cactus Air Force', 'Cactus' being the American code-name for Guadalcanal. The Solomons were to be strongly contested by the Japanese as their loss would place Rabaul under threat – their main bastion of defence in the South Pacific. The Imperial Navy and Army Air Forces therefore committed, and ultimately lost, the bulk of their fully trained units in the defence of the Solomons. The campaign became a defeat from which they would never recover.

The bitter struggle for the Solomons was far from decided when VMF-124, under the command of Maj William E Gise, arrived on Guadalcanal with the Marines' first Chance Vought F4U-1 Corsairs on 12 February 1943. Boasting twice the range of the F4F, the Corsair enabled the hard-pressed 'Cactus Air Force' to attack the Japanese further up the Solomons chain. They were now also able to escort USAAF heavy bombers on long-range strikes, as well as perform sweeps against enemy airfields in the central and northern Solomons.

One of VMF-124's original cadre of pilots sent to the Solomons was Lt Kenneth A Walsh, a determined Marine who was soon to become the first aviator to achieve ace status in the Corsair. Here, he describes VMF-124's combat debut.

'Delivery of the F4U commenced in late October 1942. There were many refinements that had to be

The first prototype XF4U-1 took to the air on 29 May 1940 and a production order was issued on 30 June 1940. The design incorporated the use of the largest and most powerful radial engine of the time, the Pratt and Whitney R-2800, which was to turn the largest propeller ever used on a single-seat fighter. To gain the necessary ground clearance for the prop, Chance Vought incorporated an inverted gull wing which avoided the use of an exceptionally long main undercarriage and had the added bonus of reducing drag. As the wing met the fuselage at roughly right angles, it did not require the usual large fairing associated with the standard design (*via Phil Jarrett*)

carried out before the planes were combat ready, which delayed our proper conversion to the type. After we gained a complement of 24 aircraft and 29 pilots, we deployed to the Pacific, having only averaged about 20 hours in the F4U. We completed one gunnery hop, an altitude hop, one night flight and then we had to go – they needed us bad. We would have to learn through experience. The F4F Wildcats were out there at Guadalcanal doing a marvellous job of defence, but no way could they

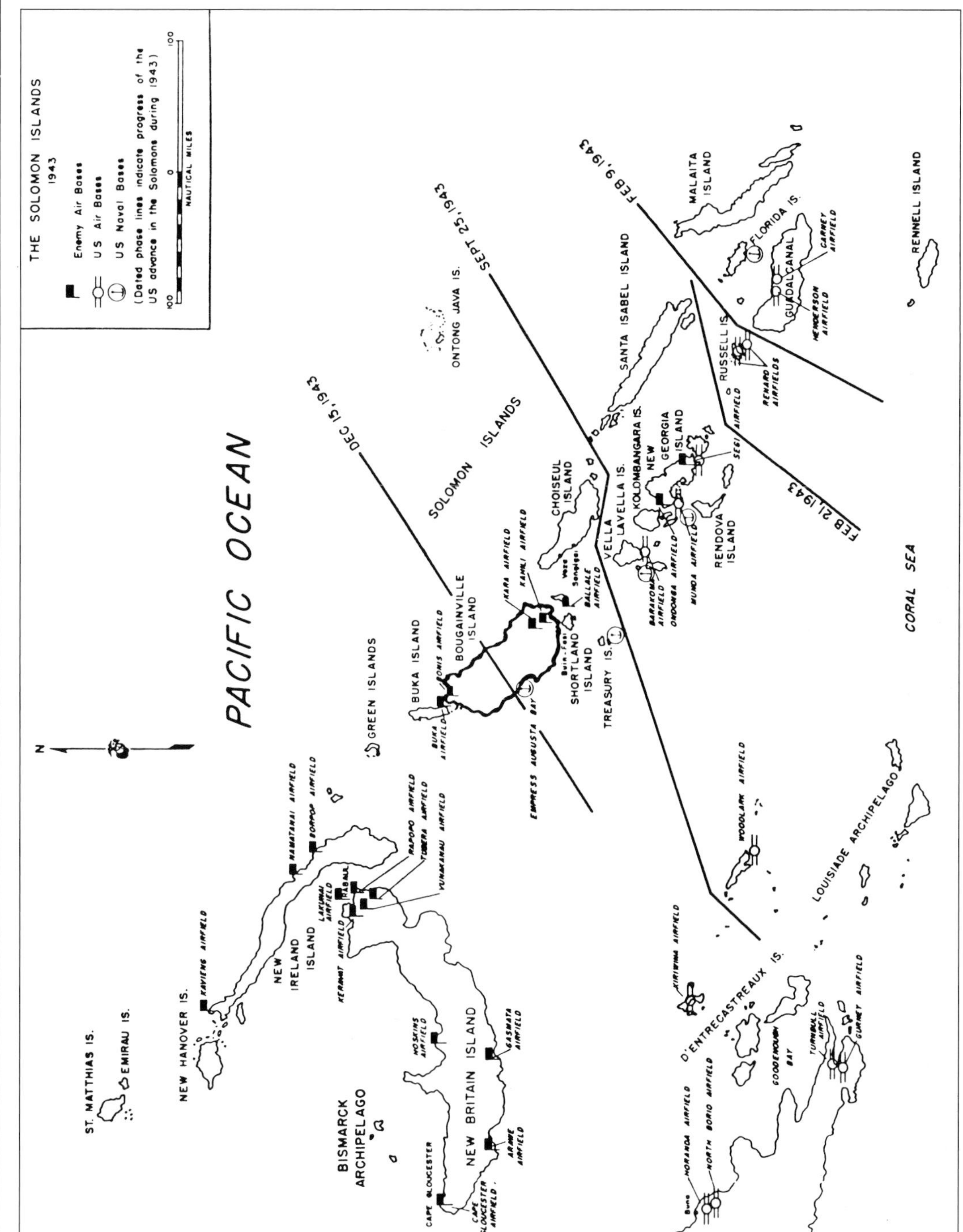

This detailed theatre map has been officially produced by the US Navy for its own publications, and clearly shows the central area of operations in and around the Solomons (*reproduced courtesy of the US Navy's FPO office*)

The XF4U-1 on an early test flight. There were major differences between the prototype and the first production aircraft. For example, the armament of one .30 cal and three .50 cal guns was revised to six .50 cal Brownings, three in each wing. The resultant loss in the wing's fuel capacity necessitated the incorporation of a fuel tank forward of the cockpit. This in turn required the cockpit to be moved further aft by three feet, thus worsening forward visibility – to counteract this problem the seat was raised by six inches. Other minor differences included the canopy arrangement and the lack of a tail hook (*via Phil Jarrett*)

take the offense. The Zero would play with the F4F like a cat with a mouse. The Wildcat also didn't have the range or the combat capability for escort missions. At that time there were only two planes that could do the job – the Corsair and the Army's P-38.

'We deployed in the first week of January 1943. Our 24 F4U-1s went aboard the jeep-carrier *Kitty Hawk*. We went on a cruise liner, rendezvousing with our aircraft at Espiritu Santo in the New Hebrides. We then waited for about 12 days before moving up to Guadalcanal, arriving on 12 February 1943 ready for combat. We took-off early in the morning to fly the 550 miles northwest to the Solomons, escorted by PB4Ys, the Navy version of the B-24. Seventeen F4Us went the first day and the balance followed the next. We landed before noon and immediately we discovered we had been slated for a mission even before we arrived. One hour later we set off from "Fighter Two" strip. The mission was a *Dumbo* escort; protecting a PBY Catalina. Two F4F-4 pilots had been shot down in the Kolombangara area, 200 miles north of Guadalcanal. Having been rescued by coast-watchers, they were moved to Sand Fly Bay, Vella Lavella, from where we were to rescue them. Twelve of our pilots achieved nine hours flight-time that day.

'The two downed pilots we picked up were Lt Jefferson DeBlanc (8 F4F kills) of VMF-112 and SSgt James A Feliton of VMF-121. For the former this was the end of a hair-raising sortie which saw him awarded the Congressional Medal of Honor – DeBlanc had "splashed" five aircraft attempting to dive-bomb Guadalcanal, before being downed himself.

'On the way back the Navy PBY crew also made an unscheduled rescue of an Army P-38 reconnaissance pilot who had ditched off the south coast of New Georgia. During that mission we were only about 50 miles from a large Zero base, and I hesitate to think what might have happened had they known we were coming up – our pilots were so inexperienced and we were at low altitude. We could have lost most, if not all of them, but we lucked out and got them back.

'I had thought that when we got up to the Solomon Islands we would have a chance to familiarise ourselves with the area, ascertaining exactly where Tulagi, Savo, Cape Esperance and the Russells (all the places I'd heard about) were. Not so, as our next mission followed the day after our *Dumbo* sortie! We were to go from Guadalcanal through to Bougainville, 300 miles up "The Slot", escorting B-24s that were to attack Japanese ships in Buin Harbour. I was leading the third four-plane element, and it soon became my usual position to lead the last flight. If there were four flights the aircraft I was flying would be numbered "13". Not being superstitious, from then on I

1st Lt Kenneth Ambrose Walsh prepares for a combat mission. Selected for Naval Flight Training in March 1936, he had experienced seven years of frontline flying before deploying to Guadalcanal with VMF-124 at the age of 26. He became the first Corsair ace, opening his score with two victories on 1 April 1943 (*National Archives via Pete Mersky*)

would always fly "No 13". During this second mission we again got lucky as only one Zero came out and he just looked us over.

'My first combat mission proper was flown on 14 February as this time the Japanese knew we were coming. Again we were escorting B-24s, but this time they were to hit Kahili aerodrome. The Japanese coast-watchers reported us long before we got there, and the Zeros were waiting when we arrived. We lost our first two pilots that day, along with two B-24s, four P-38s and two P-40s. We got three Zeros in return, one the result of a head-on collision with one of our F4Us. This, our first introduction to combat, became known as the "St Valentine's Day Massacre". Another similar mission was planned for the next day, but it was cancelled before take-off.

Ken Walsh's 'No 4 Flight', pictured at Guadalcanal in February 1943 at the start of their respective combat careers. Left to right, 1st Lt William Johnston, Jr, 2nd Lt Ken Walsh, 1st Lt Dean Raymond and MSgt Troy Shelton. These pilots would account for the destruction of 27 Japanese aircraft during the Solomons Campaign, Johnston and Raymond claiming two, Shelton three and Walsh twenty. F4U-1 'No 20' shows how VMF-124's aircraft appeared at the start of the tour. The Corsairs were soon repainted with more visible white numbers further aft on the fuselage (*Walsh Collection*)

'Being the first unit to go out in the Corsair, we didn't know exactly how to employ it, so we had to establish a doctrine. We knew that there would be many other Corsair squadrons following us, and they would want to know what we did, and how we did it. They would then be able to augment our experience and develop their own tactics. I had asked one very experienced Wildcat pilot, who had made a great name for himself during the early days of Guadalcanal, how to go about combat with the Zero. All he said was "you've gotta' go after them". Well, we knew it would take more than that!

'I learned quickly that altitude was paramount. Whoever had altitude dictated the terms of the battle, and there was nothing a Zero pilot could do to change that – we had him. The F4U could out-perform the Zero in every aspect except slow speed manoeuvrability and slow speed rate of climb. Therefore, you avoided getting slow when combating a Zero. It took time, but eventually we developed tactics and employed them very effectively. When we were accustomed to the area, and knew our capabilities, there were instances when the Zero was little more than a victim. I came to know the Zero, and I learned how to attack it. Being in my seventh consecutive year of frontline flying, I knew how to fire the guns and how to use our Mk 8 gunsight. The guns were boresighted to 1000 ft. The electric sight had rings covering so many mils, 1000 ft equalling one mil. If the Zero covered 40 mils, you knew he was 1000 ft away. We had six .50 cal guns with 400 rounds per gun, and a rate of fire of 800 rounds per minute. Our belt loading was one incendiary, one tracer and one armour piercing. A two-second burst would fire 150 rounds, and the Zero, like most Japanese aircraft, had no armour plating or self-sealing tanks. So, if you hit them, they'd burn, with their aluminium construction including magnesium parts which added further fuel to the fire. You can imagine what would happen if you got 30 or 40 hits on them.

'There were times, however, that I tangled with a Zero at slow speed, one on one. In these instances I considered myself fortunate to survive a battle. Of my 21 victories, 17 were against Zeros, and I lost five aircraft as a result of combat. I was shot down three times, and I crashed one that ploughed into the line back at base and wiped out another F4U. I was shot-up at least a dozen times, but usually the aeroplane could be repaired. The times that I really got in trouble came about due to the Zero that I didn't see, and conversely, I'm sure that with most of the kills I got they didn't see me. So, when new units came up behind us we told them what we had learned. Everything was a calculated risk, but I had a lot more to tell them about than just "you gotta' go after them".

Ken Walsh seen in one of his 'No 13s' on 1 September 1943. F4U-1 BuNo 02189 was his favourite aircraft, but it was written off by a VMF-213 pilot before his second tour. If his own aircraft was unserviceable he would take whichever aeroplane was available. Although this particular F4U has 'Captain' painted on the starboard undercarriage door, Walsh at that time was still a 1st Lieutenant. He was promoted to Captain the same day he was awarded the Medal of Honor – 8 February, 1944. The aircraft is also adorned with false gun ports, a practice carried out by VMF-124's armourers in an attempt to convince the enemy that the aircraft was more heavily armed than it actually was! Some of VMF-213's aircraft were similarly painted, as that unit used -124's ground-crews for a time (*USMC*)

'By July-August 1943 we had eight squadrons in the Solomons equipped with the Corsair. Our first combat tour lasted around seven months – our first mission was on 12 February and the last on 7 September. During that time we destroyed 68 enemy aircraft, but lost some 30 F4Us due to combat and operational causes. Of the 11 pilots lost, three fell in combat and four during operations. One of the pilots killed was our CO, Maj Gise, who was lost during an air battle on 14 May 1943.

'The date of my first kill was 1 April 1943. We were on patrol, going from the Russell's, which were 50 miles north of Patterson Field, to another little island called Baroku, the latter being a good navigational fix from which we could maintain our prescribed combat air patrol area. After an uneventful two hours going round and round, we were relieved by six P-38s, and as I turned to head back to Guadalcanal with my seven Corsairs, the Lightnings climbed right up past us. Within a minute they were jumped by a number of Zeros. There was no warning – we never had them on radar and they weren't reported by coast-watchers. They probably flew well to the south of the Solomons' cloud cover and came in for a surprise attack. I heard radio chat and realised the problem immediately. Looking over my left shoulder, I was surprised to see that the P-38s had formed a defensive Lufbery circle. I put my flight on alert and I told them to prepare for combat, which involved checking that their guns were armed and main fuel tank switched on until expended. Later we would switch to reserve, thus allowing us enough fuel to return to Guadalcanal.

'The Zeros and P-38s were in a wild melée by the time we arrived, and therefore didn't see our approach. We proceeded to climb up into the battle, and suddenly a Zero dived right across my bow. For a split second I couldn't help but marvel at the beauty of the configuration of the plane – it was clean and polished, a truly beautiful looking bird. But we were out for a kill so I lined up for a full deflection shot. I tried to get enough lead and was well within range, but it wasn't enough. My wingman, Lt Raymond, who was on the inside of the turn, fired at the same time as me as he did have the lead and he duly straddled the Zero with a burst of .50 cals – it went down burning. Raymond continued to stick right with me as I came in at a second Zero that was above us at 12 o'clock. He didn't see me and I hit him – he also went down burning.

'We began operations from Munda on the evening of 14 August. The following day, after my third combat for the 15th, I was sent to remain on station with five Corsairs covering the invasion of Vella Lavella. We were to prevent dive-bombers coming in and hitting our troops on the beach. I got on station and I was soon warned by the fighter director aboard one of the supporting destroyers – "Red 1. We have a bogey coming from the north west – it's a large bogey". I replied, "Roger. Request advise Munda to scramble what they can". I was low on oxygen so I couldn't reach high altitude where I would have preferred to have been, so I vectored my second section leader, Capt Wally Sigler (5.333 kills), to go up to high altitude instead. He was to be the top cover while I stayed down low with my wingman. Then the Zeros came in with some *Vals* and I got underneath the latter, shooting down two before a Zero clobbered me. He got on my tail and hit me with cannon shells, one of the rounds exploding in my starboard wing tank – fortunately the wing didn't blow off.

Armourers reload an F4U-1 with .50 cal ammunition following a raid on the Japanese airfield at Munda Point, Guadalcanal, in June 1943. The aircraft was equipped with six Colt-Browning M2 machine guns, with 400 rounds for the four inboard guns and 375 for the two outboard weapons, making for a total of 2350 rounds (*USMC*)

'Taking evasive action to escape the Zero shooting at me, I "split-S'ed" into a hard right turn, doing a 360° roll. During the manoeuvre I flew into cloud and suffered an attack of vertigo. We didn't have non-tumbling gyro horizon instruments in those days, so I had to try and bring the Corsair back to level flight using the turn and bank indicator. I was spinning around doing 400-500 kts, and as I came out of the cloud I realised that I was commencing an outside loop, inverted, going down at 45°. I barely missed the rim of an extinct volcano, and with one aileron gone, I just managed to roll the aeroplane back into level flight. I made it back to Munda, but they couldn't repair the Corsair so it had to be scrapped and used for spares. One of the 20 mm shells had entered the wing, severed all the hydraulic lines and hit the main spar, rendering it beyond repair – we couldn't change wings due to our poor field conditions. Although outnumbered six to one on this sortie, we thwarted the attack as the remaining *Vals* aborted the mission.

This was the aircraft that Ken Walsh was flying on 15 August 1943, seen here consigned to Munda's 'junkyard' having been damaged beyond repair by enemy fire. VMF-124 pooled their aircraft when operating from Munda and Vella Lavella, and as such '114' would have been a pool aircraft that may have previously been assigned an aircraft number by a different unit (*Walsh Collection*)

'By late August we had returned to Guadalcanal. By then there were eight squadrons of Corsairs out there, not to mention additional USAAF P-38s and P-40s, and we were beginning to make a good show of both offensive and defensive operations. On 30 August VMF-124 performed a bomber escort, but as we left Russell Island (our refuelling point) my super-

A close up of the damage sustained by '114'. One of the 20 mm cannon shells entered the upper surface of the starboard wing, exploding inside the fuel tank with shrapnel exiting the wing undersurface and leading edge. Ken was surprised that it held together, and that he was able to make it back to Munda (*Walsh Collection*)

Wreckage of an A6M Zero and a Corsair scattered next to the runway at Munda. VMF-124 was based here from 14 August, and participated in the invasion of Vella Lavella. At that time the unit was commanded by Maj William A Millington, who remained the CO until March 1945 (*Walsh Collection*)

charger malfunctioned. Leaving the flight, I headed for Munda, where I was given a replacement F4U-1 by VMF-215. I took off and headed for Kahili alone. When I found the B-24s they were were being attacked by some 50 Zeros in th target area, and we soon lost one which crashed with no survivors. I dove into the Zeros and got a couple of them at high altitude. During the long fight I heard a distress call from some of the B-24s that were then near Baga Island, having departed Kahili at low altitude. I tangled with two Zeros in the target area before I was attacked and shot up. There were four of them, and they soon had me boxed in and began shooting the hell out of me. I tried to get down low to escape, and if I'd had enough altitude I would have baled out. I finally shook them off by getting down to wave top height and heading for Munda, but the engine had been hit so I couldn't make landfall. I rode it in and crashed off Vella Lavella, from where a Higgins boat was despatched to fish me out the sea.

'My flight usually comprised 1st Lts Johnston and Raymond, and SSgt Shelton. Johnston was my wingman in the thickest battles, and he was always there when I needed him. I ran up the higher score naturally, being a division leader – leaders usually had the highest scores because they got the first shot. Johnston was shot down on 1 April, having been set on fire by a Zero. He bailed out and I saw him going down, although I didn't know immediately who it was. He landed in the water and returned to base the next day. He was very angry as he got sunburnt swimming on his back for three miles. He flew with me from then on and was a great wingman. I owe my life to him as he saved me on a couple of occasions.

'On one escort mission on 12 August he came in and flicked a Zero right off my tail. He had to put my plane in his gun sight to get the lead, which was uncomfortable for him. The Zero had already put seven 20 mm and 37 0.7 mm rounds into me, and another split second and it would have been curtains. The aircraft was on fire and the cockpit was full of smoke. I said out loud, "Please God, not here", knowing that I would have certainly been captured by the Japanese if I had gone down in that area. As I was preparing to bail out, I pulled back the canopy whilst travelling at 300-400 kts and there was a great rush of air. The smoke cleared and the fire blew out, so I pulled up under a B-24 for protection and flew back to the emergency strip at Segi, New Georgia. The Corsair was badly shot up, but I managed to blow the gear down and land. I wasn't able to control it though, and the aircraft piled into the line, taking another F4U-1 with it.'

1st Lt Howard Finn also made ace with VMF-124 at this time;

'The first aircraft I shot down was a *Betty* bomber on 10 June 1943. It was a fluke, with me being in the right place at the right time. One of our troopships had been torpedoed during the night and she could only make two or three knots. The coastwatcher informed us that they had

F4U-1 Corsair 'No 4' *My Bonnie* of VMF-124 throws up a spray of water from Munda's runway in August 1943 following a tropical storm. Although neither Finn nor Walsh can recall any of their unit's aircraft being adorned with names, VMF-124 did utilise some of VMF-213's F4Us, and vice versa. As such, this may have been a former VMF-213 aircraft. This machine again has two false gun ports on each wing (*National Archives via Pete Mersky*)

seen three bombers on the ocean side of Choiseul, and we were directed to go out 100 miles, orbit and wait for them. We were completing the first orbit when I saw three specks in the distance. I rocked my wings to get Capt Earl Crowe's (7 kills) attention, and I pointed and he saw them too. I got one and the other members of my flight the other two. It was a satisfying sortie as we had stopped the enemy attacking the ship, which was quickly towed into Tulagi harbour to offload its precious cargo.

'My second kill was almost embarrassing – you feel bad about doing something this way. There was a big Japanese raid on Guadalcanal on 16 June, and nearly everybody launched to try and intercept the raid. We were nearing the end of our CAP when Earl Crowe, Tom Mutz and I were ordered to orbit the Tulagi Harbour area. Crowe spotted enemy aircraft and radioed "Bogies low on the water". The reply from our director was "Go get them", so we dived down to the water and took after a couple of Zeros. I slid in behind one and shot him down, then moved over to a *Val* whose rear gunner was shooting at me – I downed him too. The dive-bomber was very slow, being a fixed-gear type, so I just sat behind it with my far superior weapons and fired at will – they didn't stand a chance. In training we were taught they were "little Oriental bastards" and that kind of stuff, but I still had respect for them as pilots.

VMF-124's 'D Flight' ('No 5 Flight') consisted of 1st Lt Howard J Finn (6 kills) standing at left, 1st Lt Mervin L Taylor (1.5 victories), flight leader Capt William E Crowe (7 kills) and 1st Lt Tom R Mutz, who claimed three victories. Finn was on the 14 February mission when the unit first saw combat. He chased a lone Zero and was immediately jumped by more enemy fighters. For protection he positioned himself below one of the B-24s he was supposed to be protecting – 'Some big hero!', as he said recently when interviewed for this volume (*Finn collection*)

'When we first got there the Japanese had some good quality pilots. They could handle those Zeros, pulling really tight turns. Even a *Val* tried to pull a turn on me once, but he was too low and I shot him down as I could turn inside him. The ones we encountered in February 1943 were highly skilled, but their attrition was taking its toll and the skill of the pilots became considerably less as time went on. You could tell by the type of manoeuvres they would make. They would loop and roll when we first arrived, they were so confident. They were good pilots and they knew it. By the time I left in October, however, the quality had deteriorated. I would guess they had lost many good pilots, and that was to be the trend for the rest of the war.'

MORE F4Us ARRIVE

Marine fighter units converted to the F4U as aeroplanes became available. New squadrons arrived from the US, whilst the veteran F4F units took charge of their aircraft in-theatre. Following VMF-124 came -213, -121, -112, -221, -122 and -214. Finally, with the conversion of VMF-123 in early July, all the Solomons-based units were now equipped with the Corsair. During countless air battles all these units would amass scores against the Japanese, producing many aces in the process. VMF-213, commanded by Maj Britt, had arrived at Espiritu Santo on 2 March equipped with Wildcats. They were soon to re-equip with the F4U, however, before entering combat. Capt James N Cupp was to become the unit's third highest-scoring ace with 12.5 kills during his three tours in the Solomons. Here, he describes some of his experiences.

'Being given the chance to fly Chance Vought's new aeroplane was one thing, whilst actually physically doing so was quite another. There was only one squadron of Corsairs already on Guadalcanal, and there were absolutely no spare parts nearer than the United States. Therefore, the three planes we were given to check out in were quickly grounded as they all badly needed replacement parts. We had come down south armed to the teeth with spare parts for our Grumman F4Fs, but even before we had time to unload them they were no longer of any use to us – the Corsair even used a different starter cartridge. Lts Hartsock and Kuhn from VMF-124 came down from Guadalcanal to give us all the information they could about flying the Corsair in combat, and with their encouragement, added to the midnight oil burned studying handbooks, we soon thought ourselves competent to sit behind the controls of the beast.

'When we were all successfully checked our base CO sent the squadron to New Caledonia to collect a shipment of new Corsairs. We found them aboard the small carrier that had brought them from the US, but not one of them had been made ready to fly after the trip. When we finally got the planes to Tontouta Field in New Caledonia, our troubles really started. We were hampered by the fact that none of the mechanics knew about the new plane. After a week we gave up and started for home, with only six of the 28 planes we had taken from the carrier. Within two hours after we got off the transport at Espiritu, we were back on it again headed for Guadalcanal to relieve VMF-124. Our six new planes had to be left behind and so did our men, who were really sorry to see us go off without them. They were as anxious as we were to get into combat.

'We landed on Guadalcanal 1 April and were to operate from "Fighter Strip No 1", which was to one side of Henderson Field. When we relieved VMF-124 we took over

F4U-1 of VMF-213 catapults from USS *Copahee* on 29 March 1943. Capt James Cupp relates this novel experience in the following quote: 'When we got to New Caledonia we found our Corsairs aboard the small carrier that had brought them from the US – not one of them had been made ready to fly after the trip. Moreover, we had to be catapulted, this being a rather experimental process as we had no information as to the performance of the plane under such conditions. They had no head rests (as most Navy planes do), so the first day was spent getting the ship's carpenter to make us a wooden head rest for each plane. All of us except one made it off – a lone Corsair suffered engine failure and plunged off the bow of the ship' (*National Archives*)

their aeroplanes, and although they were now old, their men were well acquainted with them and could keep them in a dependable condition for us. We had 14 of these veteran F4U-1s to use, and if we got eight of them off the ground at once, we were extremely lucky.

Capt Cupp standing on the wing of F4U-1 'No 7' ***DAPHNE C***, BuNo 02350. He claimed his first two victories in this aircraft (a ***Betty*** and a Zero) on 15 July 1943. Although three whole kills are visible, his next claims amounted to 2.5 Zeros on the 17th whilst flying BuNo 02580. The remnants of a 'No 13' are located beneath the canopy, this having been one of Ken Walsh's aircraft during his first tour (***Cupp Collection***)

'Our first job was to learn the geography of the Solomons off by heart, a process that involved becoming familiar with each island in the group individually. This was necessary in order to evade Japanese concentrations in case of a forced landing, and to know which way to go to avoid possible patrols once we were on the ground. At that time, all of the islands to the north and west of us were dominated by the Japanese. There were, however, only a few troops to each island, and these were usually dug in along the coast. "The Slot" is the strip of open water stretching between the islands of the Solomons group from Guadalcanal to Bougainville. It is approximately 350 miles long and about 70 miles wide. Along the southern edge of "The Slot" lies Guadalcanal, with Henderson Field, together with its adjoining protective fighter strips. Next were the Russell Islands, a small group 70 miles from Henderson where additional strips were built.; then the New Georgia group (home of Munda airstrip), including Rendova Island. Kolombangara, with Vella Bomber Field., was next in line, followed by Vella Lavella, the Shortlands and then Bougainville. On the northern side of "The Slot" is Tulagi Harbour in the Florida Group; San Cristobal with Rakata Bay, and Choiseul (which extends almost to Bougainville) which only had ground troops on it. Bougainville's point of interest was the main Jap airstrip of Kahili, whilst the bay just off the strip was the loading point for shipping headed down "The Slot". Balale was a small island in that bay, and boasted a busy little fighter strip.

'The tactics that Maj Britt had been drilling into us for months were essentially the same as for other fighter squadrons. Each unit, however, had its own particular way of interpreting those tactics. This difference was usually in the air discipline, and the control the leaders had over the men flying with them. VMF-213 had trained as one unit longer than other squadrons operating in the Solomons, and because of this we enjoyed the reputable distinction of sticking together in combat. The fact that we all got along so well added a great deal to our value as a squadron. Two pilots flying together must know each other by heart, and know what to expect of the other fellow in any given situation. The wingman, flying blind on his leader, must trust him implicitly when they fly a tight formation or

This rare aerial view of an F4U-1 on a combat mission in April or May 1943 was taken by USAAF B-24 gunner Bob Lundy of the 424th Bomb Squadron, 307th Bomb Group. The aircraft has a white 'No 13' and two kill marks, together with a three-word name on the cowling. Although not known for certain, this could be a picture of an aircraft flown by Cupp or Walsh (***Cupp Collection***)

Jim Cupp, wearing his standard Solomons outfit, stands on the propeller hub of F4U-1 'No 7' *DAPHNE C* – the aircraft was named for his wife Daphne Cupp. The remnants of a 'No 13' can again be seen, this time located on the centre forward area of the cowling. This aircraft later wore four kill marks following his victories on 17 July, even though these were scored in F4U-1 BuNo 02580 (*Cupp Collection*)

when they are coming home at night through stormy weather. The leader is the only one flying on instruments, the only one that knows just where the next mountain is and just when the field will pop into view. The wingman must trust his leader more than he trusts himself. If he waivers in his decision to follow his leader into what seems to him to be a hopeless situation and goes off on his own, he will be lost sooner or later. At the very least he would be of no use to the squadron as a whole. By the same token, the leader must know what he is doing at all times, without exception.

'Our squadron of 30 men was divided into three flights of eight pilots, with the extra pilots being split over each flight. The flights were broken down into two divisions of four planes. Due to the nature of our assignments, and the scarcity of planes, usually only a division was designated for a complete mission. Once in a while, however the whole flight would go together. Later, when more planes were available and missions were more involved, three divisions were usually the order of the day, although we never sent up more than 16 Corsairs – when we had that many planes, we didn't have enough pilots! The division was flown in a stepped down formation. The leader's wingman was below, back and to his right. The second section of two planes were farther back, down and to the leader's left. Directions were passed by visual signals. When a flight was involved in a mission, the two divisions would stay in the same sky and if any direction had to be given, they were transmitted over the radio.

'Air discipline was most important during bomber escorts. There were many assignments to be had while covering a bomber formation, both above and below. The closer your assigned position was to the formation, the more immovable you became. Often fighters were assigned as forward guns for the bombers, and were stationed in close above and below the formation. While there, your job was to fire only on attacking planes approaching the formation head on. The others were to be left strictly alone. Neither could you follow an enemy plane after an attack to finish him off or see if he would burn or crash – your job was to stay put. With a plane as capable as ours, it was almost an impossible task. The divisions covering the formation 1000 to 2000 ft above us were not much better off either. They could attack incoming planes from any direction, but couldn't press home their advantage after the attackers had pulled off. If a pilot should succumb to ambition and pull away from his colleagues to go after one of the enemy, he would most likely find himself in amongst a

Jim Cupp sitting on the nose of F4U-1 'No 15' *DAPHNE C*, BuNo 03829, in which he gained his fifth and sixth victories on 11 September (a *Tony* and a Zero). The next day he strafed Kahili in this Corsair, destroying ten aircraft on the ground, plus two barges. Cupp was credited with 12 aerial victories before being shot down whilst attempting to claim his 13th victim whilst flying F4U-1 BuNo 03803 (*Cupp Collection*)

1st Lt Foy R 'Poncho' Garison on the wing of F4U-1 'No 20'. He shot down two Zeros on 30 June 1943. 'On 17 July Gregg Weissenberger's division started back from a raid on Kahili. "Poncho" was flying the No 4 position. A formation of Zeros started tagging along out of range, but he could not resist the temptation. He peeled off and attacked them. Before anyone in the division knew he was gone, he was on his back in flames.' This was how Jim Cupp described 'Poncho's' demise (*Cupp Collection*)

swarm of them in a very short time.

'The plane I was assigned was a smooth running job. With constant care on the part of my mechanics, it was ready for almost every assigned mission. It only had one drawback – the engine had never been overhauled, and by then I had some 300 hours on it. Usually a Navy plane is taken to the "cleaners" every 60 hours, but this one had been in constant service since its combat debut. So it was that at sustained slow speeds the carburettor would invariably flood out and stop the engine. Each morning during the period in question we were assigned missions to Munda escorting slow flying Dauntless dive-bombers. We never ran into any aerial opposition on these excursions, but the thing that wore me down was that temperamental plane of mine. The speed of the bombers was 120 kts and we were throttled back as far as we could to stay with them. It took just about two hours for my carburettor to flood out, and it took two hours to get right on top of the enemy airfield. Every morning at exactly the same spot, for two straight weeks my engine quit cold. A few thousand feet and a few minutes would elapse before I could get it cleared out, started, and warmed up enough to get back home. Ted (my wingman) would stay with me all the time and knew what was going on. As for the others, they always contended that I was tired of flying formation and wanted a little better view of the damage the bombs were doing.

'On 25 April Maj Peyton took his division to Munda to do a little strafing and stir things up in general. On the way home, he found himself some 10,000 ft below a sizeable force of enemy fighters and bombers. He nosed over to one side and started to climb up at them. Unfortunately they saw our four planes before they had sufficient height and started to attack. The second section had dropped behind in the attempt to gain altitude, and received the brunt of the first assault. Lt Eckart went down first, never to be heard of again, whilst Lt Peck managed to knock down one of the aggressors before receiving a burst in his engine that sent him limping home. Major Peyton and Lt Vedder (6 kills) continued weaving defensively trying to gain altitude until the latter was hit and had to set down – he returned days later with only a small shrapnel hole in his thigh. Maj Peyton came home with 82 holes in his F4U and a scratch on his wrist. They got seven of the Zeros and the bombers turned back.

'On 11 May we greeted VMF-124 as they came in to relieve us, and we had a party that night in celebration. From somewhere the mess officer drew out some steaks for the few of us left by 12 o'clock. Afterwards, every last one of us was sick – we had been living too long on *Spam*, crackers and K-rations for so long we just couldn't take "real" food any more.'

Following six weeks of R&R in Sydney, Australia, VMF-213 returned to Guadalcanal for their second tour. Capt Cupp continues:

'We knew that the campaign for Rendova and Munda was to start soon

F4U-1 'No 11' *Defabe*, seen at Guadalcanal, was flown by 1st Lt George C 'Yogi' Defabio. He claimed a Zero on 30 June and two more on 11 and 17 July 1943. 'We operated from Munda and Guadalcanal, shuttling back and forth between the two bases in ten- to fourteen-day stretches. As Munda had been our object of destruction for so long, it seemed strange to call it "home". Defabio had almost ended his days there a few weeks before. During a strafing mission an AA burst clipped 46 inches off his wing. He was practically out of the plane before he realised it would still fly if he kept up enough speed – somehow he was able to make it back to the "Canal"' – Jim Cupp (*Cupp Collection*)

and our prime ambition was to get in on it. In the meantime, our mechanics had replaced the men of VMF-124 and so, when we relieved their pilots, we were a complete outfit once more. We spent the first two weeks getting all the planes into shape for the gruelling action ahead. More F4U-1s had been added to our flight logs since we left and only a few of the old ones remained. To add to this total, factory-fresh Corsairs were being ferried up from New Caledonia, and before long each one of us had his own individual plane and mechanic. One of our enlisted men, Don Buhrmann, gave our aircraft the individual names and designs that we had so long dreamed about. Gus had a gopher painted on his fuselage, Poncho had a fierce looking eagle and Treffer, having a plane that was always out with some mechanical difficulty, had a reluctant dragon painted on his machine.

'The daily "milk-run" to Munda had completely neutralised the airstrip there and also at Kolombangara, ten miles across the channel. Thus, when the Marines landed at Rendova the opposing airpower had to come down from Kahili. The American plan was to set up a force on Rendova and later cross over to Munda. Our job was to keep a constant patrol over the area to repel anything the Japs sent down. Difficulties arose from the distances involved. Operating from the "Canal", we were 200 miles from our patrol station. It was no easy trick to shuttle back and forth on the hour-and-a-half trip and still keep fresh planes on station at all times. Each patrol would take over four hours from take-off till landing and, as we were short handed in our unit, most of us flew three patrols a day.

'Although constantly in the air, I was never able to contact enemy planes. Action always took place just while we were landing or taking off, or else we were kept out because of the screen of cumulus clouds that always hung over the islands. Soon we were the only division who had not made contact and this gave concern to Maj Gregory Weissenberger (5 kills). He wanted every pilot in the squadron to have his share of victories, but without any individual playing the hero and getting more than everybody else. After the training we had, it was mostly a proposition of being in the right place at the right time to get your bag of planes. The pilot with the high score might look good in the papers back home, but his score was likely to cause dissension among his fellow pilots, and it would become difficult to practice the teamwork necessary for an effective fighting unit.

'Our torpedo planes and dive-bomber crews have never been properly credited for the role they played. In every encounter they would go straight into the target and let the enemy try and knock them down with anti-aircraft fire. When it came to an aerial attack their slow and clumsy planes didn't stand a chance against enemy fighters. On 17 July we escorted a group of these boys to Kahili to get some troopships that were attempting to reinforce the depleted garrison at Munda. There were only three in my division that day – Ted, Sgt. Hodde and myself. This made mutual protection more difficult than with a full division of four planes.

Another 'wet strip' shot taken at Munda on 26 August 1943. 'When operating from Munda the Japanese made a determined effort to see that our forces got no farther. By then the might of Kahili was pretty well exhausted, but new enemy airfields had sprung up all over Bougainville, with reinforcements coming down from Rabaul. As Munda was subjected to shuttle bombing each night (thus, living conditions were not too good), it was thought that 14 days was a long enough dose for a fighter pilot who had to fly all day' – Jim Cupp (*National Archives via Pete Mersky*)

'A Corsair below us soon got into trouble with a Zero astern. We steepened our dive and came up behind him. Ted and I both opened up at the same time and he burst into flames. We veered away from the exploding plane and became separated. I started out to the rendezvous area just south of the Shortlands. I appeared to be the only fighter in the area so when I saw some TBFs and SBDs being molested by Zeros I turned back to fight. Three of the enemy planes, seeing a lone Corsair, decided to take care of me. It was dog-eat-dog and I was the bait. I soon found, however, that as one would get on my tail within firing range, I could roll fast to the right and come out in a "split S" manoeuvre. Invariably the Zero would pull up and stall instead of following me. It happened time after time and, if I was fast enough coming around, I could pull up behind him while he was stalled and give him a burst before the next guy got on my tail. Knowing my F4U was faster, they probably thought I was diving for home, and that it was useless to try to catch me. They never did catch on and soon there were eight Japs playing "ring around a rosy" with me. I soon thought better of tackling them single-handed and high tailed it home.

'The rest of the boys had left long ago, but I soon ran into some bombers that had been hit and were limping home. When I caught up with them they were playing cat and mouse with two Zeros that had chased them out of Kahili, going in and out of the clouds trying to avoid their assailants. One of the Zeros had just finished a pass from the rear as a bomber entered a small cloud. He pulled straight up the side of the

1st Lt Wilbur J 'Gus' Thomas standing by his F4U-1 'No 10', *GUS'S GOPHER*. He became VMF-213's leading ace with 18.5 kills. His first four kills and a probable were claimed on one mission on 30 June 1943. Thomas was a well-liked and respected pilot who was unfortunately killed in a flying accident on 28 January 1947 (*Cupp Collection*)

Groundcrew posing on ***GUS'S GOPHER*** **showing the** ***Disney*** **character nose art on the port side. Eight kills are displayed beneath the canopy, although he had reached only seven victories and one probable by 15 July – he then shot down a further three Zeros on 11 September. Thomas claimed 16.5 victories with VMF-213 in the Solomons, and was then further credited with two more Zeros on 16 February 1945 whilst the unit was aboard USS** ***Essex*** **(*****Cupp Collection*****)**

cloud to avoid over-running the bomber inside and it was a simple matter for me to catch him as he topped the cumulus – he went back down the other side in flames. His partner had nestled under the cloud to catch the bomber as it came out, and when he saw his friend fall, he turned around and went back to Kahili. I stayed with the bombers until they were back in friendly territory, and then headed home.

'After each flight, we reported to Lt Harrison, the intelligence officer attached to us, and gave him the particulars of the flight. He assembled all the combined information, but it was often difficult to get the right story from a bunch of excited pilots as our reports usually seemed like a mass of unconnected events. For example, the following action details an average mission.

'30 June 1943 – My division, Lts Brown, Votaw, Spoede and myself scrambled at 1115, and were ordered to Rendova to intercept a flight of about 30 Jap planes. We climbed to 25,000, from 1215 to 1300 but saw no enemy planes. Rendova was pretty well closed in, but we could observe the landing operations progressing without interruption. We landed at Guadalcanal early that afternoon and stood by our planes and waited. At 1350 word was received that VMF-221 and VF-11 had made contact with the enemy. At 1545 my four planes, along with Lt Sheldon Hall's division, comprising the latter (6 kills), Shaw (14.5 kills), Morgan (8.5 kills) and Jones, were scrambled and told to cover the shipping off Rendova. Hall's division was about three minutes behind mine on the take-off. The radar wasn't working well so we were told to keep our eyes open. We climbed to 15,000 ft, reporting on station at 1645. A stranger was reported at 8000 ft, coming in on the shipping. We dived to attack, but could find no enemy planes. It was cloudy and all the action that we could hear on the radio was taking place behind some clouds, so we never got a glimpse of it. At this time Rendova reported nine floatplanes to the west, but we were again unable to make contact. After searching the sky for half an hour, we continued the patrol until we returned to base at 1915.

'Maj Weissenberger, Capt Cloake and Lts Thomas (18.5 kills), Drake, Defabio, Garison, McCleary and Boag were kept on scramble alert, while we were on our first flight. They took off just as we landed and were ordered to proceed to Rendova. The Major's flight was airborne at 1400 and they arrived over Rendova at 26,000 ft at 1445. Lt "Yogi" Defabio was late. He took off at 1405 and proceeded in the hope of joining up on the Major, but was never able to locate him. However, after circling the area over Rendova, he heard over the R/T a "Tally-Ho" call signalling that the fight was on. Defabio dropped to 8000 ft, where he saw two Zeros and made a run on the leader from the Zero's left and above. He fired, causing him to smoke, burst into flames and dive into the water below. He saw many other Zeros and attempted to attack them, but could find none that were not already engaged by friendly planes. When the fight was over he was joined by Lt Garison, and they returned to base.

'Maj Weissenberger and Lts Thomas and Garison attacked a group of about 15 to 20 Zeros that they had sighted below. The Major shot down three Zeros before being shot down himself. After shooting down his first two Zeros, he met his third coming at him head on. Both fired point blank. The Zero burst into flames and exploded, while the Major's plane began to smoke and caught fire. He was able to bail out at about 800 ft, and his parachute opened just before he hit the water. Luckily, he landed near a US destroyer that picked him up and returned him to Guadalcanal. He received only minor injuries consisting primarily of painfully bruised ribs, the result of hitting the tail of the plane when he bailed out.

Maj Gregory J Weissenberger straps into his F4U-1 Corsair 'No 9', BuNo 02288. He took command of the unit following the death of Maj Wade H Britt, Jr, who was killed when his aircraft ran off the runway, hit another two Corsairs and exploded during an early morning take-off (*USMC*)

'Our workload was by now comparatively light. We only flew two patrols a day, instead of the usual three. As we were so low on pilots, other squadrons were borrowing our excess planes, thus helping us to get out of more work. The invasion of Munda was now a certainty. The Japs were coming down the slot with increasing regularity. We lost two more planes before our tour was up. It happened when we were heading off a bunch of Jap dive-bombers. We came upon them late and had to go under their formation to get at the ones that had already peeled off. Their attack was stymied, but we left ourselves open to the rear. One of Ted's adversaries took full advantage of the situation and filled his fuselage full of lead. By 26 July, Doc Livinggood had grounded us all because of fatigue.'

After another trip to Sydney the unit received new personnel in preparation for their next tour. Maj Weissenberger was replaced at this junction with a new CO, Maj J R Anderson. Capt Cupp continues the story:

'When operating from Munda our beautifully marked planes were put into a pool and assigned to different pilots from different squadrons every morning. That alone was enough to break our hearts, but when the SEEBEEs (who had been pressed into service as mechanics) asked us where to inject the gas and oil we were almost tempted to draw our pay and go home. There were a few bona-fide mechanics on the strip, but they had always worked on Grummans so our sleek little planes went without much maintenance. They rapidly became dirty and undependable. They always kept going, but little things were always cropping up to

A fine view of Maj Weissenberger's aircraft as the engine roars to life, with the crewchief standing by with a fire extinguisher in case of an emergency. The tape on the gun ports was used to keep dirt from entering the barrels during taxying and take-off. The cowl flaps were always employed on the ground to prevent the engine overheating (*USMC*)

annoy you. Some would conk out when you changed blowers. Some would run rough all the time; keeping you in suspense as to whether or not it would get you back.

'The Marines were getting ready for another objective in their stepping stone campaign up the Solomons. This time it was to be Bougainville itself and it was up to the air arm to soften up Kahili and Ballale in the same way we had with Munda. To increase our airpower, the SEEBEEs were building another fighter strip at Vella Lavella (about 40 miles up the chain). The Jap bomber strip at Kolombangara (about ten miles across the bay from Munda) was no longer in use. AA batteries would still fire on us though if we got too close. There were one or two floatplanes up one of the streams close to that strip, but they could never be located in daytime. At night they would harass the troops behind us and once in a while, aid in keeping us awake by dropping a stick of bombs on Munda. It only added to the nuisance of the shuttle-bombers ("washing-machine Charlie") which operated all night long.

Maj Weissenberger takes off from Guadalcanal's 'Fighter One' strip in June 1943. He became an ace on 18 July 1943 by shooting down a Zero – his fifth and final victory. The Major celebrated his new ace status with a 'birthday cake' later that afternoon (*USMC*)

F4U-1 Corsair 'No 5' of VMF-213 has its guns boresighted using an apparatus constructed out of coconut logs. Boresighting was a frequent topic of conversation among Corsair pilots, as the procedure needed to be carried out regularly because the guns moved slightly in their mounts each time they were fired. The distance at which the .50s were boresighted varied from unit to unit, the usual distance being around 900 feet (*USMC*)

'Walley was on my wing now, with Avery and Stewart flying the second section. They hadn't seen any aerial combat yet and were anxious for the inactivity to stop. We were on our way to patrol over Vella Lavella on 17 September when the news came in that a large formation of bogies was headed our way – their initiation was about to occur.

'The sky was dotted with white clouds that stretched up to 18,000 ft. We started to climb towards the southern tip of the island dodging the clouds all the way. We nosed through a hole and saw a massive formation of dive-bombers ploughing in about five miles away from us and at the same height. At that instant I looked up and saw a string of eight Zeros zigzagging across the sky, less than 100 ft above my head. We turned over on our backs and headed for cover, whilst we radioed the Jap position and course. The Zeros saw fit not to accompany us, so after a few thousand feet we hauled up to try it again. The second section lost a little ground in the manoeuvre. We headed along a parallel course to the bombers, looking for another hole in the overcast to poke through. By that time there was quite some distance between our two sections. It was not long before we saw an opening and headed through it. This time the Zeros were looking straight down their guns at us as we repeated the operation, and this time they

F4U-1 'No 8' *Eight Ball/Dangerous Dan.* Although this aircraft was later pictured with one kill marking under the canopy on the port side, it is uncertain as to exactly which pilot gained the victory in this machine (*USMC*)

attacked. The mistake they made, however, was to get in between our two sections. As we all headed for a lower altitude, Avery and Stewart were behind them merrily blasting away. They soon reduced the odds to "even Steven" and the remaining Zeros left my tail.

'In the meantime, the bombers were approaching their target. By the time we again regained our altitude, we found most of them already in their dives and there were only a few left at our height. They were old and slow planes and it was difficult to stay behind them long enough to get in a good burst before we passed over them. We came up from behind, cut our engines and just sat there. We could almost reach out and touch them as our six guns opened up. The one I was on looked like a toy suddenly thrown to the floor. Pieces started flying off and suddenly there was nothing there. In the distance, I saw one already in his dive and for some reason, I determined to get him if I never did anything else. At first, all that was possible was to follow him down and avoid the AA as much as possible. I was glad to notice that Stewart was with me. We levelled off just above the water and I moved over to him. I had been so focused on the one plane that I was surprised to discover another bomber flying alongside of him, and then another and then another. I looked up and discovered the whole area covered with them. We had followed my prey to the rendezvous point where all the planes assembled in formation for their return to Kahili. Their only defence was a light calibre machine gun handled by the gunner in the rear cockpit.

'I pulled back the throttle to keep from over-running them. It was almost pathetic to witness their futile efforts to evade destruction. They were already less than ten feet off the water; and all they could do was skid from side to side. I came across one with a very strong desire to live. He threw his plane around with all his might and it was hard to keep my bullets going into him. First the gunner slumped over and next the engine started to blaze. In an instant, the whole thing was one flaming torch skidding over the water. I pulled up and crossed over the top of Stewart and came down again. The plane ahead of me jerked around violently and I closed without firing. The nearer I got, the more violent were his evasive manoeuvres, until finally one wing hit the water and he crashed. Without having fired a shot, I pulled up crossed back over Stewart and continued up the line. I was disheartened to find that their gas tanks were bullet proofed, but we did well in spite of it. Everytime I looked back over our course I saw a plane hit the water. I was able to count three of Stewart's, though it was difficult to keep track of him. Four of mine hit the water, but it was impossible to watch the effect on most of them.

'We were nearing the head of the column, just finishing off one

together, when my little world began to fall apart. A 20 mm shell came through the tail and exploded the CO_2 bottle behind my seat. The noise scared me out of my wits. Another came over my head and hit the accessory section just behind the engine and a third knocked a hole in my left wing, carrying my flap away. There were four Zeros above and behind me getting ready to take turns at me. Stewart had pulled ahead and didn't respond to my radio call – undaunted, I pressed the send button, hurriedly giving my position, adding the earnest cry "Help!" I was sure I couldn't stay in the air long. I would have set the plane down right there, but I was sure my opponents wouldn't have been content just to see my plane go in. The alternative was to shove the throttle forward and pray – I did both. My beautiful, faithful, greyhound of a plane responded like a bat out of hell. They must have been surprised, for they just sat there and watched me go. I was away in no time. When I left, they turned their attention to Stewart. He was also able to outrun them, but not before his plane became hard to handle from all the extra lead he was carrying. He climbed for altitude and bailed out. He came home the next day after an eight-hour ride in a native war canoe.

F4U-1 'No 4' of VMF-213 undergoes maintenance in the open at Guadalcanal in June 1943. The tape on the gun ports appears to indicate that this aircraft was equipped with ten wing guns! Even though VMF-124's ground echelon was replaced by that of VMF-213 in early June, the practice of indicating false gun ports was continued by both units (*USMC*)

'My division was not assigned a flight on the 19th so we volunteered for the dawn patrol the next day. "Charlie" came over on the hour all that night and, as we took off at 0500, I could see his silhouette 10,000 ft. above. Making a quick join up, we started after him. The boys came in close in order to see my wings in the darkness. I kept my eyes glued to the hazy blur in the distance that was the Jap *Betty*. We knew we had a long chase ahead of us; he was speeding away and we would have a long climb to get up to him. We were almost over the mountain of Kolombangara before it became apparent that we were gaining on him.

'The plane I had grabbed checked out fine on the ground, but as we got over the water the fuel pressure gauge started wavering – the normal pressure was 15 lbs per square inch., but the needle was at eight and still going down. I checked over the gas supply and turned on the electric fuel pump, but to no avail. I called the division and told them I might have to turn back. I asked them if they were able to locate the bomber. They spread out a little in order to divert their attention to the sky ahead, but couldn't see the enemy aircraft. I couldn't disappoint them while there was still a chance as we were on the same level as "Charlie" now, and about a 1000 ft behind. Our aim was to get above and ahead of him before starting our attack, but as my needle was still going down, I wobbled my wings and started in from where we were. I wanted to pass the 13 mark on my score!

'I dived underneath him, thinking that I could make one pass on his unprotected belly and then return to base. The boys would pick him up as I passed him. My intention was to attack straight up and miss the cannon in his tail that could only fire down at an angle of 45°. The impression still remains in my mind that, as I came up, the bomb bay opened and a gun started firing down from that unorthodox position. I was hit three times before I could wink an eye. All three hits seemed to centre around the bottom of my cockpit. When I looked down, there was a small flicker of flame starting to take hold. All the experience of months of combat seemed to surge up inside me, and before I could think I had my radio disconnected, the safety belt and shoulder straps unfastened and the hood of my canopy thrown back. It was when I stood up in the seat and attempted to climb over the side that thought returned. My plane was pushing through the air at more than 300 kts and the stream over my cockpit was like a steel wall holding me in. I could not get out!

'The air whipping into the cockpit had fanned the spark into a blowtorch that swept up my legs as I sat back in the seat. The throttle arms next to my left leg were still on full, but I could not make that hand move to pull it back. I brought my left arm over to my right and hooked onto it. I watched as my right arm was dragged through the flames and deposited on the throttled which I slammed closed. I tried to get out again, but again was forced back. One thought mounted until it excluded all others – "How simple it would be just to ride her in." At that time the pain stopped in my legs and the mental turmoil subsided. Complete satisfaction and contentment engulfed me. It seems the feeling was with me for hours to account for the vivid picture it left me, but I know it was actually over in a split-second. I had been straining for freedom with my legs braced against the rudder bars and then the tail was coming at me. I raised my legs to clear the elevators and then I was on my own – the plane was gone.

'I remembered my parachute and wondered if it was still on me. I found that it was and pulled the ripcord. I didn't feel it open, but I noticed the risers braced against my back attached to something solid above. Almost at once I saw the plane crash into the water below. The sock on my left leg was still smouldering and I began to feel it. Reaching down I snuffed it out with my good hand. The rest of my clothes had not caught fire – I suppose they didn't have time. My legs were covered with a white ash that used to be skin, but they didn't hurt much at that moment. My face and right arm had not been burned so badly and the surface nerves were still working. My hair was all gone and pieces of skin hung around my lips. I hurt like the devil!'

Capt Cupp's squadron-mates managed to down his intended victim while he was picked up around 1430. Badly burned, Cupp was hospitalised for 18 months, undergoing 14 operations. His final combat tally was 12 1/2 officially credited kills.

Armourers adjust the three port-side wing guns of F4U-1 *Bubbles* to facilitate boresighting at Guadalcanal. This appears to be a VMF-213 aircraft, but again may well have also been used by VMF-124 too (*USMC*)

COLOUR PLATES

This 18-page section profiles many of the aircraft flown by the elite pilots of the US Navy, US Marine Corps and the Fleet Air Arm. Also included are notable machines that are representative of the Corsair's all-important, but often ignored, ground attack mission. All the artworks have been specially commissioned for this volume, and profile artists John Weal and Mark Styling, plus figure artist Mike Chappell, have gone to great pains to illustrate the aircraft, and their pilots, as accurately as possible following much in-depth research. Aces' machines that have never previously been illustrated are featured alongside acccurate renditions of the more famous Corsairs from World War 2.

1
F4U-1 black 17 of 1st Lt Howard J Finn, VMF-124, Guadalcanal, February 1943

2
F4U-1 white 13/BuNo 02350 of 2nd Lt Kenneth A Walsh, VMF-124, Munda, August 1943

3
F4U-1 white 114 of 2nd Lt Kenneth A Walsh, VMF-124, Munda, August 1943

4
F4U-1 white 13 of 1st Lt Kenneth A Walsh, VMF-124, Russell Islands, September 1943

5
F4U-1 white 7 *DAPHNE C*/BuNo 02350 of Capt James N Cupp, VMF-213, Guadalcanal, July 1943

6
F4U-1 white 15 *DAPHNE C*/BuNo 03829 of Capt James N Cupp, VMF-213, Munda, September 1943

7
F4U-1 white 11 *Defabe* of 1st Lt George C Defabio, VMF-213, Guadalcanal, July 1943

8

F4U-1 white 10 *GUS'S GOPHER* of 1st Lt Wilbur J Thomas, VMF-213, Guadalcanal, July 1943

9

F4U-1 white 10 *GUS'S GOPHER* of 1st Lt Wilbur J Thomas, VMF-213, Guadalcanal, July 1943

10

F4U-1 white 20 of 1st Lt Foy R Garison, VMF-213, Guadalcanal, July 1943

11

F4U-1 white 125/BuNo 02487 of 2nd Lt Donald L Balch, VMF-221, Guadalcanal, July 1943

12

F4U-1 white 590/BuNo 17590 of Capt Arthur R Conant, VMF-215 Barakoma/Torokina, January 1944

13

F4U-1A white 735/BuNo 17735 of Capt Arthur R Conant, VMF-215 Barakoma/Torokina, January 1944

14

F4U-1 white 75 of Maj Robert G Owens, Jr, VMF-215, Munda, August 1943

15

F4U-1 white 76 *Spirit of '76*/BuNo 02714 of Maj Robert G Owens, Jr, VMF-215 Munda, August 1943

16
F4U-1A white 596/BuNo 17596 of 1st Lt Robert M Hanson, VMF-215, Torokina, February 1944

17
F4U-1A white 777/BuNo 17777 of 1st Lt Phillip C DeLong, VMF-212, Vella Lavella, November 1943

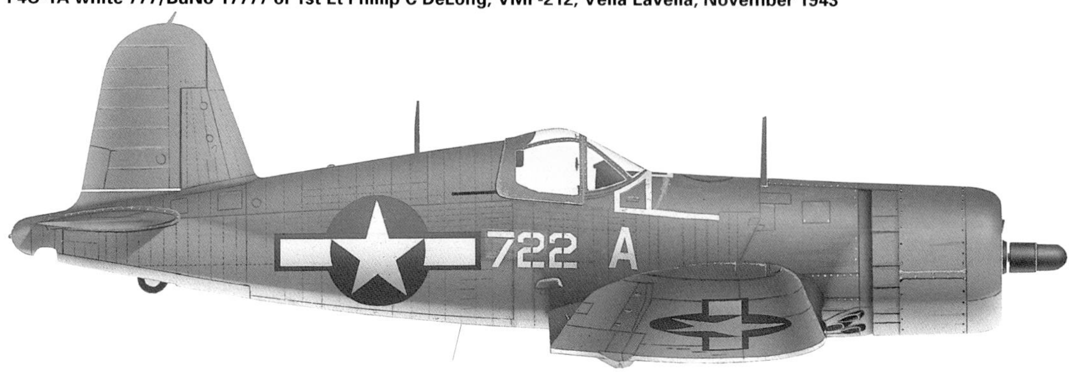

18
F4U-1A white 722A/BuNo 17722 of 1st Lt Phillip C DeLong, VMF–212, Vella Lavella, November 1943

19
F4U-1 white 576 *MARINE'S DREAM*/BuNo 02576 of 1st Lt Edwin L Olander, VMF-214, Munda, October 1943

20
F4U-1 white 93/BuNo 17430 of Capt Edwin L Olander, VMF-214, Vella Lavella/Torokina, January 1944

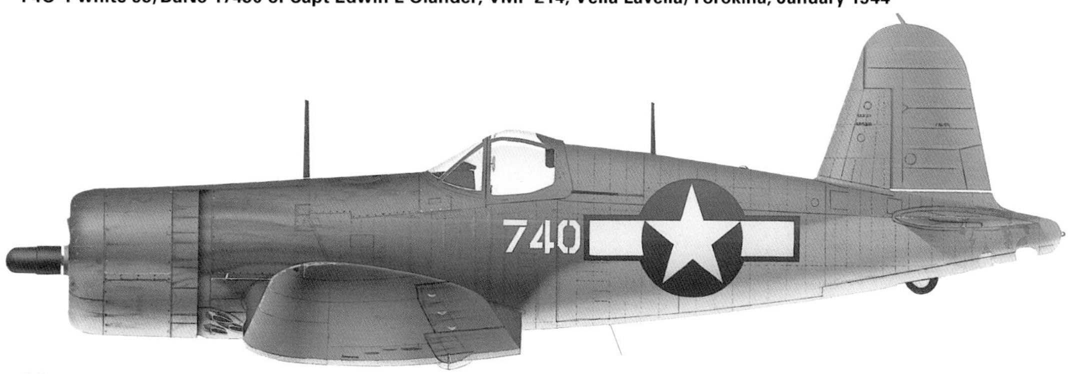

21
F4U-1A white 740/BuNo 17740 of Maj Gregory Boyington, CO of VMF-214, Vella Lavella, December 1943

22
F4U-1A white 883/BuNo 17883 of Maj Gregory Boyington, CO of VMF-214, Vella Lavella, December 1943

23
F4U-1A white 86 *Lulubelle*/BuNo 18086 of Maj Gregory Boyington, CO of VMF-214, Vella Lavella, December 1943

24
FG-1A white 271/BuNo 13271 of Maj Julius W Ireland, VMF-211, Bougainville, January 1944

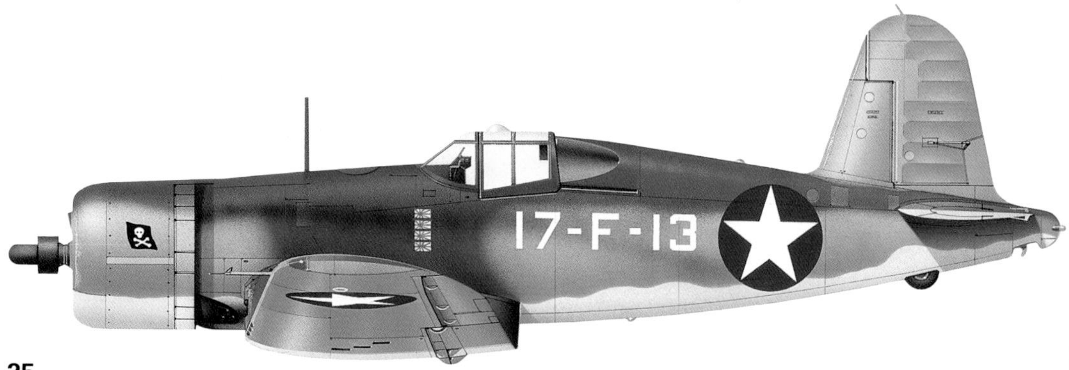

25
F4U-1 white 17-F-13 of Lt(jg) James A Halford, VF-17, USS *Bunker Hill*, August 1943

26
F4U-1A white 1 *BIG HOG*/BuNo 17649 of Lt Cdr John T Blackburn, CO VF-17, Ondonga, November 1943

27
F4U-1A white 19 of Lt Paul Cordray, VF-17, Ondonga, November 1943

28

F4U-1A white 15 of Lt(jg) Daniel G Cunningham, VF-17, Ondonga, February 1944

29

F4U-1A white 9 *LONESOME POLECAT* of Lt Merl W Davenport, VF-17, Ondonga, January 1944

30

F4U-1A white 34 *L.A. CITY LIMITS*/BuNo 17932 of Lt(jg) Doris C Freeman, VF-17, Ondonga, November 1943

31

F4U-1A white 29 of Lt(jg) Ira C Kepford, VF-17, Bougainville, January 1944

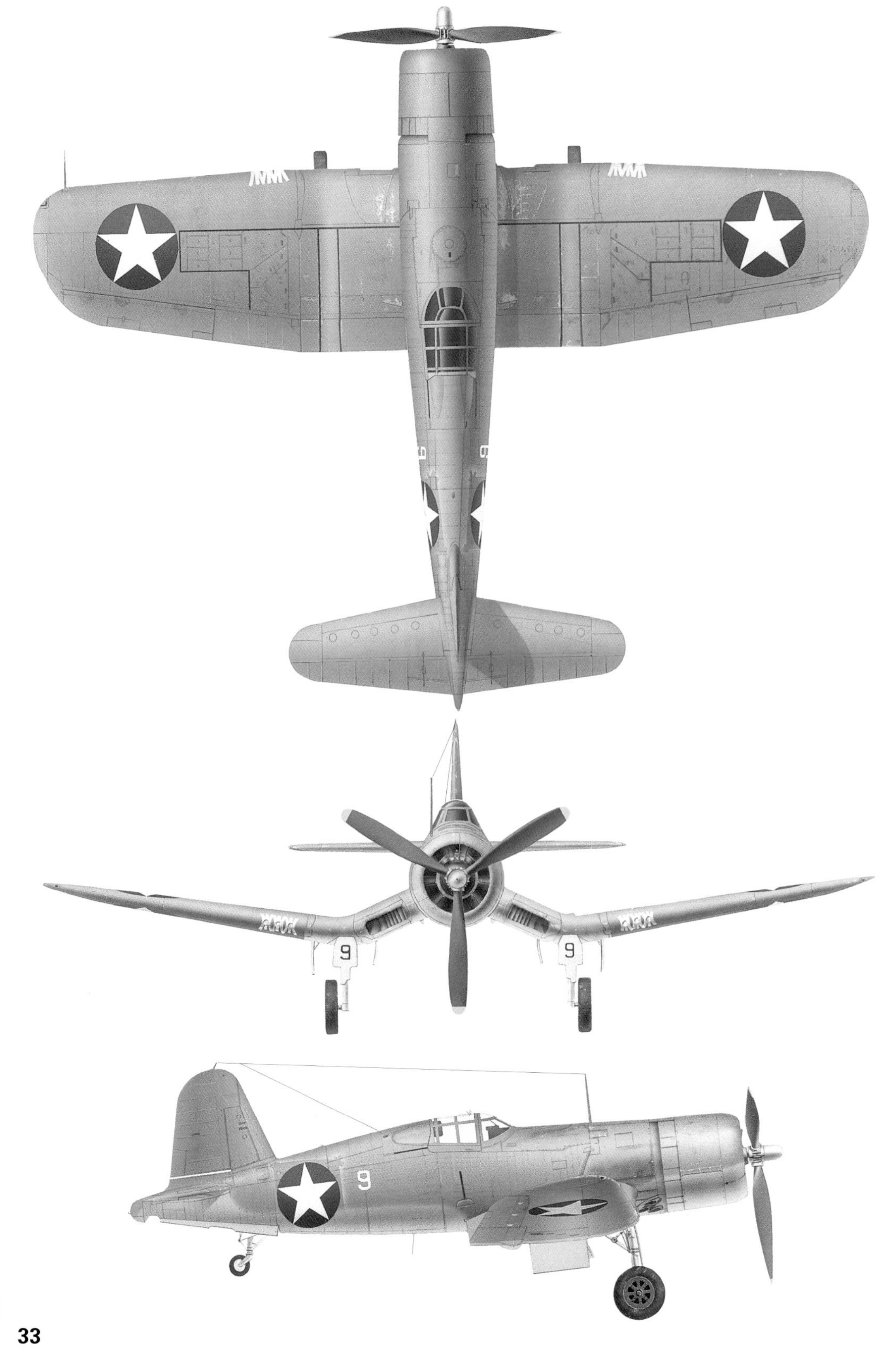

33

F4U-1 white 9/BuNo 02288 of Maj Gregory J Weissenberger, CO of VMF-213, Guadalcanal, June 1943

32
F4U-1A white 29 of Lt(jg) Ira C Kepford, VF-17, Bougainville, January 1944

34
F4U-1A white 17/BuNo 18005 of Lt Cdr Roger R Hedrick, VF-17, Bougainville, March 1944

35
F4U-1A white 25 of Lt Harry A March, Jr, VF-17, Bougainville, May 1944

36
F4U-1A white 8 of Lt(jg) Earl May, VF-17, Bougainville, January 1944

37
F4U-1A white 22 of Ens John M Smith, VF-17, Bougainville, February 1944

38
F4U-1A white 3 of Ens Frederick J Streig, VF-17, February 1944

39
F4U–1A white 5/BuNo 17656 of Lt(jg) Thomas Killefer, VF-17, Bougainville, February 1944

40
F4U-2 black 212 *Midnite Cocktail* of Capt Howard W Bollman, VMF(N)-532, Kagman Field, Saipan, April 1944

41
FG-1A yellow 056 *Mary*/BuNo 14056 of Capt Francis E Pierce, Jr, VMF-121, Peleliu, November 1944

42
F4U-1A white 108 of Maj George L Hollowell, VMF-111, Guadalcanal November 1943

43
F4U-1A black 77/NZ5277, RNZAF, Solomons, 1945

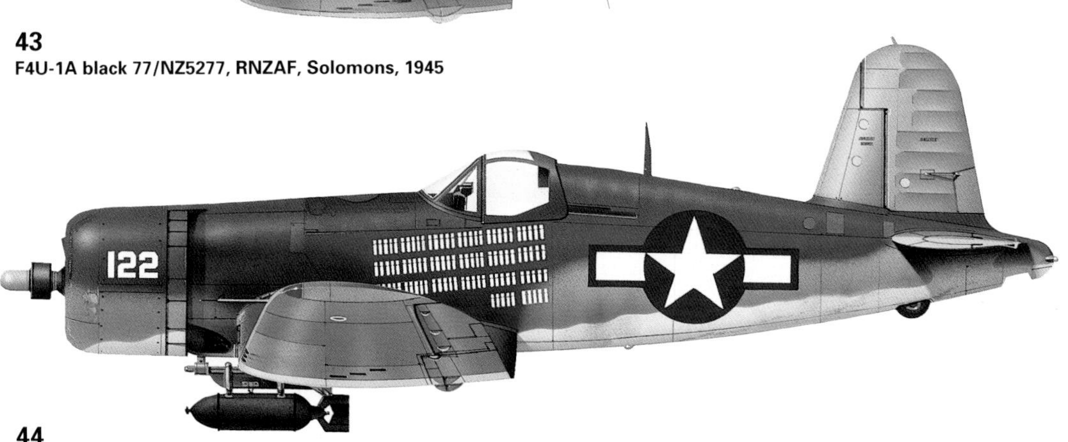

44
F4U-1A white 122 of VMF–111, Gilbert Islands, 1944

45
Corsair II white TRH/JT427 of Maj Ronald C Hay, RM, No 47 Wg, HMS *Victorious*, January 1945

46
Corsair II white T8H/JT410 of Sub Lt Donald J Sheppard, RCNVR, No 1836 Sqn, HMS *Victorious*, January 1945

47
F4U-1D white 1 of Maj Herman H Hansen, Jr, VMF-112, USS *Bennington*, February 1945

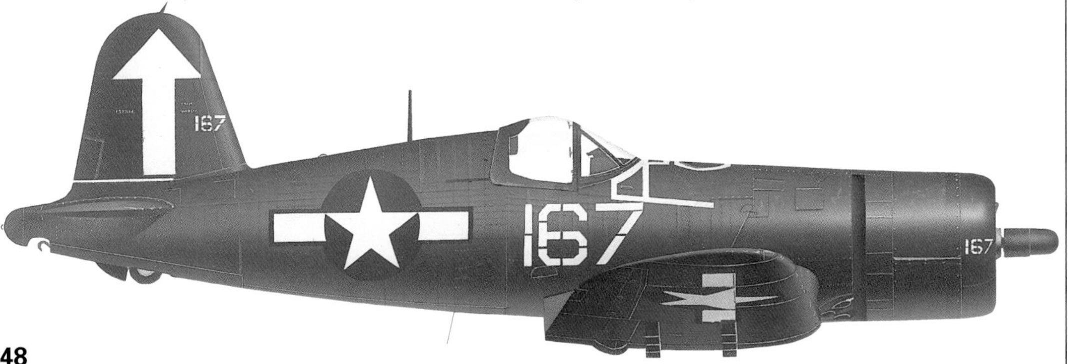

48
F4U-1D white 167/BuNo 57803 of Lt Cdr Roger R Hedrick, VF-84, USS *Bunker Hill*, February 1945

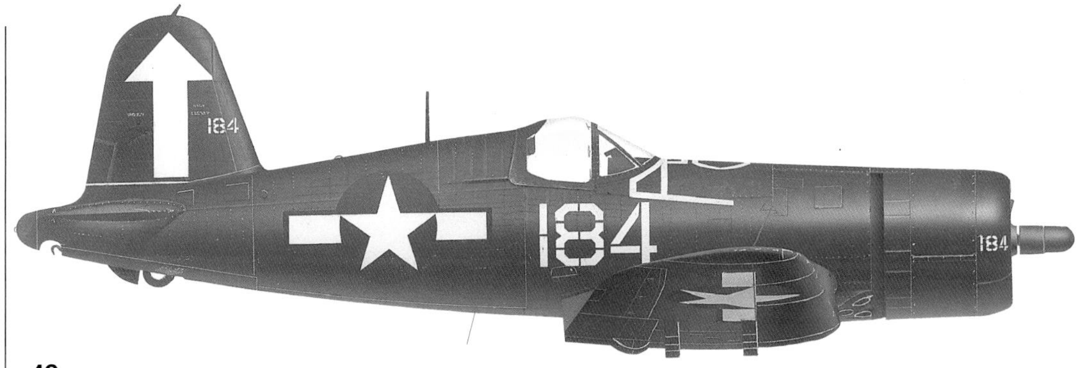

49
F4U-1D white 184 of Lt Willis G Laney, VF-84, USS *Bunker Hill*, February 1945

50
F4U-1D white 66 of Ens Alfred Lerch, VF-10, USS *Intrepid*, April 1945

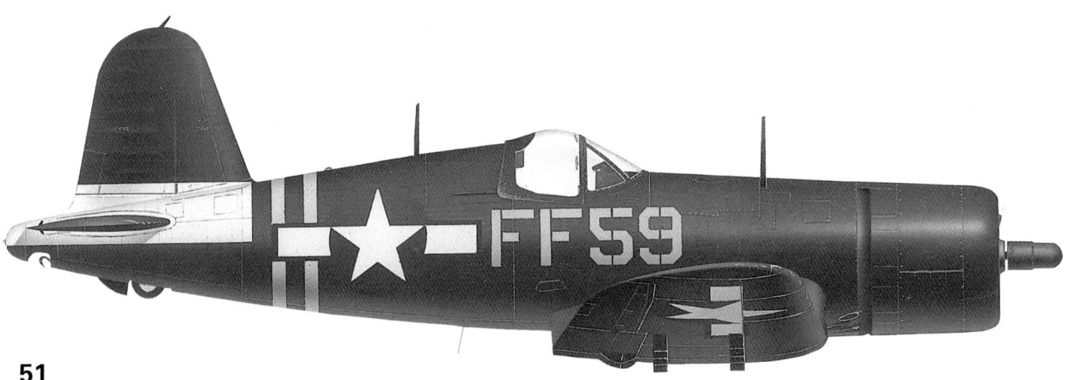

51
F4U-1D yellow FF-59 of Lt Col Donald K Yost, CO of VMF-351, USS *Cape Gloucester*, July 1945

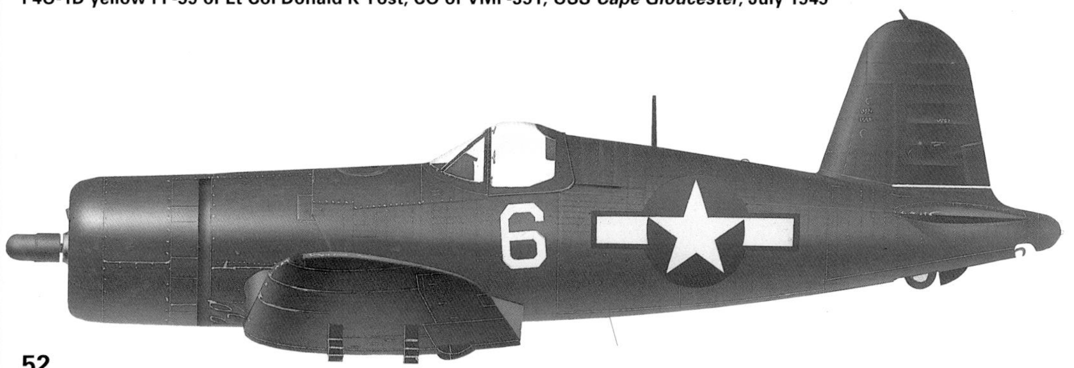

52
F4U-1D white 6 of Lt Joe D Robbins, VF-85, USS *Shangri-La*, December 1944

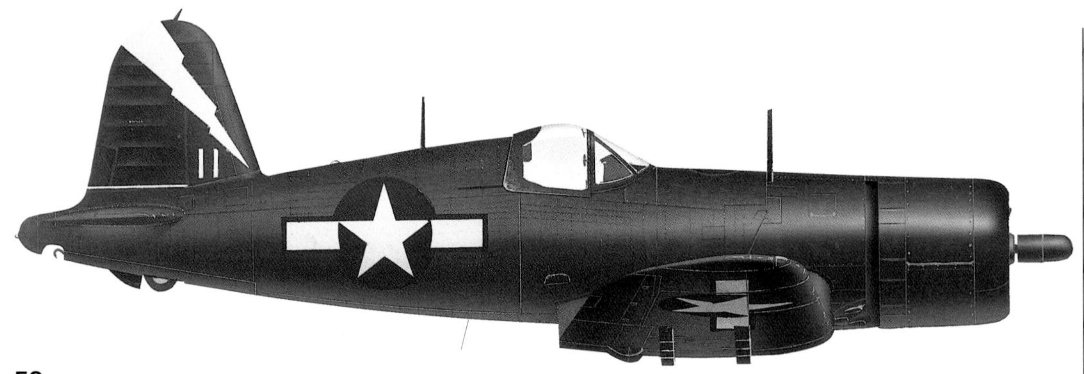

53
F4U-1C white 11 of Lt Joe D Robbins, VF-85, USS *Shangri-La*, May 1945

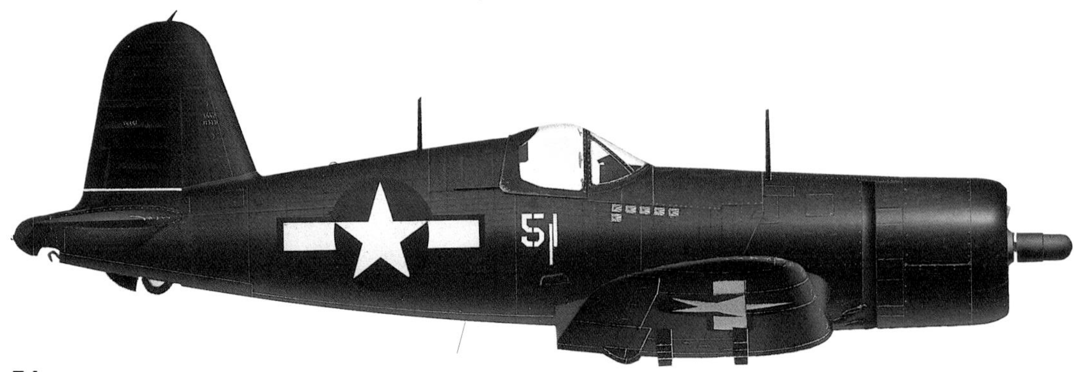

54
F4U-1D white 51 of 1st Lt Robert Wade, VMF-323, Okinawa, May 1945

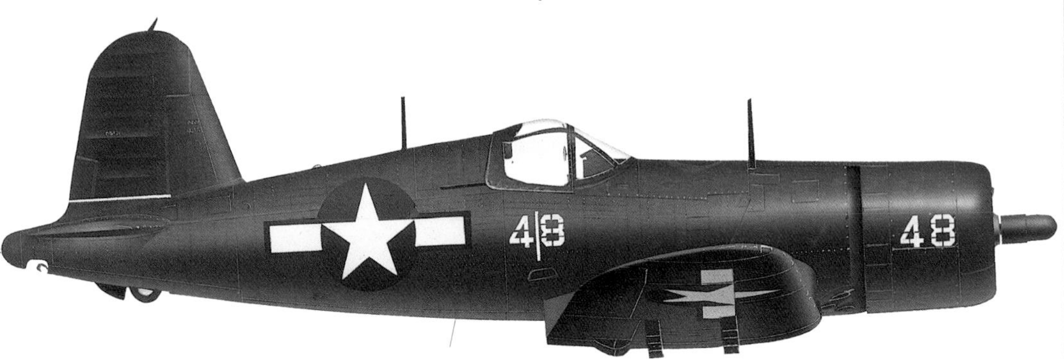

55
F4U-1D white 48/BuNo 57413 of 1st Lt Jack Broering, VMF-323, Espiritu Santo, October 1944 to March 1945

56
F4U-1D white 31 of 1st Lt Francis A Terrill, VMF-323, Okinawa, May 1945

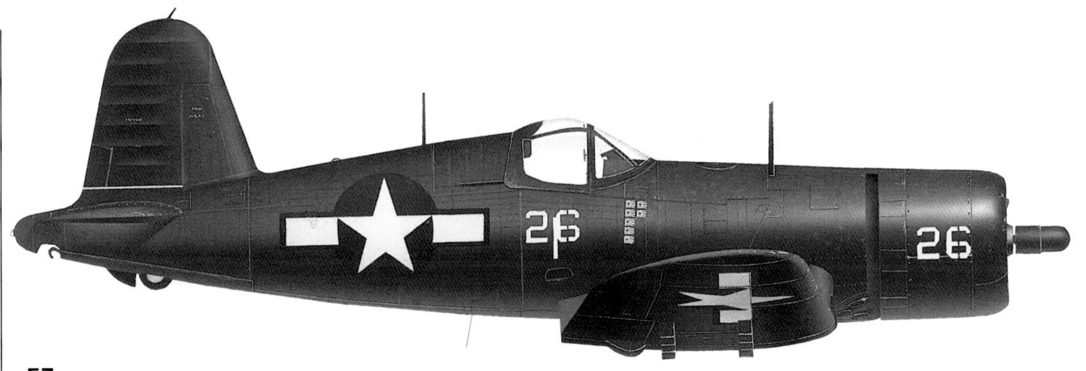

57
F4U-1D white 26 of 1st Lt Jerimaiah J O'Keefe, VMF-323, Okinawa, April 1945

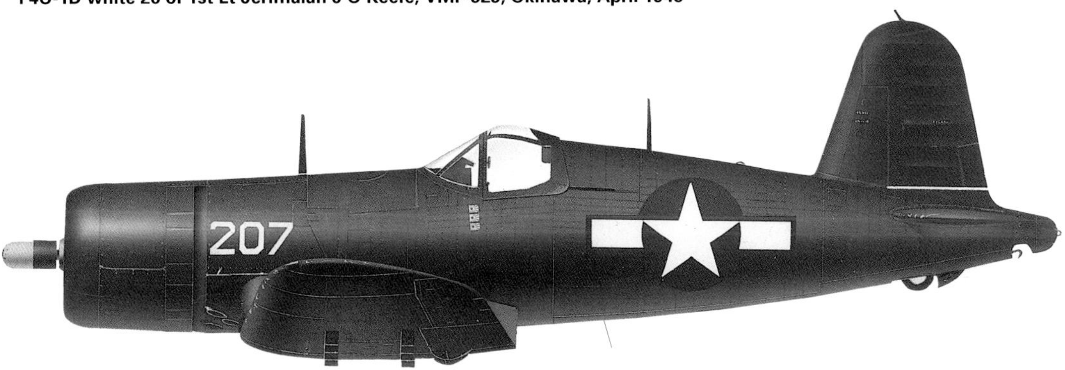

58
F4U-1D white 207 of 2nd Lt Marvin S Bristow, VMF-224, Okinawa, May 1945

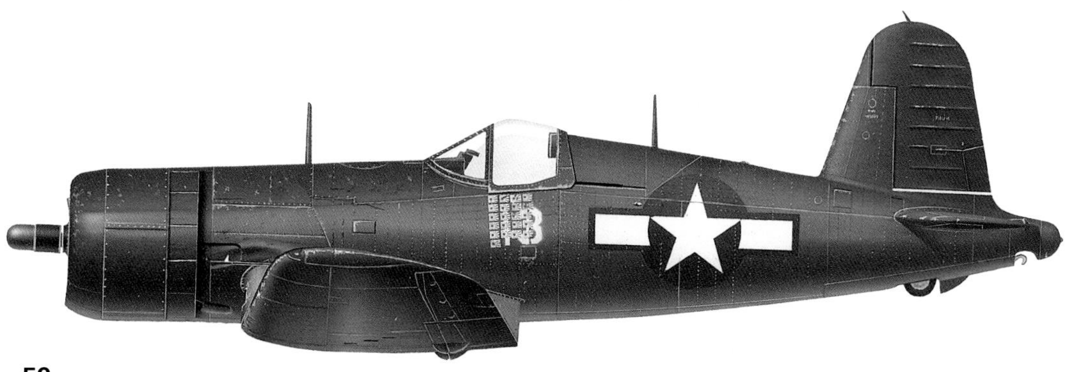

59
F4U-4 white 13/BuNo 80879 of Capt Kenneth A Walsh, VMF–222, Okinawa, June 1945

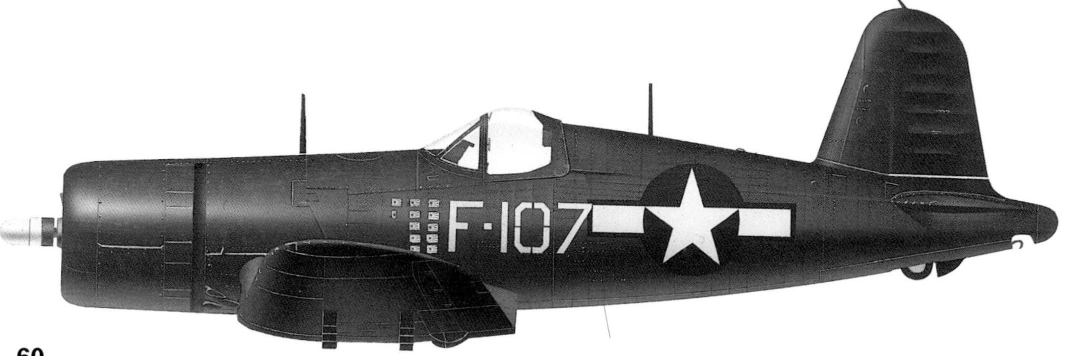

60
F4U-1D white F-107 of 1st Lt Phillip C DeLong, VMF-913, MCAS Cherry Point, North Carolina 1944

1
Capt Arthur R 'Rog' Conant of VMF-215 at Torokina in January 1944

2
Capt Harold L Spears, also of VMF-215, at Bougainville in December 1943

3
Maj Gregory 'Pappy' Boyington at Vella Lavella in December 1943

4
VMF-214's 1st Lt John F Bolt, Jr, at Vella Lavella in early 1944

5
Maj Ronnie Hay, RM, aboard HMS *Victorious* with No 47 FW in 1945

6
Lt Harry A March, Jr, of VF-17 at Bougainville in May 1944

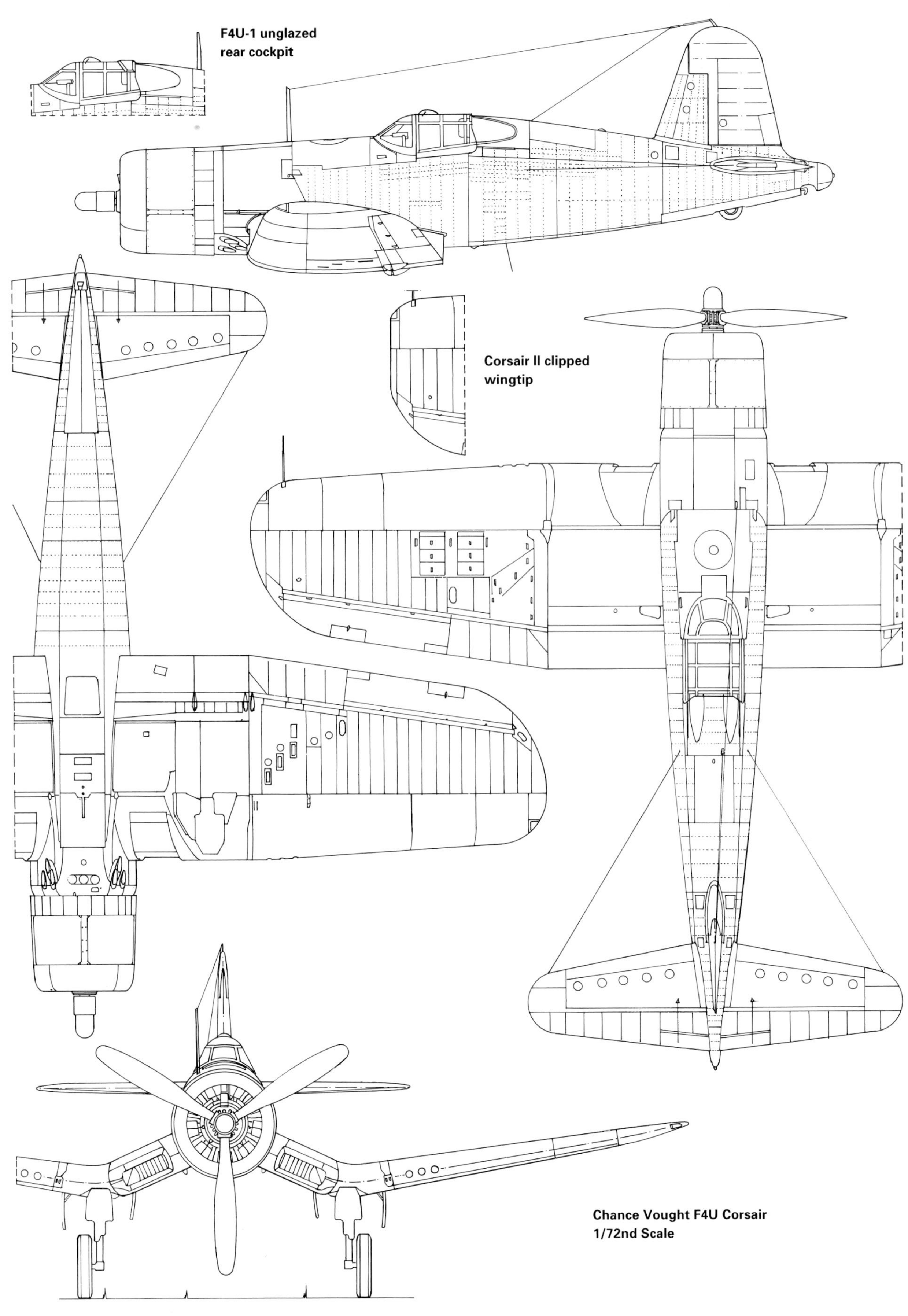
F4U-1 unglazed
rear cockpit
Corsair II clipped
wingtip
Chance Vought F4U Corsair
1/72nd Scale

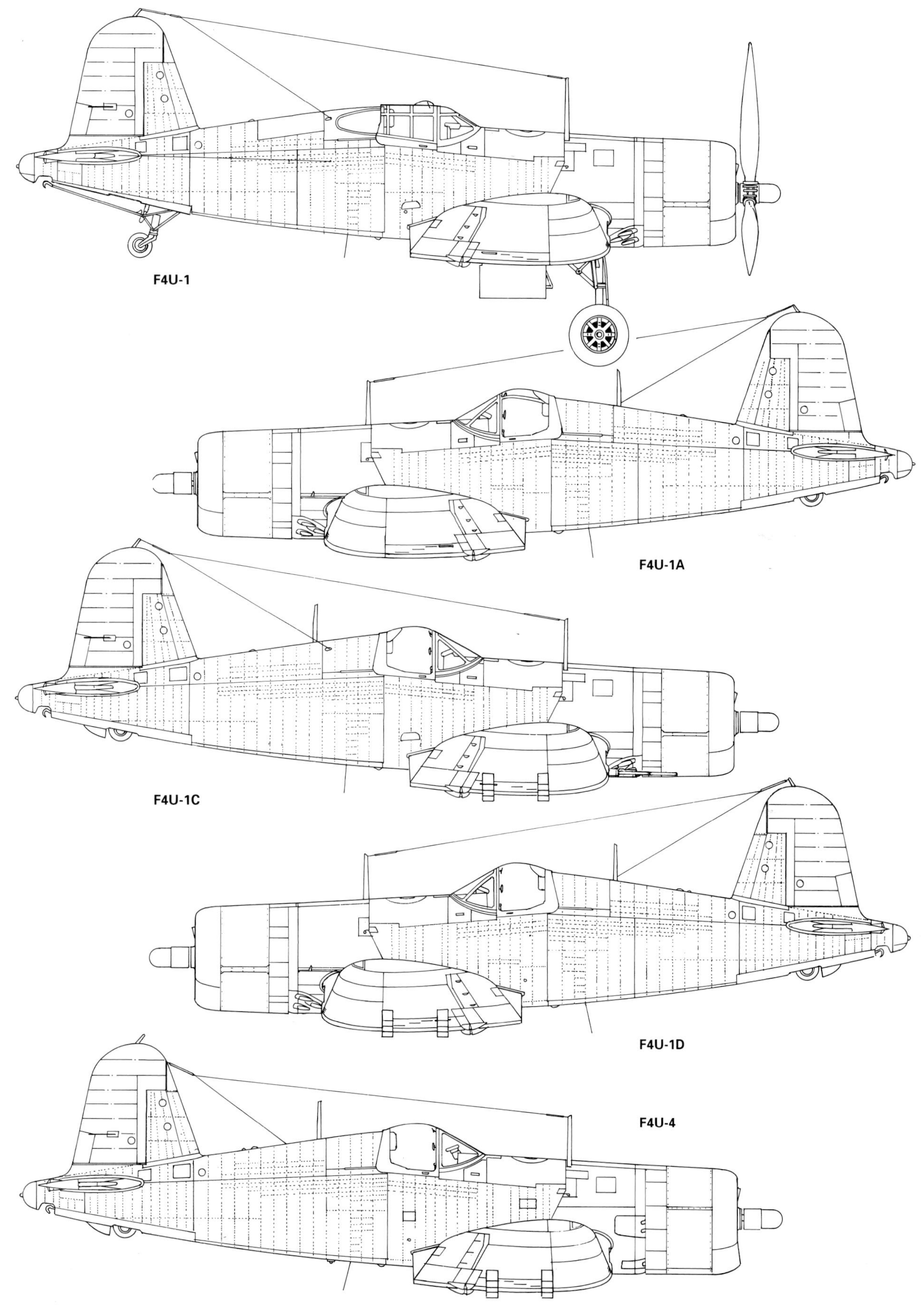
F4U-1
F4U-1A
F4U-1C
F4U-1D
F4U-4

Colour Plates

1

F4U-1 black 17 of 1st Lt Howard J Finn, VMF-124, Guadalcanal, February 1943

Finn was flying this aircraft on 14 February during the 'St Valentines Day Massacre'. He left formation to chase a lone Zero and was then attacked by more aircraft. He returned to the formation, taking refuge under a B-24, the gunners of which claimed the destruction of one of his pursuers. The next day AAF intelligence officers arrived at his base requesting that the pilot of "No 17" verify the gunners claim. This aircraft has the early style black code under the canopy as it appeared at the start of the unit's combat operations. The two-tone paint scheme consisted of Blue Grey upper surfaces with Light Grey under surfaces, except for the folding portion of the wing where the upper surface colour was also used.

2

F4U-1 white 13/BuNo 02350 of 2nd Lt Kenneth A Walsh, VMF-124, Munda, August 1943

The aircraft wears a revised white 13 forward of the national insignia. The early style black number can still be seen under the canopy and on the cowling. When VMF-124 first received their Corsairs, the CO, Maj Gise, assigned aircraft to each of his pilots, and they were required to work on the Corsair with the crewchiefs in order to familiarise themselves with the F4U-1.

3

F4U-1 white 114 of 2nd Lt Kenneth A Walsh, VMF-124, Munda, August 1943

Walsh destroyed two *Vals* and a Zero in this machine near Vella Lavella on 15 August 1943. Although his log book shows he was flying BuNo 02350, this was an error caused by the confused state of operations during the Vella Lavella campaign. White 114 was a pool aircraft based at Munda, its code not being related to its BuNo.

4

F4U-1 white 13 of 1st Lt Kenneth A Walsh, VMF-24, Russell Islands, September 1943

Walsh flew this aircraft towards the end of his third tour. It has a white 13 aft of the canopy and field-applied bars added to the national insignia. Following his tour Walsh became a Training Command instructor at NAS Jacksonville, before returning to combat in April 1945 with VMF-222.

5

F4U-1 white 7 *DAPHNE* C/BuNo 02350 of Capt James N Cupp, VMF-213, Guadalcanal, July 1943

Cupp claimed his first two kills (a *Betty* and a Zero) in this aircraft on 15 July 1943 during his second tour. The aircraft wears a white 7 in place of the previous number 13 just forward of the national insignia. The old style black 13 is just visible under the canopy and on the cowl. The aircraft bears four kill marks, representing Cupp's next victories claimed on the 17th in F4U-1 BuNo 02580.

6

F4U-1 white 15 *DAPHNE* C/BuNo 03829 of Capt James N Cupp, VMF-213, Munda, September 1943

Cupp claimed two victories (a Tony and a Zero) in this aircraft on 11 September 1943, bringing his total claims up to 7. The aircraft wears a white 15 and six whole kill marks. The cowling has been taken from F4U-1 white 7/BuNo 02350, and still bears the legend *DAPHNE* C, together with the small white 13.

7

F4U-1 white 11 *Defabe* of 1st lt George C Defabio, VMF-213, Guadalcanal, July 1943

This was the aircraft that bore Defabio's personal markings, which comprised a pair of dice and the name *Defabe*. Although not an ace, he did claim three Zeros on 30 June and on 11 and 17 July 1943. Although individual aircraft were assigned to pilots within the unit, it was seldom the case that they flew them on their assigned missions. As ops officer, Jim Cupp would allocate pilots any serviceable aircraft available, without reference to numbers and names of the fighters concerned. Defabio did happen to be flying this F4U-1 when hit by flak over Munda in July, however.

8

F4U-1 white 10 *GUS'S GOPHER* of 1st Lt Wilbur J Thomas, VMF-213, Guadalcanal, July 1943

Thomas's '*GOPHER* bears eight kill marks below the canopy and a Disney character on the cowling. The kill marks represent seven confirmed victories and a probable claimed during his second tour. On 30 June he downed his first four Zeros and one probable over Blanche Channel. His next victories, two Zeros and a *Betty*, were claimed on 15 July near Vella Lavella. Thomas went on to be VMF-213's most successful ace with 18.5 kills, 3.333 probables and 3 damaged. Most were achieved in the South West Pacific theatre during 1943, although he later bagged two Zeros and a 0.333 probable, plus damaged two Oscars, in February 1945 during a cruise on the USS *Essex*.

9

F4U-1 white 10 *GUS'S GOPHER* of 1st Lt Wilbur J Thomas, VMF-213, Guadalcanal, July 1943

The starboard side of Thomas's '*GOPHER*, showing its name. Virtually all of VMF-213's aircraft were decorated in a similar way, with a name on one side of the cowling and an artwork on the other. All F4U-1s wore white numbers on the fuselage forward of the national insignia, and a smaller black number on the undercarriage door.

10

F4U-1 white 20 of 1st Lt Foy R Garison, VMF-213, Guadalcanal, July 1943

Garison failed to reach the status of ace, but did claim two Zeros on 30 June 1943, before being killed in action on 17 July. His aircraft was adorned with a beautifully painted eagle on the cowling. Like most early F4U-ls, his aircraft was equipped with only the forward antenna mast, which in this case was the shorter of the two types employed.

11

F4U-1 white 125/BuNo 02487 of 2nd Lt Donald L Batch, VMF-221, Guadalcanal, July 1943

This was the F4U flown by Balch on 6 July when he destroyed a Zero near Rendova. He claimed two kills in the Solomons and later brought his total up to five whilst aboard *Bunker Hill* in 1945.

12

F4U-1 white 590/BuNo 17590 of Capt Arthur R Conant, VMF-215 Barakoma/Toroklna, January 1944

Conant destroyed a Zero whilst flying this aircraft on an escort mission to Rabaul on 14 January 1944. VMF-215 pilots did not have individual F4Us assigned to them, and rarely flew the same Corsair more than once. Conant's other kills were as follows - two Tonys confirmed and two probables on 25 August 1943 whilst flying F4U-1 BuNo 02371, one Zero on 1 September 1943 flying an F4U-1, one Zero on 30 January 1944 flying F4U-1 BuNo 17833, one Zero on 18 January 1944 flying F4U-1A BuNo 17735. F4U-1 white 590/BuNo 17590 lacks the curved glazing aft of the canopy, as well as the glazed canopy rear itself. The national insignia has field-applied bars, and the white aircraft number has been applied over a previous code, utilising the last three digits of the BuNo.

13

F4U-1A white 735/BuNo 17735 of Capt Arthur R Conant, VMF-215 Barakoma/Torokina, January 1944

Conant destroyed a Zero whilst flying this aircraft on an escort to Rabaul on 18 January 1944. F4U-1A BuNo 17735 appears in a very weathered three-tone scheme with field applied bars to its national insignia. This scheme followed the principle of Counter Shading/ Counter Shadowing and attempted to counteract the effects of light falling on an aircraft. As light normally comes from above, upper surfaces would be light whilst lower surfaces would be darker. Therefore, darker colours were applied to the upper surfaces, gradually blending to white on the under surfaces. Shaded areas under horizontal surfaces were to be painted white to counteract shadowing. The scheme used semi-gloss Sea Blue on the upper surfaces except where it could cause glare, whereupon it was replaced with nonspecular Sea Blue. Intermediate Blue was used on the fin and Insignia White was employed on the under-surfaces. The fuselage sides were meant to be graded from dark blue to white, but in practice Intermediate Blue was applied. This scheme was authorised on 5 January 1943.

14

F4U-1 white 75 of Maj Robert G Owens, Jr, VMF.215, Munda, August 1943

Owens gained seven confirmed kills and four probables. He destroyed a Zero on 21 August 1943 with BuNo 02656, one Zero and two probables on 22 August, another Zero on 30 August, two Zeros on 14 January 1944 whilst flying BuNo 17927 and another on the 22nd whilst flying BuNo 17937. He claimed a *Tojo* and a Zero probable on 24 January whilst flying F4U-1A BuNo 55825.

15

F4U-1 white 76 *Spirit of '76*/BuNo 02714 of Maj Robert G Owens, Jr, VMF - 215 Munda, August 1943

Although Owens authorised this F4U to be called *Spirit of '76*, it was not actually assigned to him, and he only flew it once on a 'local patrol' from Munda on 31 July 1943. It has a field-applied three-tone scheme with the intermediate tone carefully graded to intermediate white. This contrasts with the factory-applied scheme which has a distinct demarcation line between the colours. The national insignia has been updated with the application of white bars and an Insignia Blue surround to the whole design. This style of insignia came into force from 31 July 1943.

16

F4U-1A white 596/BuNo 17596 of 1st lt Robert M Hanson, VMF-215, Torokina, February 1944

Hanson was one of the most successful US aces of the war, claiming 25 kills and two probables, all of which were gained in the brief period between 4 August 1943 and 30 January 1944. When he encountered the enemy Hanson usually claimed multiple victories – on 14 January 1944 he downed five Zeros, on the 24th he claimed another four, on the 26th three and a probable, and on the 30th two Zeros and two *Tojos*. Hanson was killed by ground fire while attacking gun emplacements near Cape St George, New Ireland, on 3 February 1944.

17

F4U-1A white 777/BuNo 17777 of 1st Lt Phillip C DeLong, VMF-212, Vella Lavella, November 1943

Delong was the highest-scoring F4U ace to serve with VMF-212, being credited with a total of 11.166 confirmed victories, a probable and two damaged. His confirmed kills were as follows – two Zeros and one damaged on 9 January 1944 flying F4U-1A BuNo 17878, two Zeros on 17 January flying F4U-1A BuNo 17485, 1.8333 Zeros on 23 January flying F4U-1A BuNo 17878, one Zero on 29 January flying F4U-1A BuNo 17894, one Hamp on 31 January flying F4U-1A BuNo 17879, and three Vals on 15 February flying F4U-1A BuNo 55809. He flew white 777 on 4, 12, 13 and 18 November.

18

F4U-1A white 722A/BuNo 17722 of 1st Lt Phillip C DeLong, VMF-212, VeRa Lavella, November 1943

DeLong flew this F4U on 11 November whilst providing cover for Task Force 50, striking Rabaul. It wears the three-tone scheme with its number forward of the national insignia. When aircraft utilised the last three digits of the BuNo as an identifying code, occasionally a unit would end up with two machines with the same number. In the event of this occurring the letter 'A' was added to one of the codes, as has happened here.

19
F4U-1 white 576 *MARINE'S DREAM*/BuNo 02576 of 1st Lt Edwin L Olander, VMF-214, Munda, October 1943

Olander shot down a Zero on 17 October 1943 during a sweep to Kahili in this machine. His other kills were one Zero and a probable on 10 October 1943 whilst flying BuNo 02309, one Zero and a probable on 18 October, one Zero on 28 December while flying BuNo 17875 and a Zero and a probable on 30 December whilst flying BuNo 17792. Olander's final score was five confirmed and four probables. White 576 has a field-applied scheme, with field-modified national insignia. The aircraft lacks the curved glazing aft of the canopy.

20
F4U-1 white 93/BuNo 17430 of Capt Edwin L Olander, VMF-214, Vella Lavella/Torokina, January 1944

Olander flew a shuttle mission from Vella Lavella to Torokina on 5 January 1944 in this machine. The aircraft wears a field-applied three-tone scheme and updated national insignia.

21
F4U-1A white 740/BuNo 17740 of Maj Gregory Boyington, CO of VMF-214, Vella Lavella, December 1943

Boyington commanded VMF-214 from 7 September 1943 until he was shot down and captured on 3 January 1944. During that time he was credited with 22 aircraft destroyed and 4 probables. His unit carried out the first fighter sweep against Rabaul, a tactic aimed at destroying as many Japanese fighters as possible. The 'Black Sheep' were credited with 126 aircraft destroyed, 34 probables and 6 damaged. Following its service in the South Pacific, the unit returned to the US where it trained for carrier ops. On 18 March 1945 it commenced operations again on board the USS Franklin, but was put out of the war the next day when the ship was bombed and had to retire.

22
F4U-1A white 883/BuNo 17883 of Maj Gregory Boyington, CO of VMF-214, Vella Lavella, December 1943

Both Boyington and 1st Lt Robert W McClurg flew this aircraft on numerous occasions.

23
F4U-1A white 86 *Lulubelle*/BuNo 18086 of Maj Gregory Boyington, CO of VMF-214, Vella Lavella, December 1943

Although VMF-214 did not have any aircraft assigned to it, this F4U is marked with 20 of Boyington's kills, as well as having both the name *Lulubelle* and the Major's details painted on it.

24
FG-1A white 271/BuNo 13271 of Maj Julius W Ireland, VMF-211, Bougainville, January 1944

Ireland claimed two Zeros whilst flying '271' on a sweep to Rabaul on 23 January 1944. Earlier that day, while escorting SBDs to the same target, he had downed another Zero and a probable while flying F4U-1 BuNo 17586. Prior to that, on the 3rd (in F4U-1 BuNo 17526) Ireland got a Zero over Rabaul, and on the 17th (in F4U-1 BuNo 17924) claimed a third-share of a Zero with Capt Winfree and Lt Paradis. Ireland brought his final tally to 5.333 on the 29th (in FG-1A BuNo 13259) when he downed a Zero whilst escorting B-24s to Rabaul.

25
F4U-1A white 17-F-13 of Lt(jg) James A Halford, VF-17, USS *Bunker Hill*, August 1943

Halford got his 3.5 kills in the Wildcat in 1942.

26
F4U-IA white 1 *BIG HOG*/BuNo 17649 of Lt Cdr John T Blackburn, CO VF-17, Ondonga, November 1943

Blackburn claimed 11 kills, 5 probables and 3 damaged whilst CO of VF-17. His oufit was one of the most successful in the Solomons, claiming a total of 154.5 confirmed victories. Unlike Marine units, it also assigned F4Us to individual pilots.

27
F4U-IA white 19 of Lt Paul Cordray, VF-17, Ondonga, November 1943

Cordray claimed seven aircraft destroyed, one probable and three damaged

28
F4U-1A white 15 of Lt (jg) Daniel G Cunningham, VF-17, Ondonga, February 1944

Cunningham scored seven kills and 1.5 damaged.

29
F4U-1A white 9 *LONESOME POLECAT* of Lt Merl W Davenport, VF-17, Ondonga, January 1944

'Butch' Davenport claimed 6.25 aircraft destroyed.

30
F4U-IA white 34 *L.A. CITY LIMITS*/BuNo 17932 of Lt(jg) Doris C Freeman, VF-17, Ondonga, November 1943

'Chico' Freeman claimed two aircraft destroyed and two probables with VF-17, before going on to claim another seven kills with VF-84 in 1945.

31
F4U-1A white 29 of Lt(jg) Ira C Kepford, VF-17, Bougainville, January 1944

'Ike' Kepford was the Navy's most successful Corsair pilot with 16 confirmed victories, 1 probable and 1 damaged.

32
F4U-1A white 29 of Lt(jg) Ira C Kepford, VF-17, Bougainville, January 1944
Kepford's second white 29 wears his final tally. Unlike his first F4U (written off in a crash-landing in January 1943), this machine wore a scoreboard on both sides of the fuselage.

33
F4U-1 white 9/BuNo 02288 of Maj Gregory J Weissenberger, CO of VMF-213, Guadalcanal, June 1943
Weissenberger claimed five Zeros, the first three on 30 June 1943 and the remaining two on 11 and 18 July. White 9 was his usual mount, and was finished in the standard two-tone scheme. Walkways are bordered in black on the upper surface of the wings, and each gunport is covered with three strips of tape.

34
F4U-1A white 17/BuNo 18005 of Lt Cdr Roger R Hedrick, VF-17, Bougainville, March 1944
Hedrick gained his last three victories with VF-17 in this F4U on 18 February 1944. Earlier, a trio of kills had been scored in BuNos 17659 and 55798.

35
F4U-1A white 25 of Lt Harry A March, Jr, VF-17, Bougainville, May 1944
March gained the status of ace by shooting down two Zeros on 28 January 1944, adding to his previous three kills gained with VF-6 during August 1942 flying the Wildcat.

36
F4U-1A white 9 of Lt(jg) Earl May, VF-17, Bougainville, January 1944
May claimed eight confirmed victories, all Zeros.

37
F4U-1A white 22 of Ens John M Smith, VF-17, Bougainville, February 1944
Smith claimed three aircraft destroyed, three probables and one damaged with VF-17, and later claimed seven victories with VF-84 in 1945.

38
F4U-1A white 3 of Ens Frederick J Streig, VF-17, February 1944
Streig claimed five aircraft destroyed and two damaged. This F4U is depicted after his last kills – 2.5 Zekes claimed over Rabaul on 27 January 1944. It is unusual in that it retains the red surround to the national insignia, a colour that only appeared with the addition of white bars on 28 June 1943 – the surround was discontinued as of 31 July due to possible confusion with the enemy's *Hinomaru*.

39
F4U-IA white 5/BuNo 17656 of Lt(jg) Thomas Killefer, VF-17, Bougainville, February 1944
Killefer was not an ace but did claim 4.5 aircraft destroyed. He force landed on Nissan Island in this machine following engine failure on 5 March 1944.

40
F4U-2 black 212 *Midnite Cocktail* of Capt Howard W Bollman, VMF(N)-532, Kagman Field, Saipan, April 1944
Bollman intercepted and destroyed a *Betty* at 0112 on 14 April 1944 while flying this machine, which was assigned to Lts Caniff and Reuter. Just prior to Boliman's score, 1st Lt Bonner claimed a *Betty* probable at 0036 and 1st Lt Sovik a third *Betty* confirmed at 0111. These were the unit's only kills. F4U-2 black 212 wears a two-tone scheme. Mods fitted to this F4U included the small generator air scoop on the forward fuselage, starboard wing radome blister and the addition of a VHF whip antenna on the spine, the standard antenna mast having been removed. The canopy is equipped with extra armour plating.

41
FG-1A yellow 056 *Mary*/BuNo 14056 of Capt Francis E Pierce, Jr, VMF-121, Peleliu, November 1944
Of 'Effie' Pierce's six victories and one probable, only one was scored whilst flying the F4U – a *Betty* on 30 June 1943. His previous kills were all in F4Fs. The white area on the fin of this FG-1 served as a unit marking.

42
F4U-1A white 108 of Maj George I Hollowell, VMF-111, Guadalcanal November 1943
Hollowell achieved all his victories while flying the Wildcat with VMF-224, but had his Corsair marked up with his score, together with 25 bomb symbols. The aircraft is finished in the three-tone scheme.

43
F4U-1A black 77/NZ5277, RNZAF, Solomons, 1945
This aircraft wears an irate *Donald Duck* motif and a variety of mission marks and kill tallies, including symbols for nine large bombs, eleven small bombs, nine trucks and eight ships. It is finished in Ocean Blue with Light Grey undersides. The RNZAF roundel has been applied over the previous US insignia, and is slightly offset from the bars. This F4U-1A was brought on charge on 5 May 1944, arriving at Guadalcanal on the 20th. It served with a variety of units before being returned to New Zealand in October 1945. Whilst in the frontline it flew with No 15 Sqn/No 1 SU (Guadalcanal), No 15 Sqn/No 25 SU and No 2 SU (Bougainville), No 15 Sqn/No 2 SU (Torokina), No 14 Sqn/No 30 SU (Guadalcanal), No 16 Sqn/Na30 SU and No 21 Sqn/No 30 SU (both Nissan Island), and finally No 21 Sqn/No 30 SU (Jacquinot Bay).

44
F4U-1A white 122 of VMF-111, Gilbert Islands, 1944
White 122, decorated with 100 mission marks, was the only aeroplane to receive an official citation during the war. The Corsair was designed as a fighter, but was used in the ground attack role to great effect. At first field mods were made to allow the aircraft to carry

bombs, then Chance Vought responded by producing F4Us capable of fulfilling the role. It was this versatility that ensured the Corsair's longevity after World War 2.

45

Corsair II white TRH/JT427 of Maj Ronald C Hay, RM, No 47 Wg, HMS *Victorious*, January 1945

Hay shot down an *Oscar* and a *Tojo* on 24 January 1945 in this aircraft – on the 29th he again shared in the destruction of an *Oscar* and a *Tojo*. It is painted in Dark Sea Grey and Dark Sea Green over Light Grey. His aircraft was fitted with field-installed oblique and vertical cameras in the lower port fuselage. Delivered to the Navy in August 1944, JT427 was written off when it suffered a landing accident aboard *Victorious* in May 1945, its pilot, Sub Lt R L White (RNZN), escaping unhurt as the fighter came to rest on the deck edge.

46

Corsair II white T8H/JT4IO of Sub Lt Donald J Sheppard, RCNVR, No 1836 Sqn, HMS *Victorious*, January 1945

Sheppard was the only FAA pilot to reach the status of ace having gained all his victories in the Corsair. He downed two *Oscars* and a *Tojo* on 4 January 1945, the latter being listed as a probable although it may later have been confirmed, and on the 29th he shared in the destruction of an *Oscar* and a *Tojo* with Maj Hay – all of these scores were achieved in this aircraft. On 4 May, whilst flying Corsair 11 JT537, he downed a *Judy*, thus becoming an ace. JT410 had been delivered to the Navy in July, and was badly damaged during a heavy landing by Sub Lt Holland (RNZN) on 9 February 1945, resulting in it being declared Category X with both main wheels broken off, it was repaired at Bankstown, Australia, in June 1945, but its subsequent fate is unknown. Prior to Sheppard gaining kills in JT410, Lt J B Edmundson, also of No 1836 Sqn, used it to shoot down an *Oscar* off Car Nicobar on 19 October 1944.

47

F4U-1D white 1 of Maj Herman H Hansen, Jr, VMF-112, USS Bennington, February 1945

Hansen claimed a Zero on 30 June 1943 whilst CO of VMF-122. He re-opened his scoring on 17 February 1945 when he shot down an *Oscar* over Haramachida, Japan, and then went on to destroy another 3.5 aircraft and damage 2.5. His F4U is adorned with *Bennington's* 'Pine Tree' geometric recognition symbol, as used in early 1945. Part of the 'G' system that came into force on 27 January 1945, these markings were intended to simplify unit recognition with the large number of carriers operating together. However, they proved difficult to recognise and describe, and were replaced by a block letter system introduced in July.

48

F4U-1D white 167/BuNo 57803 of Lt Cdr Roger R Hedrick, VF-84, USS *Bunker HIll*, February 1945

Hedrick destroyed 2 *Franks* and a Zero on 25 February 1945, whilst flying this machine, to bring his final score to 12 aircraft destroyed and 4 damaged. It is shown as it appeared at the time of his kills, having had its temporary yellow nose band (employed on the first Tokyo raids) painted over. The F4U has the vertical arrow 'G' symbol.

49

F4U-1D white 184 of Lt Willis G Laney, VF-84, USS *Bunker Hill*, February 1945

Laney claimed two Zeros and a probable on the same mission that Hedrick claimed his last kills on 25 February over Inubo Point, in the Katori airfield area, Japan. Laney was credited with five aircraft destroyed, two probables and one damaged.

50

F4U-ID white 66 flown by Ens Alfred Lerch, VF-10, USS *Intrepid*, April 1945

Lerch claimed six Nates and a Valon 16 April in this F4U, which displays Intrepid's 'G' symbol. VF-10 was the only unit to use the F4F, F6F and F4U in combat, its three tours producing 27 aces.

51

F4U-ID yellow FF-59 flown by Lt Col Donald K Yost, CO of VMF-351, USS *Cape Gloucester*, July 1945

Yost gained six kills in the F4F with VMF-121, and later added to his score by downing a *Judy* and a *Francis* on 23 July and 5 August 1945 respectively, bringing his tally to eight. Yost led the MAG aboard the Cape Gloucester, being one of the first F4U units to enter combat aboard an escort carrier.

52

F4U-ID white 6 of Lt Joe D Robbins, VF-85, USS *Shangri-La*, December 1944

VF-85 boarded *Shangri-La* on 11 November 1944 for a six-week shakedown. On arrival at San Diego they were re-equipped with 36 new cannon-armed F4U-1C, which were flown into combat. Robbins did, however, fly both F4U-IDs and FG-IDs in combat. He became the only ace to serve with VF-85, adding three kills to his previous F6F claims.

53

F4U-1C white 11 of Lt Joe D Robbins, VF-85, USS *Shangri-La*, May 1945

Robbins downed three Zeros and damaged a fourth whilst flying F4U-1C BuNo 82574 on 11 May 1945. He claimed his previous kills while serving with VF-6 on USS Intrepid. He shot down a Topsy on 29 January 1944 while flying F6F-3 BuNo 66010 and a Zero on 16 February in F6F-3 BuNo 40027. This F4U-1C wears the lightning bolt symbol that was assigned to the *Shangri-La* in January 1945.

54

F4U-1D white 51 flown by let Lt Robert Wade, VMF-323, Okinawa, May 1945

Wade claimed seven kills – two *Tonys* on 15 April 1945, two *Vals*, two *Nates* and three Nates damaged on 4 May, 0.5 of a *Dinah* on 12 May and 0.5 of a *Val* on 3 June.

55

F4U-ID white 8/BuNo 57413 of 1st Lt Jack Broering, VMF-323, Espiritu Santo, October 1944 to March 1945

Broering was assigned this aircraft while VMF-323 was at Espiritu, the unit not continuing the practice of assigning aircraft to pilots following the move to Okinawa. Broering didn't get the opportunity to gain any kills as he was 'never in the right place at the right time'. He, along with the rest of VMF-323, flew endless CAPs and ground attack missions.

56

F4U-ID white 31 of 1st Lt Francis A Terrill, VMF-323, Okinawa, May 1945

Terrill claimed 6.083 destroyed and 4 damaged between 15 April and 17 May 1945.

57

F4U-1D white 26 of 1st Lt Jerimaiah J O'Keefe, VMF-323, Okinawa, April 1945

O'Keefe downed five *Vals* on 22 April and two *Nates* on the 28th, all *kamikazes*.

58

F4U-1D white 207 of 2nd lt Marvin S Bristow, VMF-224, Okinawa, May 1945

Although Bristow's F4U is adorned with three kill marks, he has only ever been credited with 1.5, these being a Zero and 0.5 of a *Kate* on 4 and 6 May 1945, respectively. The unit placed their aircraft numbers aft of the cowl flaps, the yellow prop boss serving as a squadron marking.

59

F4U-4 white 13/BuNo 80879 of Capt Kenneth A Walsh, VMF-222, Okinawa, June 1945

Walsh claimed his last kill – a Zero piloted by a *kamikaze* pilot – on 22 June 1945 in this aircraft.

60

F4U-1D white F-107 of 1st Lt Phillip C DeLong, VMF-913, MCAS Cherry Point, North Carolina 1944

DeLong, like many F4U aces returned to the US and joined Training Command to pass on his combat experience. While serving at Cherry Point he had this aircraft adorned with his full score. DeLong was later posted to VMF-312 aboard USS Bataan during the Korean War, where he downed two Yak-9s during a recce mission on 21 April 1951 whilst flying F4U-4 BuNo 97380 – for further details see *Aircraft of the Aces 4:– Korean War Aces.*

Figure Plates

1

Capt Arthur R 'Rog' Conant of VMF-215 at Torokina in January 1944. He is wearing typical 'garb' for a USMC/Navy Corsair fighter pilot in the Pacific, namely Marine Corps issue khaki shirt and trousers, a personalised US Navy lightweight flying jacket and 'Boondocker' field boots. His M40 helmet and Wilson Mk 2 goggles are also standard issue, as is the throat microphone. Conant has his parachute and survival pack slung over one shoulder, and an N2885 life preserver, equipped with a dye marker and whistle, around his other arm. Finally, around his waist Conant wears an M1936 pistol belt to which he has attached a holstered Colt 1911A1 .45 cal pistol and a pouch for magazine clips. His gloves and sunglasses are standard Navy issue.

2

Capt Harold L Spears (15 victories and 3 probables), also of VMF-215, at Bougainville in December 1943. Showing a rather more casual approach to combat flying gear than most of his contemporaries, Spears is wearing a 'cut down' pair of USMC khaki trousers and a long-sleeve shirt. Having dispensed with his boots, Spears usually flew in this dusty pair of privately-purchased suede 'desert boots'. His headgear is very much regulation issue, however, and is identical to that worn by squadron-mate Conant. Spears' life-jacket is also an N2885, but he is wearing it back to front – a common trait inexplicably perpetrated by many pilots.

3

Maj Gregory 'Pappy' Boyington at Vella Lavella in December 1943. Again wearing much the same clothing as Conant and Spears, 'Pappy's' one distinguishing feature is his early-issue life preserver, 'borrowed' from VMF-122.

4

Cigar-smoking 1st Lt John F Bolt, Jr, was also a 'Black Sheep' at Vella Lavella in early 1944. His uniform is standard issue, aside from the customised earphones within his helmet. He has also partially inflated his life-jacket, a practice adopted by a number of pilots in-theatre.

5

Although flying Corsairs with the Royal Navy's FAA from HMS *Victorious* in early 1945, Royal Marine Maj Ronnie Hay is wearing a US Navy-style one-piece lightweight overall, which was the favoured item of clothing within the BPF's flying community. His 'Mae West' is a late-war pattern issue, with additional pockets containing survival equipment. Hay is carrying a Type C helmet fitted with a late-war mask and Mk VIII goggles. Finally, he is wearing standard-issue patent leather shoes.

6

Lt Harry A 'Dirty Eddie' March, Jr, of VF-17 at Bougainville in May 1944. He is wearing US Navy/Marine Corps herringbone twill coveralls and 'Boondockers', with a leather waist belt and a Colt 1911A1 .45 cal pistol attached. His early-pattern life-vest has a survival kit (in white) slung underneath it, the former also carrying his name emblazoned across the front. Finally, his helmet and mask are very much late-war issue, compared with other USMC pilots profiled on this spread.

TOROKINA AND MUNDA

VMF-215 arrived at Espiritu Santo in July 1943. Under the command of Capt J L Neefus, they began their first combat tour by attacking Japanese bases in the northern Solomons. They moved to Munda on 12 August to complete their first tour, with their second spell in the frontline beginning in October under the command of Lt Col H H Williamson. Based at Vella Lavella from 28 November, they soon began attacks against heavily defended airfields on Rabaul. Maj Robert G Owens (7 kills) was given command of the unit on 6 December, and duly led it throughout its third tour, much of which was flown from Torokina – the unit occupied the island strip on 27 January 1944. This squadron was one of the few Marine Corsair units to keep virtually the same personnel throughout its long combat career – other squadrons would rotate back to the US, and when they returned to combat would be staffed by new pilots, thus making them in effect completely different units. During the war VMF-215 accounted for the destruction of 135.5 enemy aircraft, and produced ten aces, one of whom, Lt Robert M Hanson, was posthumously awarded the Congressional Medal of Honor.

Maj Bob Owens and his wingman, Capt Roger Conant, had served with the squadron right from the start of its combat career, and they both became aces – Owens claimed seven whilst Conant accounted for six. Here, they describe some of VMF-215's operations.

Conant – 'Our original aeroplanes at Santa Barbara had the early birdcage canopy. As soon as we had enough F4U-1s we loaded them aboard ship – a seaplane tender – and sailed to Hawaii. There we lost three pilots as they were so hot to get into combat that they volunteered to go up to the front straight away. However, they went to the mid-Pacific and never saw combat at all!'

F4U-1 Corsairs of VMF-215 fly in formation off Hawaii in early 1943. 'We flew our aircraft from Barbers Point, Hawaii, to Midway. The Corsair was almost unique in that it had wing tip tanks located inside the wing. These tanks contained 50 gallons of fuel, which we used for long flights. We would use the fuel and then open up the vents and purge the air with CO_2 so that you didn't have a combustible mixture left in them. We thought this a much better arrangement than carrying drop tanks. Midway was a great place, and being isolated there was nobody to bother you. Whilst on the island we did three months of training, which in the long run saved our lives. We had had no flight time on the Corsair until then' – Capt Roger Conant (*Conant Collection*)

Owens – 'The aeroplanes we flew in combat were sadly not those we brought over from the US. When it came time for us to go down to the Solomons, we got our orders and packed our bags. Just then, another unit arrived at Midway to relieve us – VMF-212. We went aboard the ship and they went ashore, swapping aeroplanes in the process. I was really reluctant about that. Compared to those of other units, we thought our Corsairs were the best maintained. Here we were about to go into combat and we had to give up our F4U-1s and take those of

F4U-1 'No 76' *Spirit of '76*, BuNo 02714, being pulled from the mud at Munda on 14 August 1943. Although this aircraft has been reported to be Bob Owen's machine, he only ever flew it once in combat, on 31 July 1943. His wingman, Roger Conant, also flew this machine on 1 and 4 August, and so did Ed Olander of VMF-214 on 13 October 1943. None of these pilots gained victories in it, however (*National Archives*)

VMF-212 in return. We didn't even know if their groundcrew knew how to turn a bolt correctly!

'When we went into Munda it was the first time (since Guadalcanal) that there was a group of squadrons flying similar machines. Each aeroplane had a number on the side from 1 to 16. Having been assigned to fly a mission in "No 5", I'd get out there on the line and there would be five "No 5s" – five squadrons each with a "No 5"! So we repainted the aircraft with numbers that weren't like those of other units, most squadrons tending to use the last three digits of the BuNo. From then on you were told by the engineers "You take 'No 672' and you take 'No 345'. Every time it was different, and my log-book shows that I rarely flew the same aeroplane twice. We also used other squadron's F4Us. When Maj Hugh Elwood (5.1 kills) commanded VMF-212, we had an agreement to share our aeroplanes. We decided that one day he'd take them and we'd have them the next. We'd take whatever planes were available and put our pilots in them. We pooled the aircraft because we always had more pilots than we had Corsairs. There was a time when our aircraft were painted with personalised markings. Various pilots in our unit made suggestions and the aircraft were duly painted up. I authorised the painting of an aircraft with the legend *Spirit of '76*. Contrary to what has previously been suggested, I only flew that aircraft once. Like the other pilots, I took whatever machine was assigned for any given mission.

'The Corsair was a hell of a thing to fly, particularly if you'd started on a much lighter aircraft. It had so much torque that when you "poured the coals" to 2800 rpm, it would try to walk away from you. You had to have full rudder on there in order to keep control. The F4U had a very large cockpit, so much so that the shorter guys could not hold their rudder all the way in to counteract the torque. Some pilots used to fly with a cushion – one of my pilots, Lt Hap Langstaff, used to have two of them in there in order to be able to push the rudder pedals further forward.

'We were based at Munda, New Georgia, for three or four weeks and I

It would appear that Bob Owens did, however, use this machine – F4U-1 'No 75' – quite frequently, however. Although VMF-215 pilots did not have aircraft assigned to them, Bob Owens flew another F4U-1 – BuNo 17927 – on 13 consecutive missions, during one of which he gained two victories on 14 January 1944. He also flew another F4U-1 – BuNo 02656 – on 12 different missions, during which he gained one victory and a probable on 21 and 12 August 1943, respectively (*National Archives*)

don't remember ever seeing my bed during the daytime. When we were flying in and out of there, the ground forces were still fighting. During that time Lt W D Demming was shot down in a very unusual way. As he was coming around in to land he was hit by an enemy artillery shell. They aimed at him purposely, and I heard they painted an American flag on the side of the gun! He managed to bail out of the plane but ruined his arm and was evacuated to the US. We never heard from him again.

'On 15 August 1943 we were covering the Marines landing at Vella Lavella. We were way up at altitude and up through the clouds came four Zeros. We went down after them, and as much as I'd been trying to instill into everybody (including myself) "don't shoot until you get right up on them", I started firing about a quarter of a mile away. By the time I got up close to them I'd expended my ammo and I didn't hit a soul.'

Conant claimed six kills with VMF-215 flying as Bob Owens' wingman, before going on to lead his own section. On 30 August 1943 he was on ground alert at Munda with his F4U when Ken Walsh appeared and 'stole' it. Walsh's F4U-1 (BuNo 02585) had a supercharger problem, so he landed at Munda and Capt Neefus, CO of VMF-215 gave him permission to take a readied F4U as a replacement (*Conant Collection*)

Conant – 'One of our most important tasks was bomber escort. On a typical mission we would have 50 to 70 planes stacked at three different levels – low medium and high cover. The medium cover would sometimes fly very close to the bombers, at the same level or just below them. Our divisions were made up of two pairs which would continuously weave back and forth. As a result, we always had somebody facing outwards ready for an attack. If we had spare F4Us available after a number of our aircraft had been assigned for a mission, we would also send up an extra division that we called "Roving Cover". These pilots could go anywhere they chose and could attack the enemy ahead of our formation.

'At the beginning (when I only had around 250 hours of flight time) the only thing I knew how to do was fly wing. So I'm flying wing on Bob and I'm only ten feet away. He's out shooting at planes, and the only thing I saw all day was him! We decided that I wasn't doing either of us any good just sitting on his wing so we loosened up a little bit – when he'd turn, I'd cut inside, etc. We made a mission up to Kahili escorting B-24s, weaving back and forth. After hitting the target they flew into the clouds. Once you fly into clouds, you don't get any more cover. We were free to go. Bob takes off; shooting at Zeros with me following behind him. The thing was, he was shooting and other people were tailing in on him. So when they got behind him, I'd be right behind them. I shot two of them off his tail at that time, one of which was a *Tony* (Kawasaki Ki 61).'

Owens – 'Once, we followed a B-24 down close to the water that had been shot up over Rabaul. There were two Zeros down there, and they were being flown in true fashion, being able to turn on a dime. There was also a Corsair tucked in close to the B-24. We came down from altitude making pretty good speed. I got behind one of them and followed him. He just pulled right up and kept going. I kept going after him shooting, but I never hit him. When he got to the top of his climb, we both ran out of everything. At that point I was out of speed and all

Conant destroyed a Zero on 14 January 1944 whilst flying F4U-1 'No 590', BuNo 17590, during a mission to Rabaul escorting SBDs and TBFs. Conant began the mission at Barakoma, then flew to Torokina to refuel before heading to Rabaul. The F4U was photographed whilst undergoing maintenance at Vella Lavella on 10 December 1943 (*via Jim Sullivan*)

Another view of F4U-1 'No 590', this time at Munda. It appears to be wearing a field-applied three-tone scheme, together with field-applied white bars on the national insignia. The machine lacks the curved glazed area directly aft of the canopy which was standard to most of the early 'bird cage' canopy-equipped aircraft. It is also fitted with the shorter aerial mast located aft of the cockpit, rather than the tall forward-mounted type associated with early production aircraft (*via Jim Sullivan*)

I was worried about was staying alive. He stalled I guess, and came back down. As he passed by me he was only 50 ft away, and I could see his guns flashing. There I was out of everything, and all I was trying to do was get that F4U flying again. I didn't hit him at all, so I wasn't the world's greatest shot after all!'

Conant – 'At that point Bob decided it was time to get up in the clouds. We both headed up and Bob made it. I'm going up hanging on the prop, just about to make it in, and there's a Zero over on the left. He's shooting like mad. "Shit, I ain't gonna' make it with this guy shooting at me." I just pushed it straight over and I got away too. Air combat is not a highly disciplined affair.'

Owens – 'On one mission we ended up being credited with half a plane destroyed. VF-17 was involved I think. We were escorting a B-25 flight from New Guinea on a mission to Rabaul. It got off to a bad start as we were not warned that the bombers were coming. For intelligence we had what we called "Indian Talkers". Because everybody was breaking everybody else's code, we got these guys from some tribe to come over from the US. We would have Indians on each of the islands. They would radio information back and forth by "Indian Talk". You almost couldn't break it as there was no rhyme or reason to what they said. The Indians screwed up that day and the B-25s appeared right over us, unannounced. They made one turn over Torokina and headed off to the target without escort. We were manning planes like crazy to try to catch up with them.

'We passed them coming back after they'd hit their target. The weather was not all that good. We broke out into what I call an amphitheatre, as you could see everything within a big clear area. I only saw three Japanese planes. I was shooting at one of these three and another plane came right down in between us. Finally, I said to myself "If you want to stay alive, you better get the hell out of here". We had 40+ aeroplanes trying to shoot these three little Japanese machines. I pulled off to the side and I saw two of them go down into the water and crash. The third little guy, from my perspective, actually got shot at by all 40+ aircraft. He finally went right down to just above the water. All of a sudden he hit the water and just blew up. Later, there were about ten people arguing over who shot him down. So somebody decided that we would get half the credit and so would the other unit.'

Conant – 'Although I was on the same 18 January 1944 mission as Bob, and it sounds like the same incident in which I was involved, it

Roger Conant destroyed another Zero on 18 January 1944 whilst flying this machine, F4U-1A 'No 735', BuNo 17735. The aircraft was pictured at Bougainville during February painted in a very stained three-tone scheme, with field-modified national insignia (*National Archives*)

isn't. Smitty, Jake Knight and I were a threesome that day, and the B-25s were coming out just as we were going in. We caught these three planes and they were going the other way. I'd shoot at one and he'd take off in one direction with either Smitty or Jake going after him. I'd shoot at another one and he'd go off in another direction and the other pilot would finish him off. I shot the third one and hit him good. I hit him right in the cockpit – blew the hell out of him. He circled around and I stayed with him. I pulled up alongside of him and we were only 50 ft above the water. My last vision of him was of his arms up protecting his face, with flames coming out of his engine. I didn't see him go in. This sounds so similar but it isn't because there were only three of us shooting at these planes. The interesting thing about this combat was the calibre of the Japanese pilots encountered. We had caught three of them. Only six months earlier three good pilots would have gotten' away, and they would have been shooting back at us, but we got all three of them. Furthermore, as we pulled out of this thing and all reformed, when we looked up, there were *five* Zeros all sitting in a little column above us. They had obviously seen us, and they must have seen the other guys go in. They were above us while we were low, slow and out of ammunition. They had us dead to rights, but we just turned around, got into a wild scissors and flew out. They never bothered us.'

VMF-215 personnel pictured at Vella Lavella. Bob Owens, at centre, was at that time recuperating after being shot down by his own wingman on 24 January 1944. Although initially given credit for the kill, Roger Conant (front, far left of picture) was not responsible for Bob's unplanned swim in Simpson Harbour, Rabaul (*Conant Collection*)

Owens – 'I was shot down on 24 January, but there's no mention of it in my log-book whatsoever. Roger Conant flew wing with me for a long while. When he quit flying wing he commanded a second section. One mission, when we were heading up to attack Rabaul, I had a kid flying wing – he was a really young guy. This was his first combat mission. The new guys coming out were 18 or 19 and we had to take care of them. I called them kids because I was an old man of 24! As was our custom, if there was a new guy in the outfit we'd let him fly out front. This was because the guys at the back would get hit harder if we were attacked. We were flying on a real economical power setting so that we would save all our fuel for when we got there. We were observing radio silence, but after a while this young boy finally said in a meek voice, "Skipper. Could you throttle back a little? I can't keep up". I knew who it was, and I looked over in his direction. I knew he was nervous and I motioned to him and throttled back.

'The way our attacks worked, we'd escort TBM Avengers or SBD Dauntlesses and they'd be down below us. They would go in low and we would do a big circle around

VMF-215 pilots pose next to a derelict Nakajima Ki 43 *Oscar*. This was the JAAF's most widely used fighter, and would appear to have been commonly mistaken for the Navy's Zero by Allied airmen judging by the official loss records of both Japanese services. Like most enemy aircraft, the *Oscar* was highly manoeuvrable, but it was lightly armed and lacked armour protection – unless flown by an experienced pilot, it was easy prey for the Corsair (*Conant Collection*)

them as they dived down. That particular day the Zeros were up there. The *Vals* were rolling over and peeling off to attack the ships anchored in the harbour. As we were going down, believe it or not, this kid passed me about three times. By this time I'm running wide open, and I've got the throttle pushed forward all the way to the firewall. I was really going and he couldn't stay behind me, when before he hadn't been able to keep up!

Three of VMF-215's high scoring aces pictured together at Bougainville in early 1944. From left to right, 1st Lt Robert M Hanson (25 victories and 2 probables – two of his kills took place when he was with VMF-214), Capt Donald N Aldrich (20 victories and 6 probables) and Capt Harold L Spears (15 victories and 3 probables) (*USMC via Pete Mersky*)

'Coming off the target, our tactic was to get around behind the bombers. Most of our planes would get in this position to cover any lagging planes; that's where the danger was. I pulled up, making a wide circle around so I would be behind the last guy. Lo and behold, right in front of me was a type of plane that I'd never seen before. Later I found out it was called a *Tony*, but at that time I thought it was a Bf 109. I was going much faster than this aeroplane – he was trying to get in behind the stragglers. I pulled in behind him, but I guess I screwed around a little more than what I should have, only managing to get in a short burst. He was turning, I was turning, and when I hit him again the wing came off at the root. I flipped as hard as I could to get away. Instead of just going down, the lift from just one wing flipped him up and over the same way. I had to change my direction in a hurry from going one way to getting the hell over the other way. Suddenly, there was a hell of a commotion and I was on fire. I was still a little way over the harbour at Rabaul. I got down to the water and all the guys threw their dye-markers on me. A PBY picked me up in 30 minutes. The word got out that my wingman had shot me down, which I'm sure he did. He'd been behind me and was shooting at the same guy. I know he didn't intend to do it as I flew right into where he was shooting, but he shouldn't have been shooting! I'm 99 per cent sure that's what happened, but I didn't ever say anything as it would have caused a lot of problems. They all thought it was Conant.'

Conant – 'The word went down to Headquarters that Bob's wingman had shot him down. The guy down at Headquarters had been with the squadron and knew that I was his wingman. So I got credit for shooting him down. The first *Tony* that *I* ever saw was when Bob was leading a division up the "Canal". One flew right in front of us. We were so surprised he was gone before we ever knew it. He probably never even saw us.'

1st Lt Hanson poses next to his battle-damaged F4U. This official USMC photograph is dated 4 August 1943, and claims the Japanese opponent responsible for the 20 mm cannon hits was a Zero which Hanson then shot down. On that date he scored his first victory, and his opponent was in fact a *Tony* – Hanson was then serving with VMF-214 (*USMC via Pete Mersky*)

THE 'BLACK SHEEP' SQUADRON

VMF-214 first made the transition to Corsairs in June 1943, whilst commanded by Maj H A Ellis. The squadron was to become famous under the command of Maj Gregory 'Pappy' Boyington (28 kills, 22 in F4Us). The 'Black Sheep' produced nine aces, among them the then 1st Lt (later Captain) Edwin Lawrence Olander. He gained five victories and four probables flying the Corsair during two tours with VMF-214, and recounts his varied combat experiences in the following interview.

'I was a "civilian soldier" – I began training as a naval aviator a few months prior to Pearl Harbor and returned to civilian life at the end of 1945. My military experiences were happy and exciting ones, but I never harboured a desire or intention to make the military a career. My flight training was primarily at Pensacola, after which I was assigned instructor's duty at Jacksonville Naval Air Station. Flying SNJs, my instructing consisted primarily of escorting a half-dozen pilots on a course out over the Atlantic and supervising the passes they made at a towed sleeve firing live ammunition. From a position about 1000 ft above the tow plane, and considerably forward of it, they would, one by one, turn back towards the sleeve and at the appropriate time roll into a dive and fire at the banner, returning to the formation to repeat the process.

Maj Gregory Boyington, CO of VMF-214, is handed baseball caps in exchange for kill decals whilst in the cockpit of F4U-1A 'No 740' (BuNo 17740) by second-ranking 'Black Sheep' ace 1st Lt Chris Magee (9 kills). VMF-214 pilots were to receive a cap from a World Series player for every Japanese aircraft downed (*USMC*)

'Pappy' Boyington with other VMF-214 pilots. He claimed 22 victories and 4 probables with the Corsair, preceded by six claims with the AVG in China. On 3 January 1944 whilst flying an aircraft loaned to him by Marion E Carl, his squadron was engaged by Zeros of the 204th and 253rd *Kokutai* near Cape St George, New Ireland. He claimed three Zeros whilst his then wingman, Capt George M Ashmun, scored another victory. In turn, they were both shot down, with Boyington remaining a PoW for the rest of the war (*via Pete Mersky*)

F4U-1A 'No 883', BuNo 17883, was occasionally flown by Boyington, as well as by his wingman Robert W McClurg. The latter became an ace on 23 December 1943 when he destroyed two Zeros over St George Channel. He went on to claim a total of seven confirmed victories and two probables, and following his service with VMF-214 returned to the US as a fighter instructor (*National Archives*)

I would critique and rate their performance and we would discuss the results when examining the sleeve for hits back at base. Besides this target shooting we did other things such as night formation flying and a little bit of one-on-one dogfighting, a skill we never used when later tangling with Japanese Zeros – they were much too manoeuvrable for us to engage in dogfights. Because of my instructor's duties, when I shipped out to the South Pacific in the spring of 1943 I had about 600 hours in the air, versus the 200 common for many when faced with combat. With these extra hours came increased self-confidence.

'In Espiritu Santo, in the New Hebrides, I was assigned to a pool of pilots. We were there to replace other pilots lost in combat or rotated back to the USA. However, the need soon arose for another fighter squadron in the ongoing Solomon Campaign. The then Maj Gregory Boyington, who had experience with the American Volunteer Group in China, was available for command, and thus VMF-214 was reconstituted in the field at Espiritu. The "training" we did during the few weeks before we flew to the Solomons, and combat, was really a misnomer. Some of the pilots had scarcely flown the F4U and so they had checkout and familiarisation flights. Boyington went out with all of us in two or three four-plane divisions at a time so as to judge what kind of a hand he'd been dealt when the pilots were selected from the roster. Mostly he sat and talked with us, telling us what to expect in the weeks ahead. In September 1943 we headed the 548 nautical miles north to Guadalcanal to join the aerial assaults on Bougainville.

'There were 28 of us, all pilots except for an intelligence officer (Frank E Walton) and a squadron doctor (Jim Reames). We had no ancillary personnel, and no planes assigned to us – throughout our two combat-tour existence we "borrowed" the Corsairs we flew, and the services of those who cared for them. Having no planes of our own, we simply climbed into any machine made available to us and took off, Boyington included. In the Solomons all I flew was the F4U-1, the old "birdcage" model, with its restricted visibility canopy.

'After six weeks of daily combat flights over Bougainville (mostly from Munda, New Georgia) we repaired to Espiritu again to reform. When we returned to the Solomons in November our roster had increased to 40. Once again we were all pilots except for the same intelligence officer and doctor. By this time the airfields and the Japanese air power over Bougainville had become impotent. A landing on the west coast of Bougainville had resulted in a perimeter sufficiently large enough to contain an airstrip on which fighter planes could top off their gas tanks

1st Lt John F Bolt, Jr, an ace with six victories, devised a new system of ammunition belting for VMF-214. He was convinced that the standard belt loading of one incendiary and one tracer, followed by an armour-piercing, was not the most effective arrangement for destroying Japanese aircraft that lacked protective armour. Whilst at Espiritu he carried out tests firing machine guns at wrecked aircraft and oil drums filled with gasoline, proving that the armour-piercing round was unnecessary. VMF-124 later eliminated the armour-piercing, instead using five or six incendiaries to one tracer. Other squadrons soon adopted the same loading, bringing about a temporary shortage of incendiary rounds in the Pacific (*Bolt Collection*)

Capt Edwin L Olander claimed five confirmed victories and four probables (all Zeros) from mid-September to the end of December 1943 whilst with VMF-214 (*Olander Collection*)

before attacking Rabaul, which had become our new target. We were now based back at Vella Lavella, for it was unsafe to house planes overnight on the small Bougainville perimeter which was in range of Japanese artillery back in the mountains.

'Attacking Bougainville, we flew cover for B-24 bombers and for SBD dive-bombers, as well as strafing targets of opportunity. When flying cover for B-24s, which had much more range than us, they would fly to Guadalcanal and we'd rendezvous with them over our home base (Munda, New Georgia, when the target was Bougainville, or the Empress Augusta Bay strip on Bougainville when the target was Rabaul). Customarily, there would be up to six layers of fighter cover from, say, 15,000 to 26,000 ft, with specific altitude assignments for everyone, and the four-plane divisions would weave above the bomber formation all the way to target, or until intercepted by the enemy. The same description applied when the flat-bombers were B-25s.

F4U-1 'No 576' *Marine's Dream*, BuNo 02576, in which Ed Olander claimed a Zero on 17 October 1943 during a fighter sweep to Kahili. The aircraft is seen in December following an accident at Torokina. It has a field-applied three-tone paint scheme, and utilises the last three digits of the BuNo as an aircraft number. The national insignia has also been field-modified with the addition of white bars without a blue surround (*USMC*)

F4U-1 'No 93', BuNo 17430, waits at 'Scramble Alert' at Espiritu Santo, New Hebrides. Ed Olander flew a shuttle mission in this aircraft from Vella Lavella to Torokina, and from there a CAP sortie on 5 January 1944 (*National Archives via Pete Mersky*)

F4U-1A Corsair BuNo 17736 of VMF-216 following battle damage sustained on a mission to Rabaul on 10 January 1944. VMF-216 claimed 27.33 victories (all with the Corsair) mostly on missions to Rabaul (*USMC*)

Corsair pilots scramble for their aircraft at Guadalcanal in early 1943. F4U-1 'No 68' wears a field-applied three-tone scheme and field-applied bars on the national insignia. The curved glazed area aft of the early 'bird cage' canopy has been sealed on this particular machine (*via Pete Mersky*)

'Rabaul was too distant for the SBD dive-bomber to reach, but going to Bougainville we provided them with pretty much the same staggered cover, with one crucial difference. The SBD was at its most vulnerable once it had completed its dive and dropped its bombs. It had insignificant speed and no power to regain altitude. Besides the fighter cover the SBD's only protection was a single .30 cal weapon operated by the rear-seat gunner, who literally went into combat on his back, looking up. Gawd, I felt sorry for those fellows! Our job was to weave over them all the way down and protect them as they made their way home – hard flying for all of us. VMF-214 was, of course, not the only squadron present. Usually planes from four to six Marine squadrons would be involved, as well as a couple of Navy squadrons flying F6Fs and New Zealanders flying P-40s.

F4U-1s and F4U-1As of VMF-216 are lined up next to the newly completed runway on the first day of operations at Torokina Point, Bougainville, on 10 December 1943. Sea-Bees had quickly carved three strips out of the jungle following the landings at Empress Augusta Bay. The landings were hotly contested by the Japanese as part of Operation *Ro.* During a 16-day period, ending 17 November 1943, they lost 191 aircraft from units based at Rabaul, and from the remnants of their carrier air fleets (*USMC*)

F4U-1s warm up prior to a mission at Torokina Point on 10 February 1944. There was a concerted effort by the Japanese to oust the Americans from their new base, and on 8 March shells began falling on the airfield which led to the nightly evacuation of aircraft to avoid destruction. Machines from the base flew ground attack missions against the attackers, whose offensive finally ended on 24 March (*USMC*)

Marine Corps personnel relax on the beach at Torokina Point whilst an F4U-1A departs in the background. There were three airstrips at Torokina, one right next to the beach and two more inland at Piva Uncle and Piva Yoke for bombers and fighters respectively (*National Archives via Pete Mersky*)

'Most fun of all were the fighter sweeps when we flew over their airfields to "pick a fight" – i.e., engage any enemy planes which chose to come up to meet us. Often, it was wild! Except for strafing missions the fighter sweep was the only other primary function of the fighter plane. My best description of a fighter sweep is: a bully goes into a school yard with a chip on his shoulder and says "Let's fight". Boyington led us on many of these and if we met no enemy planes over their bases he'd taunt them via radio to come up and fight. They always did and it was always a wild melée which defied description. Japanese supply lines were stretched and it was harder and harder for them to replace lost planes and pilots. Our fighter sweeps were designed to hasten the attrition, and they succeeded. Our trips to Rabaul

A relieved Maj Thomas M Coles of VMF-212 with his F4U-1A, BuNo 17937, at Vella Lavella on 20 January, 1944. He successfully landed his aeroplane even though the rudder had been shot away during an air battle over Rabaul. Three days later he got his revenge by shooting down two Zeros over Duke of York Island. VMF-212 gained a total of 127.5 victories with the F4F and F4U, all bar two of which were claimed in the South West Pacific theatre (*USMC*)

were the same. The island was a mighty fortress, being Japan's Pearl Harbor in the South Pacific, with planes coming up to greet us from four airfields. Its loss would be a very serious blow to the Japanese, and we witnessed this in the intensity of their fighting.

'Boyington was shot down in St George Channel, near Rabaul, in early January 1944, only to reappear from a Japanese prison camp at war's end. Soon thereafter, our squadron returned to Espiritu where it was soon deactivated. The "number" was sent back to the mainland where the squadron was reformed. Along with other "Black Sheep" pilots, I was assigned to VMF-211 and we did a tour based on the Green Islands, near Rabaul. I saw no more air combat, but we continued to be shot at as we patrolled New Ireland and the northern tip of New Britain around Rabaul, but that tour was relatively unexciting.

'Returning briefly to "Pappy" Boyington, whom we squadron mates were more likely to address as "Greg", "Skipper" or "Gramps" – he answered to them all – I can

1st Lt Harold E Segal of VMF-221 pictured next to his Corsair on Russell Island on 17 July 1943. At this time he had five victories, but went on to claim a further seven bringing his total to twelve. His last two victories occurred on 24 January 1944 whilst he was with VMF-211. VMF-221 were credited with 155 kills, whilst VMF-211 claimed 91.5 (*USMC via Pete Mersky*)

Capt James E Swett of VMF-221 claimed a total of 15.5 victories and was awarded the Congressional Medal of Honor. He shot down seven *Val*s during a two-hour period on 7 April 1943 whilst flying the Wildcat, and went on to claim a further 8.5 kills in the F4U (*USMC via Pete Mersky*)

Capt Donald L Balch sits beside his Corsair. He served with VMF-221 for the entire war, gaining two victories in the Solomons and another three whilst on the USS *Bunker Hill*. 'On 6 July 1943 my division was directed from the Russell Islands to New Georgia. There we were jumped by several Zeros which we broke up like a covey of quail, each division going in a different direction. I got onto the tail of one Zero and shot him down. I then started looking for the other members of my division whilst simultaneously patting myself on the back for my splendid marksmanship. All of a sudden all hell broke loose, with part of my hatch disintegrating along with some of the instruments in front of me. I immediately "split S'ed" out to the left and down, pulling out at around 6000 ft, never having seen anything. My wingman joined up with me and, because I couldn't hear anything on my radio, kept pointing at my tail. We then turned home and flew back to our base. I put my gear and flaps down on final, but I lost complete control of the aircraft on flare out. I cut the power and slammed into the runway. We found later that my controls had been badly shot up, just holding together until the moment I flared out for my landing' – Balch (*Balch Collection*)

F4U-1 Corsair 'No 465' of VMF-222 has its prop 'run through' prior to flying a mission from Green Island in 1944. This unit gained 50 victories in the South West Pacific, before participating in the Philippines campaign and then moving on to Okinawa on 22 May 1945. There, it gained its last three victories of the war (*via Jim Sullivan*)

say this with conviction, that when countries are facing a crisis such as war, inevitably some men step forward and lead when leadership is most needed. Greg Boyington was such a man. He inspired those 50 of us in his VMF-214 to achieve over and above our own most optimistic expectations. He also inspired others in squadrons with whom we fought side by side. He may have been a roughneck of sorts, he may have consumed too much whisky too often and he may not have been the classic officer and a gentleman, but he loved and supported the men with whom he fought. And, on a daily basis, he provided a quality of leadership of which few others were capable. The pity is, I guess, that he was never able to reach the heights he could have. I'm grateful that I knew Greg Boyington at his best – in combat.'

F4U-1As on a mission fly high over Espiritu Santo during March 1944 (*USMC*)

US NAVY CORSAIRS

The first US Navy unit to receive the F4U was VF-12, commanded by Lt 'Jumpin' Joe' Clifton – the squadron began to receive aeroplanes in October 1942. As the pilots trained in their new aircraft serious problems emerged that were to effect the operational deployment of the F4U. Trials aboard USS *Sangamon* showed that the aircraft was, at that time, ill-suited to carrier operations. The problems largely related to its deck landing and taxying characteristics. The undercarriage legs were found to have overly stiff oleos and would require modification to eliminate the aircraft's tendency to bounce on touchdown. There was also a tendency for a wing to drop on approach, this being due to torque stall. Bad visibility from the early 'bird cage' canopy was further decreased by oil leaking from the hydraulically actuated cowl flaps. Modifications had to be quickly introduced on the Chance Vought production line to alleviate these problems.

When VF-12 finally deployed to the Pacific they gave up their F4Us in exchange for F6F Hellcats, despite having become carrier qualified on the Corsair in April 1943 aboard USS *Saratoga*. By that time the Navy was equipping all its carrier-based fighter units with the F6F, and only had logistic support for the Grumman fighter. Because of this one-type only maintenance and spares set up adopted by the fleet, the Navy decided to deploy its third Corsair squadron, VF-17 'Jolly Rogers', as a land-based unit. They duly became only the second Corsair-equipped Navy squadron operating in-theatre, following in the footsteps of Lt Cdr W J 'Gus' Widhelm's VF(N)-75, who had commenced operations with F4U-2 Corsair nightfighters from Munda on 11 September. This unit consisted of just six pilots, but all of these men had performed

Early F4U-1 Corsairs of VF-12 on a training mission in the US in late 1942 (*via Phil Jarrett*)

F4U-1 Corsair '17-F-13' of VF-17 is seen just after a landing during the unit's Carrier Qualification cruise. The aircraft has the new three-tone scheme applied, but with the early style national insignia. It bears four kill marks, victories claimed by Lt(jg) James A Halford during his earlier service at Guadalcanal flying the F4F Wildcat. He was detached by VF-17 due to combat fatigue, gaining no further victories in the Corsair (*via Jim Sullivan*)

F4U-1 Corsair '17-F-24' of VF-17 on its back following a carrier landing mishap aboard USS *Bunker Hill* in August 1943. Although the early Corsairs (especially the 'bird cage' canopy version) were difficult to land on board a carrier, both VFs -12 and -17 did become carrier qualified in the type. Modifications to the oleos were made by VF-17 during their deployment to *Bunker Hill* which overcame the aircraft's tendency to bounce on touchdown. Nevertheless, neither unit went into combat with their Corsairs aboard a carrier, VF-12 exchanging their F4Us for Hellcats, whilst VF-17 deployed as a land-based squadron (*via Jim Sullivan*)

at least one prior combat tour, Widhelm, for example, having previously flown SBDs – most of his pilots had 2000 hours flying time on average. The Navy's wish to deploy VF(N)-75 in full squadron strength was scuppered by manufacturing delays in the construction of the hand-built radar sets fitted in the specially modified F4U-2s.

Suffering no such problems with their 'plain' F4U-1s, Lt Cdr Tom Blackburn's (11 kills) VF-17 arrived at Ondonga on 27 October 1943. They were soon to make a name for themselves during the Solomons Campaign, being officially credited with shooting down an incredible 154 enemy aircraft in just 79 days. Blackburn had chosen Lt Cdr Roger Hedrick (12 kills) to serve as VF-17's Executive Officer (XO) when the unit was formed in early in the year. The latter had completed flight school in 1936, and had gone on to serve with a number of frontline squadrons before joining VF-17 at its inception. Known as 'Rog' to all and sundry, Hedrick served with the unit for its entire combat career. In the following interview he describes his combat experiences in the Corsair.

'We sailed from Norfolk in September 1943 aboard the *Bunker Hill* for our shake down cruise, becoming carrier qualified in the early 'bird cage' model. The Air Group Commander and higher command were all happy with our performance. We soon received the F4U-1A model which was a great improvement over the earlier "bird cage" type with its lower seat. With all that canopy framing and sitting so low it was difficult with a 12 ft nose out in front of you to see a flag waver when coming aboard ship. While at sea we received a despatch ordering us to report to ComAirSols and become a land-based squadron. Naturally we were greatly disap-

F4U-1A Corsair 'No 1' *BIG HOG*, BuNo 17629, flown by Lt Cdr John T Blackburn, is seen at Ondonga after his fourth victory, which was scored on 11 November 1943. As well as four kill marks the aircraft also has four patched bullet holes, visible to the right of the aircraft number. These were the result of Blackburn's XO, Roger Hedrick, mistaking him for a Zero. The personnel are, from left to right, Wharton, Guttenhurst, March, Jr (5 kills), Blackburn, Dr Hermann and Cpl J M Taylor – the identities of the remaining two groundcrew remain a mystery (*via Pete Mersky*)

pointed, having worked hard with Chance Vought representatives to overcome some of the basically minor difficulties that any new plane has. Nobody told us at the time that the reason for the change was that we were the first Corsair squadron on board a ship in the fleet and had we blown some tyres or had to land on a different carrier there would be no spare parts for us as there were none in the logistics chain. The Marines had been based in the Solomons since February, so they did have logistic support for the Corsair. Our first base in the Solomons was to be Ondonga, 50 miles northeast of Guadalcanal. We later moved to Bougainville, from where we launched attacks against Rabaul.

'My first kill occurred on 1 November 1943 when we were covering the landings at Empress Augusta Bay, Bougainville. I was due to go on station at about 1300 to relieve Tommy Blackburn as top cover. Shortly after leaving Ondonga with eight planes we heard the Fighter Director at Bougainville talking about a Japanese strike coming in. We speeded up to maximum climb and just at that moment my generator went out, so I turned my radio off to conserve battery power. By the time we approached the southern end of Bougainville we were at 20,000 ft. In the distance towards Buka, where there were some Japanese airfields, I saw three tiny little dots and I knew that we didn't have anybody over there. I got up sun, towards Rabaul, and got above them. They didn't see us and I was able to make an easy high side run on them. I rocked my wings rather than notify my flight over the radio; I wasn't sure if my guns would fire. In fact, I planned to just use the four inboard guns rather than the full six; I wasn't sure if there was even enough power for those. This was our first combat and I was alone out front. I had a good look at these jokers, I saw the red meatball and knew for sure that they were the enemy. Coming down I picked out the leader. We had our guns boresighted to 900 ft – at that point the wingspan of the Zero filled the 50 mm ring of our gun sight. Knowing that their gas tanks were in the wing root I tried to hit that area. In this particular case, which was like almost all the others that followed, I pressed the trigger for two to four seconds and she went up like a torch. As soon as mine went up they all "split S'ed" and headed for the deck. We kept them away from Tommy Blackburn's flight by chasing them for a while, but that was about all we got out of it.

'One week later we were directed out to intercept a large Japanese strike – bombers escorted by 29 fighters. It was the first occasion that I experienced when our radar was effective. Again I had six planes with me flying top cover above Empress Augusta Bay. We again got above them – they were flying in three-plane sections and they hadn't spotted us. I remember thinking, "Here's when we find out how good the F4U is". Diving down on them, we passed through the formation and I was astounded to seem them break up into two Lufbery circles, a completely defensive tactic devised during World War 1 by the first truly American ace of them all, Maj Raoul Lufbery (17 kills). All they needed to do was spread out, as they had a higher rate of climb than we did, at least at low altitude. We chased them and made runs across the circles and after a couple of passes they broke up. All of them against six of us. We took on one after another, and I was involved in a series of head-on runs, making three or four individual passes. I was hitting each of them in turn, and I could see pieces of their engines coming off, about two cylinders at a time, flying by me. But

Lt Cdr Roger R Hedrick, XO of VF-17, relaxes in the cockpit of F4U-1A 'No 17' BuNo 18005. He gained nine victories with the unit (all Zeros) using three different 'No 17s'. His first three were gained on 1, 11 and 17 November 1943 in F4U-1A BuNo 17659, whilst the next three occurred on 26, 28 and 30 January 1944 in F4U-1A BuNo 55798. His last three were gained in this aircraft featured here on 18 February (*Hedrick Collection*)

Hedrick again seen with Corsair 'No 17' BuNo 18005. The 'skull and cross bones' motif on the fuselage was not actually carried on this aircraft – it was scratched onto the negative for publicity purposes! It only carried the standard motif on the cowling, similar to other aircraft in the unit (*Hedrick Collection*)

F4U-1As of VF-17 fly in close formation. The nearest aircraft was piloted by Lt(jg) Ira C Kepford (16 victories), 'No 8' by Lt(jg) Earl May (8 victories) and 'No 3' by Lt(jg) Frederick J Streig (5 victories). All of these machines lack antenna masts, the second two having a whip aerial instead of a spine-mounted mast (*Chance Vought*)

I never saw anyone of them open fire on me. There were no fire flashes along the wings or from the prop area. We chased each other until their survivors headed back towards Rabaul and we headed back home.

'On 11 November our mission was to cover a Task Group consisting of three carriers that was to hit Rabaul. We put our tail hooks back on our planes, which we had taken off to lighten them slightly. Our job was to fly out to the Task Group and cover them while they launched their own planes, which were to strike against shipping and airfields at Rabaul and the Simpson Harbour area. We got up before dawn and again we observed radio silence. There was a certain amount of cloud cover and we were hard pushed to even find the Task Group, although we knew fairly well where they were. We did locate them at about 0900 and landed aboard shortly after they'd launched their aeroplanes. VF-17 and an F6F squadron were providing cover for the ships, and I went aboard *Essex*, flagship of the Task Group Commander, with half the squadron, whilst Tommy Blackburn went aboard our old fiend *Bunker Hill* with the rest of the unit. At 1300 we launched again, as this was the time we expected the Japs to attack. A very large raid that came in from Rabaul and some of our boys did a great job by stopping their attack planes from getting through to the carriers. I was again involved in a big melée that went on for quite some time. My wingman and I were chasing one lone Zero that was heading back to Rabaul. This guy kept managing to escape into a cloud, just about keeping outside of firing range, so we'd have to wait for him to emerge – this was repeated time and again, I was primed waiting for him to reappear. Suddenly, a plane appeared and I set myself up for a full deflection shot. Just as I pressed the trigger, I realised I was shooting at an F4U. I instantly released the trigger and I couldn't see if I had had any effect on the plane at all. Then we did a join up signal and the F4U joined up on me. I was then looking at *BIG HOG*, F4U-1A "No 1" – my CO's aeroplane!

'I didn't know if I'd touched him until we landed at the field where we had to refuel before heading down to Ondonga. Then he showed me these damn holes in his plane. He said "You lousy shot, Roger. When those six .50s hit me, it moved the plane sideways". That's all he ever said to me about it. I never guessed that Tommy would be hiding out in the cloud – he'd been hit by about four or five Zeros and his windshield had fogged over. Being practically blind he'd ducked into the cloud to wait for his canopy to clear.

Lt Merl W 'Butch' Davenport with his F4U-1A 'No 9' at Bougainville in February 1944. The aircraft bears five kill marks (only four are visible) following Davenport's victory over a Zero on the 5th – he had previously been credited with a quarter share in the destruction of a *Betty* on 6 November, followed by two Zeros on the 21st and another pair on 30 January 1944. Davenport went onto claim a further Zero to bring his total number of confirmed victories to 6.25 (*Killefer Collection*)

'We found that about 80 Japanese aircraft were always up above us, waiting for our arrival. Every day, regular as clockwork, a fresh group would come in from Rabaul. Our bosses at ComAirSols who were responsible for the strikes going into Rabaul had to provide a certain number of fighters to protect the bombers going in. We escorted Navy dive- and torpedo-bombers, as well as USAAF B-24s and B-25s. We would provide 16 planes on a given strike, and if we had more in commission that weren't required then Tommy Blackburn and others came up with the idea to send up extra fighters to surprise the Japanese by getting above them for a change. At Rabaul they had four active airfields whilst on Bougainville we only had the one strip on the 125-mile long island. The Japanese coast-watchers would radio a warning telling the defences how many aircraft we had and when to expect us. As we approached the target we would see clouds of dust on their fields indicating that their fighters were coming up to meet us. The pattern of cover over the bombers took the form of three layers. Marine F4Us and Navy Hellcat squadrons flew below us whilst VF-17 was invariably in the top cover position – the first one the Japs had to come through. The fact that we had to be tied there when the enemy was always coming down on us got a little frustrating after a while, so we usually sent four, but on occasion two, aeroplanes to patrol outside of the main strike group, coming in low from another direction so as not to be picked up on radar. They would then climb up to as high as 35,000 ft, whilst the Japanese were usually at around 20,000 ft, although one time we paid the penalty for having this height advantage as the oil in our guns froze up – I was making some runs and nothing happened, so I had to turn the lead over to somebody else, which really annoyed me.

'I was pumping those charges as fast as I could. We were able to surprise the defenders as they were totally unsuspecting. They never bothered to look up above, being dependant on their fighter directors down below for help. I was once leading the top cover flight when we had four of our boys go on ahead. Approaching the target I looked up and two burning Zeros came down out of the clouds, almost as if they were flying in formation. Then came two more followed by yet another pair. There were just two Corsairs up there, one being flown by Ike Kepford (16 kills), and they were doing a wonderful job. We then knew that we wouldn't have to contend with quite so many of the enemy. It was a very effective tactic.

'In a January 1944 I found myself totally alone, lagging behind everybody else when we were heading back home. I encountered a Zero heading back to land at Rabaul – we weren't far off shore over Simpson Harbour. He was doing what I considered to be a victory roll and I thought "That son-of-a-bitch isn't gonna' get away with that", so I went after him and clobbered him. As usual his aircraft burst into

Lt(jg) Doris C 'Chico' Freeman with his F4U-1A 'No 34' at Ondonga in November 1943. The aircraft bears two kill marks following his victories over two Zeros on 21 November. He only claimed two further probables with the unit, but later became a 9-kill ace with VF-84 in 1945. Freeman lost his life on 11 May 1945 when USS *Bunker Hill* was struck by a *kamikaze* (*Killefer Collection*)

F4U-1A Corsair 'No 5', BuNo 17656, flown by Lt(jg) Tom Killefer. The aircraft was pictured on Nissan Island (in the Green Island group) following a forced landing due to engine failure on 5 March 1944. The aircraft bears what look likes five kill marks, but the scoreboard actually represents Killefer's 4.5 total (*National Archives*)

Another picture of F4U-1A 'No 5', this time being worked on by Marine mechanics at Bougainville on 8 February 1944. VF-17 were one of the few Corsair squadrons to assign aircraft to individual pilots, each machine having a number between '1' and '36' which helped to distinguish individual flights within a squadron, numbers '1' to '4' making up the first flight and so on. For a time the aircraft also had their spinners and first 18 inches of their props painted in different colours to denote each flight – Blackburn's flight were marked with red, Hedrick's white and so on. This practice was soon abandoned, however, as the system proved impractical to sustain in combat due to aircraft losses and poor serviceability (*USMC*)

flames, then he baled out, and I decided that he wasn't going to be there to get us the next day. I came around and tried to boresight him – I did actually fire my guns but I was too close and I must have straddled him. He flashed by on his descent, and I swear he was shaking his fist at me as I almost ran into the canopy of his 'chute. I hauled ass and by the time I finally woke up and looked around there were three of his buddies right on my tail – one on each flank and one dead astern. Luckily, I was flying

VF-17 pilots pose in front of the squadron scoreboard in January 1944. Standing, from left to right, are Lt Harry A 'Dirty Eddie' March, Jr (4 victories with VF-17 and 1 with VF-6), Lt(jg) Carl W Gilbert (1 victory) and Lt Walter J Schub (4.25 with VF-17 and 2 with VF-10). Kneeling are Lt(jg) Whitney C Wharton (2 victories with VF-10), Ens Frank A Jagger (2 victories) and Lt(jg) Harold J Bitzegaio (2 victories) (*Hedrick Collection*)

one of the new planes that we had picked up from Espiritu which was equipped with water injection that added about 25 hp – a few more knots of speed. Every time I saw one of them fire I could only change my altitude so as not to lose my speed. I gradually pulled away from them, and although they seemed to chase me forever, it actually wasn't more than ten minutes. I made it back to celebrate another day.

'On another occasion I was diving on somebody and he went into a snap roll. Lord knows what his thinking was, but it simply allowed me to catch up with him faster. It didn't bother me a bit as he was jiving around right there in front of me. That same flight I got another one that did the same thing. Maybe the section leader had decided that this might be a great tactic, but it didn't work too well. The Corsair was good at rolling and was a very stable gun platform – it could dive-bomb and so forth. I've flown the Hellcat and you'd be busy cranking on your tabs all the way down as torque and forces change, but with the Corsair there was very little, if any of that. You could whip it back and forth very easily. I know that I pulled over 9gs a few times. Our aeroplanes had accelerometers – a secret design in those days – and I once saw it register 11gs, although that wasn't in combat. It was when we were withdrawing from Rabaul covering the landings on Green Island and there was no opposition on the mission. Again as top cover, on the way back we encountered clouds above Empress August Bay. Usually in the afternoons in the Solomons there would be about 200 miles of thunderheads stretching across the area – hot and humid weather. Flying at about 2000 to 3000 ft, I looked at the clouds and decided to climb above them. If you got down on the water, which we had to do regularly, you had to sometimes fly about 15 ft above the water if you were to keep any type of contact at all. And then you'd be wondering where each little island was, as you could never be certain exactly where you were – we had no navigational aids at all. Unfortunately we got into the vortex at the top of the thunderhead, and all six of us were going in all directions, with wind shears taking us up and down, and that's where I got that 11gs. We all managed to get back safely, but it was by the grace of God on that one!'

War-weary F4U-1A Corsairs of VF-17 arrive back in the US on 7 August 1944 following their service in the Solomons. These aircraft would be overhauled and then used by a training squadron. From left to right is Killefer's 'No 5', Strieg's 'No 3' and an anonymous 'No 38' (*National Archives*)

SUCCESS IN THE SOUTH WEST

Following the American seizure of New Georgia, landings were made at Cape Torokina, Bougainville. on 1 November 1943. At that time there were four Marine Corsair units available to support the assault, namely VMFs -211, -212, -215, and -221. Bougainville, together with Green Island and Emirau (secured at later dates) helped to form a ring which enabled the strangulation of Rabaul, the main bastion of Japanese defence on New Britain, situated in the Bismarck archipelago. Airpower was used to neutralise the stronghold's air defences and to attack its lines of supply.

1st Lt Phillip C DeLong served with VMF-212, gaining his first two victories – a pair of Zekes – over Tobera airfield, New Britain, on 9 January 1944. His last three kills took place on 15 February against a formation of D3A *Val* dive-bombers, and here he describes the latter action.

'We covered the landings at Green Island on 15 February 1944, getting there just as the day was breaking. The ships were down below and then I saw the *Vals* – there were 15 of them. They were dive-bombers equipped with a rear seat gunner. I saw them starting quite high and rolling in. I couldn't see any sense in letting them get down to the ships, so I pulled in behind them. I got a good view of the gunner and shot him up. Then the aeroplane blew up. I got another two of them. My wingman had an armament fuse missing. Unable to use his guns all he did was go along for the ride!

'We strafed everything; trucks, barges, boats, natives in coconut trees, etc. Our guns were set up to fire at a fixed point where the bullets from all six guns would meet. If you got too close you didn't hit anything, but after the bullets had passed through the fixed point they would, in effect fan out in a large cone. This enabled you to spray a pretty large area.

'I was credited with 11.166 kills, the shared kills being split between three of us – Maj Hugh Elwood (5.166 kills), 1st Lt Allan Harrison and I. On 23 January, over Keravi Bay, Elwood made a run on a Zero and smoked him. I pulled up firing and got some flame out of him. Har-

F4U-1A 'No 777', BuNo 17777, following a landing accident at Bougainville on 14 December 1943. 1st Lt Phillip C DeLong had previously flown this aircraft on four of his missions during November. The machine wears a three-tone scheme with a stencilled number forward of the national insignia. The marking on the wing has been applied in the early style adopted in-theatre, with locally painted white bars. The tape applied forward of the canopy was used to seal the fuselage fuel tank access panels in order to stop fumes from entering the cockpit (*USMC*)

rison pulled up and managed to blow him up. Minutes later the same thing happened for the next plane up, so we split two kills between three of us. That same afternoon I shared another kill with Elwood.'

VICTORY CLAIMS

With the benefit of hindsight (and official Japanese loss records captured after the war) it has been established that the enemy lost less aircraft in air combat than the Allied forces had actually claimed to have destroyed. For example, in the two-month period 17 December 1943 to 19 February 1944 (the Imperial Navy's 11th Air Fleet was withdrawn on 20 February), the Allies claimed the destruction of 730 aircraft. By contrast, the Japanese Navy lost around 400 aircraft to all causes during the period. The Japanese Army Air Forces fared equally as badly, some units being totally annihilated during the campaign. Vast numbers of Japanese aircraft did not even see air combat, being destroyed on the ground by air attack. Figures cannot be accurately assessed but it can be estimated that the Allies claimed roughly twice the amount actually destroyed. This discrepancy is remarkably accurate compared to claims made in other theatres. Over claiming usually occurred during air combat and can largely be attributed to the confusion of battle. Claim inaccuracies and aircraft recognition mistakes are of little consequence compared to the overall results achieved. During the Solomons campaign the Japanese were to suffer such enormous losses that their Air Forces were, from then on, virtually incapable of taking on the Allied forces with the hope of achieving any kind of strategic success in air combat. It was because of these losses that the Japanese would later have to resort to suicide attacks in order to try and halt the American advance.

The Corsair units in the Solomons produced the highest scoring aces on the type during the whole conflict. Lt Robert M Hanson scored 25 victories with VMFs -214 and -215, before being killed in action on 3 February 1944 – he was posthumously awarded the Medal of Honor for kills achieved on 1 November 1943 and January 24 1944. Maj Gregory Boyington, commanding VMF-214, added to his previous six claims whilst flying with the 'Flying Tigers' in China, scoring 22 victories in the Corsair. He was awarded the Medal of Honor for actions on 17 October 1943, but was shot down and captured on 3 January 1944. Lt Kenneth A Walsh scored 20 victories whilst serving with VMF-124, being awarded the Medal of Honor in February 1944. He claimed his 21st, and final, victory on 22 June 1945 whilst serving with VMF-222. Capt Donald N Aldrich of VMF-215 achieved 20 victories, his last kill being scored on 9 February 1944. Capt Wilbur J Thomas of VMF-213 scored 16.5 victories during this campaign, before claiming a further two with the same unit on 16 February 1945, thus bringing his total claims to 18.5. VF-17 produced the Navy's top scoring ace of the theatre in the form of Lt Ira C Kepford, who was credited with 16 victories.

Three weather-beaten RNZAF F4U-1As are parked up between missions on Guadalcanal in mid-1944. By the time this shot was taken the threat of Japanese air attacks had subsided to the point where squadrons were confident that they could park lines of aircraft out in the open, rather than have them individually hidden away amongst the palm trees in revetments. The three-digit fin tip code was taken from the last three numbers in the aircraft's individual serial – 'No 393', for example, was actually NZ5393 (*via Jim Sullivan*)

RNZAF F4Us

Rabaul was deemed too difficult a target to attack by direct assault and was thus allowed to 'wither on the vine'. Following the destruction of Japanese air strength in the Solomons and Bismarcks, Navy and Marine Corsair units continued to harass the Japanese strongpoint by attacking ground targets. The Japanese evacuated the last of their shattered air-power on 20 February 1944. The Americans were joined by Royal New Zealand Air Force (RNZAF) units equipped with the Corsair at Bougainville on 14 May 1944 – the first unit to arrive was No 20 Sqn. Veterans of the P-40 Kittyhawk in the Solomons in 1943/44, these Kiwi units brought experience to the front, having gained a total of 99 aerial victories against the Japanese in operations to date. By the time the Corsairs arrived, however, enemy airpower in the Solomons was almost non-existent, and the RNZAF was unable to achieve any further aerial victories. Not to be deterred, they made their contribution to the war effort in the South Pacific by carrying out escort and ground attack missions in the area, which ended only in August 1945 with the final Japanese surrender.

A total of 13 RNZAF units received Corsairs in 1944/45, being numbered between 14 and 26. Spread across the South Pacific, these units utilised the F4U-1A, -1D and FG-1D versions of the Chance Vought/Goodyear fighter. Of the 424 airframes issued to the Kiwis (364 -1As/-1Ds and 60 FG-1Ds), no less than 150 (35 per cent) were lost, although only 17 of these were officially credited to enemy action. Squadrons were rotated into the frontline for three-month tours from bases in New Zealand, pools of aircraft being left at frontline strips by outgoing squadrons for use by their replacements. Unlike the British, who disposed of their massed ranks of Corsairs almost immediately after World War 2 (see the Fleet Air Arm chapter for details), the RNZAF valued their aircraft, and kept several units in service with the FG-1Ds particularly. The last unit flying the Corsair in the frontline was No 14 Sqn, who performed occupation duty with their FG-1Ds in Japan until the Allies pulled out in October 1948. Following the wind down of the squadron, the Corsairs – all weary veterans of war – were unceremoniously piled together and burnt, thus abruptly ending the RNZAF's association with the Chance Vought fighter.

Three-letter codes were rarely seen on Kiwi Corsairs, with this formation boasting a mix of combinations which perhaps denotes the presence of three separate squadrons within this strike force, seen heading for its target in early 1945 (*via Jim Sullivan*)

BRITISH CORSAIRS

Thanks to a less than impressive range of fighter and attack aircraft on offer from dedicated naval manufacturers like Fairey and Blackburn, the Fleet Air Arm (FAA) was forced to turn to fleet-modified RAF fighters in the form of the Sea Hurricane and Seafire to initially re-equip its carrier air wings during the dark days of 1941-42. Although both of these types were a great improvement over the Fulmar and Skua, neither boasted a truly sufficient range to operate at distance from the task force, or possessed truly sound deck landing characteristics.

Fortunately for the FAA's hard-pressed naval aviators, the first examples of a true carrier-bred fighter in the form of the Grumman Wildcat (Martlet) had begun to reach Britain in serious numbers by late 1941. Here was an aircraft that had a more than adequate range, was docile in the landing pattern and could hold its own in combat – its only real drawback was a rather modest top speed of 315 mph. Nevertheless, it was quickly accepted by the Navy, who in turn cast an envious eye westward across the Atlantic in search of a machine to supplement the Wildcat.

At about that time the Chance Vought company of Connecticut was putting its radical new fleet fighter – the XF4U-1 Corsair – through its paces prior to delivery to the US Navy. Wickedly quick, this machine became the target for a lend-lease deal between the British and American governments. Indeed, so popular was the 'bent-winged bird' that no less than 2012 Corsairs, divided into four marks, were eventually utilised by the FAA, which gave the aircraft the distinction of being the most populous US type to see service with the Royal Navy in World War 2.

Over the years much has been said about the aircraft's 'sporting' handling characteristics around a carrier deck, with pilots' opinions seemingly divided according to their own experiences of the Corsair. Senior US naval aviators were convinced that the F4U-1 was too difficult an aircraft for the average pilot to master in 1942, possessing incipient bounce due to overly stiff oleos, a tendency to torque stall without warning and a poor view over the nose during landing approach.

These factors resulted in carrier-based US Navy units being almost exclusively equipped with the docile Hellcat until the F4U was finally cleared for deck ops in late 1944 – by this stage FAA Corsair units had accrued almost a year's flat top experience, as well as having seen combat from carriers in both Europe and the Pacific since April 1944.

Never phased by the aircraft's 'wild' reputation, the British went

Fresh off the 'boat' from the US, a recently arrived Corsair II is taxied gingerly along the Peri track at an anonymous airfield in Britain in early 1944, its wings askew. The pilot's head can just be seen behind the cowling flaps as he leans out the cockpit in order to see what is ahead of him. Lurking in the winter mist behind the Corsair is a solitary Swordfish, plus a pair of Martlets. Despite its ascendancy over all previous FAA fighters, not all naval aviators in the Senior Service were enamoured with the Corsair, as Capt Eric 'Winkle' Brown attests to in the following quote. 'Oddly enough, the Royal Navy was not quite so fastidious as the US Navy regarding deck landing characteristics, and cleared the Corsair for deck operation some nine months before its American counterpart. The obstacles to the Corsair's shipboard use were admittedly not insurmountable, but I can only surmise that the apparently ready acceptance by their Lordships of the Admiralty of the Chance Vought fighter for carrier operation must have been solely due to the exigencies of the time, for the landing behaviour of the Corsair really was bad' (*via Phil Jarrett*)

Having completed the landing on cycle, deck crews busily manhandle a trio of Corsairs into their appropriate spots under the watchful gaze of a clutch of senior officers in the middle of the photograph. Both the carrier and the unit are sadly unknown, although the '7' code denotes that the Corsairs belong to one of the many training squadrons equipped with the type in 1944. Standing behind the cockpit of '7T', map in hand, is the carrier's Commander (Flying), who had just flown one of the aircraft aboard (*via Aeroplane*)

about re-equipping with the Corsair I from mid-1943 onwards, squadrons being trained for 'blue water' ops from the word go. Subtle mods to the aircraft included the clipping of the wings by eight inches due to the smaller confines of the hangar decks on British carriers. This change in span brought with it the unexpected bonus of improved sink rate, thus partially eradicating the aircraft's propensity for 'floating' in the final stages of landing. However, despite this mod some senior FAA pilots expressed fears akin to their American cousins.

Nevertheless, by early 1944 eight units had been formed expressly for carrier operations with both the Home and Far East fleets – this number would eventually reach a staggering 18 units by VJ-Day. The original F4U-1 'birdcage', known as the Corsair I (95 delivered), was the initial version supplied to Nos 1830 and 1833 Sqns in the US, but none of these ever saw combat. This honour fell to the more definitive Mk II, an anglicised version of the F4U-1A that was delivered to the tune of 510 airframes. Work ups were complete by the end of 1943, and the Corsair IIs were loaded aboard escort carriers for shipment to Britain.

By April 1944 the Home Fleet felt confident enough to blood the Corsair II in combat, and 28 aircraft from Nos 1834 and 1836 Sqns duly provided top cover on the 3rd of that month as No 47 Naval Fighter Wing (FW) for Operation *Tungsten* – an air strike by six carriers (121 aircraft) on the German battleship *Tirpitz*. Part of HMS *Victorious*'s air wing, the Corsair pilots encountered no enemy aircraft during the dawn raid, and returned to the carrier without having had their combined mettle tested – the Corsair's contribution to the war against Germany was restricted to supporting Home Fleet strikes against this target through to August.

The Corsair's combat debut in the Indian Ocean took place concurrently with the first *Tirpitz* strike in April 1944, although the former action was a far less orchestrated affair than *Tungsten*. Nos 1830 and 1833 Sqns, who formed No 15 FW aboard HMS *Illustrious*, were used to sweep the area east of Ceylon clean of commerce raiders, and although little real combat was met, it did give the FAA a chance to operate closely with the US Navy in the form of USS *Saratoga*, and her embarked air wing.

The Corsair force in-theatre effectively doubled in July with the arrival of *Victorious*. No 1837 Sqn also arrived in Ceylon to join *Illustrious*, increasing the embarked strength per vessel to 42 Corsair IIs each, split evenly between a trio of units. This enlarged force got the chance to show its worth on 25 July when Sabang Island was hit, although the Corsairs took a backseat to three battleships, seven cruisers and two destroyers which shelled the port and oil storage site.

Whilst covering the force withdrawal, a trio of units were given the chance to blood the Corsair in aerial combat when a handful of enemy aircraft attempted to attack the warships. No 1830 Sqn claimed three Zekes, whilst fellow No 15 FW unit No 1833 Sqn downed two Zekes and a Ki 21 *Sally* bomber. Finally, the sole kill to fall to *Victorious* was yet another Zeke, which was destroyed by a Corsair from the temporarily-assigned No 1838 Sqn. Aside from being the FAA's first of nearly 50 kills in the Corsair, these successes were also the first deck-based victories for the fighter, although its land-based score was nearing four figures after 17 months in combat with the USMC and Navy.

After more aerially unopposed target strikes, Corsair pilots again encountered the enemy in the skies over the Car Nicobar Islands in October 1944, although this time only *Victorious*'s units flew the Corsair flag. A handful of *Oscars* defending the islands were downed in the one-sided duels that took place, seven Army fighters being downed for the loss of two Corsairs and a Hellcat. Canadian Lt Leslie Durno,of No 1834 Sqn, claimed four of this total, destroying one fighter single-handedly and sharing three with his wingman – some confusion exists as to the correct identity of this pilot as a Scot by the name of Lt Alec Durno was also reportedly serving with No 1834 Sqn as Senior Pilot at this time!

One last operation was performed by the Corsair in this theatre on 4 January 1945 when *Victorious* operated in support of the strike on the refinery at Pangkalan Brandan, again on Sumatra – this raid was viewed as a dress rehearsal for the bigger Palembang strike three weeks later. The pilots of No 47 FW were tasked with providing top cover (along with *Indefatigable*'s Seafire F IIIs) for the Avengers, and duly ran into a force of *Oscars*, as well as a handful of *Dinah* recce aircraft and *Sally* bombers. Twelve aircraft were downed for the loss a single Avenger, with seven of these kills falling to Corsair pilots – Lt Durno shared a *Dinah* and a *Sally*, whilst No 1836 Sqn's Sub Lt Don Sheppard (also a Canadian) claimed two *Oscars* as the unit downed five Nakajima fighters.

With the creation of the British Pacific Fleet (BPF) in January 1945, the Royal Navy moved its force from Trincomalee to Sydney, and en route to their new home, senior staff officers decided to make use of the massed ranks of four large fleet carriers to hit the sprawling ex-Shell refinery at Pladjoe, near Palembang in Sumatra – this raid had been planned since early December 1944. Codenamed *Meridian One* and *Two*, 144 sorties were launched on 24 January, followed by more raids five days later – the former attack was the second largest force put up by the FAA in World War 2. Included in the first strike were 32 Corsairs from *Illustrious* and *Victorious*, performing bomber escort duties (16 close in with the bombers and an equal number flying as top cover), and a further 24 on a *Ramrod* sweep of the local airfields.

Flak took a heavy toll of the *Ramrod* raiders, who failed to prevent the Japanese *Tojos*, *Nicks* and *Oscars* from launching against the main strike force. Five Corsairs were lost, but in return 34 Japanese aircraft were destroyed on the ground – little evidence of the enemy in the air on these

Solitary Royal Marine ace of World War 2, then Maj (later Lieutenant Colonel) Ronnie Hay enjoyed a remarkably successful combat career flying all manner of FAA fighters, including both the Skua and Fulmar I. After scoring kills in both these less than impressive fleet fighters, Hay revelled in the power and manoeuvrability of the Corsair, stating that 'for the first time in four years of war we were on top in combat – the masters of the air – as no others could touch us, and that made our morale "Ace High"' (*Ronnie Hay*)

The early morning storm clouds that have left puddles on HMS *Victorious*'s steel deck are left behind as the carrier steams on towards the East Indies. Sailors can be picked out between massed ranks of Corsair IIs from Nos 1834 and 1836 Sqns, preparing the aircraft for their next strike on Sumatra in January 1945. The Corsairs wearing a number '7' on their starboard undercarriage door and a letter on the opposing oleo are from No 1834 Sqn, whilst those with '8A' to 'T' on both gear legs are from No 1836 (*via Phil Jarrett*)

attacks meant that the escorting Corsairs were the only ones to engage in combat. Over 20 Army fighters attacked the force, but the Corsair pilots flying top cover were well up to the task at hand and claimed eight for the loss of a single No 1833 Sqn Corsair (downed by a *Tojo*) in a battle fought around the edge of the Avengers.

Leading scorer with an *Oscar* and a *Tojo* on this sortie was veteran Marine ace, Maj (later Lieutenant Colonel) Ronnie Hay, who was serving as Wing Leader of No 47 Wg at the time. A frontline FAA fighter pilot since 1939, Hay had scored a shared kill in Skuas in 1940 during the Battle of Norway with No 801 Sqn from *Ark Royal*, followed by seven individual or shared victories in the Mediterranean in 1941 as part of Force 'H' in Fulmar Is with No 808 Sqn, again aboard the *Ark*.

His role in the Palembang strikes was a unique one for he was designated the Air Co-ordinator, which meant he oversaw all the various strike formations as they hit the refinery at their schedules times from a variety of directions as briefed – Hay had been one of the few FAA pilots sent by the Navy on the RAF's exclusive Wing Leader course at Charmy Down in April 1943 Full bottle on the etiquette of massed air strikes, he was despatched to the Mediterranean to lecture on the subject, before being sent to Ceylon as Commander Flying at China Bay. With the arrival of the Corsair in-theatre in early 1944, Hay sensed that the former 'back water' of a conflict in the Far East was at last being viewed with the seriousness it deserved, so he duly wangled his way out from behind a desk back onto operational flying, and was adopted by *Victorious*, who welcomed both his combat experience and strike tactics background. Palembang at last saw him putting theory in to practice on a grand scale.

The strike went on for some while, and during this time Hay, and his flight of three other pilots (including the FAA's sole all-Corsair ace of the conflict, Canadian Sub Lt Don Sheppard) drawn predominantly from No 1836 Sqn, patrolled as an integral flight between the Corsairs of the strike force and those flying top cover. Hay was flying his field-modified Corsair II JT427 – appropriately coded 'TRH' – which boasted oblique and vertical cameras to enable him to record views of the target for post-strike evaluation (Hay was also a graduate of the RAF's photographic interpretation course at Benson, where he had learned to fly high altitude vertical line overlap missions, and thereby achieve the most accurate post-strike evaluation photographs). Indeed, all four of his kills in Corsairs were scored in this machine, and due to its special fit it was probably the only one of its type aboard either *Victorious* or *Illustrious* assigned to one pilot. Hay reflects on this mission, and the Corsair in general in this theatre, in the following interview, undertaken specially for this volume.

'With the Corsair you felt like were literally strapped into an armchair in your sitting room, the cockpit was that large. You honestly felt like a "king" sitting up there, with virtually unlimited visibility through the bubble canopy of the Mark II. We flew those aircraft very hard, and just to illustrate this point, a little after the Sumatra show we ventured northward to Okinawa for *Iceberg*, where I came across an airfield full of the latest spec F4U-4s in glossy sea blue at Manus, in the Admiralty Islands, awaiting shipment back to the US. I came across the US Navy Officer in charge of this operation and asked him what was occurring. He told me that they were being returned to the 'States for overhaul and repair prior to being sent to the frontline again. I enquired as to their individual service use per airframe and he replied that they had seen about 500 hours of flying each. I was astonished, and replied that our Corsair IIs had accrued nearly 2000 each and were no nearer an overhaul or deep service than the day they were built! I ventured a swap whereby I took one of his non-serviced machines in place of my old crate, and he replied, "Sure bud, you can have any one you like. Any guy going up to the "sharp end" can take anything he wants!" Sadly, I fear my admiral would have spotted the F4U-4's glossy blue scheme sat amongst the ranks of sea grey Corsair IIs on *Victorious*!

Once airborne the squadrons would be tasked with providing fighter cover for Avenger IIs and Firefly Is, one unit sticking close by the vulnerable bombers, whilst the second squadron would patrol at height above the formation. This impressive view shows aircraft of No 6 FW being lead by Maj Ronnie Hay on a formation flypast of RNAS Colombo, Ceylon, in May 1944. The Corsairs are wearing a mix of codes and odd-sized national markings (*Ronnie Hay*)

'Returning to Palembang, all the Corsairs despatched to the target carried drop tanks which gave a maximum of five hours flight time. We used the external fuel first, and jettisoned them as soon as we got into action. I had my own four-aircraft flight adopt a loose formation over the target, with Sheppard to my rear. We sauntered around checking on where the Japs were, and how they were responding to the raid in progress.

'The first strike on the refineries was a bit hit and miss in terms of targets destroyed, and because of the sheer number of aircraft involved, my ability to co-ordinate formations of Avenger IIs, Firefly Is, Hellcat Is, Corsairs IIs and Seafire F IIIs was rather limited, particularly after the fuel dumps were hit and the site became obscured in dense black smoke. I therefore moved my flight into a position where we could protect the Avengers should enemy fighters show up. The next thing I knew a *Tojo* came flashing past my bows hell bent on attacking the bombers, and I quickly lined him up in my sights and fired a two-second burst in his direction. I must have hit a fuel tank because the aircraft blew up. An *Oscar* was spotted soon afterwards and I led the flight down after him to jungle level, but unlike the *Tojo* he refused to burn, instead crashing into the ground at high speed.

'Five days later, in the immediate aftermath of *Meridian Two*, I was attempting to perform a series of post-strike vertical line overlap photographic passes on the refinery site when we ran into a mixed flight of

Corsair II JT422 is typical of the 36 Chance Vought fighters that made up No 47 FW aboard HMS *Victorious* in 1944/45. The two-letter code of No 1836 Sqn is clearly visible, as is the crudely chalked on letter T to the left of the number 8 – all squadron machines eventually had this second letter painted on by the time of the Palembang raid in late January 1945. Its paint lustreless and stained, JT422 was being flown on this occasion by a Lt Knight (*Ronnie Hay*)

four *Tojos* and *Oscars*. This immediately stopped the recce work, and Sheppard and I quickly despatched one of each for two half-kills apiece. In combating the Jap fighters you simply used your superior speed to make solitary diving passes at them, restricting the temptation to turn with them at all cost. We enjoyed such a speed advantage over both types it was pointless slowing down in order to try and dogfight.'

Typical of the shots taken by Ronnie Hay in his specially-modified recce-Corsair II, this view shows the Japanese airfield on the island of Miyako, in the Sakishima Gunto chain, under attack by FAA Avenger IIs and Corsair IIs in March 1945. During the raids the Navy bombers concentrated on cratering the runways, thus restricting the airfield's use as a staging post for aircraft being flown into Okinawa from Formosa (*Ronnie Hay*)

Having fought long and hard for a 'piece of the action' in the Pacific, the Royal Navy was determined to up a good showing, which in turn meant tough escort and strafing sorties for the units – Nos 1830 and 1833 on *Illustrious*, Nos 1834 and 1836 on *Victorious* and Nos 1841 and 1842 Sqns on *Formidable*. Typical squadron strength throughout the eight months of combat in 1945 was 18 Corsair IIs, although with the arrival of *Formidable* in April the Goodyear-built Mk IV made its combat debut.

Returning briefly to the *Meridian* strikes on the Pladjoe refineries for the final time, aside from Hay and Sheppard's single kills, a further three aircraft were shared between Nos 1830 and 1834 Sqns. However, Lt Durno, who had scored one and four shared kills all in Corsair, was one of two pilots lost on the raid – he was shot down attacking an airfield and captured. Sadly, he was beheaded in Changi prison in August 1945, along with several other FAA aircrew downed in the Palembang raid.

After a spell in Sydney, the BPF joined forces with the US Fifth Fleet to form Task Force 57, and of the 270 FAA aircraft (split between five carriers) contributed to the force 110 of them were Corsairs. The battle for Okinawa, codenamed *Iceberg*, was the BPF's first Pacific combat proper, and commencing 26 March strikes were launched against Sakishima Gunto. Aside from flak suppression and strike work, Corsair units were kept busy repelling *kamikazes*, as Ronnie Hay witnessed at first hand.

'The biggest aerial threat to life posed by the Japanese came in the form of *kamikaze* attacks in the final months of the war. We experienced some

Another strafing mission over, pilots of Nos 1834 and 1836 Sqns head for the crewroom in line abreast formation. The pilot third from the right is Canadian Lt Don Sheppard, the only all-Corsair ace the FAA produced in World War 2 (*Ronnie Hay*)

very unpleasant moments with carrier decks full of bombed up and fuelled aircraft waiting to turn into wind before being cleared to launch. I can remember sitting there in my aircraft as the deck slowly healed over, moments away from take-off, when all of a sudden the ship's guns would open up and I would crane my neck skywards searching for a Zeke or a *Val* hell bent on burying itself in the bowels of the carrier. I can remember sitting in the cockpit watching one *kamikaze* just miss the *"Indom"* which was about to launch her air wing less than half a mile away from us. I was first off, fortunately, and as soon as the signal was given I was gone, followed by my flight – pity the poor sods behind us!'

Ten Japanese aircraft were claimed by Corsairs during these attacks – which lasted till mid-April – split evenly between *Victorious* and *Illustrious*. Entering the fray once again on 4 May, the BPF Corsairs intercepted a formation of 20 assorted enemy aircraft as they attacked the carrier force. Amongst the defenders was Don Sheppard, who downed a *Judy* to achieve ace status – three other aircraft were claimed by *Victorious*'s Corsairs. The following day a Corsair IV from the recently arrived No 1841 Sqn shot down a Zeke to claim *Formidable*'s first aerial kill.

Eventually, after a month of strikes the defenders of Okinawa were beaten, but not before much damage had been inflicted on Task Force 57's carriers – two-thirds of the 270 aircraft despatched from Sydney had been destroyed or damaged, a large percentage through *kamikaze* attacks. Following a spell of R&R, the carriers returned to the war zone for the last time in July, with Corsair units employed predominantly on *Ramrod* strikes on airfields as all aerial opposition had by now gone. Indeed, only two more kills were scored prior to VJ Day, and both fell to No 1841 Sqn – a *Kate* was claimed at the end of July, followed by a *Grace* on 9 August.

Later that momentous day, just when it appeared that the final FAA act with the Corsair had been played, a veteran Canadian flight commander from No 1841 Sqn by the name of Lt Robert Hampton Gray made the ultimate sacrifice during a shipping strike on the Honshu coast. Hit by flak, he nevertheless closed to within 50 ft of his target – a trademark approach he had used time and again firstly in the Norwegian campaign in April 1944, and then throughout *Formidable*'s final weeks of war against mainland Japan. This time luck was not on his side and he was lost in the resulting explosion when his target blew up. Gray was awarded a posthumous VC – only the second naval pilot to receive Britain's highest military award in World War 2.

Thus ended the FAA's Corsair war. Of the 18 squadrons eventually equipped with the type, 8 saw combat. Only two of the four marks operated by the FAA were used in action, and of the 2000+ received, roughly 40 remained in service until August 1946.

***Victorious* despatched Corsair II/IVs and Avenger IIs on strikes to the Japanese mainland up until 11 August 1945. With her aircrew suffering fatigue, and her supplies running low, the carrier was 'chopped', along with the bulk of the BPF's Task Force 38, and ordered to return to Sydney. Prior to departure, the vessel was resupplied at sea (RAS) by fleet support vessels, and this shot was taken soon after this had taken place. Parked on the deck amongst the Corsairs and Avengers is a solitary No 1701 Sqn Sea Otter (*Ronnie Hay*)**

THE CENTRAL PACIFIC

Whilst land-based units had carried out most of the work in the South West Pacific the vast Central Pacific theatre became primarily the preserve of the carriers. Corsairs were, however, based on various islands in the Pacific, and these units were mainly required to attack enemy units by-passed by the carriers during the island hopping campaign. Marine F4Us carried on the effort in the Gilbert and Marshall Islands for instance, with the majority of missions flown here being of the ground attack variety – there were very few Japanese aircraft left operating in these areas by now. It was here that the Corsair would perfect its new ground attack role, first developed in the Solomons, which would be put to good use as the Americans advanced towards Japan.

The Marine F4Us also missed out to a large extent on the air combat associated with the occupation of the Marianas, aircraft (Hellcats mainly) from TF-58 destroying some 200 enemy fighters gathered on Saipan and Tinian in what became known as the 'Marianas Turkey Shoot'. Land-based units in this theatre would, however, see more aerial engagements with the advent of the Philippines campaign, where they would fly CAP missions for the carriers taking part in the invasion of Leyte in October 1944. Marine Corsair units would go on to help with the liberation of the Philippines by launching ground attack missions in support of the advancing forces. As the campaign progressed Adm Chester Nimitz's fast carriers would continue the drive into the Central Pacific.

VF-17 had first demonstrated the Corsair to be suitable for carrier operations before their final deployment as a land-based unit. They had worked with Chance Vought technicians to improve the Corsair's shortcomings, and the resulting improvements helped to convince the Bureau of Aeronautics of its worth – the F4U was cleared for carrier use in April 1944. By that time, however, the availability of the F6F had led to the latter's widespread use by the fast carrier fleet, instead of the more versatile Corsair.

The first US Navy Corsair combat deployment aboard a carrier began on 9 January 1944 with USS *Enterprise*. VF(N)-101 (actually the second half of VF(N)-75, left behind in late 1943 because of equipment delays), equipped with

The first US Navy Corsair deployment began on 9 January 1944 when VF(N)-101, commanded by Lt Cdr Richard E Harmer, boarded USS *Enterprise* as part of Air Group 10. Equipped with F4U-2 night-fighters, the unit was tasked with defending the fleet against Japanese attacks at night. VF(N)-101 was credited with the destruction of five enemy aircraft, one probable and three damaged. Here, an F4U-2 is raised to the deck in the late afternoon, whilst VF-10 Hellcats can be seen in the background (*National Archives via Pete Mersky*)

four F4U-2s, beginning operations as part of Air Group Ten whilst under the command of Lt Cdr Richard E 'Chick' Harmer (formerly the XO of VF(N)-75, Harmer was an F4F Guadalcanal vet, having served with VF-3 aboard *Saratoga* in 1942). A second four-Corsair VF(N)-101 det was also established aboard *Intrepid* with Air Wing Six at this time. *Enterprise*'s first night interception took place on 19 February 1944.

F4U-1A 'No 122' of VMF-111 was the only aircraft to receive an official award for its combat service during World War 2. Operating from the Gilbert and Marshall Islands, the aircraft is pictured with 100 mission marks to denote the number of sorties it completed with the same engine – it never had to turn back due to mechanical trouble. VMF-111, along with other land-based units, was tasked with the destruction of by-passed Japanese garrisons, and saw very little air-to-air combat (*via Phil Jarrett*)

Operating from a carrier at night is possibly the most difficult task that a Naval aviator has to perform. This being so, it was ironic that the US Navy first ushered the 'unruly' Corsair into fleet service in this role, particularly when one considers staff attitudes towards the aircraft. Night-fighter variants of the F4U also served with land-based VMF(N)-532, commanded by Maj Everett Vaughn, and VF(N)-75 led by Lt Cdr William J Widhelm. In total these units were to be credited with 14 aircraft destroyed, 4 probables and 3 damaged.

Marine Corsair carrier deployments were a direct response to Japanese suicide strikes against Allied naval targets. The *kamikaze* attacks began in strength during the Leyte invasion that took place in late October 1944, and although this form of attack was born out of desperation, it appeared to the Japanese to be very effective. Even though they greatly overestimated the results of their attacks, they were nevertheless inflicting serious damage. *Kamikaze* attacks only occurred for a short period, but were to become the cause of over one-fifth of all sinkings and almost half the damage sustained by American shipping during the whole of World War 2.

There was only one way for the Americans to defend themselves from the new menace, and that was through increased fighter cover. The Navy needed as many fighters as it could get, and the carriers from which to operate them from. However, they simply did not have enough pilots to meet the requirement as their training programme had been cut back as the tide of the conflict had turned globally – therefore, the Marines were called in to fill the gap. Marine aviators began carrier training in the summer of 1944 at the beginning of the CVE programme. The plan was for them to operate Corsairs from escort carriers, their operational emphasis being based on supporting Marine Ground Forces. However, the first Marines actually deployed on board the big fleet carriers – ten squadrons eventually saw deck service during 1945. The urgent Navy requirement for extra fighters again meant that F4U pilots were committed to the combat theatre with insufficient training, and

F4U-1As of VMF-222 on Samar in the Philippines. The unit was based here from January 1945 until it moved to Okinawa on 22 May. This aircraft is adorned with the emblem of the Navy's Construction Battalions, the SEABEEs, who were responsible for the construction of all their airfields. The unit was credited with destroying 51 enemy aircraft and 20 probables in the South West Pacific, and gained a further two kills whilst based on Okinawa (*USMC*)

Capt Francis E 'Effie' Pierce of VMF-121 poses next to his FG-1A BuNo 14056, nicknamed *Mary* after his wife, on Peleliu on 18 November 1944. Pierce had claimed a total of six victories earlier in the South West Pacific – four in the Wildcat and one in a Corsair (the unit converted to the F4U in April 1943). VMF-121 claimed 204.5 kills in this theatre, the last occurring on 18 July 1943. Only one more was claimed – on 28 April 1945 a *Myrt* was destroyed near Ulithi. Whilst on Peleliu the unit flew mostly ground attack missions against Yap (*USMC*)

F4U-1Ds of VMFs -124 and -213 from *Essex* escort TBM Avengers on a strike against Formosa on 3 January 1945. This was the first Marine Corsair combat mission to be launched from a carrier, both F4Us and TBMs attacking Kagi airfield. Returning from the target Lt Col William A Millington, VMF-124's CO, destroyed a Japanese *Nick*, this being the unit's first kill of the cruise (*USMC*)

early sorties were marred by operational losses around the carrier.

VMFs -124 and -213 began deck ops soon after they returned to the Pacific equipped with 36 brand new F4U-1Ds in late 1944. The units boarded *Essex* as part of Task Force 38 at Ulithi on 28 December 1944, and launched their first combat sorties on 3 January 1945 when elements from both squadrons escorted TBMs attacking Kagi Airfield, on Formosa. Next they hit Okinawa, then the fleet moved down to the northern Philippines, attacking northern Luzon on 6/7 January. Passing through Luzon Strait, they sailed into the South China Sea, from where a massive strike was then launched against Saigon, in French Indochina, followed on the 16th by attacks against Hong Kong, Amoy, Swatow and Formosa again. Following a second strike on Okinawa, the fleet returned to Ulithi on 26 January. Adm Halsey was relieved by Spruance and the fleet set sail on 4 February as Task Force 58. This time the fleet boasted four large carriers – the *Bennington, Wasp, Essex* and *Bunker Hill.*

Each carrier was equipped with two Marine Corsair squadrons, whilst *Bunker Hill* also had the Navy's first day fighter Corsair squadron (VF-84, now commanded by VF-17's former XO, Roger Hedrick) embarked. The fleet was ready to attack the Japanese homeland for the first time. On 16/17 February they launched strikes against Japanese airfields, with the intention of destroying as many aircraft as possible so that they could not be used against the Iwo Jima invasion force. The fleet then travelled south and carried out attack sorties against 'Iwo' itself. They continued missions in support of the invasion until the 22nd, and then launched a strike against Chichi Jima. More sorties were flown against Japan on the 25th and Okinawa on 1 March, before the fleet returned to Ulithi.

Lt Col William A Millington, CO of both VMFs -124 and -213 claimed their first victory on 3 January 1945 whilst flying CAP during the initial Okinawa strikes. Six-kill ace Capt Howard Finn had earlier served with VMF-124 in the Solomons, and relates some of his experiences of the *kamikaze* period:

'I never had an accident either taking off or landing aboard a carrier, although landing at night was a pretty wild experience. The radar put you in position and then you would get into that imaginary cone at the rear of the ship. We would approach from the stern from two miles out until we picked up the little blue lights and then if our approach was correct they would turn on the meatball. We'd keep the meatball centred as you couldn't see the LSO and hopefully fly right in. In darkness, during bad weather it's the most precise flying you can do.

'We were warned about the *kamikazes* – indeed the *Essex* had been hit by one just before our cruise. We would have to shoot them down before reaching the fleet for it was their tactics that were doing the most damage. As a result, we abandoned defensive tactics when we went after the *kamikazes.* The Navy really feared the them, more so than on the Marines. They used destroyers as pickets and we

'Finn's Fools' pictured before a flight on board the *Essex* in December 1944. From left to right are Capt Edmond Hartsock (2 victories), 1st Lt George B Parker, standing, (1 victory), Capt Howard J Finn (6 victories) and 1st Lt William McGill (3 victories). Whilst on his first cruise with VMF-124, Finn increased his tally of five kills gained in the Solomons by downing an *Oscar* and sharing the credit for damaging another with 2nd Lt Don Carlson during a mission to Kumagaya airfield, in Japan, on 25 February 1945 (*Finn Collection*)

flew CAP over them. The *kamikazes* would go after the pickets, these being the first ships they came across. By the time of the Leyte and Okinawa operations they were no longer trying to establish air superiority, merely trying to destroy ships with *kamikaze* tactics.

'We hit the dock facilities at Formosa and we then strafed a destroyer that was later sunk by Navy planes. The destroyer tried to escape to the north, and after we had attacked it I flew over the vessel to take pictures. I had a camera in the side of my aeroplane and the plan was for me to photograph the ship in preparation for another strike. Just at that time a Navy plane must have hit the ship with a 1000-lb bomb because it sank within two minutes. We then flew raids against targets in Indochina, losing several pilots to AA. Joe Lynch was one of the pilots shot down, and he walked out of the jungle on foot. Both Okinawa and Taiwan were hit before we returned to Ulithi.

'We then supported the landings on Iwo Jima and then the fleet was sent north to attack Japan for four or five days, covering the airfields so that the enemy could not send down *kamikazes* to attack the invasion force. We were assigned airfields north of Tokyo. On the way in we kept seeing these aircraft drop down out of the clouds and then go back up. I took my flight around and waited for them to drop down. One appeared and I shot him down. Another one dropped down and we chased him until he flew into the side of a mountain.

'Our "Offensive Fighter Sweeps" against enemy airfields were conducted without external ordnance – we just used our guns. When attacking airfields we would go in *en masse* to dilute the anti-aircraft fire. Sometimes we would do a second sweep, depending on the defences, dividing the airfield up and each flight taking a different segment. Later, we conducted ground attack missions using rockets and bombs as well as our machine guns. At that time we also had the 20 mm cannon which was a more effective strafing weapon than the .50 cal gun, although they were not as reliable. They seemed to get jammed more often, and it was not uncommon to only have one of the four cannon able to fire. They were also prone to freezing at high altitude.'

Task Force 58 hit Japan again on 18 March, and this time the Navy had a lot more Corsairs available. *Essex* and *Wasp* had had their Marines replaced with Air Groups 83 and 86, both having F4U-equipped VBF squadrons. The fleet was enlarged with the addition of *Franklin* and *Intrepid*, sharing five Corsair squadrons between them, whilst the *Hancock*, with one, brought the total to 13 in all. When *Franklin* and *Wasp* were hit by air attack on the 19th this total was quickly reduced to nine. The fleet also acted in support of the Okinawa invasion, and from the

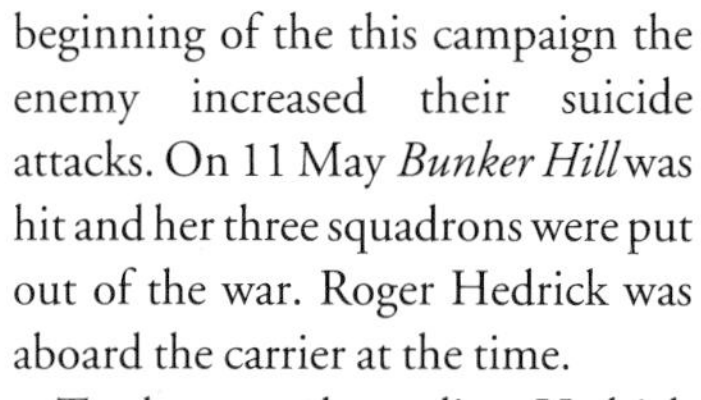

F4U-1D 'No 176' launches from USS *Bunker Hill* on 19 February 1945. Roger Hedrick commanded VF-84 until he assumed command of the Air Group following the death of the previous commander who was killed in action. He added two victories (*Franks*) to his score with VF-17, bringing his final tally to twelve on 26 February 1945 while flying F4U-1D BuNo 57803 (*National Archives*)

beginning of the this campaign the enemy increased their suicide attacks. On 11 May *Bunker Hill* was hit and her three squadrons were put out of the war. Roger Hedrick was aboard the carrier at the time.

Twelve months earlier, Hedrick and VF-17 had been relieved in the Solomons by VF-34 on 7 March 1944, the former having personally accounted for the destruction of nine enemy aircraft during some 250 hours of combat flying. His next tour was aboard *Bunker Hill*, were he served as CO of VF-84. His first credit with the unit occurred on 17 February 1945 when he damaged a *Tony* over the Nakajima factory at Mushashino, in Japan. Hedrick gained his last victories on the 25th of that month when he destroyed two *Franks* and a Zeke during attacks in the Katori airfield area, bringing his total official credits to 12 confirmed victories and four damaged. Hedrick takes up the story.

'Air Group 84 was equipped with the F4U-1D with which we were very satisfied. "Fighting 84", together with the two Marine squadrons, VMFs -451 and -221, had a total of 72 Corsairs. The had Marines had 18 planes each and we had 36, all tasked with countering the *kamikazes*. There was no new or very different tactic devised when they started throwing their hundreds of planes at us. The fleet would be surrounded by picket destroyers 100 miles from the main Task Group. They took a lot of damage, even though we were doing our best to protect them. It was an almost impossible task because our radars weren't effective.

'On one of our early fighter sweeps over a Japanese airfield my Corsair was hit by ground fire. The only way I could control the aeroplane was by flying with two hands on my stick the whole time. I found later that a control cable and my prop control had been kinked and I couldn't reduce my blade speed. I then encountered and shot down two *Franks*, finding that they exploded in the same way as the Zero. If fact one of them exploded right in front of me and I flew right through the fireball. I was hunched down, wondering where its damned engine was as I went through the ball of fire. My last kill came shortly after. I caught another Zero and after I'd fired on him, he was going down and I passed right over him. I looked right down into the cockpit as I wasn't more than 20 ft away from him. I don't know why he didn't bail out – he must have been injured or something. After all our hassles we were getting low on fuel, and I was charging on ahead due to the damage to my controls. I had to let go of the stick and with both hands I yanked back the throttle. The tube that contained the cable had been bent, but I managed to get the wire past it and got down to a

Rocket-armed F4U-1D 'No 183' launches from *Bunker Hill* on 19 February 1945. VF-84 and VMFs -221 and -451 all shared the same aircraft while aboard the carrier. Following the *Bunker Hill*'s retirement, many of the Corsairs went to Okinawa, where some were used by VMF-323 (*National Archives*)

lower prop setting. At a lower speed I was able to make it back, where they found nine holes in the plane. Those were the last three kills I got. The whole time I was there I never got to fire my guns at anything else.

Task Force 58 heading towards Japan in March 1945. In the foreground are F4U-1Ds of Air Group 84, parked on the forward deck of *Bunker Hill*. At that time the Air Group was made up of five squadrons, three Navy and two Marine, with a total of 71 Corsairs (*via Phil Jarrett*)

'The only way to counter the *kamikazes* was to put lots of CAPs up, the best we could provide. At night it was the closest I ever came to claustrophobia. We had VF(N)-76 and their handful of F6F-3N nightfighters aboard, and their sole job was to take care of Japanese nocturnal attacks. We daylight-only pilots would be buttoned up down below the hanger deck in the wardroom playing cards, or reading, when we'd hear the five-inch guns start up and we knew there was a run coming in. So everybody is puffing like mad on their cigarettes and the room would soon be full of thick smoke. Then the 40 mm opened up and you knew they were getting close, followed by the 20 mm and .50s, by which time we were just holding on, wondering where the damned thing was going to hit. As far as I was concerned there was nothing worse than being buttoned up like that. The *kamikazes* were pretty effective, and I believe they sank 38 ships, with some carriers being hit repeatedly.

'On 11 May we were finally hit aboard *Bunker Hill.* I had led a pre-dawn strike on Okinawan airfields in my role as air group commander, with the sole intent of having a crack at some of these guys before they had the chance to hit us. Adm Mitcher was aboard our carrier as we were his flagship, and after every flight I would go up and report to him for a debrief. He ordered us to restrict ourselves to defence as far as aerial combat was concerned. Flying over Okinawa we operated exclusively in certain areas at pre-determined altitudes in order to avoid tangling with our own defences on the ground, but they were getting clobbered day and night and our avoidance tactics seemingly made no difference – the Marines on the ground started shooting at us as soon as I lead the strike in. We halted our attack, made a large circuit around our target, and waited until it had lightened up so that our guys could see who we were.

Bunker Hill burns following a *kamikaze* hit on 11 May 1945. Many of her planes were destroyed on the flightdeck whilst preparing to launch a strike. Marine Corsairs in the air at the time of the attack had to land on other carriers (*Robbins Collection*)

'Following the strike we got back aboard the ship at 0900. The vessel was at general quarters, and they had movies playing – it went to "Condition One Easy" at 1000, and I went down to my office which was just below the hangar deck, near the ready room. I had made a change to the torpedo squadron's schedule for that day, and I told the skipper that he could leave his general quarters station. We had just started to discuss the change in the schedule when we felt the impact of the first *kamikaze.* It landed, plane and bomb, whilst our next flight was getting ready to launch. The bomb landed a short distance from the F4U flown by VF-84's CO, Ted Hill. It took out just about all the planes on the flightdeck.

'Less than three minutes later a second *kamikaze* came in, hitting at the

An F4U-1A aboard USS *Franklin*. In March 1945 this carrier boasted three Corsair squadrons – VF-5 and VMFs -214 and -452. Lt(jg) James E Schiller of VF-5 became an ace on 18 March by downing a Zeke, adding to his previous four kills gained in F6Fs. The next day *Franklin* and her Corsairs were put out of the war by a conventional bombing attack (*National Archives*)

junction between the island and the flightdeck. His bomb went off, opening up the deck and killing most of the guys in the ready room. Ted later told me that the flightdeck just folded right up over him. The first thing I did after the initial hit was to grab my recent poker winnings, saying "If I go swimming, this damned money's going with me!" We got out in the passageway. A replenishment group had come in the day before and the place was stacked with crates up to the wardroom. I grabbed some oranges and put two or three in my pockets – we headed through the smoke caused by burning gasoline going down through several levels from the deck above. People were trapped in compartments and so forth. We arrived at the fo'c'stle and I remember a British Navy pilot who was on board as an observer, and with whom I had had discussions about our air operations, fighting the fires alongside us. I have difficulty with the English accent, but I remember him shouting "Get us some more f...ing hose down here!"

'We got the fires under control at about 1800, and soon after we finally managed to get to the engineering crew, who had been passing out like rats in the engine room due to the terrific heat and smoke – despite this hardship, the ship never went below 10 kts. We then set about trying to get the vessel back up to full speed as the Japs would be all over us due to the horrible pall of smoke we were putting up, advertising where we were. Somewhere along the way I ran into our Chief Engineer and he was in shock, wandering around just like a zombie. All I could think to do was hand him these oranges I'd picked up a while before. He had done such a marvellous job keeping *Bunker Hill* mobile. It wasn't till the next morning that all the fires were finally put out. From the wardroom I came up to the hanger deck, totally forgetting that that was where all my unit's casualties were laid out – the image that greeted me will stay etched in my mind forever. We buried them at sea the next day. The *kamikaze* strikes put an end to our combat tour.'

Ens Alfred Lerch of VF-10 accounted for six *Nates* and a *Val* northwest of Okinawa on 16 April 1945. On that day his unit destroyed 33 *kamikazes*, and their escorts, heading for US picket destroyers. Other aces involved in this action were Lt Cdr Walter E Clarke, who accounted for three, Lt(jg) Charles D Farmer (4), Lt(jg) Philip L Kirkwood (6), Ens Horace W Heath (3) and Ens Norwald R Quiel (4) (*National Archives via Grant Race*)

MARINE F4Us ON OKINAWA

Marine Corsairs arrived on Okinawa on 7 April in the form of MAG-31 – similarly equipped MAG-33 arrived two days later. Capt Perry Lin Shuman's (6 kills) VMF-311 of MAG-31 were equipped with F4U-1Cs, and operating from Yontan, they gained a total of 71 kills during the campaign. Even more successful was Maj George C Axtell's (6 kills) VMF-323 'Death Rattlers' of MAG-33 who, whilst flying from Kadena, amassed the highest kill tally by claiming 124.5 planes destroyed for no loss to themselves, producing seven aces in the process.

This unit was the last USMC Corsair squadron formed during World War 2. They flew ground attack missions against targets on Okinawa and Japan, as well as tackling *kamikazes*. In the following interviews, three of the unit's pilots, George Axtell (the unit's first CO), Jerry O'Keefe (7 kills) and Jack Broering describe some of VMF-323's operations.

F4U-1D Corsairs of VMF-323 head back to base following a ground attack mission on Okinawa. The second aircraft still has two of its 5-in rockets left on the racks. Corsairs based on Kadena and Yontan flew both close air support missions for the ground troops and Combat Air Patrols, defending primarily against *kamikazes*. It was the Corsair's close air support at this time that earned it the appellation 'The Sweetheart of Okinawa' (*USMC via Pete Mersky*)

George Axtell – 'I was a flight instructor at Cherry Point in 1943, conducting instrument training in SNJs. I was a junior Major whilst my commanding officer in charge of MAG-32 was Guadalcanal Medal of Honor winner Lt Col John L Smith (19 kills on F4Fs). We flew together and became close friends. At that time Marine aviation was expanding rapidly, and although young and believing myself to be unqualified, Smith gave me command of VMF-323. I took it on and decided that the group I had was going to be the best. We didn't know what the hell we were doing, but we thought we could whip everybody else. We had no doubts in our abilities and confidently took on Guadalcanal veterans during our combat training. We also did intercepts on Army Air Force B-24s and B-25s, making regular attacks on them. I told my men that when they made vertical runs all they had to do was keep their pipper on the nose of the bomber, and they would then pass right by its tail and miss the bomber behind. We also made runs from the low front quarter, coming in to their noses, then rolling over and down. The first time we did this I rolled over and dived to attack first, followed by my unit. The bombers scattered all over, as they must have been green pilots. They didn't want us to fly any more intercepts against them!

'Most of our kills were "flamers" – a big red fire ball. The aircraft on fire would normally blow up, usually just as you went past him. We had gun cameras, but unfortunately they weren't the best, and we had a hard time seeing exactly what we had caught on film. Furthermore, Intelligence took most of them away from us, so we could only use what little we were left with. I wished at the time that we could get copies of them, as we could have learned a lot more, and would therefore had been able to further improve our tactics. A pilot would describe what they saw, but their accounts would often differ from what showed up on the film. The pilot might for instance say that he was about 100 yards behind an enemy aircraft when the film would demonstrate that he was at least 300 yards away. The film also enabled us to co-ordinate times and positions, and by comparing them we could also verify victory credits.'

Maj George C Axtell, Jr, was the youngest CO of a Marine fighter unit when he took command of VMF-323 in 1943. During April 1945 he was credited with the destruction of six Japanese aircraft – on the 22nd he destroyed five *Vals*, damaging three more, and on the 28th he destroyed a *Nate*. Following a ground attack mission he would always unnerve his wingman by flying very low over the target to assess the damage so he could give his commander an accurate report of their mission (*Axtell Collection*)

Jerry O'Keefe – 'We were sent to the South Pacific after several weeks in Hawaii, doing little to affect the war effort until we arrived at Okinawa during Easter 1945. I was then 21 years old and I believe our CO, Maj Axtell, was either 23 or 24 years old. I believe I was one of the youngest aces at age 21. Axtell, our XO, Jefferson D Dorroh (6 kills), and I all became aces on one flight. Dorroh got six, and Axtell and I five each. This was the first time the three of us had ever encountered the enemy in aerial combat – the date was 22 April 1945.

'On 28 April Axtell was leading a 16-plane flight and I was his section leader, which was my normal place. I spotted "bogies" at three o'clock, well below us and headed south toward the ships at Okinawa. Apparently no-one else in our flight saw the "bogies", so I asked permission to have the formation with my wingman, Lt Bill Hood (5.5 kills). As we turned to our right and began a shallow dive, it became clear that these were "bandits", instead of merely "bogies". I relayed this info back to our flight, which was then to our rear. With hand signals, Hood and I separated, Hood to the right and rear of the "Bandits" and me to the left, rear and also above. The enemy apparently never saw us until we began shooting. Hood got two on his first pass and I got one. I then turned and followed another as he dove straight down, destroying my second enemy. I never saw any enemy planes in flight again. The second action gave me seven victories, and for a time I was the leading ace on Okinawa. Later, Lts J W Ruhsam and R Wade each scored seven kills. as well'

Jack Broering – 'The frontline was only six miles away from the field on Okinawa so we could see other Corsairs making their runs. We were also close enough to take ground fire but, as the campaign progressed, we got further and further out of their range.

'Bombing and rocket attacks were quite similar, differing in only by the amount of lead you give the target. Our rockets – 3 1/2 and 5 in rounds – were fine weapons. I liked them as I thought they were the most effective weapons we had. We usually fired them whilst in a 45° dive, making about 400 mph. If you went too fast you'd start losing the covering on the elevator. You could put your "pipper" on the target with rockets, whereas with bombs you had to judge the correct lead so that it landed where you wanted it to. With Napalm we'd make a flatter approach, trying to spread it over a large area. We dropped at about 100 ft, Napalm being contained in our fuel tanks – they weren't too accurate. We used it to effect against tunnels and caves, sometimes managing to put it right into the entrances.

'All of us were trained as fighter pilots, and the ultimate was to go out and shoot somebody down. So we all hoped for that opportunity, but it was a matter of being in the right place at the right time. On 22 April our squadron shot down 25 planes in about 20 minutes. My flight was returning from a routine CAP when they started calling out all the bogies. We had quite a bit of fuel left, but the command ship wouldn't let us return and join the fight as schedules had to be followed. Another time we were on our way out onto station when I spotted four *Tonys* coming by us at a lower altitude. I kept calling them out, but my section leader couldn't see them and wouldn't turn the lead over to me. Other members of my flight also saw them and we were all screaming over the radio and jumping up and down in our cockpits, but to no avail. I couldn't assume the lead, nor leave my position so we had to go sailing on by. It would have been a perfect opportunity for me to gain a victory, but it wasn't to be.

'Fortunately a flight behind us picked them up. On 28 May after a pre-dawn take off we were patrolling our station when the controlling ship kept calling out a bogey. It remained in the same relative position to us all the time and it became apparent that an aircraft was shadowing us in the cloud layer above us. We broke up; two of us going above the clouds while the other two waited below. The enemy must have thought the whole flight was coming up so he went down below. The other section called out that he was down there so we went down too. A path of early morning sunlight was hitting the water and the enemy aircraft was flying right down it – he couldn't get out of it. The other two were waiting for him and they shot down the *Tojo*.'

1st Lt Joseph V Dillard of VMF-323 was credited with 6.333 enemy aircraft, and he is seen here with F4U-1D 'No 51'. His victims were a mixed bag of types, including *Vals*, *Dinahs*, a *Kate* and a *Judy* (*National Archives*)

2nd Lt Robert Wade of VMF-323 again seen in F4U-1D 'No 51'. Although aircraft were not assigned to individual pilots within the unit, this machine does appear to wear Wade's first two kill marks. By the time this picture was taken he had shot down two *Tonys* on 15 April and two *Nates* and two *Vals* on 4 May. He went on to claim two half-shares in the destruction of both a *Dinah* and a *Val*, as well as damaging three *Nates*, thus bringing his final score to seven confirmed victories (*National Archives*)

Shangri-La

Following *Bunker Hill*'s retirement, *Essex* and *Bennington*'s F4Us would only be accompanied by *Shangri-La* with Air Group 85 aboard. Lt Joe D Robbins (5 kills) was assigned to VBF-8 which flew the F4U-1C. He had previously gained two victories flying the F6F with VF-6 aboard *Intrepid.*

'On 8 April 1945, we departed Ford Island and on 26 April 1945 we joined the carrier Task Force off Okinawa. We had 16 carriers making up three task groups. One Task Group would replenish each day whilst the other two would be hitting targets in Japan. On 4 May I was the flight leader for 12 F4U-1Cs flying CAP over a destroyer 12 miles north of Okinawa. The Japs were sending planes from Japan to attack our forces on Okinawa and ships at sea. At times *kamikaze* planes would be at a low altitude with fighter cover at a higher altitude. Our mission was to intercept and shoot down these aircraft. We launched in the early morning from the *Shangri-La* and took up our station. As always, we charged and test-fired our guns after take-off. My division was assigned an altitude of 20,000 ft, whilst the second division was at 10,000 ft and the third 5000 ft. We had been on station a short time when at 0830 we received a vector at distance 26 miles to a bogey, and we were told that it was below us. I had fuel in the belly tank and I didn't want to drop it until I saw the bogey.

'These flights were about four hours long so you didn't want to drop the tank until you had to. I had my left hand on the switch in preparation, ready to go to the main gas tank and drop the belly store when I saw the bogey. We were all looking down when all of a sudden about 30 Zekes came from above and attacked us. We didn't see them approach as it was hazy and we had also been told they were below us. I switched tanks and dropped the belly tank and made a sharp turn all at the same time – I had to. By doing this, however the engine was not getting any fuel, so it stopped. It takes only a few seconds to switch and get suction again, but I didn't have that few seconds. You don't get suction when you are making sharp turns and I was really making them. One plane was in my gun sight coming from the 10 o'clock position. I tried a 30° deflection shot and pulled the trigger; no guns. I was banking right and then left as steep as I could to keep them from shooting at me, still no engine. I kept recharging the guns and still they wouldn't fire. I kept banking one side and then to the other, keeping my nose down and losing altitude. I had at least four of them in my sights, but my guns wouldn't fire!

'These enemy planes were escort cover for some *kamikaze* planes below. Although I wasn't hit, they shot down my wingman, Frank Siddall, and second section leader, Sonny Chernoff, and then they left. The division at 5000 ft then intercepted them. I was at about 16,000 ft when I got my engine started, and I followed my wingman down and he made a good landing in the

'No 51' of was obviously a popular aircraft to be photographed with as here its is again, this time with 1st Lt John W Ruhsam posing on its wing. This pilot's final tally was seven confirmed victories and three damaged. Both Ruhsam and Wade flew together and shared their combat victories (*National Archives*)

VMF-323 pilots pose together on the wing of an F4U-1D, with all bar one of them being an ace. From left to right, CO, Maj George C Axtell, Jr (6 victories), XO, Maj Jefferson D Dorroh (6 victories), 1st Lt Normand T Theriault (2.25 victories), 1st Lt Albert P Wells (5 victories), 1st Lt Francis A Terrill (6.083 victories), 2nd Lt Charles W Drake (5 victories), 1st Lt Joseph V Dillard (6.333 victories), 1st Lt Jeremiah J O'Keefe (7 victories), 2nd Lt Dewey F Durnford (6.333 victories) and 1st Lt William L Hood, Jr (5.5 victories) (*Axtell Collection*)

water. I stayed over him until a destroyer picked him up 35 minutes later. The destroyer that rescued him, the *St George*, was hit by a *kamikaze* two days later while he was still aboard.

'Out of the four planes in my division, none of the guns would fire. At that time we were the only Navy unit that had the 20 mm guns. That afternoon they were tested at high altitude and it was found that they froze and would not fire at about 15,000 ft. We checked with Washington and learned that the flights that were to test them at high altitude had been cancelled! From then on we were restricted to 12,000 ft until we got gun heaters. We still flew CAPs and target strikes below this altitude. VBF-85 (.50 cal) flew the higher CAPs.

'On 11 May 1945 I was on another early morning take-off to fly target CAP over our destroyer, again about 12 miles north of Okinawa. We had 16 F4U-1Cs up, and this time because of the gun freezing problems, my two divisions were at a lower altitude – 6000 ft – whilst our XO, Lt Cdr Hubert, was the mission leader flying with two divisions at 12,000 ft. Again my wingman was Frank Siddall. After about an hour on station, we were given a vector to the north. We flew for about five minutes (25 miles) and then sighted about 16 Zekes directly ahead and a little below. They were in no particular formation – Zekes just tended to fly together. My altitude was about 5000 ft when they were sighted – they were at about 4000 ft. I was leading the two divisions and the second division was on my starboard side.

'I spotted them first and made a left turn. During the turn I broke off to make a run on them, and as I started down, they just broke up going in all directions. The rest of the formation followed me down, each picking out a plane. I picked out one on the outside of my dive. He just took off heading west and dove down to about 1000 ft. I was on his tail and there were others going in the same direction. This is not the desired type of attack, but we had to get them quickly before they got to our ships. We couldn't make runs on them and pull up because there wasn't enough time. A Zeke and I were going about the same speed. I was in range, about 600 ft behind him, so I opened fire with no deflection. I aimed at the middle of his fuselage. Firing one medium burst, I saw the bullets hit the aircraft, every third bullet being an explosive. I could see damage to his tail, but no fire. He rolled over into a "Split S" and went down, and that's the last I saw of him. It all happened so fast I couldn't tell if I hit the pilot. Since I was firing 20 mm they should have gotten through to him. I don't think there was any way he could have survived, but I didn't claim a kill because I didn't see him crash or burn – he was listed as damaged.

'I looked left and there was the second Zeke. He just came over and parked in front of me as they were split up and flying all over the area. I had made a slight left turn and he had probably been trying to make a run on us and ended up there. He was about 750 ft away and within range so I fired a medium burst. He

1st Lt Jeremiah J O'Keefe of VMF-323 indicates his final tally of seven victories whilst in the cockpit of F4U-1D 'No 26'. On 22 April, during a 20-minute engagement, VMF-323 pilots destroyed 24.75 aircraft, O'Keefe downing five *Vals*, one of which attempted to ram his F4U before hitting the sea (*O'Keefe Collection*)

F4U-1D 'No 31' of VMF-323 undergoes maintenance on Okinawa in late April 1945. This aircraft was one of the machines flown by 1st Lt Francis A Terrill, and it appears rather worn with its underside splattered with mud (*Broering Collection*)

caught fire and the gun camera film later showed a parachute. Except for the fire, I saw no damage to the plane. Again I looked left and there was a third Zeke. I didn't think all of the planes were *kamikazes* because they were trying to attack me – *kamikazes* carried bombs but no guns or parachutes. Some probably were *kamikazes*, but from above I did not see any bombs. I would rather have got the *kamikazes* if I could tell which ones they were, since they were the ones that went after our ships.

'The third Zeke was at 10 o'clock but out of range (about 2000 ft away) at about the same altitude as I was (1000 feet). I turned left about 20 ° and started chasing him. We chased him for about 10 miles when we came to the island of Tari Shima. He got down to about 100 ft off the water and close to the island. I didn't tell my wingman, Frank Siddall, to keep on his tail – I didn't have to. He saw what I was doing, and that this way one of us would get him. He had been my wingman for a long time, and a good one. He was always there with me, and most of the time I didn't have to tell him what to do. We had the Zeke boxed in, and if he didn't go around the island then Frank would be on his tail. The island wasn't very high, reaching 300 ft in places over its two-mile length.

'I assumed the Zeke was going around the island because he made a 30° left turn. He was very close to the island and low, at about 100 ft. He had started a left turn at the other end of the island. The only chance he had was to try to trick us into following him around low. You didn't make tight turns in the F4U at low altitude as it would stall and spin. The Zeke could out-turn us and gain distance, then try to pull away from us and go home. I pulled up making a left turn, then a right and got him on a head-on. He was about 800 ft ahead of and slightly below me when I fired. This makes an easy shot because you can aim ahead of him; he would run into the bullets, without deflection, just a high-to-low head-on shot. I gave it a long burst. I didn't see the bullets strike. I just pulled the trigger and he blew to hell – a big ball of fire. I took a south-east heading in the direction of our station.

'It was only a couple of minutes before I saw a fourth Zeke – he could have been coming to help the one I just shot down. He was at my eleven o'clock position. He had been heading toward me, but made a left turn and took up a course about the same as mine. I was at about 500 ft and he was lower. He dove even lower to pick up speed, getting down to between 10 to 25 ft above the water. I was then at about 100 ft, with my wingman on my right wing. I was wide open for at least ten minutes and wasn't gaining on him. After we landed, my wingman told me that at the time sparks were coming out of my exhaust. The F4U top speed was 405 mph at sea level, so the Zeke was also moving at about that speed. I was probably gaining a little on him, but I couldn't stay wide open much longer or I would burn up my engine. If I fixed my sights on him in level position my bullets would hit the water behind him. By raising my nose the bullets would go

Capt Kenneth A Walsh pictured in his F4U-4 'No 13', BuNo 80879, following his 21st kill on 22 June 1945. On this day he shot down a *kamikaze* over northern Okinawa whilst serving with VMF-222. Minutes after this picture was taken, his crewchief, Sgt Harry Ross (seen left), attached the final kill decal. The F4U-4 was the most advanced variant of the Corsair to see service during World War 2, its primary differences compared with previous models being a larger engine, four bladed prop, revised air ducts (resulting in the characteristic cowling chin), a revised cockpit, including a raised deck, armoured seat, better instrument layout and an improved bubble canopy (*Walsh Collection*)

The USS *Shangri-La* on 17 August 1945. Her Air Group 85 Corsairs have the new single letter 'Z' marking that was adopted on 27 July to replace the short-lived 'G' symbol system (a white lightning bolt) (*Robbins Collection*)

straight for about 800-900 ft, then drop downward due to gravity. Even if he was 800 ft away, I would have to raise my sights above him. When I fired, he was at the right distance, but by the time the bullets got there he had moved. Like a deflection shot, you have to aim at the point the plane will be when the bullets get there. I knew I couldn't continue wide open for much longer. I was gaining on him too slowly.

'My job was to shoot him down and I didn't want to be the one to have to land in the water. I had used up a lot of ammo already and I wasn't going to waste any – there could be several more out there we could run into. My plan was to try to lob the bullets into him so I fired another short burst. He hit the water and bounced back up and kept going. I knew I had the right angle on raising my nose so I fired again. He hit the water again and bounced back up. Again I fired and he hit the water and came back up. The fourth time he went down to stay. The gun camera showed all of this on film – the parachute of No 2, No 3 blowing up and No 4 bouncing off the water. The camera had a few seconds override so it showed things the pilot didn't see. After number four it had been a long day, and I was tired. We reported to our control ship and the two of us returned to the carrier.

'On 10 July 1945, I was part of a 16-plane fighter sweep over airfields in the Tokyo area. Our mission was to knock out the Japanese Air Force, either on the ground or in the air. Sweeps were made on Katori, Choisi, Konoiki, Ikisu, Kitaura, Hokoda, Kashiwa, Imba and Shiroi airfields. It was a successful day, with considerable damage being done to Jap aircraft on the ground. No airborne enemy opposition was encountered. From 10 July to 15 August we continued to fly sweeps on Japan, which mostly consisted of targets of opportunity in Hokaido, Tokyo, Honshu, Kyushu and Osaka. Our weaponry was usually made up four 20 mm cannon, eight 8-inch rockets and either a single 1000- or two 500-lb bombs. Each flight over Japan we would hit several targets, diving in from about 20,000 ft. In each dive we would first shoot the four 20 mm cannon, then fire a couple of 8-inch rockets and then drop a bomb.

'On 15 August 1945 at 0530 we took off with a flight of 12 planes to hit the Tokyo Shibura electric plant with a dozen 1000-lb bombs. This site was a priority target, having never been hit before. Just as we got to within sight of the coast of Japan the recall was given. "Jettison bombs and returns to base; the War is over." We dropped our ordnance in the water and headed back. It was cloudy and some people were up above the clouds and I heard people screaming "Don't drop now, we're below you!"

'We ceased offensive operations and were merely told to protect ourselves by "shooting down snoopers", not vindictively, but in a "friendly" way! Japanese planes did continue their attacks in considerable number, numerous planes were shot down, mostly by anti-aircraft fire and RAPCAPS (Patrol Fighters stationed about 20-30 miles from the fleet). On 22 August 22 I flew in a 1000-plane dress formation over the fleet to mark the end of the war.'

Lt Joe D Robbins pictured on the wing of one of VF-85's F4U-1Ds. These aircraft were soon replaced with new F4U-1Cs to serve in the fighter role, whilst VBF-85 retained their Ds for ground attack duties. Having previously flown the F6F Hellcat, Robbins thought the F4U was easier to land on board the carrier due to the better bubble canopy incorporated on the later marks (*Robbins Collection*)

On 24 July 1945 Robbins, flying F4U-1C BuNo 82749, performed a *Dumbo* escort to the Inland Sea, near Kobe. The 'X' in this shot shows the location of a downed *Yorktown* pilot, and above to the right can be seen an F6F-P. A little higher towards the centre of the picture is an F4U – both aircraft were part of the rescue effort. Whilst the flying boat landed and successfully picked up the pilot, Robbins and other members of Air Group 85 strafed gun positions firing from all around. During this mission VF-85 pilot Lt(jg) R A Bloomfield shot down an *Oscar*, whilst three VBF-85 pilots shared the credit for damag-ing another (*Robbins Collection*)

ACES MAKER

During World War 2, some 1300 American fighter pilots were credited with destroying five or more enemy aircraft in aerial combat. Of these, 371 served in the US Navy and 124 in the Marine Corps. Thus, over one-third of all American fighter aces involved in the conflict wore naval aviation's beautiful wings of gold.

Unlike the Army Air Force, which flew eight primary fighter aircraft during the war (including the British Spitfire and Beaufighter), the Navy used just three – the Grumman F4F/FM Wildcat, F6F Hellcat and Chance Vought F4U Corsair. Consequently, Navy and Marine aces were consolidated more closely by aircraft type, and that is why the Hellcat became America's all-time champion 'ace maker' with 307 pilots credited with five or more kills in type. By comparison, North American's P-51 Mustang produced some 275 USAAF aces.

On the other hand, there were relatively heavy losses among F6F pilots. Throughout the war, combat-related pilot losses totalled some 450 aviators, including 20 Hellcat aces.

Although Grumman Aircraft Company produced the Wildcat fighter and Avenger torpedo aircraft, the Hellcat unquestionably became the Long Island firm's greatest contribution to the American victory. Built in large numbers (more than 12,000 airframes in three years), the F6F proved a near-perfect weapon for the war it had to fight. With a superb engine and no serious developmental problems, it was tough enough to withstand routine carrier operations. It was also reasonably fast, well armed, easy to fly and (perhaps more importantly) easy to maintain. In short, the Hellcat was a masterpiece of carrier-aircraft engineering and design. Small wonder that it became the most successful vehicle for a generation of American fighter aces.

Whilst Wildcat pilots of the US Navy and Marine Corps were just managing to hold their own in the Pacific as the final months of 1942 slipped away, Grumman was hastily pushing its new fleet fighter through its test programme. This company shot shows second prototype XF6F-3 (BuNo 02982) on a test flight over upstate New York in late October 1942 (*Aerospace Publishing*)

As this photograph clearly shows, the first production aircraft completed at Bethpage by Grumman were finished at the factory in the Blue Grey (FS 36118) over Light Grey (FS 36440) scheme. This anonymous early-build F6F-3 is undergoing carrier trials aboard an equally unidentifiable carrier in 1943 (*Jerry Scutts*)

ORGANISATION

In 1943 the US Navy possessed 'fighting squadrons' or FitRons – the phrase 'fighter squadron' was a postwar development. When the F6F entered combat in the Central Pacific that August, each fighting squadron nominally had 36 F6F-3s aboard large (generally *Essex*-class) carriers (CVs) and about 24 to the much smaller *Independence*-class light carriers (CVLs). Land-based Navy fighter squadrons generally followed the organisational structure of the CV units.

The basic building block of a naval fighter squadron was the four-aircraft division, composed of two pairs, or sections. By 1943, naval aviators were skilled in use of mutual-support tactics based upon Lt Cdr John Thach's 'weave' pattern, proven in the Battle of Midway in June 1942. Developed to enable the Wildcat to survive against faster, more manoeuvrable opponents, the 'Thach Weave' was exploited by F6F squadrons whose aircraft was not only faster than the F4F, but climbed better as well.

Despite the success of the Hellcat in fighter-versus-fighter combat, the fleet defense mission assumed ever-greater importance as the Pacific war progressed. No other statistic better illustrates this point than the fact that, from mid-1943 to late 1944, CV F6F squadrons grew from 36 to 54 and finally to 73 aircraft. Successful *kamikaze* attacks, initiated in the Philippines campaign, placed a premium upon adequate fighter protection for the Fast Carrier Task Force.

The administrative requirements of dealing with six-dozen aircraft and 100 or more pilots finally led to the establishment of fighter-bomber (VBF) squadrons in early 1945. From a practical standpoint, the latter's operating methods remained identical, with both the VF and VBF units sharing maintenance chores and flying the same aircraft interchangeably. But making two squadrons out of one of course helped to simplify paperwork and enhanced operating efficiency. Complications only arose when carrier-based Corsair VBF squadrons flew alongside Hellcat FitRons, in which case mutual maintenance and logistics were simply not possible.

Owing to shipboard personnel limitations, Navy and Marine squadrons generally delegated collateral (i.e., non-flying) duties to most pilots. Under the three senior aviators – commanding officer, executive officer and flight (operations) officer – were relatively junior pilots in charge of gunnery, navigation, personnel, parachutes and emergency equipment, and assorted other areas. Usually a squadron contained only two non-flying officers – those responsible for engineering (primarily aircraft maintenance) and intelligence. Both were reservists, the fabled

The US Navy chose VF-9 at NAS Norfolk to be the premier fleet squadron to receive the F6F-3, the unit having only just returned to their Virginia air station following a combat cruise in the Atlantic aboard USS *Ranger* in F4F-4s – they had flown in support of the *Torch* landings on the North African coast. With its complement increased from 27 Wildcats to 36 Hellcats, VF-9 went aboard the equally new USS *Essex* on 13 March 1943 to carrier-qualify its pilots (*Jerry Scutts*)

Originator of the Commander Air Group's '00' (or 'double nuts' as the marking is often irreverently referred to by junior officers), recently-promoted Cdr 'Jimmy' Flatley, Jr, is seen climbing down from his personal F6F-3 after making the first ever landing aboard the second USS *Yorktown* on 6 May 1943 (*Jerry Scutts*)

VF-8 reformed on F6F-3s at NAS Norfolk in 1943, the squadron being commissioned on 1 June under the command of Lt Cdr William M Collins, Jr (who would eventually become the unit's ranking ace with nine kills). Seen on a training sortie over Virginia in late 1943, these F6Fs wear the newly-introduced tri-colour scheme and pre-war-style fuselage codes (*Philip Jarrett*)

'90-day wonders' being given specialised training as aviation volunteer specialists, or AV(S) officers. Even Annapolis men conceded that the Navy could not have won the war without them.

CAMPAIGNS

Beginning in late August 1943, the Grumman Hellcat embarked on the first of a half-dozen major campaigns over the next two years. In those 24 months, the F6F would become the worst enemy of the naval and army air forces of Imperial Japan, downing (by official count) some 5200 enemy aircraft. Along the way, the angular Grumman produced more American fighter aces than any other aircraft in history – 307 in all. Additionally, F6Fs participated in the invasion of southern France in August 1944, adding a truly global dimension to the type's war-winning contribution.

Cdr Flatley keeps a watchful eye on a mixed formation of Hellcats and Avengers as they head for Marcus Island on 31 August 1943 – the date of the Hellcat's combat debut. No aircraft were encountered during the raids, and VF-5 had to wait until the 5 October strike on Wake Island to achieve its first kills. This 'Dash Three' was the second F6F assigned to the CAG (*Aerospace Publishing*)

Turning the clock back 12 months, by August 1943 the United States had in place the weapons and procedures which would yield naval victory over Japan. Foremost in the 'arsenal of democracy' was a new generation of carrier aircraft embarked in new ships – the versatile, long-lived *Essex* (CV-9) class and the much smaller, but equally fast, *Independence* (CVL-22) class of light carriers. Both types operated F6F-3 fighters.

First blood for the Hellcat was drawn by a member of a veteran squadron. On 1 September Lt(jg) Richards L Loesch of VF-6 caught a Kawanishi H6K near Howland Island. It was his only victory of the war, but began a Hellcat string of more than 5200 over the next two years. 'Fighting' Six splashed another 'Emily' west of Baker Island two days later, the first victim of future ace Thaddeus T Coleman, Jr.

The F6F's first two kills were scored by carrier pilots. But on 6 September, land-based squadrons in the Solomon Islands began logging a steady string of claims. The first fell to VF-33's Ens J A Warren, who downed a Zero near Margusiai Island. By month's end, Hellcats were credited with 35 shootdowns, of which 29 were scored by Solomons-based VFs -33, -38 and -40. Perhaps the greatest irony of the Hellcat's career was the fact that shore-based pilots out-scored their seagoing counterparts in the first month of combat.

On 14 September, 16 VF-33 Hellcats took off from Munda to escort an unusually large strike force comprising 72 Dauntlesses and Avengers attacking Ballale. Ten of the F6F pilots engaged Japanese aircraft, including Lt C K 'Ken' Hildebrandt who tacked onto a Zero trying to attack the withdrawing SBDs;

'I poured lead into him and he rolled over on his back smoking, at 200 ft. Tracers went by me then, so I pulled up sharply and collected

7.7 mm slugs through the cockpit enclosure. They went into my jungle pack and my back. The Zero turned away as I turned into (Ens Jack) Fruin who had another one following him. Firing from 100 yards, I continued through his pullout and roll. He went in when his port wing was shot off.

'Then I was jumped at 100 ft by a Zero. Using the hand lever to dump my flaps, I saw the Jap go by and pull up in a turn. I just held the trigger down until he blew up. Suddenly the sky was empty. Fruin was nowhere to be seen and I headed home.'

Often wrongly-captioned as showing a VF-35 F6F-3 from USS *Cabot*, this shot actually shows a VF-6 Hellcat going over the side of USS *Princeton* on 9 September 1943. The F6F suffered a sheared tailhook, which forced its pilot to 'throttle up' and attempt to take off before running out of deck. The Hellcat stalled and fell into the sea off the port side of the ship. The pilot survived his dunking and was picked up by the plane-guard destroyer (*Jerry Scutts*)

All F6Fs returned to Munda, reporting eight Zeros destroyed, though two Grummans were written off and their pilots wounded. Ken Hildebrandt added two more victories in December to become one of the earliest Hellcat aces.

The last kill of September was the first Japanese fighter claimed by a carrier-based Hellcat. On the 25th, Lt John Magda of *Saratoga's* VF-12 got a Zero over Barakoma, Bougainville. Magda, who had survived VF-8's Midway debacle, was eventually credited with four victories. In 1950 he led the *Blue Angels* aerobatic team (equipped with F9F Panthers) into action over Korea following the unit's mobilisation, and subsequent assignment to VF-191 aboard USS *Princeton*. Magda was killed in combat over Tanchon in March 1951.

During October 1943 the fast carriers began work in earnest. A major strike on Wake not only afforded the Navy with a long-awaited chance to avenge the Japanese seizure of the island in 1941, but to also introduce some significant new squadrons to combat.

Had the Japanese on Wake Island seen a roster of pilots assigned to fly on the 10 October strikes, they might have wondered if their German allies had changed sides. Flying with *Lexington's* VF-16 were

This flightline view of Hellcats at Munda (on New Georgia Island) taken in September 1943 shows *Navy* fighters of VF-33, -38 or -40, not *Marine Corps* F6Fs as has often appeared in print. All three units enjoyed success during their stay in the beleaguered Solomon Islands, claiming a shared total of 29 kills in their first month of operations (*US Navy*)

Munda was an important ex-Japanese Navy airfield taken by the Marines in mid-1943 and turned into a main staging base for new aircraft arriving in the Solomons. Again, these aircraft could be from any one of three Hellcat units operating in the area at the time this shot was taken in September 1943. Aircraft No 2 has the name *BATTLING Bobbie* emblazoned on its fuselage, and with the other more anonymous Hellcats, shares the jungle strip with a number of USMC F4U-1 Corsairs (*Tailhook*)

aviators named Birkholm, Burckhalter, Frendberg and Schwarz. Cdr Paul Buie's squadron claimed six victories and Ed Owen's VF-5 off *Yorktown* bagged 17, while *Essex's* Lt Cdr Phil Torrey led VF-9 to four successes.

Lt Cdr E H 'Butch' O'Hare's VF-6, with VF-22, -24 and -25, flew from *Independence*-class carriers. O'Hare, who had won the Medal of Honour protecting the original *Lexington* from Japanese bombers, had not been in combat since February 1942 – this was his chance to make up for lost time (for further details see *Wildcat Aces of World War 2*, also by the author, published earlier in this series). Once the enemy formation had been sighted, he immediately led his four-fighter division into a mixed group of 'Zekes' and 'Bettys', destroying one of each while his second section got two more. One of the former fell to O'Hare's section leader, Lt(jg) Alexander Vraciu.

Always proud of having flown with 'Butch' O'Hare, Vraciu recounted his introduction to combat on the master's wing;

'I was "Butch's" section lead with Willy Callan as my wingman – "Butch" was leading with Hank Landry as his wingman. We high-sided a flight of three Zekes a couple of thousand feet below us. My radio was out completely, but I could sense what was happening. "Butch" burned the Zero on the left and I blew up the one on the right. It was my first aerial combat, and like an idiot, I was mesmerised by the Zeke. The lead Zero headed down and landed at Wake. I watched him land and burned the plane on the ground, followed by a "Betty" on the second pass.

'After our first pass, "Butch" and Hank ended up below some cloud cover, and according to "Butch" later in the ready room, ran into some "Bettys", and he got one of them.'

Including Vraciu, at least nine future aces counted their first kills among the 41 claimed at Wake that day.

Another Solomons Hellcat 'flying in the face' of authority by carrying personalised nose art was VF-33's F6F-3 BuNo 25813, the mount of Lt C K 'Ken' Hildebrandt. *MY OWN JOAN II* was a deadly weapon of war when flown by the San Franciscan, who used it to down four Zekes and a 'Hamp' between 14 September and 24 December 1943. Both looking well-used following four months of solid combat, Hildebrandt and BuNo 25813 repose on Christmas Day 1943, less than 24 hours after they had both made 'ace'. VF-33 produced two other aces during its Solomons tour – Lt(jg)s Frank E Schneider with seven kills and James J Kinsella with five, although the latter's first two kills had been scored in February 1943 whilst flying F4F-4s with VF-72 (*'Ken' Hildebrandt via Mark Styling*)

This panoramic view of *Yorktown's* flightdeck shows Cdr Jim Flatley in his '00'-coded F6F-3 heading a line up of VF-5 Hellcats being readied for launch on 5 October 1943, the day that the US Navy returned to the skies over Wake Island after a long absence. The unit claimed 17 Zeros destroyed over Wake on this date

FORTRESS RABAUL

During November two carrier strikes were launched against Rabaul, New Britain. On the 5th, Rear Adm F C Sherman's task group hastily organised a strike on Japanese warships reported in the area. The veteran *Saratoga* and the new light carrier *Princeton* put up almost 100 aircraft, almost half of which were Hellcats. 'Fighting 12' and '23' claimed 21 victories between them, with the TBFs and SBDs adding seven more. More importantly, six Japanese cruisers were damaged, thus preventing them interfering with the Allied landing at Empress Augusta Bay.

Six days later carrier- and land-based naval aviators claimed 137 victories – it was the first time that American fliers had ever claimed 100 shootdowns in a 24-hour period, and although Japanese losses were undoubtedly far less, it was still an awe-inspiring performance – and an ominous portent for the enemy of things to come.

Despite bad weather thwarting most of Sherman's pilots en route to the target, Rear Adm A E Montgomery's three carrier air groups were engaged almost non-stop throughout the day. A further indication of the intensity of the aerial combat is the fact that bomber and torpedo squadrons also claimed a dozen shootdowns.

Among the fighter squadrons, the most heavily engaged were *Essex's* VF-9, with 55 credited victories, and *Bunker Hill's* VF-18, with 38 claims. Elements of the

VF-16 'Fighting Airedales' F6F-3 is prepared aboard *Lexington* in November 1943. By the end of the year six pilots had made ace in the F6F, half of them from VF-16. The badge applied in decal form forward of the windscreen is in fact an Airedale, complete with pistol and flying helmet! (*Jerry Scutts*)

Despite their undisputed skill once engaged in aerial combat, none of the pilots featured in this, or any other, volume in the aces series could have achieved 'acedom' without the support of men like these back on the ground (or, as in this case, aboard ship). Fresh from keeping F6Fs airworthy during the Gilbert Islands campaign, plane captains from VF-18 pose for *Bunker Hill*'s photographer in December 1943 (*J D Billo via Mark Styling*)

VF-10 F4F veteran Lt 'Jim' Billo formates with his CAP leader astern of *Bunker Hill*'s Task Group in November 1943 whilst the rest of VF-18 'wages war' with Japanese forces over the Gilberts (*J D Billo via Mark Styling*)

latter carrier's original FitRon – VF-17 – paid a short visit as Lt Cdr Tom Blackburn led his F4U-1A Corsairs up from Ondonga, New Georgia, cycling aboard to rearm, refuel and enjoy a little hot food – the remaining half of the unit recovered aboard *Essex*. The 'Jolly Rogers' had added 18.5 kills to their scoreboard by day's end.

Top scorer among F6F pilots was VF-9's Lt Cdr H N Houck, with two 'Kate' torpedo-bombers and a 'Val' dive-bomber to his credit. At least 13 other Hellcat pilots claimed double kills.

Against fierce opposition the carrier aviators sank a destroyer and damaged four other warships, but the indications from the fighter battles were clear – Rabaul's days as a Japanese stronghold were numbered. Hardly had the smoke cleared at Rabaul when the fast carriers shifted targets eastward. Operation *Galvanic* – the occupation of the Gilbert Islands – was to also draw heavy aerial opposition.

Appropriately, 'Fighting Nine', the first squadron to receive Hellcats, also produced the first F6F ace. He was Lt(jg) Hamilton McWhorter, III, a 22-year-old Georgian who had first scored at Wake Island on 5 October. He added two more Zekes during the Rabaul strike and reached ace status during *Galvanic*. He splashed a 'Pete' floatplane off Tarawa Atoll on 18 November – the Navy's only victory that day – and his fifth victim, a Mitsubishi G4M 'Betty', followed 24 hours later.

Tarawa proved a brutal, bloody, fight for the Marines, but provided good hunting for the 'Airedales' of VF-16. On 23 November Cdr Buie and 11 other *Lexington* pilots were vectored into a formation of Zekes near Makin Island. Placed by the radar controller in 'a fighter pilot's dream position' 4000 ft above and 'upsun' of the 24 enemy aircraft, Buie and company chased down 17 'bandits' from 23,000 to 5000 ft. From that combat Ens E R Hanks emerged with five kills and a probable, thus becoming the first of 44 F6F pilots who would make 'ace in a day'.

Twenty-six hours later Buie led another batch of 'Airedales' into combat over almost the same spot, but this time the F6F pilots began the fight with a 2000-ft altitude deficit. Though one Hellcat went down in the Zekes' initial pass, VF-16 reversed the odds in an unusual combat which swerved upward and then down. When it was over, 'Lex's' Hellcats had splashed 12 more with Lt(jg) A L Frendberg claiming three Zekes to become the third F6F ace.

A by-product of *Galvanic* was the introduction of carrier-based nightfighters. Occasionally described in print as an impromptu effort, these 'bat teams' had in fact been organised and trained prior to their deployment. Their advocate and leader was 'Butch' O'Hare who, by November, was commanding *Enterprise's* Air Group Six. His assigned fighter squadron was temporarily VF-2, under Cdr W A Dean.

O'Hare's 'bat teams' were made up of individuals hand-picked for night interceptions, which they performed in addition to their squadron's usual daytime operational routine. The teams comprised two VF-2 F6F pilots directed by a VT-6 TBF equipped with radar. Operating in conjunction with shipboard fighter directors, the teams at least stood a chance of disrupting a nocturnal attack on a carrier force, if not actually destroying the raiders.

The acid test came on the night of 27 November following two fruitless Japanese efforts to locate the task group. O'Hare and Ens Warren Skon (himself a future 7-kill ace with VF-2) were teamed with Lt Cdr John Phillips, skipper of 'Torpedo Six'. Some 15 'Bettys' attacked the carriers, and Phillips' radar operator vectored him onto two bombers, which he shot down. He called for O'Hare's section to rejoin and, in the process, it appears that a third Japanese bomber was attracted by the Avenger's navigation lights. The TBF gunner glimpsed a strange aircraft in the dark and fired a burst, apparently causing O'Hare to take evasive action. Whatever happened, 'Butch' O'Hare's Hellcat crashed into the water, along with its pilot. It was an irreplaceable loss.

Pre-invasion strikes against Kwajalein Atoll in December completed fast carrier operations for the year. Again VF-16 had the best of the shooting, claiming 18 of the 40 credited victories over Roi Island on the 4th. A number of

Shoulder to shoulder on 'Vultures' Row', a burgeoning number of the ship's company look on as the deck crew ready VF-9's Hellcats for yet another launch from *Essex* during Operation *Galvanic* (*Aerospace Publishing*)

Catapult officer Lt Walter L Chewning, USNR, clambers onto the displaced belly tank of a VF-2 Hellcat to extricate its dazed pilot, Ens Byron 'By' M Johnson, from the flames. Both men survived this harrowing ordeal, played out aboard *Enterprise* during a recovery cycle on 10 November 1943 off the Gilberts, totally unscathed. Johnson later went on to score eight kills with VF-2 during the invasion of Iwo Jima in 1944 (*Aerospace Publishing*)

these kills were claimed by 21-year-old Texan, Ens Edward G Wendorf, who downed a 'Betty' and three Zekes (although official naval records only credit him with two Zekes and a half-share in the 'Betty', with the remaining A6M being classed as a probable) – he also very nearly became a statistic himself, however, as he explains in the following report written specially for this volume;

'My BIG day had arrived. It was 4 December 1943! We went into Kwajalein as a group with three levels of cover to protect the dive- and torpedo-bombers – low-level cover at 7000 ft, mid-cover at 12,000 ft and high cover at 18,000 ft. I was flying "wing" on the division leader, Lt Jim "Alkie" Seybert, Jr, whose nickname must have stemmed from his earlier imbibing habits for I never saw him drink excessively in the time that I knew him!

'Jim's division was assigned as mid-cover. We arrived in the target area early in the morning at around 7 am, and proceeded to sweep the area for enemy "bogies". Seeing no opposition, we were directed to strafe Roi airfield, with parked aircraft (of which there were a few) and the hangar areas as our targets.

'"Alkie" put me in a right echelon, gave me the "break" signal, and peeled off to the left. I waited several seconds and commenced my attack. I kept "Alkie" in sight, but took a lateral spacing off to his right so that I could concentrate on my strafing targets and keep him in sight as well. I fired a few long bursts into a couple of aircraft on the hangar apron, then shifted my sights to an open hangar and fired a long burst into it. It was at about this time that I experienced several jolts caused by anti-aircraft shells bursting in close proximity. I "jinked and juked" (changed altitude and direction) several times to throw off their aim. We had agreed to rendezvous to the left of the field (over the water) at 5000 ft, but the AA was so intense that I had to break to the right.

VF-16 pilots head out onto the deck in November 1943. Each had an allotted aircraft according to 6-kill ace Ralph Hanks (his was 'white 37' BuNo 08926), and pilots inspected 'their' F6F once a week. Despite this personal attention, he admits that due to deck spotting, pilots rarely flew their own F6Fs, and were not allowed to apply their names to airframes until late in the combat tour

'As I was commencing my recovery, I spotted a "Betty" bomber scooting low across the water. I don't know whether it had just taken off or was returning from another field. Anyway, I had to take off a lot of throttle as the speed from my dive was going to take me past him in a hurry. I swung out to the right and then back onto the "Betty". I fired a short burst of all six .50 cal guns which went over the top of him. I lowered my nose and sights and fired two longer bursts into the bomber. It started disintegrating and trailing heavy smoke, before commencing a slow diving turn to starboard and crashing into the sea (strangely, one of *Lexington*'s squadron intelligence officers credited a half-share in the demise of this aircraft to Lt(jg) Arnold H Burrough, an SBD-5 Dauntless pilot from VB-16 – this was his second "Betty" kill of the sortie, Ed.).

The stunted palm trees behind the taxying Hellcat show evidence of the bitter 'fire fight' that took place to secure the airstrip at Betio. VF-1 remained shore-based until 7 February 1944, claiming just a solitary Zeke kill (plus a probable) during its time on Tarawa – Japanese aerial opposition had been all but wiped out in the initial fighter sweeps of the Gilberts back in November (*Tailhook*)

'I then went full throttle and start a slow climbing turn to port, looking for Lt Seybert. As I climbed through about 7000 ft, I spotted a flight of four aircraft high in the sun, and since no enemy aircraft had been reported, I assumed them to be "friendly". We had been observing radio silence, and I hadn't heard any reports on the air. Little did I know that those "jolts" I had felt on my strafing run had been several actual hits in my fuselage of 40 mm type AA fire, and my radio had been knocked out of commission. I approached the flight of four from inside and beneath them, remaining unobserved. As I neared the formation, I was shocked to see that they all wore the red "meatball" of the Rising Sun, and were actually a flight of four Zeros!

'There was little I could do but slide out to the starboard side, line up the two outside aircraft and open fire. The outer Zero exploded almost immediately, and the second one began to burn and fell off to the right. Evidently, by this time the leader and the other wingman had spotted me and they broke in opposite directions. My only recourse was to follow one of them and I selected the leader. He turned steeply to port and I soon lost him. By this time the other wingman had pulled around onto my tail. I turned sharply to starboard and saw a couple of bursts of tracer go over my head. I dove to try and lose him but he stayed close on my tail.

'I executed a sharp pull up and as I neared the top and began to drain off my speed, for some unknown reason, I decided to pull it on through and complete a loop. As I was in the inverted position, I could see the Zero pulling through like mad and I realised that he was going to be in an excellent position to shoot me down on my recovery. It was at this time that I decided to push forward on the stick and fly inverted for a couple of seconds. The Zero was so intent on pulling inside me that I think the move surprised him and he lost sight of me, continuing his pullout instead.

'By delaying my pullout, and executing it a couple of seconds later, I found him just about in my sights on the recovery. I was slightly out of range at first and had to add throttle to close before firing. I don't think that he saw me until I opened fire, and by then it was too late as he soon began to burn, and then crashed into the sea.

Lt(jg) Ralph Hanks made history in 'his' F6F-3 BuNo 08926 on 23 November 1943 when he downed three 'Haps' and two Zeros (and possibly a third A6M) in minutes off Tarawa during his combat debut. This official shot of the young Californian was one of a number taken upon his return to *Lexington* (*Ralph Hanks via Mark Styling*)

One of the first west coast fighter units formed on the Hellcat, VF-1 had a most untypical introduction to combat during the Gilbert Islands campaign in November 1943 – it flew into action simultaneously from two separate vessels. Split between the escort carriers *Nassau* and *Barnes*, the unit performed mainly ground-attack sorties for the invading Marines, or CAPs for the task force. One of the first objectives of the Tarawa assault was the airstrip at Betio islet, for once it was captured VF-1 had orders to fly ashore to provide 24-hour close-air support for the Marines. After a bitter struggle, the runway was seized and the Hellcats flew in on 25 November – barely four days after the initial seaborne assault. This shot shows the F6F-3s arriving on this date, with a battered Zero providing a sobering reminder of the airfield's former owners (*Aerospace Publishing*)

'It had been an exciting several minutes, resulting in four victories – the "Betty" and three Zeros. There were several engagements going on so I decided to climb above the closest one, dive to get some speed advantage, and see if I could help pull an enemy aircraft off someone's tail.

'As I was climbing to get into the fray, I must admit that all of my attention was directed above me and not to my rear. All of a sudden I saw 7.7 mm machine gun and 20 mm cannon fire ripping off pieces of my wing covering, and tracer fire going past me. My first reaction was to turn my head and peek out from behind my armour-plated head-rest, but as I did so a 7.7 mm round came over my left shoulder, hit me in the the temple above my left eye and went through and out the front right-hand side of my canopy. It felt like someone had hit me on the side of the head with a 2 x 4 board. I was temporarily stunned and dazed, and I don't remember how long it took me to realise that I had been hit.

'My first thought was to "Get the hell out of there". We had been instructed that one of the best evasion manoeuvres was to dive to terminal velocity (I think the "red line" maximum speed allowed was around 400 to 425 kts) and make a sharp turn to the right. This I did and evidently it worked as the Zero pilot did not elect to stay with me, for which I was most thankful. As I pulled out from the high speed dive, I guess the "Gs" caused a draining of the blood for I noticed that the latter was spurting out and landing on my left hand, which was positioned on the throttle.

'I immediately placed my left hand on the artery leading to my wound and applied pressure. It seemed to stop most of the bleeding, but some was still running down my arm and onto my leg.

'For most of these raids a "Dumbo" (friendly submarine) was positioned a few miles off the coast to rescue aviators who had been hit. In this case, I think the sub was off the northeast coast of Kwajalein, but the vessel stayed submerged until it was notified by someone that a flyer was down in the area. Since I was alone and had no radio due to AA damage, there was no way to communicate with the "Dumbo".

'I was still bleeding quite profusely, so it was decision time! Would I retain conciousness long enough to ditch in the area of the sub, get in my raft and take a chance on someone seeing me and notifying the sub of my position. Or, would I last long enough to stay in the air approximately 45 minutes – the length of time it would take to return to the ship and recover on board? I considered my options for a few moments and then decided on the latter.

'The compass heading for my return was around 045 degrees. As I attempted to take up this heading, I noticed that my RMI (remote indicating compass) was inoperative due to the AA hit again, and that the liquid compass was swinging through 30 to 40 degrees, thus rendering any reading extremely inaccurate. I decided to bisect a north/south and east/west runway heading on Roi, line up two clouds and fly in that direction. When I passed over one of the clouds I would quickly line up two more.

'The weather was mostly clear, with scattered clouds at about 3000 ft and four to five miles visibilty, so I flew most of the way above the clouds. At the expiration of 45 minutes, I decided to let down below the overcast and commence an "expanding square" search until I spotted the *Lexington.* I had completed two legs of the search when I spotted a carrier's wake, and I felt tremendously relieved.

'Unfortunately, I noticed the vessel's fantail boasted the numeral 10 – that of our sister-ship *Yorktown.* My wound had slowed to a trickle by now, but I was still losing blood, and was therefore anxious to recover on ANY carrier. As I flew by the island I waggled my wings to indicate that I had no radio, and also noticed that they had many aircraft turning up on deck ready to launch for another strike on Kwajalein. The visibility was still four to five miles and I looked all around but did not see the "Lex". I guess the people on the *Yorktown* realised my problem and used white material of some sort to make an arrow pointing in a southerly direction, adding the numerals 12 to indicate the miles to my carrier. I waggled my wings again indicating that I understood their message, and turned to that heading in search of the "Lex".

'After only several minutes of flight, I picked up the wake of the "Lex", and upon arrival noticed that the deck was clear and ready to accept aircraft. They immediately gave me a "Prep Charlie" in Morse Code with an Aldis lamp, indicating that it was OK to begin

With *Yorktown* recovering VF-5's Hellcats in the background, elements of VF-16 are launched from *Lexington* for the next strike on the Marshall Islands on 23 November 1943 – the latter squadron downed 17 aircraft on this date. Just above the Hellcat's centreline tank can be seen the silhouette of the escort carrier *Cowpens,* whose embarked flight of F6F-3s from VF-6 (12 aircraft in total) also participated in the day's activities (*Aerospace Publishing*)

Despite being weak through loss of blood from a head wound, Ens Ed 'Wendy' Wendorf still managed to get his F6F-3 (BuNo 66064) back aboard *Lexington* in one piece following combat over Kwajalein Atoll on the morning of 4 December 1943. He had claimed two Zeros and a 'Betty' destroyed on this sortie, before being 'clobbered' by an unseen enemy fighter (*Tailhook*)

my approach, and subsequently a "Charlie" which meant it was okay to land. I turned downwind and began my approach. Much to my chagrin, I discovered that my tail hook rail had been shot away, and that I had no hydraulic pressure to lower my wheels or flaps. There was a compressed air bottle to blow down the wheels in an emergency, and since I definitely considered this such an occasion, I used it to lower my gear, and pressed on with my approach. The deck was clear, but as I approached the ramp I was given a wave-off by the LSO, who signalled to me as I flew past him that I needed to lower my tail hook and flaps. I waggled my wings again indicating that I understood, but that I was unable to do either!

'I continued upwind and began another approach. As I had opened my canopy and tried to use both hands to fly the plane, the wind blowing in my face, and the fact that I could no longer hold the pressure point on my temple, had caused the wound to bleed freely. The flowing blood was completely obstructing the vision in my left eye, and believe me it is difficult enough to land on a carrier deck with BOTH eyes functioning!

'As I neared the ramp on my second approach, I noticed there was a Hellcat crashed on deck in a "wheels up" condition. As I learned later, it was Lt Capowski, who had taken several 20 mm hits in the cockpit, and was severely wounded in the hand. They had brought him in on a "straight in" approach, and he was unable to lower his gear prior to landing.

'I was feeling OK except for the bleeding. I was not feeling faint or light-headed, and the wound above my eye was now feeling sort of numb – the caked blood was helping to stem some of the flow. Despite not feeling much pain, I did not necessarily relish the thought of circling for a while as the deck crew proceeded to clean up the crash, but I had no other choice.

'After approximately 15 minutes of circling, they again gave me the "Charlie" signal to land, and this time, realising that I had no tail hook or flaps, had rigged the barrier across the flight deck. This consisted of several strands of one-inch wire cabling to stop the aircraft on its run-out.

'I made my second approach and soon discovered that I could not see well enough to make the trap unless I held my left hand to my temple to stop the flow of blood. I made the approach in this configuration, flying the aircraft and making throttle adjustments, before eventually taking the "cut" with my right hand. I landed successfully and slowed my roll to almost a stop before I struck the barrier and nosed up. It had been an ordeal, and despite losing two quarts of blood, I had survived.'

After recovering from his wounds, Ed Wendorf completed his tour with VF-16, and went on to claim one more Zero and an unidentified bomber over Truk (29/4/44) and Guam (19/6/44) respectively. He saw out the war with VC-3 aboard the *Savo Island*, his official score remaining at 4.5 kills and two probables – all with VF-16.

Returning to the Kwajalein Atoll raids, Wendorf's CO, Paul Buie, who had already nurtured two aces among his junior officers, joined the ranks himself with three Zekes on the 4 December mission. He thereby finished the year as the top-scoring F6F pilot. The US Navy record, however, was still held by Lt(jg) Donald Runyon with nine kills, including eight as an *Enterprise* F4F pilot in 1942. At the end of 1943 he was back in combat, flying F6Fs with VF-18 from *Bunker Hill*.

Land-Based Hellcat Squadrons in 1943

VF-33	Solomons	60
VF-38	Solomons	7
VF-40	Solomons	4

Top Hellcat Squadrons of 1943

VF-9	*Essex*	65
VF-33	Solomons	60
VF-16	*Lexington*	55
VF-18	*Bunker Hill*	50
VF-5	*Yorktown*	21
VF-12	*Saratoga*	15
VF-6	various CVs	14.66
VF-23	*Princeton*	14
VF-24	*Belleau Wood*	7.50
VF-38	Solomons	7

Total by 16 F6F squadrons – 323

Top Hellcat Pilots in 1943

Lt Cdr P D Buie	VF-16	7	Total 9
Lt(jg) A L Frendberg	VF-16	5	Total 6
Ens E R Hanks	VF-16	5	all on 23/11/43
Lt C K Hildebrandt	VF-33	5	Total 5
Lt(jg) H McWhorter, III	VF-9	5	Total 12
Lt(jg) A E Martin, Jr	VF-9	5	Total 5
Lt(jg) F M Fleming	VF-16	4.5	Total 7.5
Lt(jg) J Magda	VF-12	4	Total 4
Lt Cdr H Russell	VF-33	4	Total 4
Lt(jg) E C McGowan	VF-9	3.5	Total 6.5
Lt(jg) E A Valencia	VF-9	3.5	Total 23

THE YEAR OF DECISION

In the Pacific as in Europe, 1944 was the year of decision in World War 2. First on the fast carrier agenda was the heavily defended Japanese naval base at Truk Atoll, in the Carolines, as Adm Raymond Spruance's Fifth Fleet planned a three-day surface and air bombardment in mid-February. Long aware of the mysterious, but fabled 'Gibraltar of the Pacific', many carrier aviators later admitted to suffering pre-raid nerves before the Truk strikes were flown. For example, one seasoned pilot, upon learning of his next target, confessed to the author many decades later that his first instinct was to jump overboard.

This VF-24 pilot has taken the barrier aboard the light carrier USS *Belleau Wood* after sustaining combat damage over Kwajalein on 1 February 1944. This vessel was one of 12 'flat tops' that made up Task Force 58.2 during the Marshall Islands operation (*Jerry Scutts*)

But Truk proved more daunting in reputation than in fact. The operation opened with a spectacular dawn fighter sweep on the 17th, which soon turned into a bitter dogfight involving 70 Hellcats and dozens of Japanese fighters. In the first 20 minutes Lt Cdr Ed Owens' VF-5 from *Yorktown*, supported by elements of 'Fighting 9' and '10', claimed nearly 50 kills. VF-5's boss takes up the story;

'We arrived over the target area with every advantage that could be desired: at dawn, in tactical formation and with the enemy caught by surprise with his aircraft on the ground.

'As we started to strafe airfields, quite a melée developed as the Japs began getting into the air. Actually, there were so many Jap aeroplanes moving that it was almost confusing to select a target and stay with it until it was shot down, without being lured to another target just taking off, or apparently attempting to join up in some kind of formation.

'After a few minutes it was difficult to find uncluttered airspace. Japanese aircraft were burning and falling from every quarter, and many were crashing on take-off as a result of strafing. Ground installations were exploding and burning, and all this in the early golden glow of the dawn. I guess it prompted me to recall it as a "Hollywood war". At times it all looked like it might have been staged for the movies.

'I would say that up until that time, the Truk raid was the greatest "show in town", and I wouldn't have missed it for anything!'

Intrepid's 'Fighting Six' was close behind VF-5, and Lt(jg) Alex Vraciu flamed three Zekes and a 'Rufe' floatplane, running his tally to nine. Later

VF-5 was heavily engaged in combat over Truk Atoll on 17 February 1944, downing 30 of the 124 aircraft claimed on this date. The unit did suffer losses during this bitter fighting, however, F6F BuNo 25761 coming to grief when landing back aboard *Yorktown* the following day

Intrepid's **VF-6 also enjoyed success on 17 February, claiming 16 kills. This group shot was just prior to the Truk strike occurring, and includes three aces – Lt (jg) Cyrus J Chambers (standing, second from right), who scored 5.333, three on the 17th; Ens Joe D Robbins (middle row, second from left), who finished the war with five, and claimed a Zeke on the 17th; and Lt(jg) Alex Vraciu (to Robbins' left), whose tally reached 19, including four on the 17th. The latter's 'white 32' serves as a backdrop (*via Mark Styling*)**

that morning, 'Ham' McWhorter of VF-9 claimed two Zekes and a 'Hamp' to become the first pilot to score ten kills in Hellcats. However, VF-18's very capable Don Runyon had already become the Navy's first double ace, having logged his tenth kill of the war (second in F6Fs) on 4 January. Two land-based pilots had also reached double figures by early February – Lt Cdr Tom Blackburn and Lt(jg) Ira Kepford, both of the Corsair-equipped VF-17.

At day's end, Vice Adm Mitscher's fighter pilots had claimed 124 aerial kills, while scores of other enemy aircraft had been attacked on the ground. Approximately 250 of Truk's 365 aircraft had been destroyed or damaged in one frantic day of combat, thus allowing Mitscher's SBDs and TBFs to sink 14 naval vessels and two-dozen merchant ships unopposed from the air. However, there was a price to be paid for this stunning success, as 25 aircraft of the Fast Carrier Task Force were lost, and torpedo damage was sustained by *Intrepid*. Nevertheless, the naval balance in the mid-Pacific had been irrevocably altered.

So too had the pace of Pacific air combat. Between 1 January and 31 March, the number of Navy aces had doubled, which was a phenomenal increase, as the first 25 months of the war had produced fewer than 30 'blue water' aces in total. Yet in the first quarter of 1944, nearly three-dozen Hellcat and Corsair pilots logged their fifth victories, 21 of whom flew F6Fs. The F4U aces came entirely from Lt Cdr Blackburn's land-based VF-17 (for further details see *Aces 8 Corsair Aces of World War 2* by Mark Styling).

Truk was revisited at sunrise on 29 April and, in the words of an *Enterprise* strike leader, 'We wrecked the place!' Primary target this time was Truk's remaining dockside facilities, as the harbour was nearly devoid of ships. The beneficiary of the dawn sweep was *Langley's* VF-32, led by Lt Cdr Eddie Outlaw. The CO personally gunned five Zekes while his pilots claimed 16 more. Three of those fell to Lt Hollis Hills, a former RAF pilot who, on 19 August 1942, had scored the first victory for the P-51 Mustang when he downed an Fw 190 over the Dieppe beach-head (for further details see *Aces 7 Mustang Aces of the Ninth and Fifteenth Air Forces and the RAF* by Jerry Scutts). Hills later joined the ranks of the aces with his

All available deck crew pull together to move the Hellcat up to the bow of the *Essex*. 'Fighting Nine' was the top scoring unit over Truk on the 17th, logging claims for 35 aircraft destroyed (*US Navy*)

fifth career victory in September 1944. The second Truk was by far the biggest combat in VF-32's career, amounting to half the squadron's score by the end of its deployment.

'Fighting Six' emerged with 19 kills over the big lagoon, and Lt(jg) Alex Vraciu became the Navy's fifth double ace – only the second Hellcat pilot to reach that plateau at that point in the war. His Zekes that morning ran his tally to 11, a score which would increase significantly before much longer.

In all, Task Force 58 pilots claimed 58 kills during the second Truk strike. This bastion would be revisited frequently over the next 16 months, but never again would strikes be opposedby Japanese aircraft in numbers of any consequence.

Three of VF-9's 35 kills fell to Ens John 'Tubby' Franks, Jr, who gunned down two Zekes and a 'Pete' over Truk Lagoon during the unit's first morning sweep of the atoll. He scored his fifth kill five days later over Saipan airfield, and then added a further two victories in 1945 when flying F6F-5s with VF-12. This shot was taken soon after he had made 'ace' on 22 February 1944 (*John Franks via Mark Styling*)

'An Old-Time Turkey Shoot'

VF-16 pilot Ens Z W 'Ziggy' Neff probably gave the Marianas operation of mid-June its popular name of the 'Turkey Shoot', but to the American planners of the invasion of the mid-Pacific islands, it was known as Operation *Forager*.

Although the strategic aim of seizing the Marianas was to obtain bases for the Army Air Force, the means was amphibious. Marine Corps and Army assault troops would occupy Saipan, Guam and Tinian, but first local air superiority had to be achieved. The only means of doing so was obvious – carrier-based Hellcats.

Vice Adm Mitscher brought 15 fast carriers to the Marianas, deployed in four groups – six *Essexes*, the veteran *Enterprise* and eight of the nine *Independence*-class CVLs. Altogether, the 15 air groups embarked 479 F6F-3s, including 27 radar-equipped -3N night fighters of VF(N)-76 and -77. The 'Big E's' VF(N) detachment comprised three F4U-2 Corsairs, proving how far the concept had come since O'Hare's untimely death less than seven months before.

The air superiority phase began with afternoon fighter sweeps on 11 June. During the day, seven Japanese reconnaissance aircraft were splashed during Task Force 58's approach, including a 'Judy' scout-bomber by VF-50's CO, Lt Cdr J C Strange (his second kill in an eventual tally of five). It became the first of 870 Hellcat victims during the two-month campaign.

Beginning at 1300 that afternoon, elements of 14 Hellcat squadrons began thinning the defenders. Most heavily engaged was VF-2, led by Cdr W A Dean, Jr, who claimed three Zekes and a 'Tojo' over Guam – he finished the war with 11 kills. In all, the *Hornet* pilots were credited with 26 victories, followed by *Cabot's* VF-31. Lt(jg) V A Rieger (five total) claimed three of the 'Meataxers'' 13 kills over Tinian.

Tinian was also home for Naval Air Group 321 – the Japanese night-fighting contingent in the Marianas – who were ordered to fly their Nakajima J1Ns against the task force in a mid-afternoon attack. Cdr W M Collins, Jr, (nine kills) of *Bunker Hill's* VF-8 tackled a batch of 'Irvings' from the unit as they climbed out from their airfield at Gurguan, claiming three himself while Lt(jg) R J Rosen (six kills) bagged two more. By late afternoon TF-58 had claimed 98 confirmed victories, and the Marianas campaign was underway.

Japan's defence against the invasion was two-fold. Firstly, major por-

VF-10 'Grim Reapers' also took a heavy toll of the Truk defenders on the 17th, claiming 29 aircraft destroyed and a further 11 damaged. This shot shows two sailors rapidly replenishing the almost obligatory 150-US gal centreline tank of a 'Reapers'' F6F-3 spotted on the stern of USS *Enterprise* during the height of the Truk assault (*US Navy*)

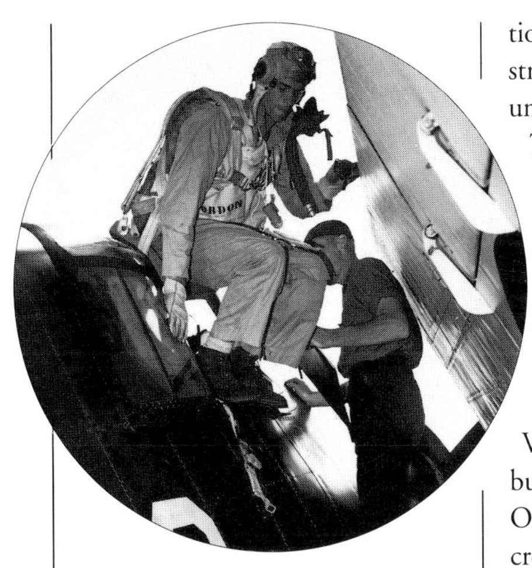

VF-10 five-kill ace Lt(jg) Donald 'Flash' Gordon squeezes out of his cockpit following a patrol over Truk on 16 February – note his personalised N2885 life-jacket (*US Navy*)

VF-32 pilots pose for the camera on *Langley* after completing a sortie over Truk that saw them down 21 Zekes. CO, Lt Cdr Eddie Outlaw (bottom row, second from right), claimed five, his wingman (front row, extreme right), Lt(jg) D E Reeves, four, Lt(jg) R H May (in sunglasses), three, Ens J A Pond (to May's left), two, Lt H H Hills (front row, second from left), three, his wingman (to Hills' right), Lt(jg) L R McEachern, two, and Lt(jg)s H C McClaugherty (behind Hills) and Lt(jg) R A Schulze (to his right), one each

tions of the 61st Air Flotilla were based in the Marianas with a paper strength of some 630 aircraft, although the actual total remains unknown. Despite this considerable force, the Naval General Staff in Tokyo placed even greater stock in the 'second string to their Marianas bow' – Vice Adm Jisaburo Ozawa's First Mobile Fleet, whose nine carriers deployed nearly 440 fighter and attack aircraft. Though smaller than the land-based component, Ozawa's force, with its greater range and mobility, was expected to prove that the balance of power was in favour of the occupying forces.

Although the Japanese boasted a larger number of aircraft than Task Force 58, the decisive factor was qualitative, not quantitative. Vice Adm Mitscher's air groups were, for the most part, not only skilled but experienced. And institutionally, the Fifth Fleet vastly exceeded Ozawa's in every quality. Aside from modern aircraft and competent aircrews, by mid-1944 American radio, radar and operating procedures were thoroughly tested. The battle could only go one way.

But Adm Raymond Spruance was taking no chances. The Fifth Fleet commander directed Mitscher to launch pre-emptory strikes against the Bonin Islands, halfway between Guam and Tokyo, to prevent aerial reinforcements from reaching the Marianas. Therefore, on 15 June Task Groups 58.1 and 58.4 attacked Iwo Jima with three heavy and four light carriers. The result was a series of frantic dogfights beneath rain-laden skies, resulting in widespread combats by VFs -1, -2 and -15. Lt L G Barnard (eight kills) from *Hornet* became an ace in his first fight as VF-2 tallied 17 of the day's 41 claims over 'Iwo'. He reported to the squadron's intelligence officer;

'I would estimate there were 30-40 Zekes in the air when we arrived over the target. We were at 15,000 when I saw several Zekes making runs on some F6Fs below us at 1000 ft. We pushed over after them and, as we did so, we saw eight to ten coming in below us. I made a head-on run on one from above. I turned as I passed to see him blow up. Wings and debris went everywhere.

'I pulled up and missed one and a Zero pulled in front of me at 9000 ft. I fired on him from six o'clock at the same level. He blew up and I went right through his fire.

'After that one, I turned around and there was a Zero on an F6F's tail. I fired a full deflection shot from nine o'clock below, and he blew up. By this time they were blowing up all over the place.

'From there I pulled around until I saw one on the water at about 200 ft altitude. I got it, level at eight o'clock, and it rolled over into the water.

'I climbed back up for altitude to 5000 ft and saw a Zero above me. It was at 8000 ft and making an over-

VF-9 pilots pose with their scoreboard for an end of tour photo on the deck of *Essex* in late February 1944. The 'Hellcats' claimed 120 kills during their second spell in the frontline, and produced ten aces in the process. No fewer than 1332 combat sorties were completed in this 1943/44 tour, and the unit lost one pilot killed in action and four posted as missing – a further seven were lost in non-combat related flying accidents (*Barrett Tillman*)

Grumman aircraft have a reputation for being well-built, and the Hellcat was no exception. This VF-15 F6F-3 had its horizontal tailplanes so badly damaged by AA fire during a strike on the Marcus Island on 20 May 1944 that its pilot was forced to land back aboard *Essex* without the benefit of flaps – with the tails shredded the deployment of the landing aids could have caused the aircraft to stall on approach (*Jerry Scutts*)

head run on an F6F at 6000. I followed it down to the water. It went into its run and pulled through faster than I did, so I went into a wing-over. Two more F6Fs closed and it turned inside them. Before they could bring their guns to bear, I pulled up in a high wing-over and shot it down from eight o'clock above, 100 ft off the water.'

A pair of *Yorktown's* VF-1 pilots scored four victories each on the 15th – Lt P M Henderson, Jr, and Lt(jg) J R Meharg – although the former, who had just became an ace in this combat, failed to return. His Hellcat was one of 12 US aircraft lost in the two-day neutralisation of Iwo Jima.

American claims were undoubtedly optimistic, but the damage inflicted was genuine. For instance, Japan's Air Group 301 put up 18 Zekes to contest the raid and 17 were lost with 16 pilots killed.

With TF-58 reunited west of Saipan, the largest carrier battle in history began on the morning of 19 June. Ozawa's force had sortied from Borneo six days before, and despite poor communications and scouting, had located Mitscher's four carrier groups and single battleship group and began launching four major raids from its three carrier divisions. The weather favoured Japan – clear skies and an easterly breeze which allowed the Mobile Fleet to continue steaming toward its targets without interrupting flight operations. However, the Americans also knew where to find Ozawa. US submarines had dogged him since he left Tawi Tawi, and before the battle was fully joined on the 19th, they had torpedoed two of his largest carriers – Pearl Harbor survivor *Shokaku* and his flagship, *Taiho*. In hours both ships had succumbed to their damage.

Of Ozawa's four main strikes, only three had the potential to harm Mitscher. The first was a 64-aircraft raid from three of his smallest carriers – *Chitose, Chiyoda* and *Zuiho*. Alerted by radar, 74 Hellcats from eight squadrons were up and waiting at 1035. Three F6F pilots were

Seen during Operation *Reckless* (Hollandia and Aitape landings) in April, the pilot of this VF-2 F6F-3 has opened the canopy to help cool his warm cockpit. Few aircraft were encountered during this op, with the VF-2 downing just a solitary 'Betty' (which fell to Lt(jg) D A Carmichael, Jr, his first of 12 kills) on the 24th

This well-used combat veteran (note the paint-chipped wing leading edges) from VF-2 was photographed aboard *Hornet* on 6 May 1944, having recently been involved in a gunnery sortie judging by the staining under its wings (*Jerry Scutts*)

killed, including the commander of *Princeton's* Air Group 27, Lt Cdr Ernest Wetherill Wood (who had claimed two Vichy French Dewoitine D.520 fighters whilst flying F4F-4s with VF-41 during Operation *Torch* in November 1942), but 'Raid I' was defeated in detail. The few Japanese pilots to penetrate the combat air patrol wasted their efforts against the battleship group.

'Raid II' registered on US radars about 40 minutes after the first strike. With 109 effective sorties from *Taiho, Shokaku* and *Zuikaku*, this strike was the largest of the day. It was also met by the greatest concentration of F6Fs as hard-pressed fighter directors vectored no fewer than 162 Grummans onto the Japanese. *Essex's* highly-proficient VF-15 benefited from being first to intercept both 'Raids' 'I' and 'II', with impressive results – by day's end 'Fighting 15' had claimed 68.5 victories. However, Ozawa's second strike succeeded in penetrating three task groups, attacking one battleship and four carriers, but inflicting minimal damage. In turn, six Hellcats and three pilots were lost in blunting 'Raid II'.

The third Japanese strike put up only 49 aircraft from *Junyo*, *Hiyo* and *Ryuho*, and accomplished nothing. By the time the strike got within range of the US task force at 1300, only 16 Zekes remained in formation. They were mauled by a like number of Hellcats, losing seven A6M5s for no F6Fs shot down.

'Raid IV' was a collaborative venture from Ozawa's Carrier Divisions One and Two. However, only 64 of the 82 aircraft despatched reached the target area, and became further dispersed in ineffective attacks or attempts to land at Guam. The latter were 'greeted' by 41 Grummans from four squadrons at about 1600, and they shot down at least 30 and destroyed a further 20 on the ground. Two F6F pilots were killed in this phase of the battle.

Double Wasps burbling away, Hellcats of VF-8 are prepared for launch from *Bunker Hill* on D-Day (15 June 1944) for the Saipan landings (*Jerry Scutts*)

Operation *Forager* involved 15 fast carriers, which combined could put aloft an awesome 479 Hellcats to patrol the skies over the Marianas, ensuring the success of the amphibious assault on Saipan, Guam and Tinian. Pilots from VF-1 were involved in this action right from the start, and are seen here heading to their Hellcats aboard *Yorktown* at midday on 15 June 1944. That afternoon the unit was embroiled in dogfights over Iwo Jima that saw them destroy 20 Zekes (*Tailhook*)

Four days later VF-1 almost doubled its 15 June score when it downed 37 aircraft on the opening day of the Battle of the Philippine Sea – the largest carrier battle in history. Two Zekes (plus a probable third) fell to the pilot of this F6F-3 (BuNo 40090), Lt William C Moseley, although he was flying another Hellcat (BuNo 41438) on the 19th – indeed, the latter machine was so badly damaged in the melée off Iwo Jima that it was pushed over the side of *Yorktown* following his recovery back aboard ship (*US Navy*)

More Combat Air Patrols (CAPs) were flown over the islands that evening, resulting in further combats. *Essex* pilots claimed nine more victories, but their skipper, Cdr C W Brewer (6.5 kills), was lost, along with his wingman.

Wearing the unit's famous 'High Hatters' emblem forward of the windscreen, 'White 5' has its engine throttled up prior to the pilot releasing the brakes and rolling down *Yorktown*'s wooden runway on the history-making afternoon of 19 June 1944 (*Aerospace Publishing*)

The 'Turkey Shoot' was a triumph of both technology and training. Including combats during long-range searches, the 15 F6F squadrons had been credited with 371 shootdowns against the loss of 14 pilots. Aside from VF-15, the most successful units were *Lexington's* veteran VF-16 with 46 victories, *Hornet's* VF-2 with 43 and *Yorktown's* VF-1 with 37. *Princeton's* VF-27 was most successful of the CVL units with an even 30 'splashes'.

Leading one of the interceptions on 19 June was Lt Cdr Frederick A Bardshar (7.5 kills), who later that day was promoted to command both VF-27 and *Princeton's* air group following the death of his CAG, Cdr E W Wood. Bardshar retained vivid memories of the inbound Japanese strike groups:

'We met a large number of escorted single-engine Japanese bombers while still climbing at about 14,000 ft. I was fascinated by the general inactivity of the Japanese escort fighters, who continued to weave above the bomber formations as the head-on confrontation of Japanese bombers and US fighters occurred.

'A melée followed, one of several. The Japanese escorts did not oppose the intercept, nor were they effective after the melee began. As I recall, I claimed two aircraft. The second, a 'Val', drew me out of the fight by diving, and after he flamed at roughly 7000 ft, the engagement was essentially over. The sky was marked with numerous burning and falling aircraft and some chutes as well as AA over the force.

'Air and communication discipline had been emphasized in VF-27 and was evident in the engagement. Section integrity was, generally, maintained, and transmissions were limited and to the point. We learned,

A combat-damaged tailhook which snapped under the strain of the arrested landing resulted in this late-build F6F-3 gently nosing over upon recovery on *Yorktown* on 19 June (*Jerry Scutts*)

COLOUR PLATES

This 14-page section profiles many of the aircraft flown by the elite pilots of the US Navy, US Marine Corps and the Fleet Air Arm. All the artwork has been specially commissioned for this volume, and profile artist Mark Styling, plus figure artist Mike Chappell, have gone to great pains to illustrate the aircraft, and their pilots, as accurately as possible following in-depth research that included corresponding with over 30 surviving Hellcat aces. Many aces' machines that have never previously been illustrated are featured alongside acccurate renditions of the more famous Hellcats from World War 2.

1
F6F-3 white 00/BuNo 04872 of Cdr James H Flatley, CVAG-5, USS *Yorktown*, 6 May 1943

2
F6F-3 white 00 of Cdr James H Flatley, CVAG-5, USS *Yorktown*, 31 August 1943

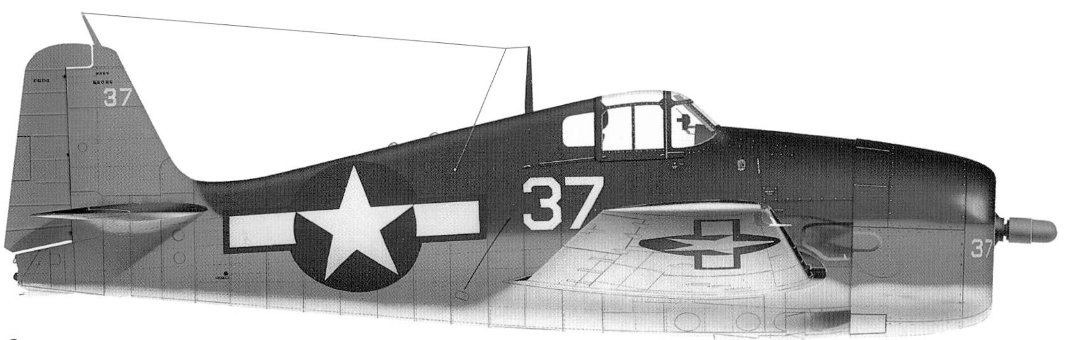

3
F6F-3 white 37/BuNo 08926 of Lt(jg) Eugene R Hanks, VF-16, USS *Lexington*, 23 November 1943

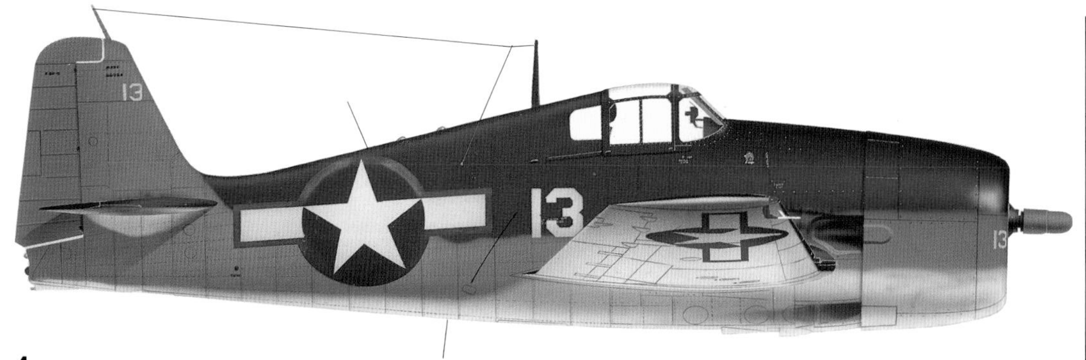

4

F6F-3 white 13/BuNo 66064 of Ens Ed 'Wendy' Wendorf, VF-16, USS *Lexington*, 4 December 1943

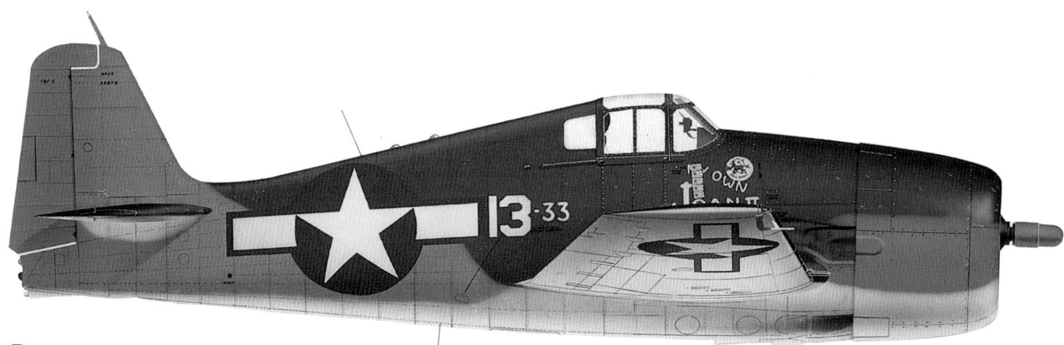

5

F6F-3 white 13 *MY OWN JOAN II*/BuNo 25813 of Lt C K 'Ken' Hildebrandt, VF-33, Ondonga, Christmas Day 1943

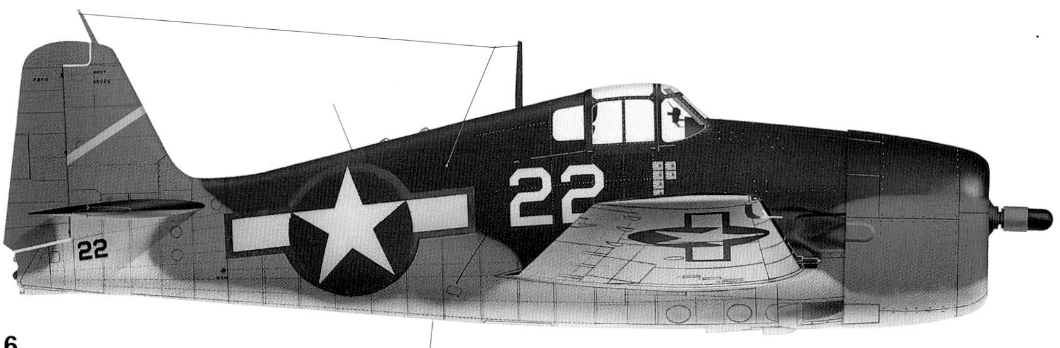

6

F6F-3 white 22 of Lt(jg) Robert W Duncan, VF-5, USS *Yorktown*, late February 1944

7

F6F-3 white 67/BuNo 40381 of Lt Richard 'Rod' Devine, VF-10, USS *Enterprise*, 17 February 1944

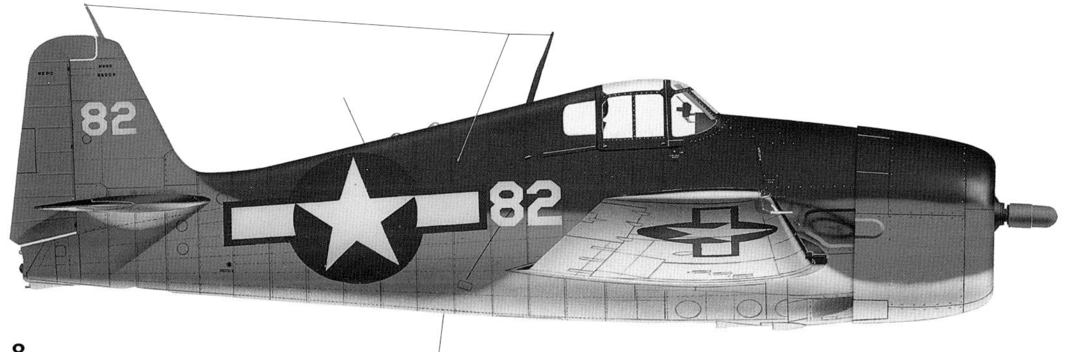

8

F6F-3 white 82/BuNo 26183 of Lt(jg) Donald 'Flash' Gordon, VF-10, USS *Enterprise*, 17 February 1944

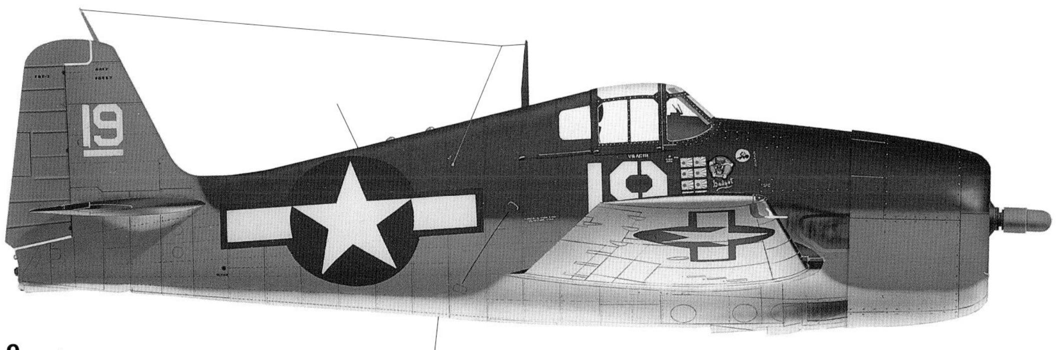

9

F6F-3 white 19/BuNo 40467 of Lt(jg) Alexander Vraciu, VF-6, USS *Intrepid*, 17 February 1944

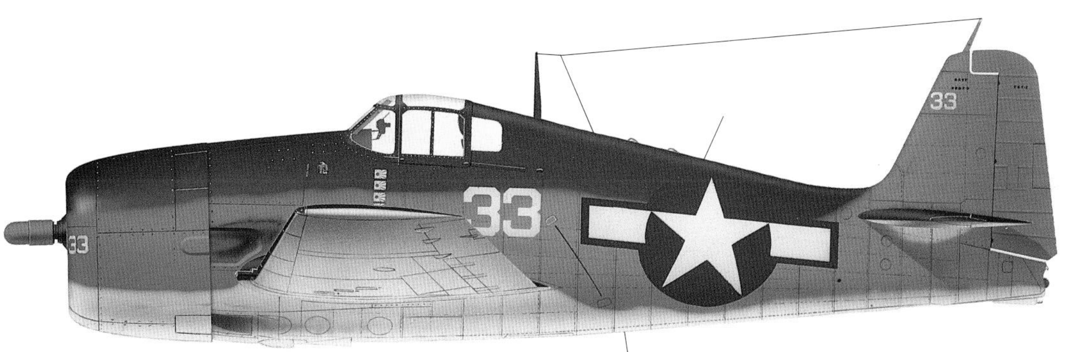

10

F6F-3 white 33 of Lt(jg) Frank Fleming, VF-16, USS *Lexington*, April 1944

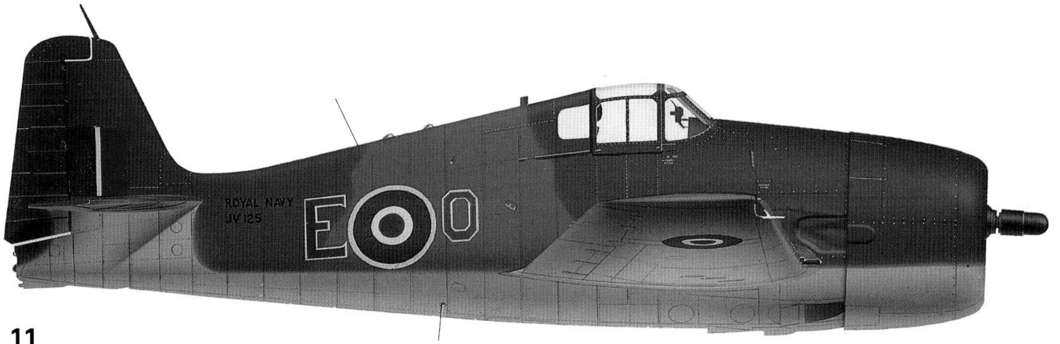

11

Hellcat I JV125 of Lt Cdr Stanley G Orr, No 804 Sqn, HMS *Emperor*, 14 May 1944

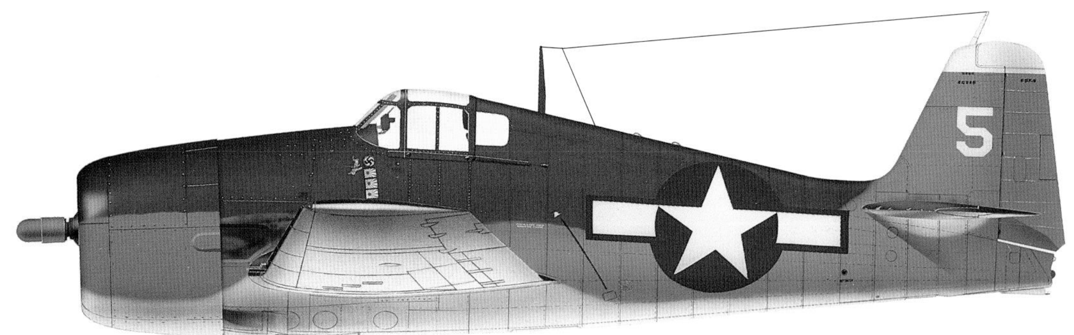

12
F6F-3 white 5/BuNo 40315 of Lt Hollis 'Holly' Hills , VF-32, USS *Langley*, 30 April 1944

13
F6F-3 white 31/BuNo 69532 of Wilbur B 'Spider' Webb, VF-2, USS *Hornet*, 19 June 1944

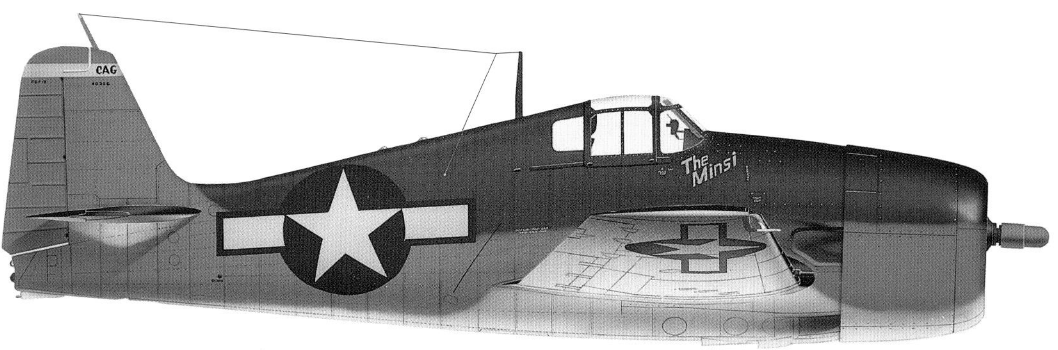

14
F6F-3 *The Minsi* of Cdr David McCampbell, Commander Air Group 15, USS *Essex*, 19 June 1944

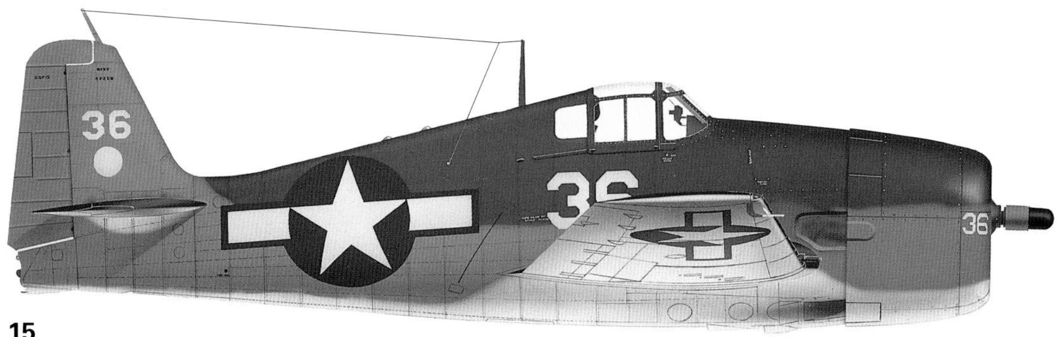

15
F6F-3 white 36/BuNo 41269 of Ens Wilbur B 'Spider' Webb, VF-2, USS *Hornet*, 20 June 1944

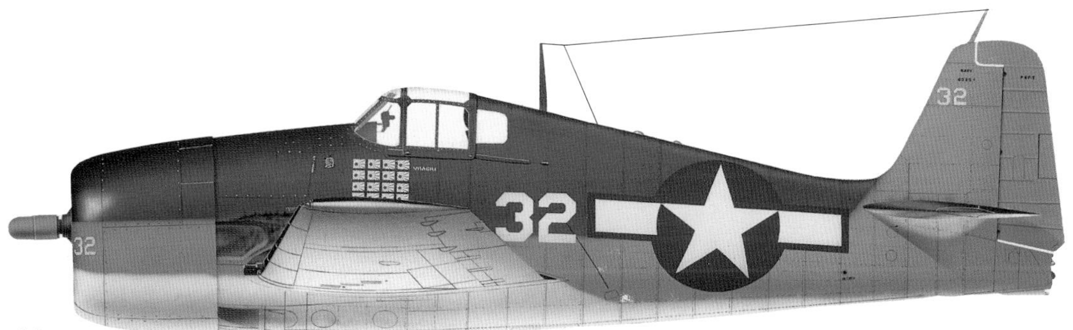

16
F6F-3 white 32 of Lt(jg) Alexander Vraciu, VF-16, USS *Lexington*, 21 June 1944

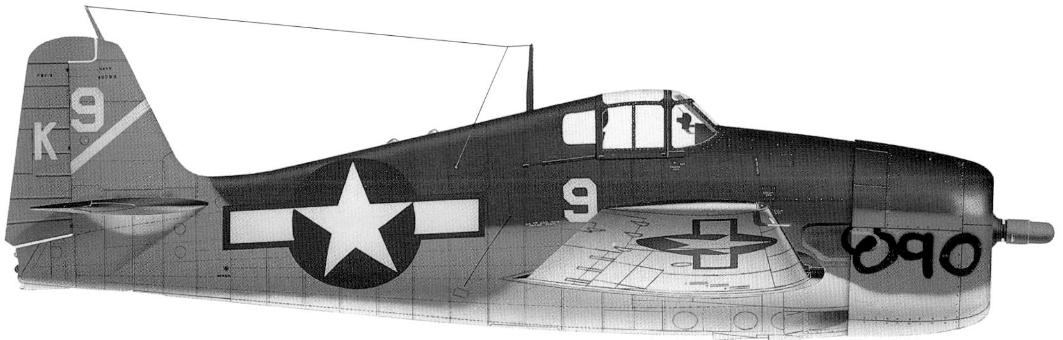

17
F6F-3 white 9/BuNo 40090 of Lt William C Moseley, VF-1, USS *Yorktown*, June 1944

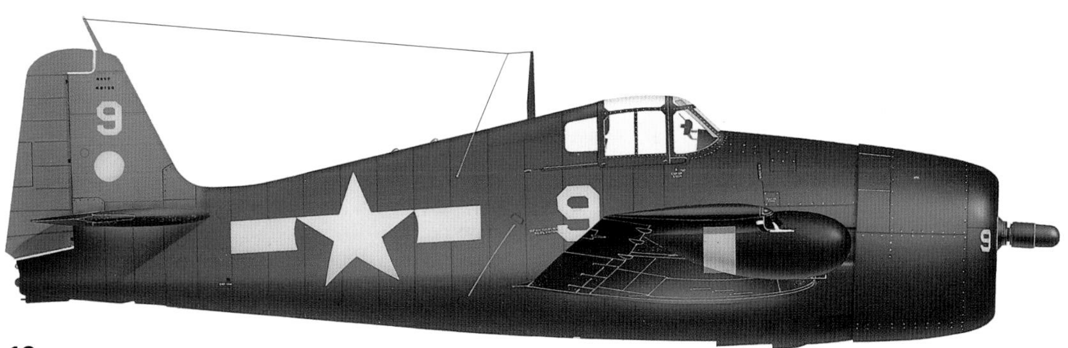

18
F6F-3N white 9/BuNo 42158 of Lt Russ Reiserer, VF(N)-76 Det 2, USS *Hornet*, 10 July 1944

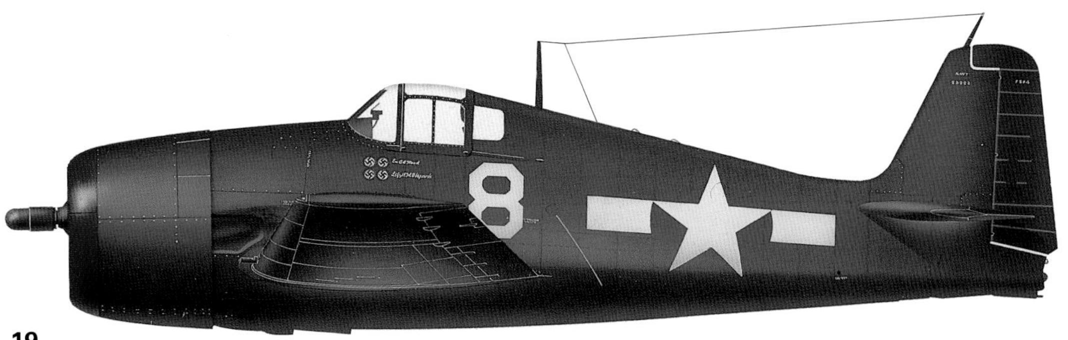

19
F6F-5 white 8 of Ensigns Alfred R Wood and Edward W Olszewski, VOF-1, USS *Tulagi*, August 1944

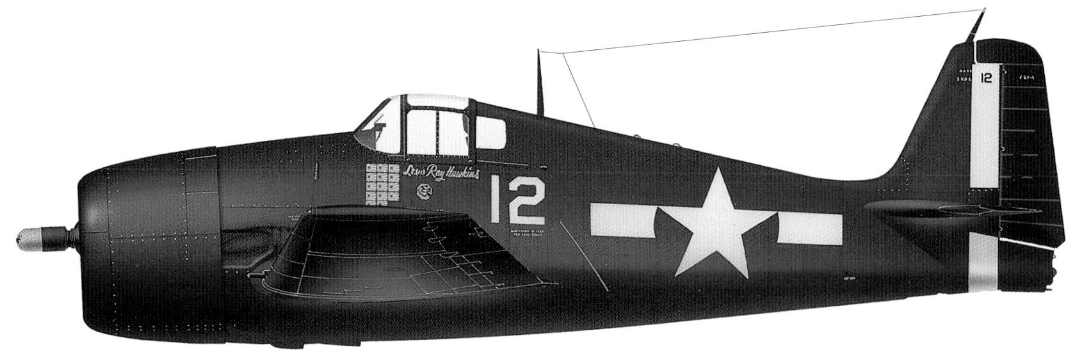

20
F6F-5 white 12/BuNo 58937 of Lt(jg) Ray 'Hawk' Hawkins, VF-31, USS *Cabot*, September 1944

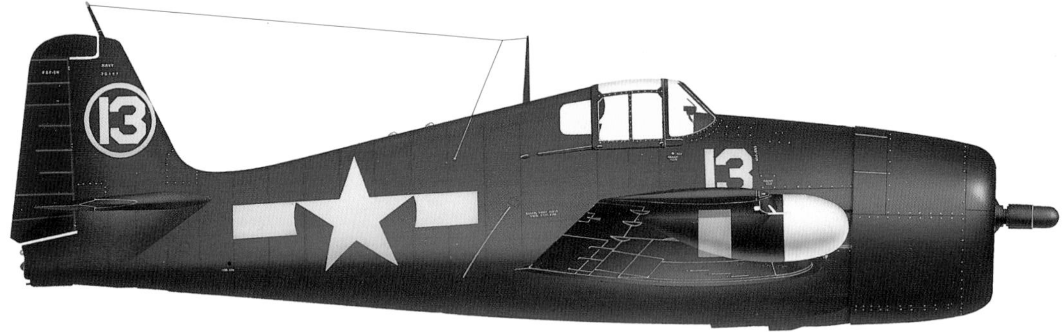

21
F6F-5N white 13/BuNo 70147 of Lt William E 'Bill' Henry, VF(N)-41, USS *Independence*, 21 September 1944

22
F6F-3 white 3 of Ens Gordon A Stanley, VF-27, USS *Princeton*, September 1944

23
F6F-3 white 17 of Lt Richard Stambook, VF-27, USS *Princeton*, 24 October 1944

24
F6F-3 white 13 of Lt William E Lamb, VF-27, USS *Princeton*, 24 October 1944

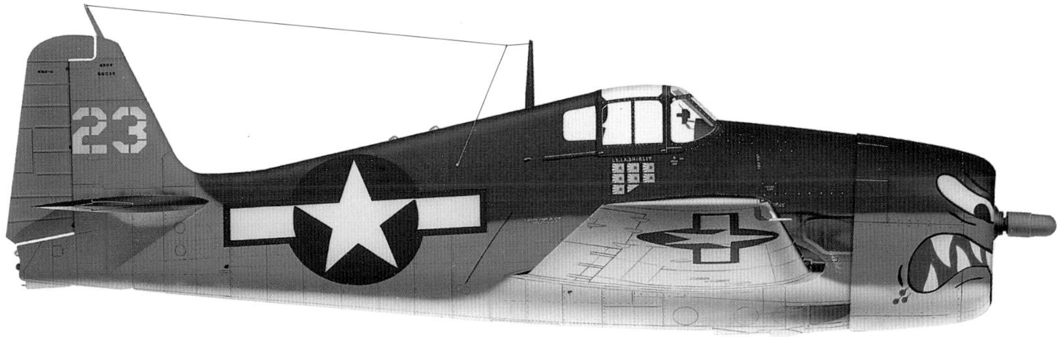

25
F6F-3 white 23 of Lt James 'Red' Shirley, VF-27, USS *Princeton*, 24 October 1944

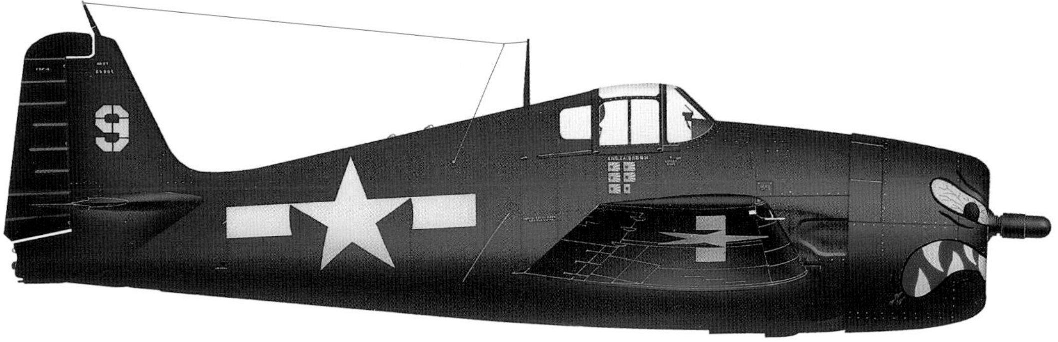

26
F6F-5 white 9 of Lt Carl A Brown, Jr, VF-27, USS *Princeton*, 24 October 1944

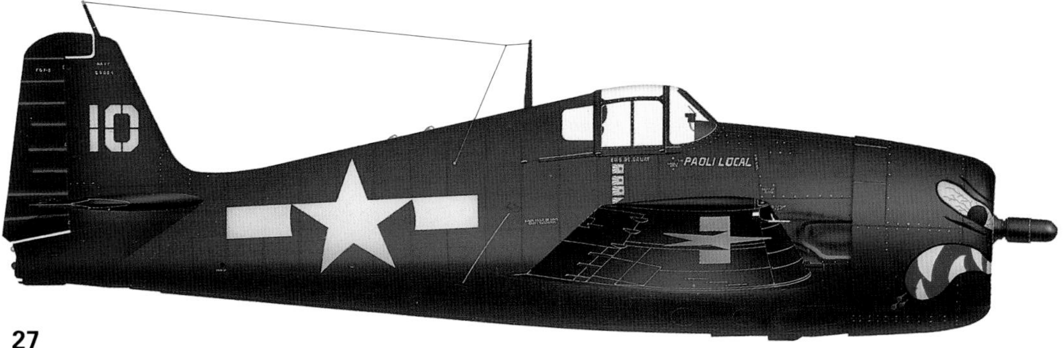

27
F6F-5 white 10 *PAOLI LOCAL* of Ens Paul E Drury, VF-27, USS *Princeton*, 24 October 1944

28
F6F-5 white 1 of Lt Cdr Fred A Bardshar, CO of VF-27/Commander Air Group 27, USS *Princeton*, 24 October 1944

29
F6F-5 white 7 *PAPER DOLL* of Ens Bob Burnell, VF-27, USS *Princeton*, 24 October 1944

30
F6F-5 *Minsi III*/BuNo 70143 of Cdr David McCampbell, Commander Air Group 15, USS *Essex*, 25 October 1944

31
F6F-5 white 28/BuNo 58069 of Ens Frank 'Trooper' Troup, VF-29, USS *Cabot*, 29 October 1944

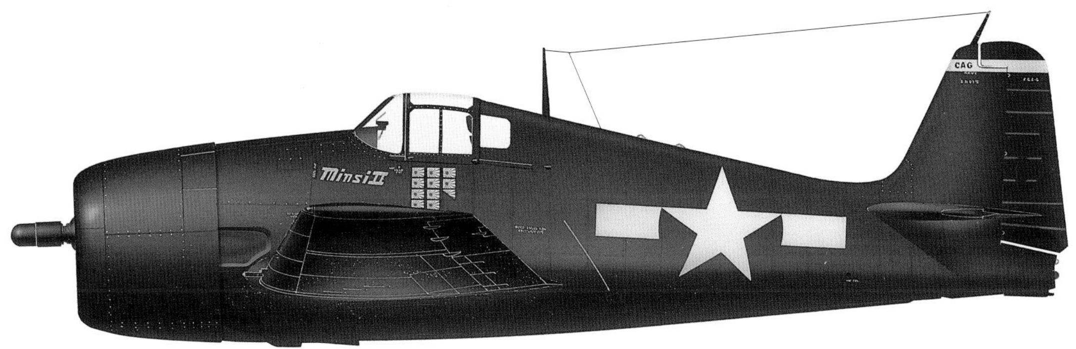

32
F6F-5 *Minsi II* of Cdr David McCampbell, Commander Air Group 15, USS *Essex*, October 1944

33
F6F-5 white 29 of Lt James S Swope, VF-11, USS *Hornet*, October 1944

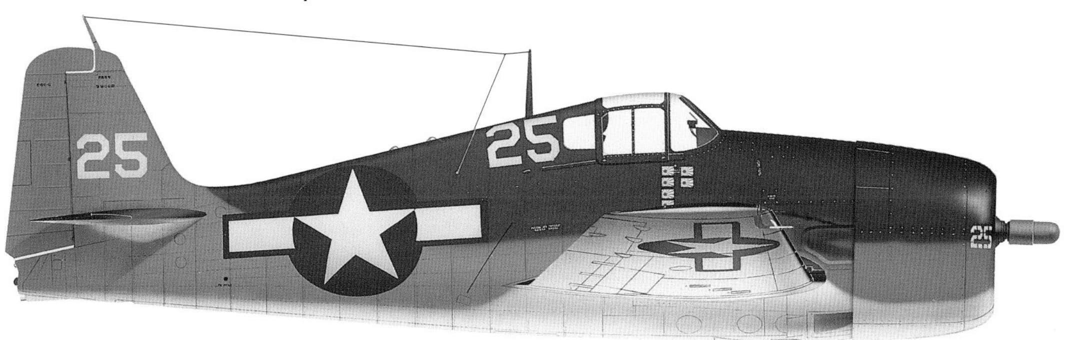

34
F6F-5 white 25 of Lt Bruce Williams, VF-19, USS *Lexington*, October 1944

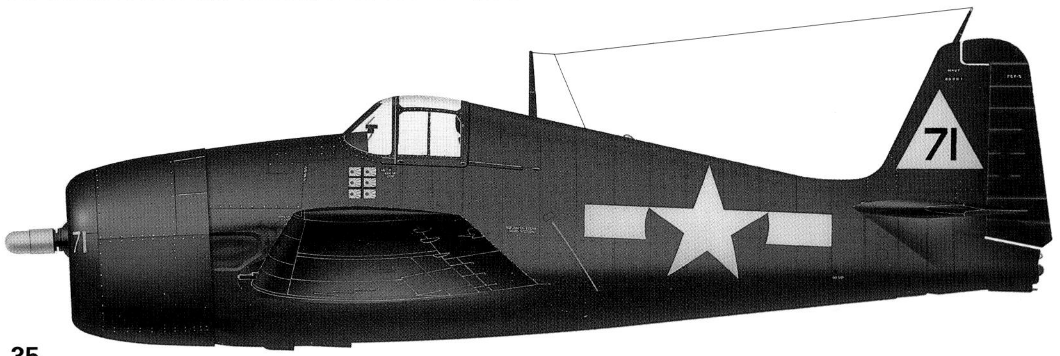

35
F6F-5 white 71 of Lt Leo B McCuddin, VF-20, USS *Enterprise*, October 1944

36
F6F-5 white 13/BuNo 42013 of Lt(jg) Ed Copeland, VF-19, USS *Lexington*, 6 November 1944

37
F6F-5 white 99 of Cdr T Hugh Winters, Jr, Commander Air Group 19, USS *Lexington*, November 1944

38
F6F-5 white 9 of Lt Charles 'Skull' Stimpson, VF-11, USS *Hornet*, November 1944

39
F6F-5 white 30/BuNo 70680 of Lt(jg) Blake Moranville, VF-11, USS *Hornet*, January 1945

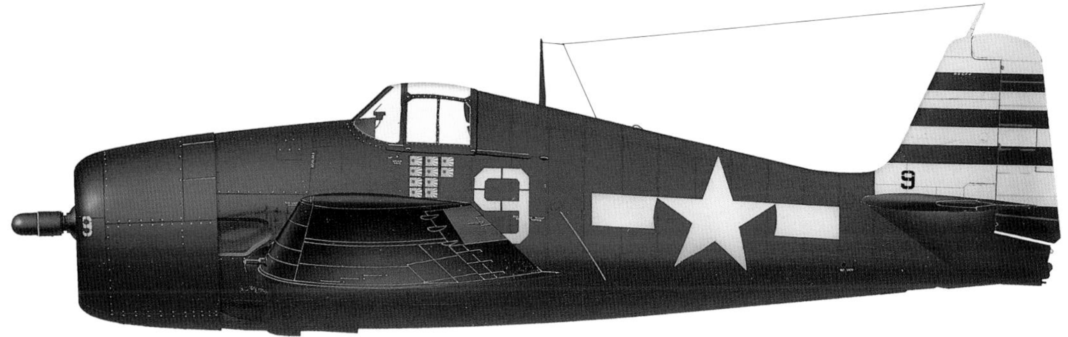

40
F6F-5 white 9 of Lt Hamilton McWhorter, III, VF-12, USS *Randolph*, January 1945

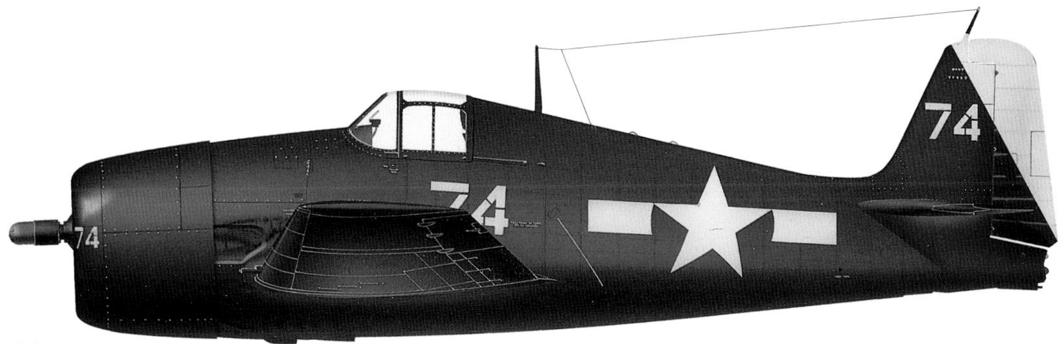

41
F6F-5 white 74/BuNo 72354 of Lt John M Wesolowski, VBF-9, USS *Yorktown*, 11 April 1945

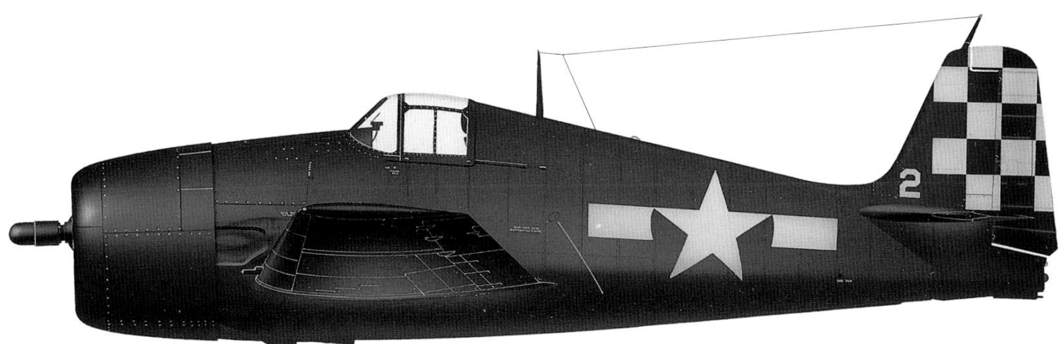

42
F6F-5 white 2 of Lt Cdr Robert A Weatherup, VF-46, USS *Independence*, 15 April 1945

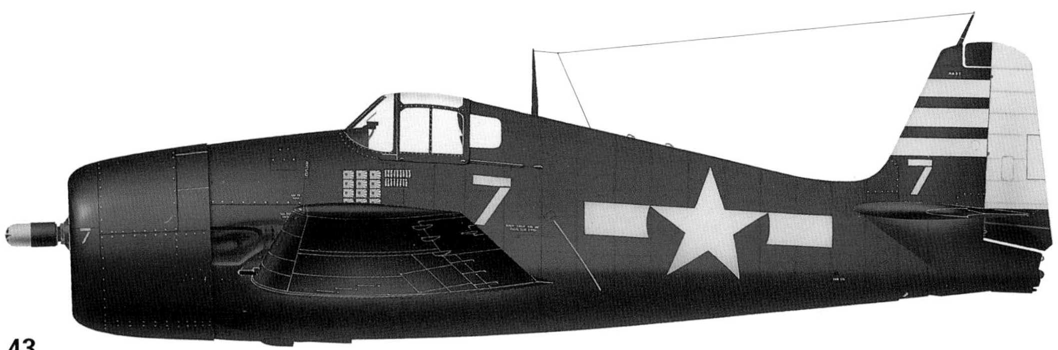

43
F6F-5 white 7 of Ens Robert E Murray, VF-29, USS *Cabot*, April 1945

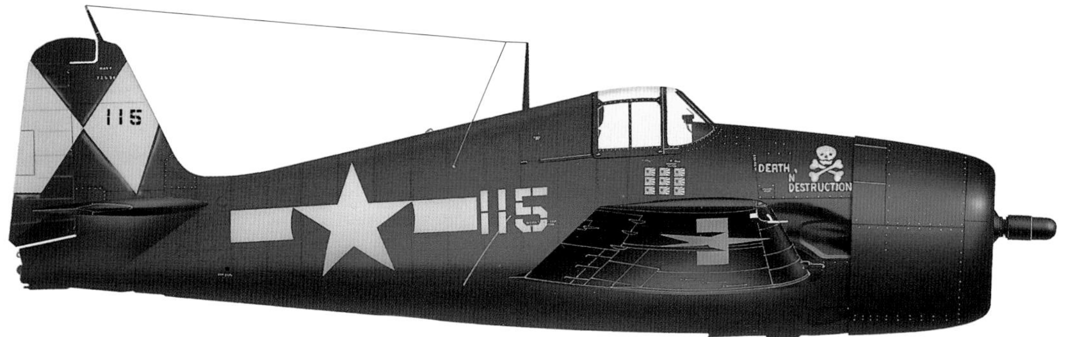

44

F6F-5 white 115 *DEATH N' DESTRUCTION*/BuNo 72534 of Ensigns Donald McPherson, Bill Kingston, Jr, and Lyttleton Ward, VF-83, USS *Essex*, 5 May 1945

45

F6F-5N white F(N)76/BuNo 78669 of Maj Robert B Porter, VMF(N)-542, Okinawa, 15 June 1945

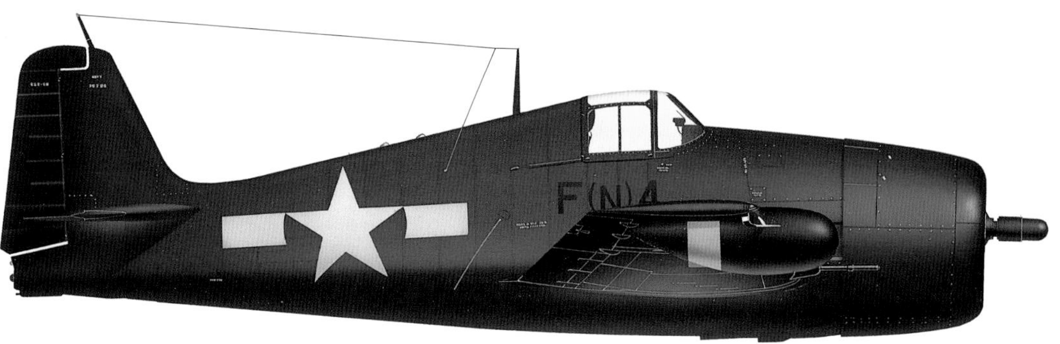

46

F6F-5N black F(N)4/BuNo 78704 of Capt Robert Baird, VMF(N)-533, Okinawa, June 1945

47

F6F-5 white VS 1 of Lt Cdr Willard E Eder, 'Victory Squadron', late 1945

1
Lt Cdr Paul D Buie, CO of VF-16 aboard USS *Lexington* in November 1943

2
Lt(jg) Alex Vraciu of VF-16 aboard USS *Lexington* on 19 June 1944

3
Lt Jim Swope of VF-11 aboard USS *Hornet* in January 1945

4
Lt Cdr Stanley Orr, CO of No 804 Sqn on HMS *Emperor* in April 1944

5
CAG-15 Cdr David McCampbell aboard USS Essex in November 1944

6
Maj Bruce Porter, CO of VMF(N)-542, on Okinawa in June 1945

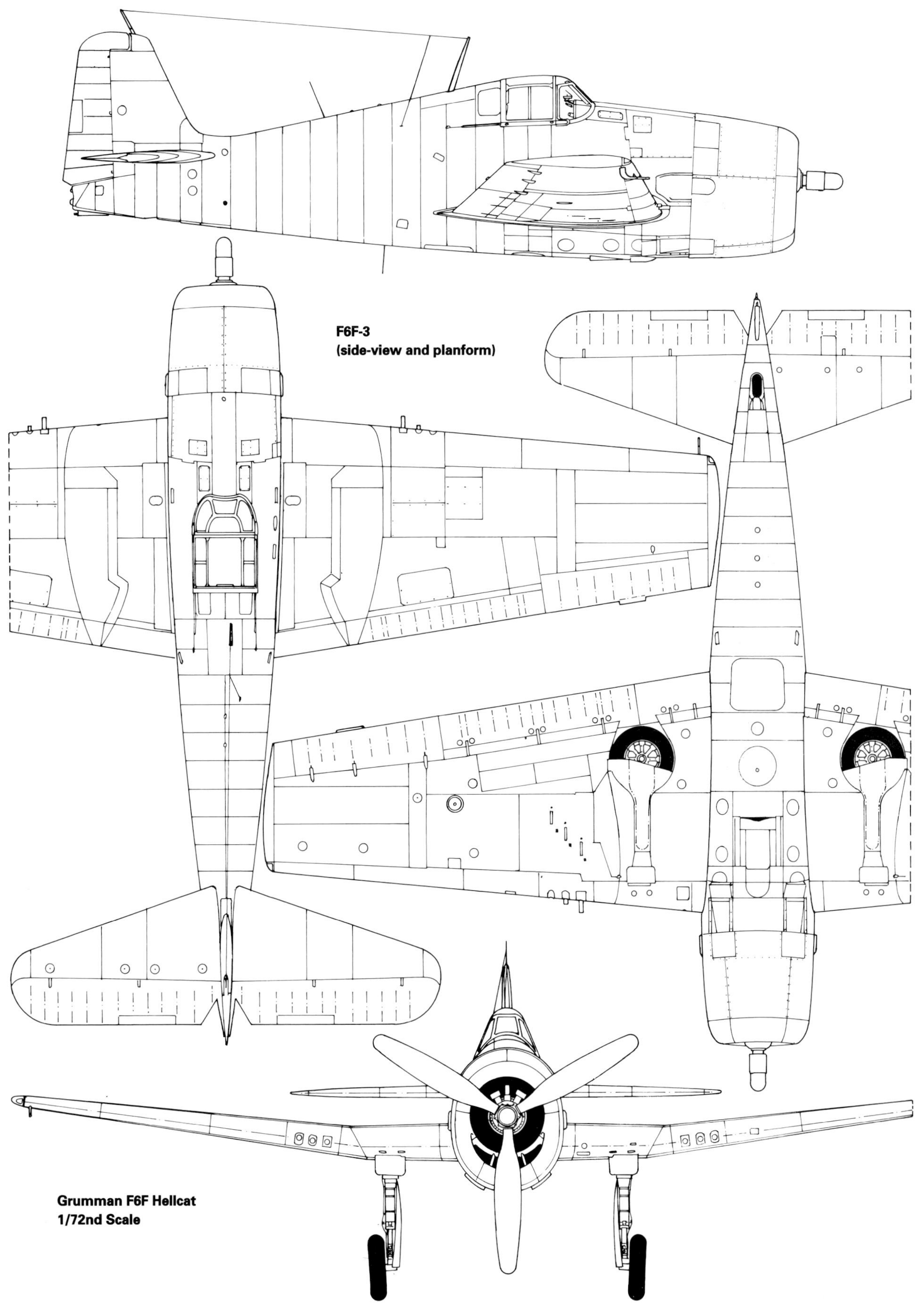
F6F-3
(side-view and planform)
Grumman F6F Hellcat
1/72nd Scale

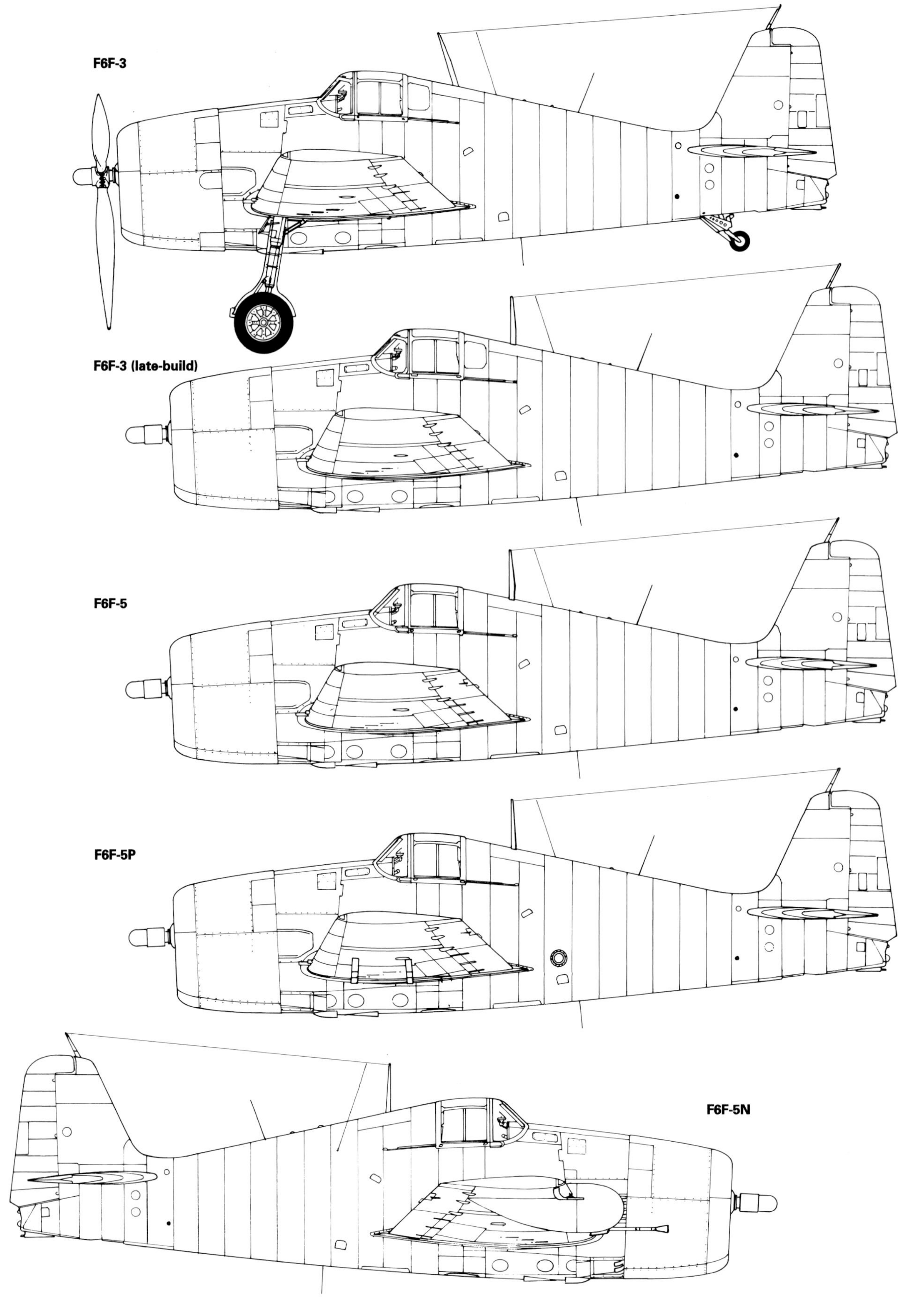
F6F-3
F6F-3 (late-build)
F6F-5
F6F-5P
F6F-5N

Colour Plates

1

F6F-3 white 00/BuNo 04872 of Cdr James H Flatley, CVAG-5, USS *Yorktown*, 6 May 1943

Widely respected as one of the Navy's outstanding combat leaders, 'Jimmy' Flatley flew this early-production F6F-3 while commanding Air Group 5 during carrier work-ups in mid-1943. Indeed, BuNo 04872 was the first ever aircraft to land aboard the second *Yorktown*, a feat it accomplished on the above-mentioned date. Note the contemporary roundels and Blue Grey (FS 36118) over Light Grey (FS 36440) scheme, and the '00' 'Double Nuts' modex, now recognised the world over as denoting the CAG's aircraft. The origin of this marking is a little vague, as most CAGs used the modex '99' to decorate their aircraft, with '00' then being used in Navy terminology to denote the admiral. Indeed, Flatley used the callsign '99 Sniper' when airborne, so as not to offend his ranking superiors who may be listening in.

2

F6F-3 white 00 of Cdr James H Flatley, CVAG-5, USS *Yorktown*, 31 August 1943

This 'Dash Three' was used by Flatley on the Marcus Island raid, and was the second Hellcat to be assigned to the CAG. Like its predecessor it wears his trademark '00' code and an LSO (Landing Signal Officer) stripe on its fin. The Hellcats greatly differ in camouflage schemes, however, this aircraft having been painted in the field in the interim tri-colour scheme of Sea Blue non-specular (FS 35042) over Intermediate Blue (FS 35189), with Insignia White non-specular (FS 37875) undersurfaces. The aircraft's red-bordered fuselage national insignia is smaller than regulations stipulated probably because VF-5 was one of the first F6F squadrons formed, and had to repaint its aircraft from the original factory-applied sea grey/light grey pattern of 1942-43. This machine was later photographed with the red roundel surround crudely painted over, as officially ordered on 31 July 1943.

3

F6F-3 white 37/BuNo 08926 of Lt(jg) Eugene R Hanks, VF-16, USS *Lexington*, 23 November 1943

Lt(jg) E R Hanks made history in his allotted F6F-3 BuNo 08926 on the morning of 23 November 1943 when he downed three 'Haps' and two Zeros (and possibly a third A6M) in a matter of minutes off Tarawa Island during his combat debut, thus making him the first of 44 Hellcat 'aces in a day'. This aircraft was soon adorned with kill decals upon its recovery back aboard *Lexington*, and Hanks photographed in its cockpit for the newspapers back in America. According to his log book, Hanks never flew BuNo 08926 again after his five-kill mission.

4

F6F-3 white 13/BuNo 66064 of Ens Ed 'Wendy' Wendorf, VF-16, USS *Lexington*, 4 December 1943

This was the aircraft that Ed Wendorf (4.5 kills) crash-landed back aboard 'Lady Lex' on this date following a frantic action over Kwajalein Atoll. It has often been wrongly described in other volumes as having a red surround to the national insignia, but research for this book has shown that the light shade around the 'star and bar' is in fact blue paint used to touch out the long-since banned red.

5

F6F-3 white 13 *MY OWN JOAN II*/BuNo 25813 of Lt C K 'Ken' Hildebrandt, VF-33, Ondonga, Christmas Day 1943

All five of Hildebrandt's victories were scored in this machine, which he flew on virtually every sortie during his squadron's spell in the Solomons between August 1943 and January 1944. The early-build F6F-3 bears the VF-33 'Hellcats' insignia forward of the windscreen, along with its nickname and pilot's scoreboard. Like most land-based Hellcats in the Solomons, it has also had its aerial mast removed.

6

F6F-3 white 22 of Lt(jg) Robert W Duncan, VF-5, USS *Yorktown*, late February 1944

Bob Duncan was the first carrier-based Hellcat pilot to shoot down a Zero, destroying two A6M5s over Wake Island during a fast carrier strike on 5 October 1943, followed by four more Zekes over Truk Atoll on 17 February 1944. He added another Zeke on the 22nd for a total of seven confirmed victories. Duncan was one of seven aces in the squadron led by Lt Cdr Edward M Owen, who contributed five of the unit's 126.5 credited victories. Like *Enterprise*'s VF-10, 'Fighting Five' returned to combat equipped with Corsairs in the final months of the war, flying briefly from *Franklin* in February and March 1945 before the ship was severely damaged in action.

7

F6F-3 white 67/BuNo 40381 of Lt Richard 'Rod' Devine, VF-10, USS *Enterprise*, 17 February 1944

'Rod' Devine used this 'plain Jane' early-build (note sloping aerial mast) F6F-3 to down a 'Sally' bomber over Truk Lagoon on this date VF-10 bagged 30 aircraft on the 17th, although Devine was the only one to down a 'Sally'. By the time the 'Grim Reapers'' tour had finished in June 1944, 'Rod ' Devine had scored eight kills, and finished as the ranking ace of the deployment.

8

F6F-3 white 82/BuNo 26183 of Lt(jg) Donald 'Flash' Gordon, VF-10, USS *Enterprise*, 17 February 1944

Like Devine, 'Flash' Gordon also got on the scoreboard on the morning of the 17th over Truk, splashing a Zeke (just one of 20) in the one-sided clash. He finished the deployment an ace with five kills, two of which had been scored on VF-10's previous Pacific tour aboard *Enterprise* in F4F-4s in 1942/43.

9

F6F-3 white 19/BuNo 40467 of Lt(jg) Alexander Vraciu, VF-6, USS *Intrepid*, 17 February 1944

In December 1943 this aircraft was assigned to Alex Vraciu, who shot down seven aircraft with it – four on this date over Truk (three Zekes and a 'Rufe'). The Hellcat sported the regulation squadron markings in addition to personal emblems. Below the canopy rail was stencilled *VRACIU*, while VF-6's 'Felix the Cat' emblem shared space with a personal insignia of unknown origin – a red-faced bull's head on a yellow background. The nickname *Gadget* was rendered in white script, presumably applied by the plane captain or other maintenance personnel. The fuselage of this very aeroplane somehow survived the wholesale scrapping of Hellcats after the war, and has been married to the wings and tail of F6F-5K BuNo 80141 and restored to airworthy condition. It is presently owned and flown by The Fighter Collection at Duxford, in England.

10

F6F-3 white 33 of Lt(jg) Frank Fleming, VF-16, USS *Lexington*, April 1944

Frank Fleming was among the earliest Hellcat pilots to gain confirmed victories against Japanese aircraft. By the end of 1943 he had been credited with 4.5 victories, and went on to complete his tour aboard *Lexington* with 7.5. Although personally-assigned aircraft were seldom flown by their designated pilot, some squadrons such as VF-16 made the effort. Aside from Fleming's kill decals, 'white 33' also wears a 'Fighting Airedale' insignia forward of the windscreen.

11

Hellcat I JV125 of Lt Cdr Stanley G Orr, No 804 Sqn, HMS *Emperor*, 14 May 1944

This drably-marked Hellcat I was used by Lt Cdr Orr to attack a formation of He 115 floatplanes off the coast of Norway on this date. Delivered to No 804 Sqn as an attrition replacement in early May following the unit's return from the April *Tirpitz* raids, JV125's service records are a little vague after its initial successes off Norway. Its only other entries of note whilst in FAA service were that it was delivered to Shorts of Belfast for repair following a Cat B accident in early 1945, and that it did not return to airworthiness until 22 December that year.

12

F6F-3 white 5/BuNo 40315 of Lt Hollis 'Holly' Hills , VF-32, USS *Langley*, 30 April 1944

Having already earned a place in the history books by scoring the first ever kill in a Mustang (see *Aces 7 Mustang Aces of the Ninth and Fifteenth Air Forces and the RAF*), Hollis Hills became a naval aviator in late 1942, and helped form VF-32. He considered himself to be a good shot, and had a chance to show his ability when his new unit went into combat in 1944. Employing German 'Yo-Yo' tactics of diving into a target, making one firing pass and then using his speed to quickly regain altitude, Hills used this aircraft, callsign 'Steele 5', to down three Zekes over Truk Atoll on 29 April.

13

F6F-3 white 31/BuNo 69532 of Wilbur B 'Spider' Webb, VF-2, USS *Hornet*, 19 June 1944

Webb flew 'White 31' over Guam during a single-handed interception of Japanese dive-bombers in the Orote Field traffic pattern on this date. In a few minutes he had shot down six Aichi D3A 'Vals' confirmed and two probables, becoming one of six Hellcat 'aces in a day' during the 'Great Marianas Turkey Shoot' – all this despite having persistent gun failure due to a lack of hydraulic pressure in the weapons' charger system. Webb landed back aboard ship with a barely functioning undercarriage, no canopy and minus his flying helmet, which had been shot off – he was unhurt, however. In all, 147 bullet and shrapnel holes were found in BuNo 69532, and after parts reclamation, it was honourably 'buried at sea'.

14

F6F-3 *The Minsi* of Cdr David McCampbell, Commander Air Group 15, USS *Essex*, 19 June 1944

The Minsi was the second Hellcat assigned to the Navy's leading fighter ace, Cdr David McCampbell. His first F6F-3 was BuNo 41692, nicknamed *Monsoon Maiden*, which he flew during his time as CO of VF-15, and which was jettisoned from *Essex* on 20 May 1944 due irreparable flak damage the day before over Marcus Island. This machine was issued to him as a replacement, and he named for his lady friend, Miss Mary Blatz. It too was stricken with flak damage over Manila in September 1944, and duly replaced by F6F-5 *Minsi II*. McCampbell flew *The Minsi* on at least one of his two sorties of 19 June, accounting for five 'Judys' in the first and two Zekes in the second. The horizontal band around the vertical stabiliser and rudder was an *Essex* trademark which remained when CVG-4 relieved CVG-15 in November. None of McCampbell's 'CAG birds' had side number.

15

F6F-3 white 36/BuNo 41269 of Ens Wilbur B 'Spider' Webb, VF-2, USS *Hornet*, 20 June 1944

This was one of four machines used by Webb during the Marianas campaign, 'White 36' being flown by the newly-crowned ace on the 'Flight after Darkness' assault on the retreating Japanese fleet staged 24 hours after his epic Guam sortie. TF-38 launched 216 aircraft to strike the shattered enemy at extreme range, knowing that the force would have to recover back aboard in darkness – few pilots were night landing-qualified in 1944. Webb returned safely in BuNo 41269, but 104 aircraft were lost.

16

F6F-3 white 32 of Lt(jg) Alexander Vraciu, VF-16, USS *Lexington*, 21 June 1944

Following the torpedoing of *Intrepid* at Truk on 17 February, VF-6 was sent back the US, but Alex Vraciu somehow managed to wangle a transfer to VF-16, and thus remain in combat until the middle of the year. He had been the leading ace in his previous unit, and went on to top VF-16's list of high scorers also. Vraciu was assigned aircraft number 32 (BuNo unknown) whilst with his new unit, which carried his name and ultimate tally of 19 victories. It is uncertain whether he flew this Hellcat during his interception of Japanese dive-bombers over TF-58 on 19 June, which resulted in six kills in only eight minutes. One source indicates that he flew number 13 on that occasion, but the origin of that statement is unknown.

17

F6F-3 white 9/BuNo 40090 of Lt William C Moseley, VF-1, USS *Yorktown*, June 1944

This machine was issued to five-kill ace Moseley in late June as a replacement for BuNo 41438, which had had to be jettisoned over the side of *Yorktown* following aerial combat (in which he downed two Zekes and claimed a third as a probable) on the 19th of that month near Guam. This machine still wears its crudely-applied ferry code (the last three numbers of its BuNo) on its cowling.

18

F6F-3N white 9/BuNo 42158 of Lt Russ Reiserer, VF(N)-76 Det 2, USS *Hornet*, 10 July 1944

This rare F6F-3N was used by Reiserer when he flew to Saipan on this date to discuss operating procedures with a USAAF P-61 Black Widow unit that was patrolling the same night skies. Three days earlier he had used similarly-marked BuNo 26077 to down his ninth, and last, kill (a 'Betty') on a night CAP that lasted almost four hours. This was Reiserer's sole nocturnal score. Note the mixed scheme on this fighter, its matt blue tail contrasting sharply with its overall glossy sea blue fuselage and wings.

19

F6F-5 white 8 of Ensigns Alfred R Wood and Edward W

Olszewski, VOF-1, USS *Tulagi*, August 1944
Incredibly, of the six Luftwaffe aircraft claimed by the gunnery-spotting VOF-1 during Operation *Dragoon*, this Hellcat was involved in the destruction of four of them – Ens Wood shared in the destruction of two He 111s near Vienne on 19 August, and Ens Olszewski downed a pair of Ju 52s near Orange two days later. Both pilots went on to score kills in the Pacific with the redesignated VOC-1 in 1945.

20
F6F-5 white 12/BuNo 58937 of Lt(jg) Ray 'Hawk' Hawkins, VF-31, USS *Cabot*, September 1944
Texan 'Hawk' Hawkins was the second-ranking ace of VF-31 'Flying Meataxes' with 14 kills, five ('Oscars') of which were scored on 13 September 1944. Assigned a mixed fleet of 14 'Dash Threes' and 10 'Dash Fives', the unit produced 14 aces during its 1944 deployment. Its overall wartime tally of 165.5 aircraft made it the top-scoring CVL fighter squadron in the Navy.

21
F6F-5N white 13/BuNo 70147 of Lt Bill Henry, VF(N)-41, USS *Independence*, 21 September 1944
The first dedicated night air group in the US Navy, CVLG(N)-41 deployed in the light carrier *Independence* in August 1944. The fighter squadron under Lt Cdr T F Caldwell shot down 46 Japanese aircraft, producing two aces, Exec Lt W E Henry with 9.5 victories and Ens J A Berkheimer, who was killed with his score standing at seven. Relatively few of the aerial victories were achieved in darkness, however, owing to slow acceptance of the night fliers' capabilities by TF-58. A perfect example of this occurred on 21 September when Henry used BuNo 70147, callsign 'Cupid 13', to score a probable 'Oscar' kill over Clark Field at 9.35 am!

22
F6F-3 white 3 of Ens Gordon A Stanley, VF-27, USS *Princeton*, September 1944
Like most of 'Fighting 27's' distinctively-marked Hellcats, this machine went to the bottom of the Pacific with *Princeton* on 24 October 1944 following the carrier's mortal wounding by a well-placed bomb dropped from a lone 'Judy'. It was the regular mount of eight-kill ace Gordon Stanley, who had the distinction of scoring all his victories in pairs! Stanley was to later die in an F9F-6 crash in 1956.

23
F6F-3 white 17 of Lt Richard Stambook, VF-27, USS *Princeton*, 24 October 1944
Stambook was VF-27's third-highest scorer on their 1944 deployment, having claimed his final kill (a 'Nick') six days prior to *Princeton*'s sinking. A seasoned pilot by the time he saw combat with VF-27 in 1944, 'Dick' Stambook had earlier served with VS-3 on Dauntlesses and VF-6 and VF-3 on Wildcats.

24
F6F-3 white 13 of Lt William E Lamb, VF-27, USS *Princeton*, 24 October 1944
A pre-war naval aviator, William Lamb served as VF-27's Exec from June 1944. This promotion seemed to inspire Lamb greatly for he proceeded to 'make ace' in the space of ten days between the 19th and 29th of that month. He went on to add a sixth kill to his World War 2 record on 18 November 1950 when he shot down a MiG-15 over North Korea whilst serving as CO of F9F-3 Panther-equipped VF-52 aboard USS *Valley Forge* (see *Aces 4 Korean War Aces*).

25
F6F-3 white 23 of Lt James 'Red' Shirley, VF-27, USS *Princeton*, 24 October 1944
This was the aircraft used by ranking VF-27 ace Shirley to down five fighters in a frenetic dogfight that occurred west of the task force on this date.The Hellcat was destined never to carry his final scoreboard of 12.5 kills as it was lost with *Princeton* later that day. Rated as an exceptional pilot, Shirley had been 'ploughed back' into the Navy's training programme at Pensacola as an instructor upon earning his wings in early 1942, and had had to fight to get a frontline posting late the following year.

26
F6F-5 white 9 of Lt Carl A Brown, Jr, VF-27, USS *Princeton*, 24 October 1944
Although assigned to VF-27's second-highest scorer, this particular Hellcat was not being flown by him on this date. Indeed, with the loss of all squadron records (and pilots' log books) on the 24th, it cannot be ascertained if this aircraft was used by him to down any of the 5.5 kills it is marked up with. This near-new Hellcat was one of six F6F-5 replacements issued to the squadron prior to the Leyte Gulf campaign, operating side-by-side with the far more common tri-colour 'Dash Threes'.

27
F6F-5 white 10 *PAOLI LOCAL* of Ens Paul E Drury, VF-27, USS *Princeton*, 24 October 1944
Like Carl Brown's Hellcat, this machine was not flown by its regular pilot, 6.5-kill ace Paul Drury, on 24 October. Such was the hurry to scramble VF-27's fighters, pilots strapped into whatever aircraft they could find serviceable – not that an unfamiliar cockpit put Drury off for he downed three fighters in the bloody clash. Named after a Philadelphia commuter train that he used to catch near his home, Drury's *PAOLI LOCAL* was flown into combat on this fateful day by recently-arrived replacement pilot Ens O L Scott, who was subsequently shot down and killed – VF-27's only aerial loss on this day.

28
F6F-5 white 1 of Lt Cdr Fred A Bardshar, CO of VF-27/Commander Air Group 27, USS *Princeton*, 24 October 1944
The pilot of this Hellcat held the distinction of commanding both VF-27 and Air Group 27 for much of *Princeton*'s combat deployment. Previously the unit's Exec, Fred Bardshar proved more than up to the job(s) thrust upon him following the death in combat of the previous incumbent, Cdr E W Wood, on 19 June 1944 – the same day the former splashed two 'Judys'. Bardshar's final score of 7.5 kills was marked in the usual fashion on the starboard side of the fuselage on this machine.

29
F6F-5 white 7 *PAPER DOLL* of Ens Bob Burnell, VF-27, USS *Princeton*, 24 October 1944
Although bearing Burnell's name, scoreboard (four kills in total) and personal marking, this F6F-5 was flown by Carl Brown, Jr, on the 24th, the latter using it to down five Zekes before landing back aboard *Essex*. Both pilot and aircraft were badly shot up in this combat, but by recovering back aboard ship rather than ditching, PAPER DOLL became one of just nine (out of 24) VF-27 Hellcats to survive the sinking of *Princeton*. Prior to the unit deploying aboard ship, Burnell had hand-painted the cat's teeth on all 24 F6Fs assigned to VF-27.

30

F6F-5 *Minsi III*/BuNo 70143 of Cdr David McCampbell, Commander Air Group 15, USS *Essex*, 25 October 1944

Easily the best-known Hellcat of them all, BuNo 70143 was an early production F6F-5 that retained the 'windows' behind the cockpit as per the F6F-3 – a feature deleted on most 'Dash Fives'. As an air group commander, McCampbell was able to fly his assigned aircraft on nearly every mission, and *Minsi III* lasted far longer than either of his previous *Minsi*s. Although McCampbell lost his logbooks after the war, it is estimated that he scored 20 or more of his 34 confirmed victories in *Minsi III*. Sadly, this machine was lost in an accident in December 1944 whilst being flown by McCampbell's replacement.

31

F6F-5 white 28/BuNo 58069 of Ens Frank 'Trooper' Troup, VF-29, USS *Cabot*, 29 October 1944

VF-29 replaced the battle-weary VF-31 aboard *Cabot* on 5 October 1944, and immediately adorned their F6F-5s in identical markings – 'G symbols' tended to be associated more with the carrier than the air group. Frank Troup used this aircraft to down a 'Jack' and a 'Tojo' over Clark Field during an early-morning sweep on this date. However, his aircraft was badly shot up by a second 'Jack' soon after he had despatched the 'Tojo', and Troup was forced to ditch the fighter during his return – he was soon rescued by the destroyer USS *Halsey Powell*, however. Frank Troup finished the war with seven kills.

32

F6F-5 *Minsi II* of Cdr David McCampbell, Commander Air Group 15, USS *Essex*, October 1944

This aircraft was one of the first F6F-5s issued to Air Group 15, and naturally was assigned to the ranking pilot aboard *Essex*. It was flown very infrequently when compared with McCampbell's previous Hellcats, as its pilot was not fond of its engine unreliability – it suffered two powerplant failures in very short order whilst the CAG was airborne in it, and following air combat damage, was renamed and passed on to a line pilot from VF-15.

33

F6F-5 white 29 of Lt James S Swope, VF-11, USS *Hornet*, October 1944

Devoid of any distinguishing markings other than the white ball 'G symbol' on the tail and a similarly-coloured propeller hub, this Hellcat was occassionally flown by combat veteran Jim Swope during the latter half of VF-11's frontline deployment on *Hornet*. A pre-war private pilot, Swope had joined the 'Sundowners' as early as September 1942 – just in time to deploy to Guadalcanal, where he claimed 4.666 kills in Wildcats. He followed up this success with a further five kills scored whilst leading his four-Hellcat division, which included six-kill ace Lt(jg) Blake Moranville as section leader.

34

F6F-5 white 25 of Lt Bruce Williams, VF-19, USS *Lexington*, October 1944

This early-build F6F-5 was one of just a handful to serve in the frontline in the old tricolour scheme of 1943. Aside from its odd shading, the fighter also boasts its modex repeated immediately aft of the cockpit – a marking unique to VF-19, and one which was decidedly non-regulation. Seven-kill ace 'Willie Mohawk' Williams was responsible for bringing one of the most gravely damaged Hellcats safely back aboard ship when he recovered in F6F-3 BuNo 42054 on 21 October 1944. He had been strafing ammunition barges off Ceram, in the Philippines, at low-level when one exploded just below his fighter. The Hellcat was 'tossed' from 50 to 150 ft as a result of the blast, freezing all the cockpit instruments and leaving Williams upside down with his right wing in shreds. Somehow he got back aboard *Lexington*, where a survey of the damage revealed twisted structural spars in the right wing, a warped tail surface, cancelling his aileron control, and a foot-long chunk of 'two-by-four' wooden plank lodged in the engine.

35

F6F-5 white 71 of Lt Leo B McCuddin, VF-20, USS *Enterprise*, October 1944

'Fighting Squadron 20' embarked in *Enterprise* in August 1944, logging combat missions over the Philippines and Formosa. Among the nine aces were Lt(jg) Douglas Baker with 16.333 victories and the CO, Cdr Fred Bakutis, with 11. The pilot of this Hellcat, Lt McCudden scored five victories over Japanese fighters in three combats, all in the space of six days. Although he flew 'White 71' at least once in combat, the six victory flags below its cockpit probably represent the aircraft's tally, rather than any single pilot. After transferring to *Lexington* in December, VF-20 completed its tour in January 1945 with 158 kills.

36

F6F-5 white 13/BuNo 42013 of Lt(jg) Ed Copeland, VF-19, USS *Lexington*, 6 November 1944

Unlucky for some, 'white 13' was ditched in Luguna do Bay by six-kill ace Ed Copeland after it had sustained AA damage over Manila on this date. Fortunately, he was soon rescued by Filipino guerillas, who hid him until he could be picked up by a PBY. All of Copeland's kills, and his sole probable, were scored against different types of aircraft, which must some kind of Navy record.

37

F6F-5 white 99 of Cdr T Hugh Winters, Jr, Commander Air Group 19, USS *Lexington*, November 1944

The original skipper of 'Fighting 19', Cdr Winters became *Lexington*'s air group commander in September 1944. He flew two 'CAG birds', both similarly-marked with 'number 99', and used the radio callsign '99 Mohawk'. The first *Hanger Lily* (a misnomer referring to the ship's hangar deck) was damaged by flak and jettisoned. The second eventually sported eight victory decals, plus the name and an appropriate flower painted forward of the windscreen – 'COMDR T H WINTERS' was stencilled below the cockpit as well. Owing to the loss of his logbooks, neither BuNo is known.

38

F6F-5 white 9 of Lt Charles 'Skull' Stimpson, VF-11, USS *Hornet*, November 1944

VF-11's leading ace on both of its frontline deployments, Charlie Stimpson scored his first six victories flying F4F-4s at Guadalcanal in 1943. A further ten kills (all fighters) were accrued by 'Skull' in four-week scoring spree in October/November 1944, thus giving him a wartime total of 16. This aircraft was specially adorned with the appropriate number of kill decals for photographic purposes only.

39

F6F-5 white 30/BuNo 70680 of Lt(jg) Blake Moranville, VF-11, USS *Hornet*, January 1945

The callsign of this F6F was 'Ginger 30', reflecting its base as

Hornet. Six-kill ace Moranville was shot down by a single well-aimed 20 mm AA round whilst strafing ground targets in this aeroplane near Saigon, Indochina, on 12 January 1945. Captured by the Vichy French, Moranville, and several other downed fliers, experienced an odyssey which took them from Saigon to Hanoi, on to Dien Bien Phu and then into China, and safety.

40

F6F-5 white 9 of Lt Hamilton McWhorter, III, VF-12, USS *Randolph*, January 1945

'Ham' McWhorter was not only the first Hellcat ace but also the first double ace as well, flying with VF-9 aboard *Essex* in 1943-44. He scored his first victory at Wake Island on 5 October 1943, his fifth in the Gilberts on 19 November and tenth at Truk Atoll on 17 February 1944. Many 'Fighting Nine' pilots later joined Air Group 12, including Armistead B Smith, Reuben Denoff, John M Franks and Harold Vita, who all became aces. McWhorter scored his 11th success a year after the Truk raid, downing a Zeke near Tokyo on 16 February 1945. He added a 'Myrt' reconnaissance aircraft on 13 May for a wartime total of 12. Aside from the distinctive white stripes on the vertical stabiliser, Air Group 12 aircraft also had white ailerons.

41

F6F-5 white 74/BuNo 72354 of Lt John M Wesolowski, VBF-9, USS *Yorktown*, 11 April 1945

Already a five-kill Wildcat ace following his tour with VF-5 on Guadalcanal in late 1942, Wesolowski then served as a flight instructor for almost two years, before being posted in January 1945 to the newly-created VBF-9 as Exec. He scored two kills over Okinawa during his second frontline tour, the first of which was against the ultimate Japanese naval fighter, the Kawanishi N1K2-J *Shiden-Kai* 'George'. Claimed on 11 April in this Hellcat, Wesolowski's 'George' was the only one of its type downed by *Yorktown*'s air group.

42

F6F-5 white 2 of Lt Cdr Robert A Weatherup, VF-46, USS *Independence*, 15 April 1945

Four days after Wesolowski bagged a 'George', VF-46's Exec, Lt Cdr 'Doc' Weatherup, went one better by downing a pair of *Shiden-Kai* over Kanoya Airfield, on Kyushu – his only wartime kills. One of the fighters was flown by Navy ace Shoichi Sugita (between 30 and 70 kills), and his wingman Toyomi Miyazawa was in the second 'George'. Both part of the elite 343rd *Kokutai* which included Saburo Sakai amongst its ranks (he actually witnessed the attack from the ground), the two Japanese pilots were caught whilst attempting to take-off following a rocket and strafing attack by VF-46.

43

F6F-5 white 7 of Ens Robert E Murray, VF-29, USS *Cabot*, April 1945

Lt(jg) R E Murray was VF-29's 'topgun' with 10.33 confirmed kills, the unit producing a further 11 aces. Operating against Japan, VF-29 claimed 113 victories, including 34 off Formosa on 16 October 1944 – Murray claimed four on this day to achieve ace status. Aside from carrying 12 flags, denoting that both Murray's shared 'Betty' claim and a damaged Zeke had also been included in the tally, 15 bombing mission symbols have been painstakingly added to the fuselage of 'Lucky 7'.

44

F6F-5 white 115 *DEATH N' DESTRUCTION*/BuNo 72534 of Ensigns Donald McPherson, Bill Kingston, Jr, and Lyttleton Ward, VF-83, USS *Essex*, 5 May 1945

Carrying gaudy nose-art and a victory tally of nine kills, BuNo 72534 was arguably the most recognisable Hellcat aboard *Essex* in the last months of the war. Predominantly flown by a trio of ensign aces, the fighter's greatest day came on 4 May 1945 when it was used by Lyttleton Ward to down three 'Alfs' and an 'Oscar' as VF-83 helped repel one of the biggest *kamikaze* raids launched on TF-58 during the Okinawan invasion.

45

F6F-5N white F(N)76/BuNo 78669 of Maj Robert B Porter, VMF(N)-542, Okinawa, 15 June 1945

Bruce Porter logged three victories while flying F4Us with VMF-121 in the Solomons during 1943. He became an ace on the night of 15 June 1945 when he shot down a 'Nick' and a 'Betty' mothership, complete with *Ohka* suicide bomb, off the coast of Okinawa. Upon assuming command of VMF(N)-542 some weeks earlier, Porter had inherited the previous CO's (Maj W C Kellum) 'F(N)76', which was the only Hellcat in the squadron fitted with cannon armament. It was then adorned with the name *Millie Lou*, but the new CO insisted upon a more warlike appellation, and chose *Black Death*. He also had a bottle of Schenley's whiskey painted on the starboard cowling. 'F(N)76' was also stencilled in white on each landing-gear door, and Porter's victories were displayed on the left side of the fuselage below the cockpit.

46

F6F-5N black F(N)4/BuNo 78704 of Capt Robert Baird, VMF(N)-533, Okinawa, June 1945

The Marine Corps' only nightfighter ace, Baird had previously flown F4U-2s with VMF(N)-532 in the Central Pacific, but had enjoyed little success with the Chance-Vought machine. He arrived on Okinawa with VMF(N)-533 in April 1945, and became an ace over a two-week period in June. He claimed his first victory, a 'Jake' floatplane, on 9 June, followed by two 'doubles' – a 'Betty' and a 'Nell' on the 16th, then a 'Fran' and 'Betty' six nights later. His sixth, and final, victim, another 'Betty', was splashed on 14 July. Like many nightfighter pilots, he preferred cannons, but only scored his last victory with the 20 mm weapons owing to previous functioning problems.

47

F6F-5 white VS 1 of Lt Cdr Willard E Eder, 'Victory Squadron', late 1945

At the end of World War 2 the Navy and Treasury Departments combined in a final bond drive to defray demobilisation costs. The 'Victory Squadron' was established under Lt Cdr Eder, who had led Air Group 29 in 1944-45. His personal Hellcat included a detailed score board depicting his seven aerial victories (one shared), plus three Vichy and nine Japanese aircraft destroyed on the ground, in addition to 39 bombing sorties. Other aircraft in the squadron were F7Fs, F4Us, SB2Cs, TBMs and two captured Japanese aircraft – a Zeke and a 'Kate'. Another ace in the unit was Capt 'Gus' Thomas, a Marine Corps Corsair ace who scored 18.5 kills during two tours with VMF-213.

FIGURE PLATES

1

Lt Cdr Paul D Buie, CO of VF-16, has unfolded his mission map and is explaining to his pilots up on the deck of *Lexington* where the next sweep will take place over Tarawa on the morning of 23 November 1943. He is wearing an AN-H-15 tropical issue flying helmet, customised in squadron colours by the unit's groundcrew. Other pilots in VF-15 had their head gear embellished with a green shamrock hand-painted on top of the cloth helmet. Buie's goggles are standard military-issue Polaroid B-8s, which had only been cleared for frontline use the previous month. As commanding officer, he has chosen to wear a khaki shirt and trousers, rather than the more common 'suit/summer/flying', and complements this smarter apparel with a pair of highly-polished black lace-up shoes.

2

Looking a little more 'combat-wise' in his well-worn flying 'coveralls' than the 'spotless' Buie, Lt(jg) Alex Vraciu displays his final score after his epic struggle against a formation of 'Judys' on 19 June 1944. His headwear consists of a later spec AN-H-15 helmet combined with an old pair of favourite AN-6530, or B-7, goggles. Like Buie, Vraciu's life preserver is a ubiquitous N2885. He is still wearing his dinghy pack, having just jumped out of his Hellcat, and his hands are adorned in fire-proof naval aviator's gloves. Finally, Vraciu is wearing standard QMC-issue 'Boondockers' on his feet.

3

Wearing fundamentally similar clothing as Vraciu, Lt Jim Swope of VF-11 in January 1945 also has his seat-type parachute strapped on his back below the dinghy pack. His helmet is similar in design to Buie's, but his goggles are B-7s. Most pilots chose to carry just a Smith and Wesson .38 revolver when going into combat, but Swope has also opted for the added protection of a jungle knife, secured in its leather scabbard.

4

Lt Cdr Stanley Orr, CO of No 804 Sqn on HMS *Emperor* in April 1944, checks over the charts prior to launching against *Tirpitz*. Although wearing a standard Royal Navy dark blue flying overall, adorned with 'two-and-a-half' rank tabs, and fully tied-up Mae West, Orr's head gear is American in origin – a modified AN-H-15, complete with B-7 goggles. He had acquired these whilst in Norfolk, Virginia, working up with the newly-formed No 896 Sqn on Martlet IVs in October 1942. His oxygen mask is RAF issue, however. In order to stave off the cold should he have to ditch in fjord, Orr is also wearing a turtle neck woollen sweater underneath his overall. The webbing belt for his .38 service revolver is attached to the bottom of his Mae West.

5

As befits the senior pilot aboard ship, CAG-15 Cdr David McCampbell is wearing a khaki button-up shirt and matching trousers similar in style to Lt Cdr P D Buie's. His equipment is all standard Navy issue, and he has a Smith and Wesson .38 revolver holstered beneath his left arm, with a bandoleer well-stocked with ammunition slung over his right shoulder beneath the life preserver. McCampbell has also chosen the later B-8 goggles in preference to the older B-7s favoured by a number of seasoned combat veterans.

6

Maj Bruce Porter, CO of VMF(N)-542, is also wearing as shirt and trousers as befits his rank. Unlike the carrier-based aviators seen on this spread, Porter has chosen not to adorn his N2885 with various dye marker pouches and flare rounds. Note too that he written his name on the crotch strap of the life preserver, thus preventing anyone from 'borrowing' it by mistake! Unlike his pilots, who would be equipped with well-worn 'Boondockers', Porter is wearing a shiny pair of dress brown leather lace ups, which look rather smarter with the shirt and trousers.

among other things, that the F6F belly tank was a critical recognition item. Those who jettisoned their tanks were subject to attack by US aircraft from other squadrons.

'The tactics of our principal intercept were not refined, and we were quite vulnerable to the escorting Zeros who had a useable altitude advantage. Having no altitude advantage on the bombers ourselves, we initiated with flat side runs followed by tail chases. My shooting was all no deflection, which I think was typical. The Japanese were unquestionably constrained by fuel limitations.'

Oil-stained 'White 30' may just be a candidate for 'Davey Jones' locker' judging by the leading-edge damage to the starboard wing sustained in this 19 June crash. A seasoned campaigner, this F6F-3 already sports a replacement rudder (which has suffered combat damage during its latest tussle with the enemy) from a previous close shave (*Jerry Scutts*)

Aside from F6Fs, CV-based dive- and torpedo-bombers crews claimed 4.5 victories, and escort-carrier FM Wildcat pilots added four more, running the day's total to 380 credited victories. It remains the greatest one-day tally in the history of American air combat.

Individually, six Hellcat pilots became aces in a day, accruing 34 confirmed victories in total. Three were *Essex* pilots – Cdr David McCampbell, the air group commander, with seven kills in two interceptions; his fighter leader, Cdr Brewer, with five; and Lt(jg) G R Carr with five – the latter went to score 11.5 kills. Two *Hornet* aviators achieved their scores in the traffic pattern over Guam, with Ens W B Webb (seven kills in total), a former enlisted pilot, claiming six confirmed and two probables, while Lt R L Reiserer (nine kills in total) of VF(N)-76 scored five. Lt(jg) Alex Vraciu of VF-16, already the top-scoring carrier aviator at the time, downed six 'Judys' for a total of 18. In the following passage, reproduced with due acknowledgement to *The Hook*, Vraciu describes this combat in detail:

'As part of the American task force protecting the Saipan operation, we were expecting an attack by over 400 Japanese carrier planes on the morning of 19 June 1944. Bogies were up on radar as they approached in several large groups and carrier fighter aircraft were scrambled to supplement the combat air patrols already aloft. I was part of a VF-16 standby group of 12 F6F-3 Hellcat fighters launched from USS *Lexington* (CV-16).

'As we climbed for altitude at full military power, I heard "Sapphire Base", *Lexington*'s Fighter Direction Officer (FDO), as he he broadcast, "Vector 270 (degrees), angels 25, pronto". VF-16 skipper Lt Cdr Paul D Buie led our three divisions

Seen aboard *Lexington* on 13 June, 'White 26' wears six kill markings. As Ralph Hanks pointed out in chapter one, all VF-16 pilots had an 'assigned' aircraft, and it is likely that this F6F belonged to Lt(jg) W E Burckhalter, as he was the only pilot in the unit at this time with exactly six kills. If this is the case, the F6F outlasted its assigned pilot, as Burckhalter had drowned off Saipan 48 hours before, having ditched a flak damaged BuNo 40676

of four planes each. I led the second division of F6F-3s.

'Overhead, converging contrails of fighters from other carriers could be seen heading in the same direction. After a while, the skipper, who was riding behind a new engine, began to pull ahead steadily until he was out of sight. We had seen his wingman, Lt(jg) W C B Birkholm, drop out – the full-power climb was too much for his engine. Birkholm's propeller froze and he headed downward to a ditching. Luckily, he was picked up by a destroyer 14 hours later.

'My engine was throwing an increasing film of oil onto my windshield, forcing me to ease back slightly on the throttle. My division stayed with me, and two other planes joined us. When I found that my tired engine would not go into high blower, our top altitudewas limited to 20,000 ft. Our predicament was reported to "Sapphire Base".

'All the way up, my wingman, Ens Homer W Brockmeyer, repeatedly pointed toward my wing while observing radio silence. Thinking he had spotted the enemy, I attempted to turn over the lead to him, but each time I tried he would only shake his head. Not understanding what he meant, I finally shook him off in order to concentrate on the immediate task facing us. I found out later that my wings weren't fully locked – the red safety barrels were showing – which explained "Brock's" frantic pointing.

'It was all over before our group reached this particular wave of attacking aircraft, and I was ordered to return my group to the task force and orbit overhead at 20,000 ft. We had barely arrived at our station when the FDO vectored us on a heading of 265 degrees. Something in his voice told us that he had a good one on the string. The bogies were 75 miles away when reported, and we headed outbound in hope of meeting them halfway. I saw two other groups of Hellcats converging off to starboard, four in one group and three in the other.

'About 25 miles out, I tallyhoed three bogeys and closed on them. In the back of my mind, I figured that there had to be more than three as I remembered the seriousness in the FDO's voice. Spot-gazing intently, I suddenly picked out a large, spread-out, mass of at least 50 planes, 2000 ft below us, portside and closing. My adrenalin flow hit high C. They were about 35 miles from our forces and heading in fast. I remember thinking that this could develop into the once-in-a-lifetime fighter pilot's dream.

'Puzzled and suspicious, I looked about for the accompanying enemy fighter cover that normally one would expect over their attacking planes, but none were seen. By this time we were in a perfect position for a high-side run on the enemy aircraft. I rocked my wings as I began a run on the nearest straggler, a *Judy* dive-bomber.

'However, I noted out of the corner of my eye that another F6F seemed to have designs on the same

Ens Wilbur 'Spider' Webb of VF-2 made ace on 19 June when he took on a large formation of 'Vals' alone at low-level over Guam, downing six. He made the now famous radio transmission, 'Any American fighter near Orote Peninsula. I have 40 Jap planes surrounded and need a little help', prior to engaging the enemy! Webb's score would have probably been even greater had he not suffered intermittent gun failure (*Wilbur Webb via Mark Styling*)

Soon after Saipan had been secured, ranking Navy ace Cdr David McCampbell replaced his late-build F6F-3, nicknamed *The Minsi*, with this factory-fresh F6F-5, shipped from America. Looking resplendent in its Glossy Sea Blue (FS 25042) scheme, McCampbell's *Minsi II* has its engine and fuel system cleared of inhibitor off Saipan prior to being officially cleared for ops (*Tailhook*)

'Judy' as well. He was too close for comfort and seemed not to see me, so I aborted my run. There were enough cookies on this plate for everyone, I thought. Streaking underneath the formation, I had a good look at the enemy planes for the first time. They were 'Judys', 'Jills' and Zekes. I radioed an amplifying report.

'After pulling up and over, I picked out another 'Judy' on the edge of the formation. It was mildly manoeuvring, and the Japanese rear gunner was squirting away as I came down from behind. I worked in close, gave him a burst and set him afire quickly. The 'Judy' headed for the water, trailing a long plume of smoke.

'I pulled up again to find two more 'Judys' flying a loose wing. I came in from the rear to send one of them down burning. Dipping my Hellcat's wing, I slid over on the other and got it on the same pass. It caught fire also, and I could see the rear gunner continuing to pepper away at me as he disappeared in an increasingly sharp arc downward. For a split second I almost felt sorry for the little bastard.

'That made three down, and we were now getting close to our fleet. Though the number of enemy planes had been pretty well chopped down, many still remained. It didn't look as if we would score a grand slam and I reported this to our FDO. The sky appeared full of smoke and pieces of aircraft as we tried to ride herd on the remaining enemy planes in an effort to keep them from scattering.

'Another meatball broke formation and I slid onto his tail, again working in close due to my inability to see clearly through my oil-smeared windshield. I gave him a short burst, but it was enough. The rounds went right into the sweet spot at the root of his wing. Other rounds must have hit the pilot or the control cables, as the the buring plane twisted crazily out of control.

'Despite our efforts, the 'Jills' started their torpedo runs and the remaining 'Judys' prepared to peel off for their bombing runs. I headed for a group of three 'Judys' flying in a long column. By the time I had reached the tail-ender, we were almost over our outer destroyer screen but still fairly high when the first 'Judy' was about to begin his dive. As he started his nose-over I noticed a black puff appear beside him – our 5-inchers were beginning to open up.

'Trying to disregard the flak, I overtook the nearest enemy bomber. It seemed that I had scarcely touched the gun trigger when his engine began to come to pieces. The 'Judy' started smoking then began torching alternately on and off as it disappeared below me.

'Before I caught up with it, the next 'Judy' was in its dive, apparently trying for one of the destroyers. This time, a short burst produced astonishing results – he blew up in a tremendous explosion in my face. I must have hit its bomb, I guess. I had seen planes explode

Lt Russ Reiserer, CO of the nocturnally-optimised VF(N)-76 Det 2 aboard *Hornet*, was another pilot who made 'ace in a day' during the "Val' Fest' over Orate on 19 June, although his 'weapon' on this occasion was a 'straight' F6F-3 rather than a -3N. He had been part of a mixed VF-2/VF(N)-76 sweep despatched in the wake of 'Spider' Webb's strike, and had responded to the latter's call for assistance (*Russ Reiserer via Mark Styling*)

Like Webb, Lt Alex Vraciu of VF-16 claimed six kills on 19 June, although his action took place in the morning almost over the task force. Like the former, who struggled to fire all six of his .50s, Vraciu was mechanically hindered in combat by an engine down on power. This shot was taken moments after he had extricated himself from his F6F, having returned to *Lexington* (*Tailhook*)

Vraciu scored his 19th, and last, kill (a 'Zeke') 24 hours after his spectacular successes over the 'Judys' This official Navy shot shows the then ranking carrier ace climbing out 'his' F6F-3 (BuNo 40467/'White 32') aboard Lexington in late July 1944, the battle-weary Hellcat displaying a full scoreboard, plus an obligatory VF-16 decal (*Tailhook*)

One of the more successful CVL-based fighter squadrons involved in *Forager* was VF-51, assigned to USS *San Jacinto*'s CVLG-51. They claimed 22 victories between 11 June and 25 July, of an eventual total of 50.5 kills for its solitary frontline det. VF-51's sole ace, Lt Bob Maxwell, scored six of his seven kills during the 'Turkey Shoot', including a triple score against Ki 61s on 15 June. This F6F boasts a rare example of nose art in the form of 'snake eye' dice and the name *Little Joe* on its cowling (*Tailhook*)

before, but never like this! I yanked up sharpely to avoid the scattered pieces od aircraft and flying hot stuff as I radioed, "Splash number six. There's one more ahead and he diving on a BB (battleship). But I don't think he'll make it".

'Hardly had the words than the 'Judy' caught a direct hit that removed it immediately as a factor to be worried about in the war. He had run into a solid curtain of steel from the battlewagon.

'Looking around, it seemed that only Hellcats were in the sky with me. Glancing back along the route from where we had come, I could see only Hellcats and a 35-mile long pattern of flaming oil slicks.

'In my satisfaction at the day's events, I felt that I had contributed my personal payback for Pearl Harbor. However, this feeling begain to dissipate in a hurry when some of our own gunners tried to shoot me down as I was returning to *Lexington*. Although my IFF was on, my approach was from the right direction and I was making the required two 360-degree right turns, it all didn't seem to matter to some of the trigger-happy gun crews in the heat of this fleet battle.

'I would like to think that the choice words I uttered on the radio stopped all that nonsense, but I know better.'

Lt(jg) Vraciu had used only 360 rounds during this legendary action, downing all six aircraft in under eight minutes. As a result of his success over the 'Judys', Vraciu assumed the mantle of top Navy ace from VF-17's Lt(jg) Ira Kepford, the latter having filled this lofty position since scoring his 16th, and final, victory whilst flying F4U-1A Corsairs in the Solomons on 19 February 1944. Vraciu would retain 'pole position' for a further four months.

Late in the afternoon on 20 June, search aircraft and submarines located Ozawa withdrawing westward. Vice Adm Mitscher, released to pursue the retreating enemy, launched a 300-mile strike from each task group. In all, 227 effective sorties were flown, including 96 by Hellcats. They escorted 131 dive- and torpedo-bombers which caught up with the Japanese fleet about two hours before sunset.

Amid billowing clouds and spectacular flak, Task Force 58's aviators pressed home the attack, opposed by roughly 70 interceptors. Dogfights erupted over each carrier group, and their supporting tankers, with F6Fs claiming 22 victories and seven probables for six losses in return.

Most heavily engaged was the *Lexington* formation, as VF-16 fought to defend its SBDs and TBFs. Alex Vraciu claimed a Zero destroyed and another damaged, running his score to 19 confirmed. Five other fighter squadrons gained victories, most notably *Enterprise's* VF-10 (seven confirmed) and *Wasp's* VF-14 (five over the oilers.) The most successful F6F pilots of the mission were Ens C S Beard (four kills in total) of VF-50, Lt(jg) R C Tabler (three kills in total) of

VF-24, and Ens J L Wolf, Jr (four kills in total), of VF-10, all with double kills.

Avengers from *Belleau Wood* sank the carrier *Hiyo*, and additional damage was inflicted on others, but at a considerable cost. During the long, dark return to the task force, some 70 aircraft succumbed to fuel exhaustion or battle damage. Within this number were 14 F6Fs, which hiked Hellcat attrition on the mission to 20. Task Force 58 had paid a price, but aerial supremacy over the Marianas now was assurred.

Iwo Jima had still to be seized, however. In order to keep the pressure on the Bonins, 'Iwo' was 'revisited' on 24 June and 3-4 July. During the first of these strikes, a 10-hour battle was conducted in two parts. A morning fighter sweep resulted in claims for 68 shootdowns by *Yorktown's* VF-1, *Hornet's* VF-2 and *Bataan's* VF-50. Lt(jg) Everett G Hargreaves (8.5 in total) of 'Fighting Two' claimed top honours with five victories. The same three squadrons were largely responsible for another 48 kills in marginal weather later that afternoon.

The two-day repeat performance in July brought another 92 claims, most notably seven credited to a pair of *Hornet* nightfighters in the predawn sweep of the 4th. Lt(jg)s J W Dear, Jr, and F L Dungan (both seven kills in total) of VF(N)-76 were armed with bombs, but stirred up a flock of 'Rufe' floatplanes at Chichi Jima. Although they had emerged from the combat as aces – Dear splashed three 'Rufes' and Dungan four – they had won their laurels the hard way, the former landing just before his engine seized and the latter having suffered a bullet wound.

Dungan's tally was matched by VF-31 pilot Lt(jg) C N Nooy off *Cabot*, who was on his way to becoming the top CVL ace of the war with 19 kills. In all, Task Force 58 added 44 new fighter aces during the month, but even that record would eventually be eclipsed.

No fewer than 28 of the pilots seen in this VF-2 group shot made 'ace' during the 1943/44 combat tour aboard *Hornet*, the unit downing 245 aircraft in a little over nine months – only three 'Red Ripper' pilots were lost in aerial combat in return. A two-thirds life size print of this photograph was used as part of a Navy recruiting exhibition staged in Radio City Music Hall, New York, soon after victory had been clinched in the Marianas (*Connie Hargreaves via Mark Styling*)

As in June, among 'Iwo's' defenders was the hard-pressed Air Group 301, which also took heavy losses in the second series of raids. Partially reinforced, the *hikotai* put up 31 Zeros on 3 July and lost at least 17. Due to the deadly combination of obsolete aircraft flown by inexperienced pilots, the Japanese rate of attrition could only increasing.

The Bonins strike also marked the debut of the ultimate Hellcat, the F6F-5. *Franklin's* VF-13 was the first squadron in the Pacific with a full complement of 'dash fives', which featured the R-2800-10W engine with water-injection as a standard feature. First blood for the new Hellcat was drawn by Lt A C Hudson (one kill in total), whose division claimed three Zekes off Iwo Jima early on the fourth. By the end of the deployment, Cdr W M Coleman (six kills in total) and three of his 'Lucky 13' pilots would be aces in the 'dash five' Hellcat.

From the beginning of *Forager* in mid-June until the middle of August, the Navy added 58 new aces to its ranks, all Hellcat pilots. Therefore, after almost 12 months of combat, the total number of F6F aces stood at 92. That number was about to explode.

Occupation of the Marianas

11 June to 10 August 1944

VF-2	*Hornet*	197
VF-15	*Essex*	100.5
VF-1	*Yorktown*	99
VF-31	*Cabot*	67.5
VF-50	*Bataan*	58
VF-16	*Lexington*	48
VF-8	*Bunker Hill*	46
VF-10	*Enterprise*	40
VF-14	*Wasp*	36.5
VF-27	*Princeton*	36

Total by 19 F6F squadrons **869.5**

Top Hellcat Pilots of the Marianas Campaign

Cdr D McCampbell	CAG-15	10.5	Total 34
Cdr W A Dean, Jr	VF-2	9	Total 11
Lt L E Doner	VF-2	8	Total 8
Lt(jg) R T Eastmond	VF-1	8	Total 9
Lt(jg) E C Hargreaves	VF-2	8	Total 8.5
Lt R L Reiserer	VFN-76	8	Total 9
Lt A Van Haren, Jr	VF-2	8	Total 9
Lt(jg) A Vraciu	VF-16	8	Total 19
Lt(jg) J L Banks	VF-2	7	Total 8.5
Lt(jg) D A Carmichael	VF-2	7	Total 12

A further 36 F6F pilots claimed five or more victories

TO THE PHILIPPINES

American grand strategy in the Pacific was decided at a conference in the summer of 1944. Gen Douglas MacArthur, Adm Chester Nimitz and the members of the Joint Chiefs of Staff chose to reoccupy the Philippine Islands rather than strike toward the Chinese mainland.

Sixteen fast carriers departed Eniwetok Atoll at the end of August with some 520 Hellcats. The ever-increasing requirement for fleet defense had resulted in big-deck carriers embarking up to 54 fighters – a significant increase over the previous 36.

Although depicting F6F-5Ns of US-based VF(N)-107 in August 1944, this shot does show the unique twin 20 mm cannon arrangement fitted exclusively to a modest number of nightfighter Hellcats – the gun barrels on these aircraft lack the cone-shaped flash suppressers worn by their frontline brethren (*US Navy*)

Thus, the stage was set for the Battle of Leyte Gulf which, if not actually the largest naval engagement of modern times, was certainly the most diverse and intense. In numbers of combatant ships engaged, the Second Battle of the Philippine Sea ran a close second to the 1916 Battle of Jutland. However, for variety and concentration of forces engaged – air, surface and submarine – no other action could match it.

During initial sweeps over Mindanao on 9-10 September, the fast carriers not only surprised a major land-based airpower, but achieved outright aerial supremacy. There was little aerial combat (only 13 shootdowns credited), but enemy airfields were bombed and strafed almost with impunity. It took three days for the Japanese to recover their poise, with the task force experiencing no serious opposition until the 12th.

The first and last of the 82 victories credited that day were claimed by a new, innovative, Hellcat squadron – Lt Cdr T F Caldwell's VF(N)-41. Flying from *Independence*, Caldwell's fighter and torpedo squadrons were wholly devoted to nocturnal interception, strike and interdiction missions. It was a bold experiment, as Caldwell's command was entrusted with proving the concept of a dedicated night air group flying from the narrow deck of a CVL. More would be heard from CVLG(N)-41 during the Philippines campaign.

A mid-morning fighter sweep over Cebu stirred up considerable opposition for VF-15 and -19, team mates in Task Group 38.3. The *Essex* fighter skipper, Lt Cdr J F Rigg (11 kills in total), claimed four

By the time of the Second Battle of the Philippine Sea, the nightfighter concept had progressed from flight-size dets aboard fast carriers, to a dedicated air group tasked with defending TF-38 after dark. CVLG-41 flew night intercepts and bombing missions between August 1944 and January 1945 from the CVL USS *Independence*. Here, VF(N)-41 F6F-5Ns lining up for launch at dusk during the Leyte Gulf action (*Tailhook*)

This impressive victory tally and bomb log denotes the career stats of Texan Lt(jg) Ray 'Hawk' Hawkins, second-ranking ace of VF-31 'Flying Meataxes' with 14 kills. The unit produced 14 aces during World War 2, and was credited with the destruction of 165.5 aircraft (*Ray Hawkins via Mark Styling*)

One of the most famous markings ever worn on a US combat aircraft, the ferocious cat's mouth applied by VF-27 to its F6F-3s and -5s was conceived by Lts Carl Brown (10.5 kills, front row fifth from left) and Dick Stambook (10 kills, standing fourth from right), and Ens Bob Burnell (four kills, to Stambook's right) whilst the unit was working up at NAS Kahului, Hawaii, in March/April 1944. Burnell hand-painted 'teeth' on all 24 F6Fs prior to embarking aboard USS *Princeton* on 29 May 1944 (*Paul Drury via Mark Styling*)

Zekes and a 'Tojo' to lead 'Fabled 15's' tally of 27 victories. Meanwhile, 'Satan's Kittens' off *Lexington* bagged 23, including three by the VF-19 CO himself, Cdr T H Winters, Jr (eight kills in total), while Lt Albert Seckel, Jr (six kills in total), went one better by claiming four Zekes.

Most of the remaining shootdowns went to *Hornet* and *Wasp* Hellcats, a number of claims by 'Bombing Fourteen' pilots who had hastily transitioned to fighters. The latter reflected the increasing need for F6F squadrons to meet expanded operations schedules. While many SB2C Helldiver pilots welcomed the chance to switch to Hellcats, the major drawback of such transitions was limited opportunity to acquaint bomber pilots with aerial gunnery and fighter tactics. Nevertheless, the VB-14 aviators did well, and on the 12th five of them combined to score eight kills over Negros Island. At least one VB-2 pilot (Lt(jg) M H Richey) in *Hornet* also shot down an aircraft (a Zeke) whilst flying a Hellcat during this period.

On 13 September nearly 100 claims, including two dozen by VF-31, were added to the F6F tally. Twenty-one-year-old Lt(jg) Arthur R Hawkins (14 kills in total) became only the second CVL 'instant ace' as the *Cabot* pilot downed five Zekes over Negros Island.

Reinforced to a strength of 60 A6M5s, Naval Air Group 201 absorbed the brunt of the combat. Based at Nichols Field and Mactan, it lost four-fifths of its strength in the air or on the ground. Included in the casualties were 10 experienced warrant-officer and NCO pilots.

Princeton's ever-aggressive VF-27 emerged with the highest score on 21 September, claiming 37 kills in the Manila area. Top honours belonged to Lt John R Rodgers, who came achingly close to acedom with 4.50 victories (all Ki 61 'Tonys') – his only score of the war.

Leading one of two fighter sweeps from six CVLs was VF-27 CO, Lt Cdr Fred Bardshar. He recalled;

'My group attacked Nichols and Neilsen Fields at Manila with 48 F6Fs. We were stacked in three sub-groups: *Princeton's* at 12,000 ft, 16 others at 16,000 and 16 more at 20,000. We arrived over the target without opposition and my wingman and I initiated action by shooting down a "Nick" over Neilsen at about 10,000 ft. We fired as a section from a high side run. The Jap did not see us. The 12 .50 cal machine guns registered on the first burst with sensational effect. Our targets included parked aircraft at Nichols and Neilsen and also on Dewey Boulevard. I had my right aileron and tailhook shot out and was diverted to a large deck carrier for a barrier arrestment.'

Despite Lt Rodgers' poor luck, three other pilots became aces in a day on the 21st, including two VF-18 aviators off *Intrepid* – Lt Harvey P Picken (11 in total) and Lt(jg) Charles Mallory (10 in total) each splashed five (a combination of 'Bettys' and assorted fighters) whilst flying F6F-5P photo-recce Hellcats.

Picken had two previous kills to his credit but Mallory had never scored before. Meanwhile, VF-31's Lt(jg) Cornelius Nooy was already an ace when he led his division against Clark Field. Attacked by a mixture of enemy fighters, he kept his 500-lb bomb on its rack whilst he gunned down four bandits and flew a fifth into the ground (two Zekes, two 'Tojos' and a 'Tony'). He then proceeded to put his bomb into a hangar on the the ex-USAAF base, and thus finish off one of the finest naval fighter missions flown in World War 2.

Cdr Dean's VF-2 finished its lengthy tour with a final combat on 22 September. 'The Rippers'' last victim (a 'Tony') fell to Ens Wilbur B Webb, the Pearl Harbor survivor who on 19 June had downed six 'Vals' over Guam. The squadron had scored 245 credited victories since November 1943, producing 24 aces in the process.

Pre-war Warner Brothers actor Lt Bert DeWayne Morris scored five of his seven kills over Leyte Gulf. He appeared in a number of films before entering the Navy in June 1941. Morris returned to Hollywood after the war, starring in Westerns and other films, but retained his naval links through the reserve. In 1959, whilst visiting his old CAG, Capt David McCampbell (who was then commanding the carrier USS *Bon Homme Richard*), Morris died of a heart attack at the age of 45

On 24 September *Essex's* CAG, Cdr McCampbell, shot down a 'Pete' floatplane with his wingman, Lt(jg) Roy W Rushing (13 kills in total). Having previously scored 18.5 victories, McCampbell was now tied with Alex Vraciu, late of VF-16, who had been the Navy's top ace since 19 June.

Then on 21 October CAG-15 shot down a 'Dinah' reconnaissance aircraft and a 'Nate' fighter near Tablas Island, thus running his score to 21 confirmed, setting three records in the process. McCampbell became not only the Navy's top fighter ace, but also the first US Navy pilot, and carrier aviator, to attain 20 victories – he was never seriously challenged for top spot for the duration of the war. It took some time for the news to spread, as Alex Vraciu, who had been the fast carriers' leading ace since late April, recalls;

'We didn't really know much about how the other fellows were doing at the time. You went out, flew some hops, maybe shot down some planes, and then came back. I don't think I knew that Dave had passed me until I rejoined the *Lexington* late that fall.'

Among the fighter squadrons quietly building steady scores was Lt Cdr Fred Bakutis' (7.5 kills) VF-20. Entering combat in August, the new *Enterprise* squadron had to wait until mid-October for its first chance to tackle the enemy. Even then, the honour went to Cdr J S Gray, Jr (six kills in total), recently skipper of VF(N)-78, who flamed a prowling 'Betty' on the night of 11 October – by this stage in the war the formerly independent nightfighter units had been absorbed into the *Essex*-class FitRons. The following day, VF-20, led by CAG Cdr Dan Smith, Jr (6.083 kills in total), destroyed 21 bandits over Formosa.

Prior to tackling the still-potent Japanese fleet in Philippine waters, Task Force 38 moved to secure its southern flank. The three-day operation aimed at beating down Japanese airpower in Formosa resulted in heavy combat on 12-14 October as carriers again went head-to-head with land-based aviation. And, as before, the carriers won.

This photograph, taken on the morning of 21 October 1944, shows CAG-15 David McCampbell taxying forward to his shutdown spot on *Essex* after completing a sweep over Tablas Island, in the Philippines, He had downed a 'Dinah' and a 'Nate' during this sortie, thus assuming the mantle of the US Navy's ranking carrier ace from Alex Vraciu of VF-16 (*Tailhook*)

With the klaxon ringing in their ears, steel-helmeted pilots of VF-20 run for their 5-in rocket-armed F6F-5s aboard *Enterprise* between strikes on Manila on 15 October 1944. Aside from the deck crew tasked with arming the Hellcats and strapping in their pilots, most other sailors seem to be busy scouring the sky off to starboard for an incoming raid of Japanese suiciders – this action off Luzon marked the debut of the *kamikaze* (*US Navy*)

Early on the 12th, VF-15 and -19 conducted a series of hard-fought combats over the Chinese island. *Lexington's* 'Satan's Kittens' claimed 27 shootdowns while Hellcats from *Essex* bagged 23 more. Their opponents were a mixture of Japanese army and navy types – mainly Zekes, 'Tojos' and 'Oscars'.

Most heavily engaged was 'Fighting Eight', which tore into a formation of 'Nicks', Zekes and 'Oscars' near Taien Airfield. The *Bunker Hill* squadron left 30 aircraft destroyed before returning to the task force. The CO, Cdr William M Collins, Jr (nine kills in total), led the list with four fighters and a bomber, but Ens Arthur P Mollenhauer of VF-18 – barely aged 20 – matched the 33-year-old Collins. It was the youngster's only score, however, as he went missing in action two weeks later after damaging a Zeke whilst flying F6F-5 BuNo 58409 over Luzon.

Most of the shooting was over by early afternoon. Portions of at least 14 carrier air groups had participated in seizing air superiority from the Japanese, with victory claims running at 224 destroyed and 27 probables. *Hancock's* VF-7 recorded its first five victories on this notable day, whilst 24 hous later its CO, Lt Cdr Leonard Check, damaged an 'Oscar' – he would achieve the status of double ace before the end of the deployment. Only 37 Japanese aircraft were reported shot down on the 13th, largely by *Enterprise's* VF-20 and *Belleau Wood's* VF-21.

The enemy bounced back on 14 October as 92 shootdowns were credited to TF-38 aviators. Over half the claims went to VF-11, -18 and -27. The 'Sundowners'' pilots, badly outnumbered by inbound raiders, claimed 14 kills against three pilots and four aircraft lost as Lt Charles Stimpson – already a six-kill Guadalcanal ace in F4Fs – became the squadron's second ace in a day, claiming three 'Hamps' and two Zekes confirmed, and two 'Tonys' as probables. *Princeton's* VF-27, the prominent CVL squadron in the 'Turkey Shoot' four months before, splashed 11 twin-engine 'Fran' bombers offshore.

In exchange for about 30 Hellcats, the Formosa strikes deprived Japan of some 350 aircraft. For the moment, the path to Leyte Gulf was clear.

During this timeframe – mid-September to mid-October – an *Intrepid* pilot had quietly, and competently, been running up an exceptional record. Lt Cecil E Harris of VF-18 had scored one victory as a land-based F4F pilot with VF-27 in the Solomons on 1 April 1943, but now, almost 18 months later, he had finally hit his stride, and in just three combats in 32 days shot down 11 Japanese aircraft – four fighters (three 'Hamps' and a Zeke) on 13 September; two bombers (a 'Sally' and a 'Lilly') and two Zekes on 12 October; and three 'Judys' on the 14th. Still more was yet to come.

On 16 October, *Cabot's* new VF-29 announced itself in spectacular fashion. Lt Cdr Willard E Eder's (6.5 in total) squadron was tasked with 'capping' two American cruisers which had been torpedoed. Japanese

An ex-VF-10 four-kill combat veteran from the 'Grim Reapers'' Wildcat tour of 1942/43, Lt Ed 'Whitey' Feightner was well into his second spell in the frontline – this time with VF-8 aboard *Bunker Hill* – when he claimed his last trio of kills (three Zekes over Taien Airfield, on Formosa) on 12 October 1944, thus bringing his wartime score to nine (*Ed Feightner*)

bombers pressed hard to finish off the cripples, resulting in VF-29 claiming 34 shootdowns, with Lt Albert Fecke (seven in total) and his number four man, Ens Robert Buchanan (five in total), each destroying five attackers – mainly 'Frans' and 'Jills'. Although USS *Houston* was torpedoed a second time, both cruisers were towed to safety.

Two days later Lt Edward B Turner (seven in total) became *Wasp's* sole instant ace during a dogfight over Mabalacat airfield, claiming four Zekes and an 'Oscar' in VF-14's total score of 16 kills.

LEYTE GULF

The Battle of Leyte Gulf (also called the Second Philippine Sea) involved nearly 550 Hellcats from the 17 carriers of Task Force 38, plus 65 more embarked in three Task Force 77 escort carriers. The battle began on 24 October with simultaneous strikes by both sides against Japanese fleet units west of the archipelago and US forces to the east.

From 270 claimed shootdowns by US carrier aircraft, an incredible nine instant aces in a day were crowned, including two FM-2 pilots flying from escort carriers. The seven Hellcat aces represented three squadrons, the first being *Lexington's* VF-19 which launched fighter sweeps over Luzon. 'Satan's Kittens' stirred up a variety of bandits, and claimed 30 victories around Luzon, paced by Lt William J Masoner, Jr (12 in total). Already an ace, the former VF-11 pilot more than doubled his wartime total by downing six twin-engined bombers around 0730. In his combat report Masoner wrote;

'My division was escorting four SB2Cs on a 300-mile search. As we came up to join them over the eastern shore of Luzon, they spotted a group of "Bettys" and I saw them shoot down two. I saw four or five "Bettys" scattering in all directions, so I picked one and went down on it with my division. I opened with a quartering shot and rode up on his tail. I observed his 20 mm gun firing from his turret. My incendiaries hit his fuselage and right wingroot. He burst into flame and hit the water.

'I pulled up and saw eight "Dinahs" about 100 ft over me. They turned and spread slightly. I came up from below the right-hand plane and put a long burst into his starboard engine. It started to burn—the flames spread and it fell a mass of flames.

'By this time no more planes were available so we rendezvoused and continued our search. After abut 50 miles one of the bombers tally-hoed two "Nells". We dove down after them and chased them five or six miles. I dropped my bomb and then caught up with them. I made a run from above and astern and his right wing burned, exploded and fell off. He dove into the water and burned. I started to make a run on the other "Nell" but he was already burning and crashed. My wingman got him.

'We then joined the SB2Cs, flew our cross leg and started home. As we approached the shoe of Luzon we spotted five "Nells" at about 500 ft. My wingman and I went down on them and he burned one which crashed. His guns then stopped and he pulled up. I made a high quartering run on one "Nell" and observed hits. I did a wing-over and came up under his tail to avoid his ball turret, which was firing. I hit him in the fuselage at very close range. He exploded and pieces flew all over. He nosed straight down and hit the water.

'I came up from behind and above one the next "Nell" and, hit in the

VF-20's Lt(jg) Melvin 'Pritch' Prichard claimed 2.25 of his 5.25 kills over Manila Bay on 15 October, but perhaps his most daring victory was claimed two days earlier – although it has never been officially credited to him. 'Pritch' downed a 'Betty'at low-level well within TF-38's inner flak cordon, the bomber catching fire and crashing just several hundred feet away from his carrier (*Steven Prichard via Mark Styling*)

Leading VF-11 ace Lt Charles R 'Skull' Stimpson poses for an official photograph in a 'Sundowners" F6F-5 specially adorned with his final combat tally of 16 kills and an appropriate unit decal. He was without a doubt one of VF-11's most experienced pilots, having made ace in F4Fs over Guadalcanal (*US Navy*)

A VF-29 Hellcat is prepared for a catapult launch from *Cabot* on 10 October 1944. On this date the squadron scored its first victories when future 5.5-kill ace Lt Bruce D Jaques and Ens Frank A Wier downed a pair of twin-engined bombers in an early-morning interception. The former had opened his account back in November 1942 when he downed a Vichy French Bloch 174 or Potez 63/11 whilst flying a Wildcat with VGF-29 (VF-29's previous designation) from USS *Santee* during the *Torch* landings

VF-11's Guadalcanal tour in 1943 produced a number of outstanding pilots who went on to compile big scores in F6Fs. One of these individuals was Lt William J Masoner, Jr, who, upon returning to the US, was sent to VF-19 to help the unit get up to speed tactically. Once his the squadron entered the fray in mid-1944, he showed that he hadn't lost the 'combat edge', and when Masoner departed VF-19 in December, he left it as top ace with 10 F6F kills

wingroot, he exploded, throwing large pieces by me as I pulled up. He burned and crashed.'

Masoner's wingman, Lt(jg) W E Copeland, ran his own tally from three to six and reflected, 'Mr Masoner always found a way to get me into trouble'. Copeland may have set a record for diversity, as his six victories represented six aircraft types – 'Val', 'Oscar', 'Nate', 'Nell', 'Betty' and 'Lily'.

An hour after VF-19 tied into the Japanese bombers, *Princeton's* VF-27 engaged a variety of single-engine fighters over Polilo Island in Lamon Bay, off Luzon's east coast. Twelve of Lt Cdr Fred Bardshar's highly-capable pilots splashed 36 bandits, with Ens T J Conroy (seven in total) claiming six, while Lts J A 'Red' Shirley and C A Brown, Jr, and Lt(jg) E P Townsend, all bagged five apiece – the latter pilot's only kills.

Upon return to TG-38.3 around 0940, the victorious Hellcat pilots were shocked to find their ship aflame. 'Sweet P' had taken two bombs through the flight deck, and fires raged out of control. She was abandoned and scuttled – the first American fast carrier sunk in two years, and the last ever.

VF-27's Ens Paul E Drury was to feel the highs and lows of combat on this fateful day, making ace trying to repel the huge morning attack against the task force, and then having to 'jump ship' when *Princeton* was mortally damaged;

'My greatest and most dramatic exposure to the Battle of Leyte Gulf occurred all wrapped up in one day – 24 October 1944, the longest day of my life. Actually, I guess it started the night before on the evening of the 23rd, as the Japanese had all kinds of observation planes out trying to locate our task force. In fact, I think they already had us located, and they were just keeping track of us until the next morning when they were going to attack.

'Our task group comprised two large carriers, the *Essex*, which was Adm Sherman's flagship, and the *Lexington*, with Vice-Adm Mitscher aboard, the fast carriers *Princeton* and *Langley*, the battleships *Massachusetts* and *South Dakota*, the cruisers *Birmingham*, *Reno*, *Mobile* and *Sante Fe* and 13 destroyers.

'Eight of us from VF-27 were told that evening that we would have CAP duty the next morning, and that we could expect a lot of activity. So we were awakened on the 24th at about 4.00 am, and it was still dark when we took off. Due to a combination of the excitement on the flightdeck, the blacked-out carrier and the fact that we were in a hurry to get off because there were already bogies on the radar screen, I didn't get to fly in my regular plane, the *PAOLI LOCAL*, nor did I get to fly in my regular division (led by Lt Carl Brown, Jr, who bagged five Zekes in this sortie to take his score to 10.5 kills, Ed.).

'I found myself as wingman on Jim "Red" Shirley, who was the leading ace in our squadron (as mentioned earlier, he was to see his score rise from 7.5 to 12.5 kills during the course of the sortie, Ed.). But this was no big deal because I thought as soon as the sun came out I'd slide over to where I belonged, and still maintaining radio silence, I would signal for that pilot to get back where he belonged. That scenario, however, never came to pass, because as soon as we had rendezvoused after take-off the four of us were vectored out on a bogie, which we quickly took care of. As soon as we got back on station, Carl Brown's division of four was vectored out onto a contact, and so the routine continued – I never did get back into my regular division (two *Nicks* were downed in these fleeting battles, one apiece to "Red" Shirley and Ens Robert Blyth, Ed.).

'Following these snooper intercepts all eight of us were given a vector to go on at full speed to tackle a larger formation of aircraft, and as Carl Brown's section had tackled the last snooper, we had a height advantage over his division going into the dogfight. We duly spotted the enemy first, and as the sun had now fully risen, I could clearly see just how large this attack was.

'"Red" Shirley quickly radioed back to *Princeton*, "Tally-ho – Eighty Jap planes", and then thoughtfully added, "better send help".

'The carrier responded "Affirmative", and stated that they could send another 12 fighters to help out, plus contact *Essex* to launch a few more. Our job on CAP was to make sure that the enemy didn't get close to the task force. At this point in the mission we were about 60 to 70 miles away from the carriers, and as our job was to protect the fleet, we really had little choice as to what to do next – we just hoped that those planes being launched would hurry up and get here. However, I knew that it would take quite some time for the fighters to be made ready for take-off and then launched, but it was nevertheless a comforting feeling knowing that help was on its way.

'With this thought firmly in mind, the four of us dived into this Japanese formation. I think that we each downed one plane on that first pass, then after that all hell broke loose and it was just one huge mass of aeroplanes trying to see who could shoot who down. I think the four of us shot down 15 Jap planes that morning (the division's score was officially recorded as 14, with Drury bagging two Zekes and a "Tojo", Shirley a "Nick", a Zero and three "Tojos" and Ens Thomas J Conroy three Zekes and three "Tojos" – the fourth member of the flight remains anonymous, Ed.), and then we were out of ammunition and short on fuel, so we were ordered back to the task force.

'I believe I was one of the last pilots to land on the *Princeton* before it was bombed, as I had just gotten out of my plane and returned to the ready-room for a debrief when a tremendous volume of black

Toting a full complement of rockets, a contrailing VF-7 Hellcat departs USS *Hancock* for a raid on Clark Field on 29 October. High Velocity Aerial Rockets (HVARs) were widely used on F6Fs, being launched from 'zero length' rails beneath the wings. A full load of six gave the Hellcat a weight of fire equivalent to a destroyer's broadside. The original HVARs possessed 3.5-in warheads, but in 1944 the 5-in variety became available. With extraordinary penetrative ability, the ogive warheads could easily puncture the steel plates of most ships, and were also effective against some types of bunkers. The weapon's major drawback was inaccuracy, requiring a long, straight, approach to the target (*Tailhook*)

smoke came billowing into the compartment through the ventilating system. An announcement was soon made that yes indeed we had been bombed, and that all aviators were ordered up to the flightdeck to stand beside their aeroplanes – I think the captain had at first thought that we might be able to launch, but the bomb had gone through the deck and exploded in the hangar bay.

'Unfortunately, just at that moment all our our torpedo planes were below decks being armed and fuelled up, and one solitary bomb that wouldn't have normally done all that much damage, started a chain reaction of destruction. One of the torpedoes exploded and blew up the aft elevator right near where I was standing beside my Hellcat on the flight deck, whilst another took out the forward elevator. The captain immediately realised it was time to abandon ship and instructed all crew, other than the fire control party, to do so. I went over the side down a rope, and swam over to the destroyer *Irwin*, where I collapsed from exhaustion. After surviving another air raid, my "new" ship was ordered to finish *Princeton* off with torpedos, but the two launched failed to hit the target due to a damaged torpedo director, so the cruiser *Reno* finished the job off.

'There was great explosion and a huge mushroom-shaped cloud rose up over a thousand feet, and when the air cleared enough for us to try and figure out where the carrier might be located, the *Princeton* was gone. By this time it was 6.00 pm, and the longest day of my life was coming to a close.'

Like Paul Drury, Carl Brown, Jr, also lived a lifetime of aviation adventure in the course of this one mission. Slightly wounded, and flying a badly-damaged aeroplane, he experienced an epic of carrier flying;

'I don't know exactly how long the fight lasted. It was a long one – my guess is three to five minutes. I finished the fight with four Zekes on my tail arguing about who'd kill me. I used my last ditch manoeuvre: shove the stick forward as hard as I can with the throttle two-blocked and pitch full low. Nobody can follow that and shoot, so you gain at least a few seconds to think. As soon as I was headed straight down, I put the stick hard to the right for a spiral because the Zero couldn't turn well to the right at high speed. I lost them.

'*Princeton* was hit and the "Lex" and *Langley* refused to take me aboard because I had too much damage and might foul their deck. My instrument panel was well shot up, one fuel line in the cockpit was cut, and I had two to four inches of gas in the bottom of the bird. My port elevator hardly existed, and my tailhook was jammed, and I couldn't get it out with my emergency extension.

'I had two small shrapnel wounds in my left leg, but that was minor. I asked "Hatchet" (*Princeton*), who was still on the air although hit and burning, to tell the lead destroyer that I was going to ditch in front of him and to please pick me up.

One of the most dramatic photographs of a Hellcat ever taken, this 24 October shot shows a wounded Lt Carl Brown, Jr, of VF-27 gingerly taxying battle-damaged (164 holes) F6F-5 *PAPER DOLL* forward on *Essex*'s deck, having just completed a landing without hydraulics. Brown's former 'home', the *Princeton* (visible in the original print), had been mortally wounded by a lone bomb dropped through its flightdeck by a single 'Judy' which VF-27 had failed to intercept – as detailed in the text, Brown's division had accounted for 21.5 of the 36 aircraft downed by the unit as they blunted the early-morning strike on TF-38. *PAPER DOLL* had destroyed five Zekes in what was to be its pilot's last aerial combat (*US Navy*)

Hatchet said he'd pass the word. At that time *Essex* came on the air and said, "Hatchet 31. If you'll land immediately, we'll take you". You can imagine my relief.

'I lowered my gear with the emergency bottle – had no hydraulics, so I wouldn't have flaps for landing, nor an airspeed indicator (shot out), or cowl flaps or hook. The *Essex* captain had compassion and guts. I made a "British" approach from 500 ft. The LSO held a "Roger" on me til I was at the ramp when he gave me a fast, a high dip, and a cut. I had tested my controls and couldn't get the stick all the way back. I took the cut and snapped the stick as far as it would go. My tail hit the ramp hard, knocked the hook out, and I caught the first wire.'

Whilst Carl Brown, Jr, was taken below deck to the sick bay for treatment, his Hellcat was quickly pushed towards the bow in order to allow VF-15 to land back aboard. Just nine VF-27 Hellcats were airborne when *Princeton* was bombed, the remaining 16 aircraft having landed aboard the carrier to refuel and rearm, their pilots thinking that they had seen off the attack. The surviving F6Fs were soon pressed into service with their new units, who quickly painted out the distinctive cowling decoration and thus restored the Hellcats to regulation fleet finish (*Tailhook*)

Despite appalling losses, the Japanese kept throwing airpower at TF-38. About the same time VF-27 was engaged off Luzon, *Essex* launched fighters to intercept another large raid. Though he had been cautioned against personal involvement, Cdr David McCampbell led the scramble with VF-15's last seven Hellcats. Already the Navy's leading ace, his experience was badly needed.

The fighter director put McCampbell and his wingman Lt(jg) Roy Rushing onto a raid estimated at 80 hostiles. Lighting a cigarette, McCampbell assessed the situation and went to work. Maintaining altitude, and picking his targets carefully, he began whittling down the huge aerial armada. By the time he disengaged 90 minutes later through a lack of ammunition and fuel, he had claimed nine confirmed (five Zeros, two 'Oscars' and two 'Hamps') and two probables (a Zero and an 'Oscar'). Rushing flamed six more (four Zeros, an 'Oscar' and a 'Hamp'), while other *Essex* pilots downed a further ten Zekes or 'Vals'.

Meanwhile, Task Force 38 had struck repeatedly at powerful Japanese surface units approaching the Philippines from the west. Strike co-ordinators concentrated their dive- and torpedo-bombers on the enemy battleships, sinking the 64,000-ton *Musashi* and damaging six other ships.

By sundown the Japanese were withdrawing westward and the US carrier groups remained largely untouched. Hellcats had claimed nearly 200 kills during the long, frantic, day, including 21 by the three CVE squadrons – primarily VF-60 aboard *Suwannee*. Most heavily engaged were VF-19 with 53 kills, and VF-15 with 43.

The next day, 25 October, was one of mixed fortunes for the US Navy. It started badly and worsened through the morning as the Japanese central force unexpectedly emerged into Leyte Gulf, threatening Gen Douglas MacArthur's amphibious shipping. The battleship-cruiser force had reversed helm during the night, with merely an escort-carrier group in its path. Against awesome odds, and helped by other CVE units, 'Taffy Three' fought off the assault, losing one 'baby flattop' to surface gunfire and another to the newly-formed *kamikaze* corps.

Safely back in the USA, three veterans of VF-27's brief, but bloody, combat deployment point out to the press photographer exactly where their former 'home' can now be found. The young pilot with his finger on the globe is Ens Paul Drury (six kills), who is flanked by Ensigns Hugh Lillie (left, five kills) and Bob Burnell (right, four kills). The location for this shot is Drury's home at Ardmore, in Pennsylvania (*Bob Burnell via Mark Styling*)

Meanwhile, Adm W F Halsey steamed north in response to reports of Japanese carriers off the north-eastern tip of Luzon. His aviators found Vice Adm Ozawa's sacrificial four carriers and immediately went to work. The small, but spirited Japanese CAP, which numbered no more than 25 Zekes, was quickly swept aside as VF-15 splashed nine defenders. Four fell to Lt J R Strane, who ran his score to an even dozen – he scored his final kill (an 'Oscar') over Luzon on 5 November.

As McCampbell assigned targets from his lofty vantage point, a light carrier was damaged and a destroyer was sunk. He was then relieved as strike co-ordinator by Cdr Winters, who directed his own *Lexington* aircraft and other air groups against the survivors. By the time Winters departed, all three enemy flattops had been sunk or were sinking, including *Zuikaku*, the last of the Pearl Harbor attackers.

The Battle of Leyte Gulf effectively neutralised Japan's once powerful fleet. In four days between 23 and 26 October, the Imperial Navy lost 24 warships, including four carriers, three battleships and nine cruisers, and although submarines and surface combatants accounted for some of the Japanese losses, the huge majority succumbed to carrier airpower. Navy pilots and aircrews claimed 657 enemy aircraft shot down in exchange for 140 of their own number lost to all causes.

Liberation of the Philippines was no longer in doubt, if ever it had been, but the emergence of the *kamikaze* was an unsettling event. It would occupy the full attention of Hellcat pilots and fighter directors for the remaining ten months of the war.

Cdr McCampbell's nine-kill haul partially offset the news of the loss of *Princeton* that same morning for the 'folks back home'. *Minsi III* (BuNo 70143) was quickly polished up and decorated with 30 flags, and its pilot photographed in various poses for the national papers (*Tailhook*)

THE LONG HAUL

Japanese airpower in the Philippines, severely crippled at Leyte Gulf, lingered another two weeks. On 29 October fighter sweeps to Manila and fleet CAPs netted nearly 70 kills by Hellcat squadrons, including 38 by VF-18. Six days later VF-80 marked its debut as Lt Cdr Albert Vorse, Jr's (11.5 in total) *Ticonderoga* pilots notched their first dozen kills. Day-long combats over and around Clark Field accounted for 97 total victories. Thereafter, aerial encounters with Japanese aircraft dwindled to virtually nothing by early January.

That same day resulted in the loss of an outstanding FitRon as a suicidal Zero pilot boresighted *Lexington* and impacted near her island. She withdrew for repairs, prematurely ending VF-19's highly-successful cruise, accomplished without the loss of a bomber or 'torpecker' to enemy fighters. The 'Kittens'' 155 victories ranked them eighth among all F6F squadrons in the number of kills scored on a single deployment.

Despite losing the services of experienced squadrons and air groups, the task force possessed a

Pilots from VF-18 aboard *Intrepid* mill around the tail of a replacement F6F-3 prior to manning their Hellcats and heading off to strike Clark Field for the second time that day – 29 October 1944. A dozen enemy fighters had been downed on the first mission, and the unit went on to double that score in the afternoon sweep (*Jerry Scutts*)

depth of talent. As mentioned earlier, a perfect example of this was VF-18's Cecil Harris, who had splashed two floatplanes on 24 October, and logged his third 'quadruple' on the 29th. He added a lone Zero on 19 November, then downed four more enemy fighters on the 25th, running his wartime total to 23. With four quadruple kills, Harris was arguably the most consistently exceptional fighter pilot in the US Navy. He made maximum use of each opportunity, and only the battle damage sustained by *Intrepid* prevented him from challenging McCampbell's spot as 'topgun.'

Wearing a white 13 on its fuselage and tail, this VF(N)-41 F6F-5N (seen being attached to the waist catapult on *Independence* in October 1944) was the mount of leading Navy nightfighter ace Lt William E Henry, who scored 9.5 kills between September 1944 and January 1945. His unit claimed a total of 46 kills whilst in the frontline, producing two aces in the process (*Tailhook*)

Another stand-out was VF-20's Ens Douglas Baker, a 23-year-old Oklahoman who demonstrated exceptional ability from the start. He flamed four fighters in his first combat on 12 October, and had run his tally to an even dozen by 14 November – the highest score ever attained by an ensign. That same day Cdr McCampbell destroyed one 'Oscar' and damaged another over Manila Bay, thus ending not only his own kill tally, but VF-15's as well.

By mid-November the most experienced Hellcat squadrons were finishing their tours, or were already en route home. These included several units which had been in almost constant combat since the Marianas campaign or before – VF-8, -14, -15 and -28, plus VF-27, which had been orphaned since the loss of *Princeton* the previous month.

'Fabled Fifteen' had recorded an eye-watering record since May. Through a combination of training, leadership and unprecedented opportunity, not only the fighter squadron but the entire air group had achieved extraordinary success at the 'Turkey Shoot', in the Philippines and beyond. Lt Cdr James F Rigg's unit (the latter had succeeded Cdr Brewer who was killed at Saipan) had scored 310 aerial victories and produced 26 aces, one of whom was his CAG, David McCampbell – the latter was now unassailable as the Navy's top ace with 34 victories. Later McCampbell was awarded the Medal of Honour for his spectacular success, thus becoming the only F6F pilot accorded that distinction, and the only carrier aviator so honoured in the last three years of the war.

Another ace's aircraft, F6F-5 'Ginger 29' was the occasional mount of VF-11's Lt Jim Swope, who claimed five kills whilst flying Hellcats from *Hornet*. Like his great friend Charlie Stimpson, Swope had been land-based with the 'Sundowners' in Guadalcanal in 1943, where he claimed 4.666 kills whilst flying the Wildcat – his combined score placed him second in VF-11's aces listing behind Stimpson (*Jerry Scutts*)

While many top scorers rotated home, other aces were returning for a second and even third tour. One such pilot was Lt Alex Vraciu, formerly of VFs -6 and then -16. Though recently married, Vraciu

VF-15 pipped VF-18 to the title of 'Topguns' for the Leyte action by a mere 1.5 kills – 140.5 versus 139! This group shot of 'Fighting Fifteen' was taken days before they were replaced on *Essex* by VF-4 on 17 November. VF-15 produced 26 aces during its seven months at sea. The backdrop for this photo is provided by *Minsi III* (F6F-5 BuNo 70143)

Armed up with four 5-in rockets apiece, VF-15 F6Fs are marshalled forward past the waist hangar lift on *Essex* prior to launching for a strike on shipping in Subic Bay on 5 November. Seven aircraft were downed during the sweep, including kills 31 and 32 to Cdr McCampbell in *Minsi III*. Aside from the CAG's success, the remaining victories were shared by five VF-15 aces (*Jerry Scutts*)

was anxious to return to combat, and when he reported to *Lexington* in November, the ship was still recovering from *kamikaze* damage and preparing to bid farewell to Air Group 19. Vraciu remained aboard just briefly, before joining VF-20 in *Enterprise*. There was a fitting symmetry to this assignment, as Vraciu's friend and mentor, 'Butch' O'Hare, had been the 'Big E's' CAG when he was lost off Tarawa in 1943.

However, on 14 December Vraciu was shot down while flying his second mission with 'Fighting Twenty', Japanese AA gunners succeeding where 19 of their aviators had failed. He bailed out of F6F-5 BuNo 58831 near Bamban Airfield, and was quickly scooped up by friendly Filipino USAFFE guerillas. He remained on the ground, gathering information on the Japanese defences around Clark Field for a further six weeks, before returning to US control. Despite eventually making it back to his carrier, Vraciu was soon sent back to America as the Navy policy at the time dictated that servicemen who had spent time behind enemy lines were not allowed to return to combat for fear of capture.

The 14th was a bad day for Hellcat aces generally, as Vraciu's squadron-mate, the recently-promoted Lt(jg) Douglas Baker, went missing soon after he had destroyed three Zekes and an 'Oscar' – Vraciu was eventually given Baker's dogtags as proof of death. With 16 victories to his credit, the latter was well on his way to the upper ranks of the Navy aces. That same day five-kill VF-29 ace Lt(jg) W D Bishop bailed out of his F6F following a mid-air collision over Subic Bay. He was seen on the ground the next day, but mysteriously disappeared before he could be rescued.

On a more positive note, Lt R H

Anderson (8.5 in total) of VF-80 became the 28th, and last, Hellcat instant ace of 1944 on this date. His unit, nicknamed 'Vorse's Vipers', tangled with a mixed formation of Zekes and 'Oscars' over the Philippines, and Anderson claimed five in as many minutes. The potent team of Lts Patrick D Fleming (19 in total) and Richard L Cormier (eight in total) added four apiece en route to acedom, while their *Ticonderoga* squadronmates accounted for ten more. It was the realisation of a dream for 'Zeke' Cormier, who had previously flown Avengers on mundane anti-submarine patrols in the Atlantic.

Occupation of Leyte – *10 October to 30 November 1944*

VF-15	*Essex*	140.50
VF-18	*Intrepid*	139
VF-20	*Enterprise*	135.16
VF-19	*Lexington*	127
VF-14	*Wasp*	87.50
VF-11	*Hornet*	82
VF-8	*Bunker Hill*	74
VF-29	*Cabot*	72
VF-13	*Franklin*	67.50
VF-27	*Princeton*	59

Total by 22 F6F squadrons – 1300.16

Top Hellcat Pilots of the Leyte Occupation

Lt C E Harris	VF-18	18	Total 23
Cdr D McCampbell	CVG-15	15	Total 34
Ens D Baker	VF-20	12.33	Total 16.33
Lt W J Masoner	VF-19	10	Total 12
Lt C R Stimpson	VF-11	10	Total 16

VF-80 was one of a number of newly-formed squadrons to make its combat debut over Luzon in November 1944. Flying from USS *Ticonderoga*, the 'Vipers' enjoyed considerable success during their solitary frontline deployment, having claimed 159.5 kills by the time they returned to the US on 1 April 1945. This shot was taken on 5 November – the date on which VF-80 claimed its first six kills – as the Hellcats are lined up for launch. Half of the day's victory tally fell to future aces (*Tailhook*)

In response to the increasing suicide threat, big-deck air groups experienced a profound change shortly before year's end. Fighter complements were raised from 54 to 73 Hellcats – the fourth increase since June 1942 – with Marine Corps F4U units also helping to fill the gap. *Essex* was the first to embark one of these composite air groups, as two Corsair squadrons augmented Lt Cdr K G Hammond's (two kills in total) VF-4 in December.

The increase in fighters meant that fewer SB2Cs and TBMs could be embarked, and normally the VB and VT squadrons were reduced to 15 aircraft apiece. However, as a

This panoramic view, taken from *Ticonderoga*'s bridge, shows TF-38 *Essex*-class carriers (from left to right) *Wasp, Hornet, Hancock* and *Yorktown* at anchor of Ulithi Atoll on 2 December 1944. The original caption for this shot read 'Murderer's Row'! Each carrier boasted an air group of 100 aircraft, approximately half of which were Hellcats assigned at that stage to one almost unwieldy (at least administratively) squadron

Three of VF-11's most successful pilots recount their experiences in the wardroom pantry following the 'Sundowners'' awesome display of aerial supremacy in the environs of Clark Field on 5 November. Jim Swope (left) and Blake 'Rabbit' Moranville (right) both scored kills on the early-morning Strike Able, sharing four 'Tojos', plus a 'Betty' for the latter. 'Charlie' Stimpson's two 'Oscars' and a 'Tojo' were claimed two hours later during the follow-up Strike Baker sweep

temporary measure *Essex* and *Wasp* 'beached' their Helldivers and operated 91 fighters with 15 Avengers.

Indochina Interlude

The fast carriers bade farewell to the Philippines on 10 January 1945 when VF(N)-41 splashed four bandits. The first major operation of the new year was an anti-shipping sweep of the East China Sea, where no Allied warships had steamed in three years. Though intelligence indicated significant Japanese fleet units along the Indochina coast, none turned up. Fighter sweeps and CAPs of 12 January netted 14 shootdowns for Hellcat squadrons, including 11 by VF-3. It was a significant boost, as Lt Cdr W L Lamberson's (three kills in total) pilots had claimed just eight kills aboard *Yorktown* since October. Near Saigon a 'Tony' and a 'Hamp' fell to Lt John L Schell (five kills in total), who was destined to become one of only two F6F aces produced by the squadron – Lt(jg) James M Jones was the other pilot, and he scored two of his eventual seven kills with VF-3. He eventually attained ace status with VBF-3 (the only pilot to do so) following reassignment to the latter unit after VF-3 had split in two on 1 February 1945.

As usual, F6F squadrons flew the huge majority of missions on the 12th, Hellcats logging 1065 of the task force's 1457 combat sorties, or nearly three-quarters of the total. Twenty-one carrier aircraft were lost in the process.

VF-11's 'Ginger 13' prepares to be loaded with two 500-lb bombs in readiness for a strike on Tan Son Nhut airport in French Indochina. F6Fs could carry two bombs beneath the wings, but a single 500-pounder was the most frequent option. A standard techniques was to letdown from 15,000 ft in a 50-degree descent, releasing at 3500 ft. Skip-bombing was also performed by Hellcat units against thin-skinned ships. Flying low, pilots released their ordnance in level flight and pulled up over the target as the delayed-action bomb skipped off the water and penetrated the ship's hull

Among the dozen F6F pilots shot down was Lt(jg) Blake Moranville, a VF-11 ace with six kills. The engine of his F6F-5 BuNo 70680 was holed by flak while strafing Tan Son Nhut, and he was forced to belly-land in a rice paddy. Captured by the Vichy French, he and five other downed fliers were moved to a compound near Hanoi just prior to open hostilities erupting between the French and Japanese. Moranville then embarked on an epic adventure capped by an overland march to Dien Bien Phu with a Foreign Legion unit. Eventually flown to Kunming, in China, he safely returned to the US. There he resumed his duties as keeper of 'Gunner', VF-11's Boston Terrier mascot.

Packed into VF-11's ready-room deep in the bowels of *Hornet*, pilots on the Indochina strike make notes on their flight maps prior to walking to their aircraft. The pilot with 'Gunner' (the squadron mascot) on his lap is Lt(jg) Bill Eccles (four kills), whilst to his left is Lt Jimmie 'Doc' Savage (seven kills)

Moranville was one of only two Navy aces known to have been taken prisoner in the Pacific War, the other being VF-15's 20-year-old Ens Kenneth A Flinn (five kills in total), who was shot down near Nansei Shoto on 13 October 1944. He survived more than nine months of captivity only to die of malnutrition three weeks before Japan capitulated.

By January 1945 the new 73-plane/110-pilot organisation of *Essex*-class FitRons was recognised as being administratively unmanageable. Therefore, Commander Naval Air Forces Pacific authorised air groups to divide their fighter-force into two squadrons. Generally, the existing CO retained the VF organisation, while his executive officer – normally another lieutenant commander – formed a fighter-bomber unit, designated VBF. Maintenance remained as before, with both squadrons flying the same aircraft. However, some air groups later deployed with mixed complements of Hellcat fighters and Corsair fighter-bombers.

The VF/VBF split was described in the following terms by Lt Cdr Marshall Beebe (10.5 kills), commanding officer of the reformed VF-17;

'The fact that the F6F was equipped with wing bomb racks and a centreline rack made it doubly useful as a fighter-bomber. During training at NAS Alameda, California, the squadron was increased from 36 to 54 aeroplanes. Then during the short period in Hawaii the complement was increased to 72 aircraft with 102 pilots.

'The aircraft and pilots were transferred from VF-6, which fortunately had received some inter-squadron tactical training on the west coast. In January 1945, while at Guam, the squadron was divided into two 36-aircraft squadrons – VF and VBF – for administrative purposes. The two squadrons flew almost identical operations.'

The first ace of the new year was Lt C M Craig, VF-22's acting CO aboard *Cowpens*. On 21 January he led his division into a formation of *kamikazes* off Formosa and returned to 'Mighty Moo' with five confirmed 'Tojos', for a wartime total of 11.75 kills.

That month Cdr T F Caldwell's Night Air Group 41 completed its deployment aboard *Independence*. Though slow to gain acceptance, the night-flying Hellcats and Avengers eventually proved the validity of the

As mentioned earlier, Lt William E Henry of VF(N)-41 was the leading Navy nightfighter ace of the war, with six of his 9.5 kills being scored in full or semi-darkness. He later led F4U-5N Corsair nightfighter-equipped VC-3 Det C on USS *Valley Forge* during the first year of the Korean War (*Barrett Tillman*)

Smaller CVL-based F6F units contributed a great deal to the overall victory in the Pacific. One such outfit was VF-22 aboard USS *Cowpens*, whose 24 pilots downed 50 aircraft between 13 September 1944 and 21 January 1945. This shot was taken just prior to the unit being relieved, and shows VF-22's 'Sockeye 7' division which comprised; Ens Ben C Amsden (standing, far left) with five kills; Lt(jg) Bob A Richardson (standing, middle) with 3.25 kills; Ens Mike J Roche (standing, right) with 3.5 kills; Ens Arthur 'Ike' DeSellier (front row, left), 0.25 of a kill; and Lt(jg) Joe A Degutis, also with a quarter-kill (*Ben Amsden via Mark Styling*)

This VMF(N)-541 'Bat Eyes' F6F-5N was photographed at Peleliu prior to the squadron heading north to the Philippines (*Tailhook*)

dedicated nocturnal air group, both in offensive and defensive measures. VF(N)-41 closed its account with an 'Oscar' splashed off Canton on 16 January – the squadron's 46th confirmed kill. It was also the tenth victory for former SBD pilot Lt William E Henry, who was one of the unit's two aces. The other was Ens Jack S Berkheimer, who had scored to 7.5 kills before disappearing during a mission over Luzon the previous month.

Bill Henry's combat was not limited to night interceptions, however, as VF(N)-41 also engaged in nocturnal strike and heckler missions. Ironically, in some ways the most trying experience for the aircrew of the 'Indy' was not the stress of a night combat, but having to play the passive role of spectator on the deck during daylight *kamikaze* raids, as Henry explained;

'A few days out of the China Sea the day fighters were hitting Formosa and we did CAP or standby all night until the second day, then suicide planes came out by the dozens. Therefore, it was decided to put some of us VFN up to help.

'I was sitting in my plane, turning up, parked in the landing area when I saw everyone get off the flightdeck. I soon saw why. A 'Judy' was heading for us from the port quarter. All I could do was sit and look. As he flew over the battleship next to us, they got him and he rolled over on his back and crashed in our wake. They decided not to launch me.

'Later in the afternoon they decided to try to put some of us up again. This time I was in the plane on the port catapult. I was not turning up. Here came a Zero heading for us. He had trouble pushing over to hit us, and was going to overshoot, so he flattened out and flew into the side of a CVL right next to us, probably *Langley*. He burst into flames but most of the plane fell into the water and the fire went out. Again they cancelled the launch. About 30 minutes later I saw a CV burning in formation off our starboard bow. It was the *Ticonderoga* (143 killed and 202 wounded).'

Relieving CVLG(N)-41 was the fleet's first big-deck 'night owl' unit, Air Group 90 aboard *Enterprise*. The CAG was Cdr William I Martin, a veteran SBD and TBF pilot who had pioneered the night attack role for torpedo- and dive-bomber units in US naval aviation. With 30 F6F-5Ns and -5Es (plus two photo-birds), VF(N)-90 was led by Lt Cdr R J McCullough, whose pilots would shortly be introduced to combat.

About this same time, Marine Corps night Hellcats were carving a reputation for themselves in the Philippines. Lt Col Peter Lambrecht's VMF(N)-541 arrived at Tacloban Airfield in December and, in barely a month, shot down 23 enemy aircraft that had proved too fast for USAAF P-61 Black Widows to engage. Ironically, most of the kills were scored in daylight, as the initial night kills evidently dissuaded Japanese fighter-bombers from snooping around. The top shooters were 1st Lt Harold T Hayes and Tech Sgt John W Andre, each with four kills. Later commissioned, Andre became an ace with another nightfighter victory (this time in an F4U-5N Corsair of VMF(N)-513) seven years later, in Korea (see *Aces 4 Korean War Aces* by Robert F Dorr, Jon Lake and Warren Thompson).

TOKYO BOUND

The new organisation in Task Force 38 had just been implemented when the fast carriers attacked Tokyo. With barely time to 'shake out' the VF/VBF split and absorb the new night fliers, 16 fast carriers aimed their bows at the Japanese homeland for two days of strikes in mid-February.

A predawn launch on the 16th kicked off a day-long series of combats over and around the Japanese capital. Strenuous opposition, combined with poor weather – as low as 1000-ft ceilings – conspired to produce a major challenge for the relatively inexperienced carrier pilots. In fact, for seven of the embarked air groups, the Tokyo strikes were their introduction to combat.

Other than two roving 'Betty' bombers splashed by the CAP, the first overland combat was found by VF-9, now riding *Lexington* on their third deployment in less than two-and-a-half years. Over Katori, Lt Cdr Herbert N Houck's (six kills in total) pilots found a mixture of Zekes and 'Nates', claiming 12 confirmed and four probables. This was just the beginning, as 'Fighting Nine' logged eight more victories during the day.

Ens Wiliam G Bailey, USNR, of VF-33 was lucky to step from the wreckage of his F6F without a scratch following this rather dramatic landing back aboard USS *Sangamon* on 26 February 1945. The small confines of the escort carrier greatly reduced the pilots' margin for error when landing back aboard. Bailey's predicament was caused by a 'floating' landing, which saw him catch a wire too late to avoid hitting the island (*Philip Jarrett*)

However, the *Lexington* Hellcats paid a price for their success. One pilot failed to appear at the rendezvous after the first sweep, and two more were lost on the second – apparently the victims of Japanese fighters. One was the CAG, Cdr Phil Torrey, Jr, (two kills in total) who had led VF-9 during the 1943-44 cruise. He was last seen making a head-on pass at a 'Tojo', but was then lost to sight during the erratic manoeuvres.

Most heavily engaged was VF-80, which found repeated opportunities in the Katori and Imba areas. The 'Vipers' claimed two-dozen victims in the morning, paced by Lt Cdr L W Keith (5.5 kills in total) with five, while their original CO, *Hancock's* CAG, Lt Cdr 'Scoop' Vorse, Jr, led other divisions to 13 more victories over Chiba Peninsula. During the fight Vorse gained four victories, running his wartime total to 11.5. Only one Hellcat was hit by enemy gunfire.

VF-80 fought four more combats during the day, including a dogfight over Imba Airfield that saw Lt A L Anderson (5.5 kills in total) destroy five fighters representing four different types – two 'Oscars', a Zeke, a 'Tojo' and a 'Tony'. In the same area Lt W C Edwards, Jr (7.5 kills in total), also emerged as an instant ace, downing two 'Nates', two Zekes and an 'Oscar'.

Then, shortly past noon, five pilots intercepted more Zekes and 'Oscars' between Imba and Mobara Airfields. Lt Pat Fleming shot down five of the former, while his section leader, 'Zeke' Cormier, got three more. Other 'Vipers' claimed seven additional kills. Then, late that afternoon, three pilots claimed four more victories for a squadron total of 71 confirmed and 15 probables throughout the day. It was a record unsurpassed in American aviation, made possible by the fact that CVG-80 did not distinguish between VF and VBF units.

The day's top personal scores included five by Cdr Gordon Schecter (five kills in total), skipper of VF-45. He gunned three Zekes and shared two other kills in the morning (a 'Dinah' and an ancient 'Claude'), then added an 'Oscar' late that afternoon. Ens R R Kidwell, Jr, also claimed five kills in two missions, these being his only scores of the war. In fact, the *San Jacinto* squadron made an extremely-impressive showing with 28 kills, second only to VF-80's record tally. Though every fighter squadron in the task force achieved kills, most of the CVL units had to be content with flying ForceCAP patrols over the carriers.

Fire is the thing most feared on a carrier, and the Hellcat's ability to set itself alight was further 'fuelled' by the gas stored in its external tank, which invariably ruptured if the aircraft suffered a heavy landing. This VF-9 F6F-5 had its belly tank ripped off by the arrestor wires as it landed back aboard *Lexington* on 25 February 1945, the pilot running down the wing and jumping to safety. Note how the fabric-covered elevators have already burnt through and that the prop is still turning

Two-tour veteran Jim Swope scored his fifth, and last, F6F kill on 15 January 1945. His 'Jill' was one of six victories credited to the 'Sundowners' on this day as they patrolled off the coast of Hong Kong. Tour-expired, he returned to the US in February 1945 (*Tailhook*)

This operation marked the first time that F4Us were embarked in strength, as *Bunker Hill's* air group included not only VF-84, but two Marine Corsair outfits also, while *Essex* too boasted a pair of 'Leatherneck' squadrons. In all, the F4Us accounted for 27 of the day's total of 291 aerial claims.

Although 17 February had brought significant combat, it was clear that Japanese airpower had taken a beating the day before. Another 97 shootdowns were claimed as 11 Hellcat squadrons accounted for all but 29 of the total. Leading the pack was *Yorktown's* VBF-3, adding 13 victories to the previous day's 23. In fact, the two-day Tokyo strike represented the fighter-bomber outfit's only aerial claims of the deployment.

Wasp's VF-81 claimed 11 kills on the 17th and also crowned its sole ace – on the 16th and 17th Lt(jg) H V Sherrill added 4.5 victories to his one previous credit. *Essex's* 'Fighting Four' counted 22 shootdowns during the operation, of which three went to Lt D E Laird, running his Pacific War tally to five. Combined with his two shared Luftwaffe kills (0.5 of a Ju 88 and 0.25 of a He 115) from *Ranger's* 1943 Norway strike, 'Diz' Laird became the only Navy ace with confirmed victories against both Germany and Japan – although indisputably a five-kill ace, Hollis Hills of VF-32 is technically not a US Navy ace as his first kill was scored against the Luftwaffe whilst he was part of the Royal Canadian Air Force.

Back in a big way was VF-80, as Pat Fleming continued to add to his burgeoning tally. He took three divisions on a sweep south-west of Katori airfield, stirring up 'Nates', 'Oscars', Zekes and 'Tojos' in the process.

The *Hancock* pilots shot down 12, of which Fleming claimed four. He had downed nine Japanese aircraft in well under 24 hours, running his score to 19. He remained tied as the Navy's fourth-ranked fighter ace for the rest of the war. Moreover, the 'Vipers' were credited with 83 kills during the Tokyo strikes – more than one-quarter of the two-day total. In all, TF-38 lost 88 aircraft, including 28 to operational accidents and poor weather.

VF-17 was one of the most successful units involved in the final carrier push into Japanese home waters in 1945, scoring 161 kills between February and May. Its primary weapon throughout this period was the F6F-5 Hellcat (72 machines split between VF- and VBF-17), although as this shot clearly shows, a handful of late-build -3s also saw service into the Okinawan campaign – indeed, 'White 41' was probably one of the last of its type in TF-58. Twelve pilots achieved ace status on this deployment with VF-17, plus a further eight with 'twin' unit VBF-17 (*Jerry Scutts*)

The fast carriers were back off Japan on 18 March, launching far-ranging sweeps of airfields and searching for enemy warships. *Hornet's* VF-17 found repeated combat around Kanoya as CO, Lt Cdr Marshall Beebe, and Lt Robert C Coats (9.333 kills in total) each claimed five victories. Formerly CO of VC-39, Beebe had swum away from the torpedoed escort carrier *Liscombe Bay* in 1943, but was now well on his way to double ace status. Bob Coats, who later admitted to being the only non-swimming ace in Navy history, downed five Zekes. In all, the squadron claimed 32 victories that morning.

The next day *Essex's* new VF-83 logged its first nine kills. Its VBF 'twin' squadron, flying F4Us, had already been blooded the day before, and both outfits would be heard from repeatedly in the ensuing five months.

That same morning, approaching Kure Naval Base, *Hornet* Hellcats were intercepted by a small force of enemy fighters flown both competently and aggressively, which effectively tied up the strike escort. One of the pilots was Lt Robert A Clark (six kills in total), who quickly downed a 'George' and a Zeke early in the fight. By that point, 'the radio was a scrambled jabber of pilots screeching for help and yelling advice. I noticed about 3000 ft above us a circle of Jap planes apparently loafing through the fight, but I soon saw their game. They'd formed a "Lufbery" circle, World War 1 style, and were waiting until a Hellcat got on some Jap's tail. Then they'd jump him in section and shoot him down, and return to the upper circle. This tactic worked as one Hellcat went screaming by me in a plunging dive with his belly tank on fire. Someone was yelling on the radio, "Drop it! For God's sake, drop it – you're on fire!" The sky was a flaming kaleidoscope of burning aeroplanes, flashing insignia and lancing tracer. Four or five chutes floated gently downward.

'After getting back to the *Hornet*, we rendezvoused the survivors of our ill-fated sweep. We had lost eight. We had accounted for 25 Japanese aircraft, and also discoverd that our dive-bombers and torpedo aircraft had

Texan Lt(jg) Tilman E Poole was one of 12 VF-17 aces on its Hellcat deployment, claiming six kills and one probable during roving sweeps of southern Japan between 18 March and 12 April. He had earlier seen combat in F6F-3s as a replacement pilot with VF-39 in the Marshalls, dive-bombing pockets of Japanese resistance on bypassed islands in the region (*Tilman Pool via Mark Styling*)

The outstanding fighter squadron of the Okinawan invasion in terms of aerial kills was VF-83 aboard *Essex*. Between 1 April and 23 June its pilots downed 122 aircraft, whilst naval aviators of the 'twinned' VBF-83 claimed a further 60. Both units used identically-marked F6F-5s, the carrier embarking 70+ Hellcats decorated with Air Group 83's 'hour glass' motif on the fin and upper wing surfaces. This 19 April shot shows Hellcats being marshalled into position prior to launching against the island of Ie Shima, off the west coast of Okinawa

had excellent success at the Kure base with minimum losses', Clark later related.

Two days later VBF-17 again led the *Hornet* hit parade. Lt(jg) Henry E Mitchell (six kills in total) led an interception offshore which resulted in eight kills – five 'Bettys' by Mitchell and two 'Bettys' and a Zero shared by his division.

Ordeal off Okinawa

Operation *Iceburg*, the invasion of Okinawa, began on Easter Sunday, 1 April 1945. Officially, it lasted 83 days until 23 June, and in that period carrier-based F6Fs splashed on average ten enemy aircraft a day.

In 12 weeks the embarked Hellcat squadrons claimed 837 shootdowns, led by *Essex's* VF-83 (122 kills) and *Yorktown's* VF-9 (93), while the F6Fs of VBF-9 added 44 more. In fact, 'Fighting Nine' was so heavily engaged that it produced the top three scorers of the campaign. Lt Eugene A Valencia was already a seven-kill ace when he took his division into combat as a thoroughly well-drilled team. During 'turn-around' training at NAS Pasco, Washington, Gene Valencia had bribed sailors with alcohol in exchange for more fuel, thus allowing additional flight time. His methods may have been unorthodox, but the results would speak for themselves.

The fourth-heaviest day of air combat in the carrier war occurred on 6 April, resulting in 257 Navy victories. The stats for this day came as no surprise to fighter pilots and radar controllers, who counted ten major raids during the afternoon. Some 355 *kamikazes* and 340 bomber or escort aircraft were flung at the task force, not all of which found their targets. Still, there were enough to keep all hands busy past sunset. *Belleau Wood's* VF-30 accounted for 47, and three ensigns claimed 16.5 kills among them – C C Foster got six (8.5 kills in total), K J Dahms 5.5 (seven kills in total), and J G Miller (eight kills in total) bagged five. That same day VF-17 splashed 25 as Lt(jg) W E Hardy (6.5 kills in total) ran his score from zero to five in 70 frenetic minutes, returning to *Hornet* at dark – VBF-17 added 21 more.

The major beneficiaries of this intense activity were Cdr J J Southerland II's VF-83 pilots, as *Essex's* Hellcats splashed 56 raiders in six combats around the Ryukyus. The CO bagged two 'Tonys' en route to scoring five kills exactly – a long way from his VF-5 days over Guadalcanal where he had duelled with Saburo Sakai in early August 1942 – Southerland scored his final kill (a Zeke) on 29 April whilst serving as CO of VF-23 aboard *Langley*. Three other pilots claimed four kills each – Lt(jg)s H N Batten and S J Brocato (both scored seven in total), plus Ens J M Barnes (six kills in total) – they all made ace on this day.

Despite the tireless efforts of the F6F and F4U pilots, enough attackers penetrated the CAP to hit 19 ships, sinking six. No carriers were damaged, but radar picket destroyers sustained heavy damage with ten hit and three sunk.

On 7 April TF-38 intercepted a very different type of suicide mission. Japan's greatest remaining battleship, the 64,000-ton *Yamato*, was found off the south-west coast of Kyushu, en route to Okinawa with her screen of nine escorts. Unopposed from the air, the task force sent day-long strikes of dive- and torped-bombers under lowering skies against the dreadnaught, and although AA gunners downed nine carrier aircraft (including two F6Fs), *Yamato*, a light cruiser and four destroyers were sunk.

Braced onto the forward catapult, a VF-29 F6F-5 is just seconds away from being shot off the bow of USS *Cabot* at the start of a dawn sweep along the Japanese coast in mid-February. The unit scored 113 kills and produced 12 aces during its seven-month stint in the Pacific

During the day Hellcats splashed 32 bandits, although one put a bomb into *Hancock*, before following the ordnance through the flightdeck. Badly damaged, the ship and Air Group Six were forced out of action until early June. 'Fighting Six' had claimed 15 kills since arriving in March, but the two-month enforced lay-off prevented the veteran squadron from producing any further aces.

During interceptions on the 12th, VF-30 ace Michele Mazzocco (five kills in total) tangled with a well-flown 'Tojo' near Okinawa, and learned just how rugged the F6F really was. Although the *Belleau Wood* pilot inflicted early damage on the Nakajima, its pilot continued the fight. After chasing tails downward from 18,000 ft, Mazzocco and the Japanese flier approached one another head on. Both began firing, and both scored hits. Then the New Yorker realised, 'he wasn't going to veer off, and a collision was not only inevitable, but planned by him.

'I waited until the last possible moment, my heart in my throat, then pulled up hard and to the right. His left wing came through the bottom arc of my prop and debris flew all over the sky. The concussion was tremendous, and jarred me to the bone, and I lost control of my plane for a moment that seemed an eternity.

'When I recovered, I could see him spinning slowly down toward the sea. My wingman checked my plane and told me my belly tank had taken most of the punishment in the collision. I managed to jettison it and made an emergency landing on the carrier. "Mr Grumman" surely built a tough one when he built that Hellcat. God bless him.'

On 16 April the *kamikazes* tried hard again, but failed to match the strength of their efforts ten days earlier. VF-17's Lt(jg) J T 'Stump' Crosby nevertheless capitalised upon a long-awaited opportunity. Having completed a previous deployment with VF-18 in 1943/44, during which he had claimed a quarter-kill of a 'Betty', Crosby had further damaged two fighters on this tour and was ready for 'acedom'. That morning he chased down three 'Jacks', a Zero and a 'Val' to become *Hornet's* tenth, and last, instant ace – a record for all carriers. TF-38 carrier pilots claimed 157 victories during the day, which was exactly 100 fewer than their total on 6 April.

Joint second top-scorer in VF-29 was Ens Franklin 'Trooper' Troup, who downed seven aircraft between 15 October 1944 and 4 April 1945. His tally of 20 bomb markings alongside the kill symbols denotes that VF-29 could also carrying out the fighter-bomber role – a task that assumed greater importance as more and more Hellcats were thrust into the frontline (*Franklin Troup via Mark Styling*)

'Valencia's Flying Circus' of VF-9 holds the record as being the highest-scoring fighter division in Navy history. Lt Eugene Valencia's team was credited with 43.5 kills during their 1945 det. This shot shows from left; Lt(jg) H E Mitchell ten kills); Lt(jg) C L Smith (six kills); Lt(jg) J B French (11 kills); and Valencia, whose first tour score of 7.5 combined with his 15.5 in 1945 to make 50, all without the loss of a single Hellcat (*Barrett Tillman*)

Ens Donald M McPherson was just one of 12 pilots to score five or more kills with VF-83 during its 1945 deployment. His first aerial kills came on 6 April when he downed two 'Vals' near Kikai Jima, followed on 4 May by three 'Alf' biplanes that had been re-rolled from recce floatplanes into *kamikaze* bombers – over 100 aircraft were downed in one frantic hour on this date as the Japanese launched a huge assault on TF-38 (*Donald McPherson*)

During the Okinawa campaign, 'Fighting Nine's' Gene Valencia added 12.5 victories to his own score while all three pilots in his division became aces. His section leader, Lt(jg) James B French (11 kills in total), and wingman Lt(jg) Harris E Mitchell (ten kills in total), both became double aces, whilst the number-four man in the team, Lt(jg) Clinton L Smith, shot down six Japanese aircraft.

The division's combat debut had occurred during the February Tokyo strikes, but their next taste of action could hardly have been more spectacular. Patrolling over a picket destroyer on 17 April, Valencia was vectored onto 'ten-plus' bogies which quickly grew into 25 Zekes and 'Franks'. Attacking from the 'perch', Valencia ignored the odds and led his three pilots into the swarm of Japanese, his first burst exploding the topmost 'Frank' and thus signalling the start of a ten-minute dogfight. During that time Harris Mitchell shot three Zekes off his leader's tail, allowing Valencia to concentrate on his own shooting.

When burning aeroplanes stopped falling into the sea, the team regrouped and circled the combat area. Valencia and company counted eight parachutes still in the air among the 17 kills claimed. 'Only' 14 were confirmed – six by Valencia, four by French, three by Mitchell and one by Smith. The only damage sustained by the F6Fs was superficial dents and scrapes caused by the debris of disintegrating enemy aircraft.

TF-38's next major action occured on 4 May when task force fighters splashed 105 bandits throughout the Ryukyus. The shooting started well before dawn as VF-9's nightfighter detachment dropped four snooping 'Bettys', three of which fell to Ens John Orth, taking took his final score to six. *Yorktown's* 'day shift' also contributed by claiming a further 29 kills, including 11 by Valencia's well-drilled team.

VF-83 splashed two-dozen suiciders near Izema Shima where, in his second and last combat, Ens Myron M Truax (seven kills in total) claimed four Type 93 trainers, a 'Val' and an 'Oscar'. By mid-morning the scoring was over, with VBF-12 and VF-46 bringing the day's Hellcat tally to 73 – *Essex, Bunker Hill* and the new *Shangri-La's* Corsairs added 30 more.

Come the dawn of 11 May, the task force's air defence had proven invincible for three full weeks, but that record sequence was tragically ended in a combined *kamikaze* and dive-bombing attack which knocked *Bunker Hill* out of the war. After controlling terrible fires, CV-17 limped away with some 650 casualties, including 389 dead. Elsewhere, VF-9 claimed 20 more kills and Lt Bert Eckard (seven kills in total) became the 46th, and last, Hellcat ace in a day when he splashed five Zekes north-east of Okinawa.

Despite appalling losses among their ranks, the suiciders kept coming. Their persistence ended *Enterprise's* superb career on 14 May, prematurely stopping Night Air Group 90's tour. The Night Hellcats of

Although officially frowned upon, nose art was worn very occasionally on Pacific theatre Hellcats, with this previously unknown example being one of the gaudiest. F6F-5 BuNo 72534 was christened *DEATH N' DESTRUCTION* by a trio of ensign aces serving with VF-83 in April 1945, the name being further embellished with a skull and cross-bones! Donald McPherson, Bill Kingston, Jr, and Lyttleton Ward each flew the fighter on numerous occasions over Okinawa, with the latter definitely shooting down three 'Alfs' and an 'Oscar' in it during the 4 May mass attack, and becoming an ace in the process (*Bill Kingston via Mark Styling*)

VF(N)-90 had claimed 31 shootdowns by this stage, including 4.5 by Lt Owen D Young (three 'Jakes', a 'Tony' and a shared 'Pete'), all of which were destroyed in an 83-minute spell on the morning of 12 May.

However, with repeated scoring opportunities came unrelenting operations, and the constant strain of CAPs, strike escorts and occasional close air support quickly used up squadrons and air groups; units deploying for an expected six-month tour were worn out in four.

In June VF-9 ended its second Pacific deployment, turning over to VF-88 in *Yorktown*. Against the loss of five pilots, the original Hellcat squadron had claimed 128.75 aerial victories and 47 on the ground during 1574 combat sorties. In compiling its record, VF-9 expended 543,600 rounds of .50 cal ammunition, over 300 bombs and 750 rockets. In all, 'Fighting Nine's' two F6F tours totalled 250.75 aerial kills (plus six Vichy aircraft during *Torch* in 1942). Thus, VF-9 became the Navy's second-ranked Hellcat squadron behind VF-15. 'Fighting Nine' produced 20 aces throughout the war, a tally only exceeded by VF-2 (27 aces) and VF-15 (26 aces). At war's end VF-9's Lt Gene Valencia was the Navy's second-ranking ace with 23 victories, being tied in this position with Lt Cecil Harris of VF-18.

Another notable achievement by a VF-9 pilot was the consistent record of Lt Marvin J Franger. Originally a 23-year-old ensign aboard *Ranger* for

Late in the afternoon on 3 April 1945, Lt(jg) Mel Cozzens was part of a VF-29 division that intercepted a small force of Zekes and 'Tonys' inbound to TF-38 south of Kikai Jima. Five pilots shared ten kills, Cozzens claiming the lion's share with two Zekes and a 'Tony' falling to BuNo 71972's guns – this almost doubled his score from 3.5 to 6.5 kills (*Mel Cozzens via Mark Styling*)

VF-6's second Hellcat tour in the frontline was badly affected by a serious *kamikaze* strike on *Hancock* off Okinawa on 7 April 1945, resulting in the squadron claiming just 20 victories (14 prior to the strike and six after returning in July), and producing no aces. This shot shows the surviving Hellcats being flown off to Maui on 21 April as the carrier limped towards Pearl Harbor for repairs (*Tailhook*)

the *Torch* landings, he used his F4F-4 to shoot down a Vichy French Curtiss Hawk 75A, plus a second fighter as a probable, over Morocco. During the squadron's *Essex* cruise in 1943-44 he added four Zeros and a 'Kate', then finished his last tour with a further three Japanese fighter kills in 1945. His nine victories over Axis aircraft included six different enemy types – Hawk 75A, 'Kate', 'Hamp'/Zeke, 'Nate', 'Jake' and 'Tony'.

Okinawa Campaign – *1 April to 23 June 1945*

Top-Scoring F6F Squadrons

VF-83	*Essex*	122
VF-9	*Yorktown*	93.25
VF-17	*Hornet*	89
VF-30	*Belleau Wood*	77
VBF-17	*Hornet*	76
VBF-83	*Essex*	60
VF-82	*Bennington*	60
VF-47	*Bataan*	56.50
VF-45	*San Jacinto*	45.50
VBF-1	*Randolph*	45
VBF-9	*Yorktown*	44

Total by 21 F6F squadrons – 837.25

Top Hellcat Pilots of the Okinawa Campaign

Lt E A Valencia	VF-9	12.5	Total 23
Lt(jg) J B French	VF-9	10	Total 11
Lt(jg) H E Mitchell	VF-9	9	Total 10
Lt(jg) J M Johnston	VBF-17	8	Total 9
Ens C C Foster	VF-30	7.5	Total 8.5

The Okinawan campaign also saw land-based Hellcats in the form of Marine F6F-5Ns taking a toll of Japanese nocturnal raiders, with two of the pilots in this group shot attaining ace status over the beleaguered island – Maj Bruce Porter, in the middle of the front row, and Capt Wally Sigler, to the former's left. Both pilots were flying with VMF(N)-542, and both had earlier scored the bulk of their kills in F4U-1s over the Solomons in 1943

Maj Porter's favoured mount, BuNo 78669, is readied for a sortie at Yontan in July 1945. Porter made ace in a rare double night kill on 15 June, using a mix of machine gun and cannon fire to down a *Ohka*-toting 'Betty' and a 'Nick' twin-engined fighter. Most nightfighting Hellcats kept the standard six-gun .5 cal armament – indeed, only Porter's -5N had cannon. Despite his success, most units experienced jamming problems with their cannon. Indeed, the Corps' only all-Hellcat night ace, Capt Robert Baird of VMF(N)-533, was able to use his 20 mms for just one of his six kills

Marine Corps nightfighter Hellcats also came into their own at Okinawa. Three Squadrons operating from Yontan and Kadena Airfields scored 69 kills, led by Lt Col Marion Magruder's VMF(N)-533, which accrued half of the total. The squadron also produced the Marine's only Hellcat ace, and also their only night ace – Capt Robert Baird, who shot down six aircraft during five interceptions in June and July.

Additionally, two former Corsair pilots became aces at Okinawa as VMF(N)-542's Maj Bruce Porter and Capt Wallace Sigler each logged their fifth victories while flying F6F-5Ns.

'Old 76', as BuNo 78669 was known to its groundcrew, had been the chosen aircraft of Porter's predecessor, and as such nose-art in the form of a big red heart with the name 'Millie Lou' emblazoned across it. He immediately ordered that it be removed, and a 'big fifth of Schenley's whiskey', accompanied by the words *Black Death*, be applied in its place. Note the flash suppresser on the cannon muzzle

Hellcat Nightfighter Squadrons at Okinawa – *April to August 1945*

VMF(N)-533	35
VMF(N)-542	18
VMF(N)-543	16

VMF(N)-533 'Crystal Gazers' was the most successful nightfighter unit in the Corps, downing 35 aircraft. Like most USMC Hellcats, BuNo 72627 wears nose-art on its cowling, and is in immaculate condition on Ie Shima on 27 June 1945. Marine Corps pilots initially felt that the Hellcat would make an inferior nightfighter when compared with the F4U-2 Corsair then being developed for the role, but the former soon proved to be the better machine in a combat environment (*Tailhook*)

FLEET AIR ARM AND ANVIL-DRAGOON

In British service the Hellcat had limited opportunity for aerial combat. However, since the Fleet Air Arm (FAA) only logged 455 aerial victories in six years of war, the F6F's contribution of 52 kills is not inconsiderable. In fact, American-built fighters accounted for more than one-third of the total, including 67 by Martlet/Wildcats and 52.5 by Corsairs.

A quartet of recently-arrived Gannet Is (later renamed Hellcats to avoid confusion with Britain's US allies) of No 800 Sqn patrol over the Irish Sea during a training sortie from Eglinton in September 1943. FAA Hellcats remained in this drab Dark Sea Grey/Extra Dark Sea Grey scheme throughout their time in Home Fleet service (*Charles E Brown*)

Originally, the Royal Navy called the F6F the 'Gannet', after a large seabird found in northern waters. The new Grumman was badly needed, as for a variety of political and economic reasons, Britain failed to field a satisfactory home-grown single-seat carrier fighter during the war. Granted, the Seafire Mk III was unquestionably the finest low-level naval fighter the Allies produced, but it lacked the range, offensive capability and, most importantly, carrier suitability of the rugged American types.

Beginning in the summer of 1943, the Royal Navy acquired the first of 1263 F6F-3s and -5s, called Gannet Mk Is and IIs, respectively. This little-used name was changed back to Hellcat in March 1944, by which time F6F-5N nightfighters were also becoming available.

Flying from the light carrier HMS *Emperor*, No 800 Sqn introduced the F6F to combat in British colours in December 1943. The occasion was a series of anti-shipping patrols along the Scandanavian coast, and Gannets were later charged with providing top cover for several large strikes against the German battleship *Tirpitz* during the following spring and summer.

Throughout these operations the only significant aerial combat experienced by FAA F6Fs occurred on 8 May 1944 when *Emperor's* Hellcats engaged a small number of Fw 190s and Bf 109Gs from JG 5 over Norway. Despite the *Luftwaffe* fighters' superior speed (30 kts or more), two Messerschmitts and a Focke-Wulf were claimed destroyed, the latter

Lt Cdr Stanley Orr's No 804 Sqn found few problems in operating from the tiny deck of HMS *Emporer* in all but the fiercest of gales. Indeed, two squadrons of Hellcats (24 aircraft) were usually embarked during the Norwegian campaign in 1944 (*Stanley Orr*)

falling to veteran fighter pilot Lt Blyth Ritchie – the Scot joined the squadron in late 1941, and had been credited with 3.5 victories in Sea Hurricane Is and IICs in 1942.

On the 14th, Ritchie caught an ungainly Heinkel He 115 seaplane 'wave-hopping ' along the Norwegian coast and quickly shot it down, then joined seasoned ace, Lt Cdr Stanley G Orr, CO of No 804 Sqn, in splashing another – these kills made the Scot an ace, with his score standing at five destroyed and two shared destroyed, one damaged and one shared damaged. Sadly, Ritchie was killed in an operational accident soon after achieving this milestone.

PILOT PROFILE

Commander Stanley Orr DSC and two bars, AFC

Stanley Orr, like Blyth Ritchie, was also an ace, although he had achieved this status as early as November 1940, flying unwieldy Fairey Fulmar Is with No 806 Sqn in the Mediterranean aboard HMS *Illustrious.* When his carrier was badly damaged by German dive-bombers on 10 January 1941, Orr's squadron was put ashore at Malta, and he became one of the island's original defenders. Fighting pitched battles against overwhelming numbers of German and Italian fighters and bombers, the sub-lieutenant's score had risen to six destroyed and four shared by the time he returned to the UK in late 1941.

After a spell as an instructor, he was sent to America in August to take command on No 896 Sqn, which was forming on Martlets. Embarked aboard *Victorious*, the squadron sailed into the Pacific in March 1943, but Orr was struck down with polio and sent back to the UK. He made a full recovery, and in August of the same year was sent to RNAS Eglinton, in Northern Ireland, to take charge of No 804 Sqn, which was in the process of exchanging its veteran Sea Hurricane IICs for the FAA's first Hellcat Is (then called Gannets). Cdr Orr's experiences with the big Grumman, detailed in the following interview conducted specially for this volume by series editor Tony Holmes in October 1995, give the British side of the F6F story;

'The Hellcat was without a doubt the best, and most popular, naval fighter of the period. It suffered none of the Corsair's stall and visibility problems, being an easy aircraft both to fly and to deck land. It bestowed upon its pilot immense confidence, which was an important thing in those days as you usually had your hands more than full coping with the enemy! Indeed, it was such a stable platform to fly that following the *Tirpitz* raids we recommended that bomb racks be fitted to the aircraft. In no time at all this modification had been carried out, thus allowing us to attack targets on the

Lt Cdr Orr (left) and two of his pilots check their mission route prior to manning their Hellcats for the strike on *Tirpitz* on 3 April 1944. Note that all three naval aviators are wearing different flying gear, with perhaps the Bomber Command-style Irvin jacket adorning the pilot on the right being the most unusual. Most FAA aircrew preferred not to fly in their Irvins as they became waterlogged should the wearer be forced to ditch. This photograph appeared on the front page of *The Evening News* (the forerunner of today's *Evening Standard*) on 8 April 1944 (*Stanley Orr*)

ground when we weren't required to act as fighter cover for our Barracudas and Avengers.

'In fact, following the departure of the larger fleet carriers following the big *Tungsten*, *Mascot* and *Goodwood* strikes in April, July and August 1944 respectively, the Norwegian campaign was left to the smaller escort carriers, whose principal strike aircraft was the Hellcat.

'Aside from its marvellous airborne attributes, the Hellcat also boasted an enviable reliability record. The aircraft rarely went unserviceable, which was crucially important as the escort carrier squadrons usually had only eight to ten Hellcats on strength at any one time – 50 per cent unserviceability could really hit your mission effectiveness!

'Unserviceability was one of the first problems I encountered with my new squadron at Eglinton when I arrived in August 1943, however. The unit's brand new Hellcat Is had only just arrived from America by ship, and had been sent ahead of the vessel carrying their spares! Despite this rather unfortunate state of affairs, we got on with our conversion to the fighter, but the first thing that happened was that the tailwheel tyres quickly began to wear out and burst due to our intensive programme of deck-landing practice.

'The squadron was on the verge of being permanently grounded when we came up with the idea of laminating strips of old truck tyre rubber together into a 12-in solid disc, which we then bolted onto our tailwheels – much to the chagrin of the FAA's engineering staff! Two months after our Hellcats had arrived, packing cases turned up with our long-awaited spares.

'We completed carrier qualification aboard *Ravager* in October 1943 and were then assigned to No 7 Naval Fighter Wing. A one-off convoy patrol to America aboard HMS *Emperor* then followed in December, and we used this trip both to thoroughly familiarise ourselves with the fighter around a carrier, and stock up with spares upon our arrival at Norfolk naval yard in Virginia in the New Year.

'Once we returned to the UK, we continued our training on the new fighter, both ashore and at sea, before heading north to Hatston, in the Orkneys, where we operated as a wing with other Barracuda and Avenger squadrons, rehearsing for the *Tungsten* strikes on *Tirpitz*. When the time came for the mission proper to be flown on 3 April 1944, we had practised the sortie so thoroughly that it all went like clockwork.

'The day dawned "gin clear", and No 804 Sqn was tasked with protecting the second strike on *Tirpitz*, which was to be performed by 19 Barracudas of No 52 Torpedo, Bomber, Reconnaissance (TBR) Wing an hour after the first attack – No 800 Sqn had helped escort the first assault. Six carriers were involved in the strike, with aircraft launching from a predetermined point 120 miles north-

Hellcat I FN340 came to grief during No 804 Sqn's carrier qualification period aboard HMS *Ravager* when its pilot struck the stern of the ship on landing. Dated 22 October 1943, this accident was the only one suffered by the unit during its intensive 'blue water' shakedown cruise. The crestfallen pilot of FN340 can be seen to the right of the photo beneath the port wing roundel. This particular airframe was the first ever Hellcat flown by Lt Cdr Orr upon his arrival at No 804 Sqn, the new CO performing a brief familiarisation flight in the fighter on 12 August 1943 (*Stanley Orr*)

west of Kaafjord. No less than 40 fighters, comprising Corsairs, Wildcats and Hellcats, provided the escort for the Wing, and my squadron took up station on the starboard side of the force.

'We experienced some difficulty in keeping station with the bombed-up Barracudas, which could barely make 135 kts. Some 20 miles from the coast, the strike force climbed to a height of 10,000 ft, and I positioned the Hellcats 1000 ft above them, weaving at about 190 kts. The squadron kept together well, with Green and White flights continually crossing over the centre section so as to keep an all-round lookout.

'Above us, the Corsairs seemed split up into groups of threes and fours which, in my opinion, would have made the immediate location of enemy fighters extremely difficult if there had been any around. Upon arrival over *Tirpitz*, it was found that the smoke screen generated by the Germans had risen half way up the mountains on either side of Kaafjord, but the heavy AA gun position Able was clear and firing repeatedly. Three or four other flak batteries were also shooting in our direction, so each flight attacked their pre-briefed gunsites once it was clear that no enemy fighters were in the area – I later heard a story after the war that most of the Luftwaffe fighter wing (JG 5) that was supposed to protect the battleship had returned briefly to Germany for re-equipment just days prior to the attack, and had been stuck there due to bad weather. However, I can't vouch for the truth of this tale!

'We dived from 8000 to 1000 ft at an angle of 50 degrees, firing three- to five-second bursts, and gun positions Able, Dog, Easy and Fox all temporarily fell silent. White section attempted to attack the smoke-obscured Baker AA site, and in so doing passed near to the stern of the *Tirpitz*, which was pouring smoke from its aft end. A flak and merchant ship were also strafed as the squadron flew out of the Kaafjord, before the flights reformed over the sea and proceeded to escort a number of Barracudas back to the task force at low-level.

'The Hellcat proved itself to be an excellent gunnery platform on this mission, and I wrote in my combat report to the captain of the *Emperor* on 5 April that "if we had been carrying bombs – the Hellcat is well suited for this purpose – we could possibly have contributed to the damage of the *Tirpitz*".

'Just over a month later we headed back into Norwegian waters in search of more targets of opportunity, and on 9 May we flew Operation *Hoop Dog* in search of a convoy near Gossen Island – I was leading eight Hellcats and a similar number of Wildcat Vs from *Searcher's* No 898 Sqn. We combed the area for a short time, but soon realised that there were no ships to be found, so I headed south. On passing over Fjortoft Island two Luftwaffe BV 138 floatplanes were spotted

Wearing its three-number serial crudely sprayed on its cowling, No 804 Sqn's JV145 is carefully positioned for launch from *Emperor* during the *Tirpitz* strikes. This type of hurried recognition marking was also seen on a number of F6F-3s in the Pacific in 1943/44, often being applied for ferry flights between land bases and the carrier task force (*Stanley Orr*)

taking off, so I ordered Black flight (comprising No 898 Sqn Wildcats) to attack, and both aircraft were quickly despatched – we were carrying bombs on our Hellcats, and thought it rather pointless to tackle the enemy in this configuration when we had the Wildcat Vs flying as fighter escorts.

'We then continued on with the sortie, and various targets ranging from oil tanks near Aalesund to a fish-oil factory and warehouse on an island off Kvalsvik were hit. A single Hellcat, flown by Kiwi Sub-Lt R A Cranwell, was lost to flak.

'On 14 May both Hellcats squadrons launched nine aircraft apiece as part of *Potluck Able* – a strike against enemy shipping off Rorvik. Eight of the Hellcats were configured as bombers and a similar number as fighters, whilst the remaining two aircraft carried out an armed recce of the target area five minutes prior to the strike force. As I led the formation in a climb to 5000 ft following landfall near Vikten Island, the recce pilots reported sighting several large ships off Rorvik.

'We ran into the target area from south to north, and whilst the Hellcat "fighters" strafed AA batteries in the harbour, I led the bomb-toting No 804 Sqn aircraft against two ships to the north of Rorvik, whilst the similarly-configured No 800 Sqn machines attacked two vessels to the south.

'Whilst all this was going on, No 800 Sqn's flight of four Hellcat "fighters" had sighted five He 115 floatplanes, whose pilots quickly realised they stood little chance against the marauding Grummans, and tried to alight on the water. Two Heinkels were shot down on the first pass – one fell to the guns of White flight leader, Lt Blyth Ritchie – and the remainder made panic landings north of Rorvik. Having successfully bombed our targets, I led Red Flight into the fight with the Heinkels, and I believe I made one pass at Ritchie's He 115 just prior to it crash-landing.

'By the time we had knocked our speed off and turned around to run in at them again, the three remaining floatplanes we bobbing up and down on the water like sitting ducks. White flight had since exhausted their ammunition after strafing the remaining He 115s, and it was left to us to finish them off – I shared in the sinking of one and then set another alight. A No 800 Sqn aircraft flown by Sub-Lt Hollway was hit by return fire from one of the He 115s and the pilot was forced to bale out on the return trip to *Emperor*. Sadly, he was never found.'

After D-Day No 804 Sqn was absorbed into No 800 Sqn, and duly disbanded – it later reformed on 1 September 1944 in South Africa on Hellcat IIs, prior to heading to the Far East where it saw more action. For Lt Cdr Orr, however, the 'shooting' war was over, being posted as Chief Flying Intructor to RNAS Henstridge in September 1944, before being accepted into the Empire Test Pilots' School at Boscombe Down – a move which was to feature prominantly in his postwar FAA career.

The He 115 successes on 14 May 1944 were the last aerial victories scored by the Hellcat against the Luftwaffe, despite Hellcat-equipped escort-carrier squadrons supporting the invasion of Southern France that August.

The top scoring Hellcat unit in the FAA by some considerable margin was No 1844 Sqn, whose pilots achieved 32.5 kills during their time aboard HMS *Indomitable* in 1944/45 – indeed, all six of the highest scoring Commonwealth Hellcat pilots saw service with this outfit. Initially equipped with Mk Is (F6F-3s), the unit was the recipient of some of the first Mk IIs (F6F-5s) delivered to the FAA in February 1945. These later aircraft were retained in their US Navy factory finish of overall Glossy Sea Blue, and the latter American-style roundels were also applied, as worn here on JZ935 (*Ray Sturtivant*)

Royal Navy Hellcats were thrust into combat against Japan that same month when the East Indian Fleet launched strikes upon the Sumatran oilfields. Sporadic aerial combat occurred on 17-19 October, when Hellcats and Corsairs claimed seven 'Oscars' for three losses, including one F6F. Logging the first Pacific victories for British Hellcats were Sub-Lts E T Wilson and E Smithwick of *Indomitable's* No 1844 Sqn, the two pilots combining to destroy three 'Oscars'. The squadron added a 'Sally' bomber on 20 December.

Meanwhile, the FAA's only dedicated photo-reconnaissance unit in the region was also active at this time, No 888 Sqn flying Hellcat PR IIs (F6F-5Ps) from *Emperor*.

The heaviest aerial strikes flown against the Dutch East Indies occurred in December 1944 and January 1945, and included *Indomitable's* Nos 1839 and 1844 Sqns flying Hellcat Mk Is (F6F-3s) as part of No 5 Naval Fighter Wing. The *Meridian* strikes against petroleum targets around Palembang, though short in duration, evoked a serious response from the Japanese Army Air Force.

Three missions flown during late January brought a measure of success to FAA Hellcat pilots, with a trio of 'Oscars' being destroyed over Sumatra on 4 January, followed by five assorted fighters on the 24th and 5.5 victories on the 29th. All of these kills were recorded by *Indomitable's* two fighter squadrons, Nos 1839 and 1844 scoring four and 9.5 victories respectively. The most successful individual was Sub-Lt E T Wilson of the latter unit, with 2.5 kills.

Indomitable's monopoly on British Hellcat victories against Japan ended on 1 March. No 804 Sqn, still flying from the escort carrier *Emperor*, engaged Japanese Army aircraft off Rangoon, and seven pilots split two 'Oscars' and a 'Dinah' among them.

During the Okinawa and Home Island campaigns the British Pacific Fleet functioned as a semi-autonomous element of Task Force 38. There was a good deal of commonality, as both the US and British navies flew Hellcats, Corsairs and Avengers, while RN escort carriers also had Wildcats. However, the FAA also retained significant numbers of generic Barracuda, Firefly and Seafire aircraft.

On 8 April 1945 No 888 Sqn off HMS *Khedive* 'splashed' three snoopers which approached the task group, but AA guns and operational crashes all took a toll in the last months of the war – both Nos 808 and 896 Sqns lost their COs in this way. The best day of the war for FAA Hellcats occurred on 12 April, whilst units were supporting strikes against Formosa. No 1844 Sqn splashed six enemy fighters, including two by Sub-Lt W M Foster.

Aerial combat largely eluded BPF Hellcats during May and June, with only three victories by *Indomitable* pilots on 4 May. On 25 July No 1844 Sqn made a high-altitude interception of four Aichi 'Grace' torpedo-bombers approaching the task group. Three were soon shot down, and the fourth escaped with a serious mauling. It was the Hellcat's final combat in British service. Of all the FAA fighter units involved in combat in the Far East, No 1844 sqn was clearly the highest scoring with 32.5 kills – next highest was the Corsair-equipped No 1836 Sqn with 17. The only other Hellcat unit to accrue a score of note was No 1839 Sqn with seven kills.

FAA pilots recorded only 18 aerial combats in Hellcats during the 15 months from May 1944 to July 1945, with the peak scoring period, not surprisingly, occurring during April of the latter year at the time of the Okinawa invasion. No less than 19 of the Hellcat's 52 victories were logged in that month alone.

At the end of the war the FAA boasted 12 Hellcat squadrons split between Home Stations, the East Indian and Pacific Fleets. Though not the most successful Royal Navy fighter, the Hellcat surely proved itself one of the most versatile.

Top FAA Hellcat Units

No 1844 Sqn	*Indomitable*	32.5
No 1839 Sqn	*Indomitable*	7
No 800 Sqn	*Emperor*	5.5
No 808 Squn	*Khedive*	4
No 804 Sqn	*Emperor*	3

Top FAA Hellcat Pilots

Sub-Lt E T Wilson	No 1844 Sqn	4.83
Sub-Lt W M Foster	No 1844 Sqn	4.50
Lt W H Atkinson	No 1844 Sqn	3.33
Sub-Lt R F Mackie	No 1839/1844	3
Sub-Lt W Fenwick-Smith	No 1844 Sqn	3
Sub-Lt MacLennan	No 1844 Sqn	3

ANVIL-DRAGOON

The Hellcat's only European combat in US service occurred in an unlikely venue – the stylish vacation coast of Southern France. Two months after the Normandy landings the Anglo-American operation called *Anvil-Dragoon* (the code-name was changed just before the commencement of 'D-Day South') initiated a giant pincer against German forces in Occupied Europe. Assault troops went ashore on 15 August.

Whilst huge carrier battles were raging in the Pacific that often involved hundreds of Hellcats, a modest force of two 10,400-ton *Casablanca* class escort carriers combined with two small Royal Navy 'flattops' to support the Allied invasion of Southern France in mid-August 1944. Two US Navy Hellcat units were involved – VOF-1 aboard USS *Tulagi*, who were tasked primarily with target spotting for naval gunners, and VF-74 embarked on USS *Kasaan Bay*. This photograph shows a bomb-toting F6F-5 of the latter unit being launched on a close-air support sortie on 15 August. Four days later elements of VF-74 downed a Ju 88 and a Do 217 attempting to bomb Task Force 88. The unit flew 289 sorties in 11 days in support of Operation *Dragoon*, losing five aircraft in the process (*Tailhook*)

Supporting the landings were two American escort carriers, each operating an independent F6F-5 squadron. Embarked in *Kasaan Bay* was Lt Cdr H B Bass's VF-74 while Lt Cdr W F Bringle took VOF-1 (Observation-Fighter) aboard *Tulagi*. The latter unit was specially trained in artillery and naval gunfire spotting, which was a skill much in demand for an amphibious operation.

In concert with British carrier squadrons, the Hellcats' primary missions were close air support, interdiction and gunnery spotting. However, a handful of aerial encounters developed, and the F6F pilots made the most of their limited opportunities.

Two combats occurred on 19 August – the second anniversary of the Dieppe landing in northern France – with Lt Cdr Bass and his division downing a Junkers Ju 88 in the morning, followed in the afternoon by two *Kasaan Bay* pilots shooting down a Dornier Do 217 north-east of Issiore. No other *Luftwaffe* aircraft presented themselves to 'Fighting 74', but Bass was shot down and killed by flak – one of 11 US Hellcats lost in the operation.

Bringle's *Tulagi* pilots claimed six victories – three Heinkel He 111s fell near Vienne on the evening of the 19th, followed by three Junkers Ju 52 transports on the 21st. Top scorer was Ens Edward W Olszewski who downed two of the latter despite having only one operable gun. He and three others added to their Axis tallies against Japan in 1945 flying FM-2 Wildcats with the redesignated VOC-1.

Top Hellcat scores of *Anvil-Dragoon*

Ens Edward W Olszewski	VOF-1	2
Ens Alfred R Wood	VOF-1	1.5
Ens Richard V Yentzer	VOF-1	1

Eight other VOF-1 and VF-74 pilots scored partial victories.

END GAME

The final phase of the Pacific War began in early July 1945. With the Imperial Navy long removed as a threat, carrier task groups were free to concentrate on strike operations against coastal and shore-based targets, including Japanese industry. Hoarding remaining aircraft and aircrews for the expected invasion, Japan ceded air superiority to the Allies. Consequently, aerial combat dropped dramatically, with naval aviators claiming 265 shootdowns in May, compared with a mere 20 in June. However, the final series of strikes, especially against remaining enemy fleet units, prompted a brief resurgence in July.

Aerial combat only occurred on six days of that month, with 56 of the total 59 kills being claimed on the 24th, 25th and 28th. The latter three dates involved strikes against naval targets at Kure, Kobe and elsewhere in the Inland Sea. Japan's remaining battleships and aircraft carriers, lacking fuel and air cover, lay immobile and open to attack almost at will.

These operations marked the return of some veteran squadrons. 'Fighting Six' was back in the repaired *Hancock* while VF-16 arrived for a second deployment, now aboard *Randolph*. Both units scored on the 24th, but VF-31, also newly returned to combat, starred the next day. The *Belleau Wood* pilots claimed eight kills over Yokaichi Airfield, four 'Franks' falling to Lt(jg) C N Nooy – despite this action being his only aerial combat of his second cruise, it raised his wartime total to 19 confirmed.

Also back was VF-27, displaced from *Princeton* in October. Now aboard *Independence*, Lt Cdr Bardshar's unit was back in combat in May – a turnaround period of only seven months. He found Home Island operations both bigger and better organised than was previously the case.

'During July and August 1945 we hit Kure, Niigata, Muroran, Yokosuka and Utsunomiya, among others. Kure's defenses were, I think, the strongest and certainly the most spectacular. They used coloured bursts for air spotting as we did with surface naval rifles. Concern with flak at Kure was somewhat tempered by concern with mid-air collisions. The raids were large, rather well co-ordinated and concentrated, and the density of US aircraft over the targets was high.'

On 28 July Hellcat pilots accounted for another 22 airborne bandits, including 13 by VF-16. That morning a dozen 'Franks' were claimed, including three by Lt Cleveland R Null and one by Lt John W Bartol. They became the last ever Hellcat aces, raising their respective scores to seven and five – their previous kills dated from 1943.

Following the atomic bomb drops on Hiroshima and Nagasaki on 6 and 9 August, TF-38 sailors and fliers anxiously awaited Japan's response. When no surrender was forthcoming, the carrier men urged their Army Air Force counterparts

Wearing distinctive rudder stripes and boasting all-white ailerons, the F6F-5s of VF-/VBF-12 were amongst the most colourful Hellcats in the Pacific in 1945. Based aboard USS *Randolph*, the 'twinned' squadrons boasted a combined fleet of nearly 60 fighters, and between them downed 125 aircraft in five months of near-solid action in Japanese home waters – pilots from the VBF unit actually outscored their VF rivals 74 to 51. Twelve aces flew with the squadrons on this tour, with six achieving this much coveted status during the 1945 deployment (*US Navy*)

Air Group 16 relieved Air Group 12 aboard *Randolph* at Leyte Gulf on 17 June 1945, and returned to the frontline the following month. By this stage in the war, aerial opposition had all but disappeared, so it came as something of a surprise when an eight-strong flight of VF-16 F6Fs was tackled by a large force of 'Franks' and 'Georges' over Ozuki on 28 July. Twelve 'Franks' and a solitary 'George' were downed without a single Hellcat being lost. Two pilots made aces during this action – Lt C L Null, whose trio of 'Franks' added to his four kills from VF-16's 1943/44 det; and Lt J W Bartol, who bagged a 'Frank' to take his tally to five. The plane-guard destroyer in this shot is HMS *Verulam* (*US Navy*)

to drop one or two more A-bombs, hoping to hasten the war's end. Instead, the endless routine of strikes and CAPs continued as before.

In the 30 days preceding the surrender – 14 July to 14 August – 89 Japanese aircraft fell to Navy pilots, this tally representing 24 units, of which 14 claimed 65 kills. With more opportunity than the others, VF-16 and -31 easily led the month-long scoring tally with 18 and 12 victories, respectively.

On the morning of 15 August, strikes were inbound to Japan when an urgent recall order was radioed. Emperor Hirohito had decreed surrender, leading to an order for the immediate cessation of hostilities. It was very much a mixed blessing. While most airborne pilots and crews gleefully dropped their ordnance offshore and returned to their carriers, others were fighting for their lives. VF-31 tangled with Zekes offshore and splashed six while *San Jacinto's* VF-49 claimed seven more A6M5s west of Mito. About the same time VF-6 shot three fighters into Sagami Bay, just before the imperial announcement.

However, VF-88 was jumped near Atsugi and was forced to fight some determined, aggressive, 'Franks' and 'Jacks'. Nine Japanese fell to the outnumbered *Yorktown* pilots, who lost four of their number.

The task force reinforced the CAP, now alerted to other recalcitrant Japanese aviators. Between 1120 and 1400, Corsairs shot down two intruders while VF-86 Hellcats off *Wasp* splashed another pair. The last Hellcat victory of the day was also the last of World War 2, Ens Clarence A Moore beating the remaining elements of his VF-31 division to gun range and duly despatching a 'Judy' dive-bomber at 1400. It was Moore's first victory, and the Hellcat's 5271st by Allied pilots.

Veterans of some of the first action seen by the Hellcat in the Pacific at Tarawa in late 1943, VF-1 returned to the frontline aboard USS *Bennington* in time to witness the death throes of Japan. Indeed, so spent a force was their once formidable enemy that only a solitary kill (a 'Judy' on 13 August) was scored on this tour. Photographed in early August, Hellcat BuNo 71351 still displays *Bennington*'s distinctive 'Christmas Tree' 'G'-symbol on its tail and ailerons, despite the carrier having been issued with the more mundane 'TT' codes the previous month (*US Navy*)

Top F6F Squadrons – July to August 1945

VF-31	*Belleau Wood*	19
VF-16	*Randolph*	18
VF-88	*Yorktown*	13
VF-49	*San Jacinto*	12
VFN-91	*Bon Homme Richard*	9
Total by 13 squadrons –		88

Top-Scoring Hellcat Pilots – July to August 1945

Lt J A Gibson	VF-49	4	Total 4
Ens P T McDonald	VF(N)-91	4	Total 4
Lt C N Nooy	VF-31	4	Total 19
Lt C L Null	VF-16	3	Total 7
Lt(jg) M Proctor	VF-88	3	Total 3
Lt(jg) G M Williams	VF-49	3	Total 3

WARTIME HISTORY OF VF-19

Fighting Squadron 19 was established at Naval Auxiliary Air Station Los Alamitos, California, on 15 August 1943. The commanding officer, Lt Cdr T Hugh Winters, was born and bred a Navy man; his father, T H Winters, Sr, had graduated from Annapolis in 1909, and was 25 years old when baby Hugh was born in South Carolina on 11 March 1913.

Winters graduated in the Naval Academy class of 1935, a prime year group for combat in World War 2. Two won the Medal of Honour, including one posthumously – in total, some 40 of Winters' classmates perished during the War, including 15 as aviators. Members of the 'Class of '35' died at Pearl Harbor, Coral Sea and Midway, whilst fellow fighter aces included Fred Bakutis (VF-20), Leonard 'Duke' Davis (VMF-121), Noel Gayler (VF-3), Eddie Outlaw (VF-32), Gordon Schechter (VF-45) and Malcolm Wordell (VF-44).

When VF-19 'stood up', Winters 'owned' one F6F-3, a J2F-5 Duck amphibian and a Piper Cub. By early September there were seven Hellcats, with 29 on hand by year's end.

In seeking a name, the squadron decided upon a way of honouring its aircraft. Therefore, 'Fighting 19' became 'Satan's Kittens,' and the name remained for three-and-a-half decades. The emblem was designed by Walt Disney Studios, and showed an angry, caped, cat astride an airborne spear holding lightning bolts in one paw.

Winters' pilots were not representative of most newly-established fighting squadrons, as his aviators included several senior- and junior-grade lieutenants happy to be out of instructing billets, some cast-offs from other squadrons, and a few former dive-bomber and floatplane pilots.

Because new *Essex*-class carriers experienced some inevitable 'slippage' in reaching the fleet, Air Group 19 had time on its hands. In seeking diversions, VF-19's intelligence officer, Lt Jack Wheeler, acquired a slot machine. Instead of mundane cherries, bells and fruit

VF-19's commissioning CO, and later its CAG, Cdr Hugh Winters, Jr, was an inspirational leader of men who was in the thick of combat throughout Air Group 19's *Lexington* deployment in 1944. He claimed eight kills and one probable during his time in the frontline, using two identically marked F6F-5s christened *HANGER LILLY* – Winters also had a flightdeck tractor similarly adorned with both this sobriquet and his familiar 'Mohawk 99' modex. This photograph was taken in late October 1944, just days prior to CAG-19 scoring his eighth, and last, kill – an 'Oscar' downed on an anti-shipping strike over Manila Bay on 5 November
(*Hugh Winters via Mark Styling*)

gum, this device was altered to ring up Zekes, 'Bettys' and 'Vals'. Officially the 'one-armed bandit' was dubbed the 'Visual Aid Recognition Machine', or 'VARM' for short.

Prior to the creation of VF-19, Los Alamitos had been a pleasantly dull little field where nothing much happened. As an elimination-training base, it allowed aviation cadets to 'bounce' in Stearman N2S biplanes, while all hands adopted genteel manners in keeping with Navy Regulations.

However, it did not take long for the unconventional Hugh Winters, or his boys, to stand out from the crowd. One pilot was caught running from a hangar to bachelor officers' quarters, wearing flight gear. This was bad enough, but the culprit failed to halt when challenged by the duty petty officer. Then, when the base commander tried to confiscate 'VARM', Winters decided enough was enough. He flew down to NAS San Diego and straightened things out with Commander, Fleet Air. After explaining the importance of 'VARM' to VF-19's morale and efficiency (not to mention the squadron party fund), a compromise was reached. 'Fighting 19' could keep the controversial gadget if Winters would accept two lieutenants (junior grade) whom no other squadron wanted.

One of the miscreants was unable to get aboard a carrier at night and the other had made an unauthorized landing at Anaheim. Winters quickly agreed, saying, 'I've got worse than that putting 60 holes in the banner target'. VF-19 continued its 'recognition training' and then carrier-qualified aboard *Altamaha* (CVE-18).

By the end of February 1944, Air Group 19 was headed for Hawaii as passengers aboard *Lexington.* Winters and company established itself on Maui and concentrated on gunnery, formation and instrument flying, as well as the obligatory socialising. The unit was dealt a cruel blow in late March when 20 pilots were ordered to VF-100 – the fleet fighter pool – and were replaced by less well-trained aviators. Many of the new men had never flown an F6F, but they were quickly assimilated into the squadron as wingmen and generally proved capable.

The squadron was shaping up well. Air discipline and radio procedures were good, and gunnery scores stood above average. Satan's Kittens were combat ready, but officialdom proved difficult. During a blackout two VF-19 ensigns 'borrowed' the base executive officer's jeep and proceeded to the Maui *Shimbun*, 'a happy place where the girls served saki and stuff'. Quickly retrieved by the shore patrol, the errant aviators faced possible return to the US, but 'skipper' Winters took punitive action by immediately grounding the pilots – from operating jeeps! His judgment proved correct, as both offenders finished the tour as aces.

The air group rode *Intrepid* to Eniwetok at the end of June and, on 9 July, flew aboard *Lexington* in Task Group 38.3. 'Lady Lex' would be VF-19's home for the next four months, the most important 120 days in the squadron's 35-year history. 'Satan's Kittens' embarked upon their combat cruise with a full complement of 37 F6F-3s, including two -3P 'photo birds'.

With only four combat-experienced pilots, including Winters, the squadron flew its first missions during strikes on Guam between 18 and 21 July. The Hellcats were armed with 500-lb bombs on nearly every flight, and encountered no enemy aircraft. Although Japanese AA fire was described as 'light,' it could not be discounted, as VF-19 lost two pilots during this period.

During late July and early August, strikes were launched against the Palaus and Bonins. A VF-19 photo pilot, Lt John Hutto, tangled with a Rufe over Urukthapol on 25 July and claimed it probably destroyed. In the latter missions on 4 and 5 August, VF-19 scored its first confirmed victories – two Zekes shot down near Iwo Jima, scored almost one year after forming at Los Alamitos. But, according to the squadron history, the flak was 'by far the most severe yet experienced'. Three pilots and four F6Fs were lost, including Lt H R Burnett, previously one of the fleet's finest SBD pilots. He had shot down two Japanese aircraft in the Solomons during 1942.

Despite the losses, morale remained high as the pilots participated in flightdeck athletics and anticipated large-scale combat. Their training stressed deflection shooting, and most felt confident that they would do well against Japanese aircraft. But squadron doctrine emphasised the importance of teamwork. As Winters said, 'On CAP: keep quiet, listen and look. On escort: no VF pilot can ever leave his VB or VT to shoot down planes that are not committing to attack same, or you'.

With the invasion of the Philippines, these concepts were put to good use. The first day of the operation was 9 September, when Winters led his Hellcats from *Lexington* to shoot up Japanese airfields in the Cagayan Vally of Mindanao. Twenty-seven enemy aircraft were claimed destroyed on the ground.

Three days later VF-19 got in its first large dogfight and won 14 to nothing. Topguns were Lt Albert Seckel with four kills and Winters with three.

As the fast carriers sent strikes over the length of the Philippines, VF-19 ranged far afield. Over 30 aircraft were strafed on Cebu during 12 September, a pattern that was set to continue during the next 48 hours as a further 80 were claimed destroyed on airfields on Negros and Panay Islands. Some of these missions involved round trips of 600 nautical miles. Following the injury of CAG Cdr Karl Jung during a ditching near the task force, Cdr Winters 'fleeted up' to become CAG-19. On 10 October, he intercepted a twin-engine Japanese aircraft 30 miles west of the task force. He closed the range, identified it as a 'Fran', and easily shot it down. Thus began the most successful 30 days in the history of American fighter aviation, that 'Fran' being the first of 1229 enemy aircraft credited to US Navy squadrons during the month.

Personally-assigned aircraft were unusual on the *Essex*-class carriers, owing to the near impossibility of properly 'spotting' (positioning) a pilot's assigned machine on the deck

'Satan's Kittens' relax in their ready room awaiting the call the main their aircraft in October 1944. The pilots visible in the front rows are, from left to right; Lt(jg) Clarence E Bartlett (one kill); a cigar-chewing Lt Roger S Boles (four kills); Lt(jg) Israel H Silvert (two kills); Lt(jg) 'Moose' Dawson; Lt 'Lin' Lindsay (eight kills); and Ens William H Martin (four kills) (*Elvin Lindsay*)

Lt(jg) Ed Copeland was one of 11 aces produced by VF-19 during their solitary frontline tour, having joined the unit soon after it was established at Los Alamitos in mid-1943. Five of Copeland's eventual tally of six kills were scored in two actions – he downed an 'Oscar' and a 'Nate' over central Formosa on the morning of 12 October 1944, and bagged a 'Nell', a 'Betty' and a 'Lily' 12 days later over Luzon, again on a morning sweep. Any chance of adding to this tally was dashed on 6 November when Copeland was shot down by AA gunners over Manila. Fortunately, he was rescued by Filipino guerrillas and returned to VF-19 on New Year's Eve (*Ed Copeland via Mark Styling*)

for launch. However, the exception to this rule was provided by air group commanders, and as CAG-19, Winters had a pet Hellcat. The combination of *Lexington's* call sign and the CAG side number rendered his airborne identity as '99 Mohawk'.

However, number 99 gained another identity, as the plane captain dubbed the F6F-5 *Hanger Lilly*, with an appropriate flower emblem. Despite the spelling error (referring to the hangar deck), '*Lilly* became a notable fixture, spotted at the head of almost every major mission flown by Air Group 19. When Winters' first CAG bird was jettisoned with battle damage, his plane captain, John Uhoch, quickly produced a duplicate, complete with both name and artwork.

Winters was succeeded as CO of VF-19 by Lt Cdr Franklin E Cook, Jr, who led 'Satan's Kittens' against Formosa on 12 October. It was the squadron's hardest combat to date. Outnumbered as much as six to one, the *Lexington* Hellcats claimed 28.5 kills for the loss of two pilots and three aircraft, with several other F6Fs damaged. One of the missing fliers was Lt Cdr Cook, who was replaced by the next senior pilot, Lt Roger Boles. Three small combats later in the day raised the squadron tally to 33.5 victories. The 'Kittens'' first aces were crowned on 12 October as Cdr Winters and Lt Joseph J Paskoski logged their fifth aerial victories. Lt(jg) William J Masoner, Jr, dropped three Zekes on this day which, combined with two prior victories scored with VF-11 in 1943, also made him an ace. Two days later Lt(jg) Luther D Prater ran his score to 5.5 victories, all with VF-19.

Undoubtedly, the two busiest days in the squadron's history were 24-25 October 1944, otherwise known as the Battle of Leyte Gulf. On the 24th the squadron had expanded to 41 Hellcats, including 24 new F6F-5s. In addition to its two-aircraft photo section, VF-19 also now boasted a flight of three nightfighter Hellcats as well. To find employment for all these aircraft, 'Fighting 19' sent search teams across the central Philippines looking for Japanese fleet units and targets of opportunity. On one of these searches north of Manila, Lt Masoner hit the aerial jackpot. He came across four hostile formations and shot down six twin-engined aircraft (four 'Nells', a 'Dinah' and a 'Betty'), all confirmed by gun camera. The rest of his division accounted for a further seven aircraft, including three which fell to his wingman, Ens William E Copeland. Besides Masoner and Copeland, three other VF-19 aces emerged from the day's combats. They included Lt Elvin L Lindsay, whose team met heavy fighter opposition over Clark Field and shot down ten bandits. In all, VF-19 search teams had claimed 30 victories.

Meanwhile, TG-38.3 was coming under heavy attack. A scramble was ordered, and as VF-19 pilots sprinted down the flightdeck to man aircraft, 'Lex's' AA gunners actually cheered them on. Lt Boles' Hellcats splashed a dozen raiders during this attack, although the F6F CAP failed to prevent the light carrier *Princeton* from being mortally damaged.

By mid-morning CAG Winters was leading a strike against Japanese warships in the Sibuyan Sea. The fighters strafed to suppress flak as the carrier bombers attacked under low clouds which restricted visibility. During this mission, and subsequent flights, another 12 bandits were splashed, which helped establish a squadron record of 52 kills and nine probables during a single day's operations, against the loss of one pilot.

Twenty-four hours later Cdr Winters was again target co-ordinator, directing several strikes against the Japanese carrier force off Cape Engano, Luzon. The targets were one heavy and three light carriers, plus two battleships and several escorts. Air opposition was weak, but Lt Boles downed a Zero while leading an attack against a CVL. *Lexington* aircraft were credited with shares in sinking or damaging four enemy warships, as VF-19 had attacked with bombs.

A brief study of just one pilot's activity during this period indicates the sustained nature of VF-19's operations. From 22 September to 25 October Lt Bruce W Williams shot down seven enemy aircraft, bombed a battleship and won the Navy Cross, three DFCs and the Air Medal. A pre-war law student from Salem, Oregon, Williams got to fighters via OS2Us. Because *Lexington's* callsign was 'Mohawk', Williams became known in the task force as 'Willy Mohawk'.

During this time, Williams was flying a damaged Hellcat back from a bombing mission 'clear to hell and gone west of Palawan'. Concerned that the task group would have departed the prebriefed recovery site, he tried a maximum-range radio call, 'This is "Willie Mohawk". I'm hit and I'm trying to make it in.' When he reached Point Option, 'Lady Lex' was still there to take him aboard. Bruce Williams felt that Vice Adm Marc Mitscher, riding in *Lexington*, had kept the force steaming west in order to retrieve the lone Hellcat pilot.

On 5 November Lt Boles led a fighter sweep over Luzon, and Lt Herman J Rossi made ace. However, 'Smiley' Boles was hit by AA fire and crashed south of Manila. He was succeeded by 25-year-old Lt Elvin Lindsay. 'Lin' Lindsay became VF-19's third skipper in three weeks – undoubtedly the youngest squadron CO in the US Navy.

Whilst the Luzon raid was occuring four suicide Zekes attacked *Lexington*. AA gunners splashed three, but the fourth proved both determined and skilful. He struck astern of the island, to starboard, killing 50 men, including 11 from the air group.

Ed Copeland was still evading capture in the jungles of Luzon when this shot of the remaining ten aces in VF-19 was taken in December 1944. Standing, left to right, are; Lt B W Williams (seven kills), Lt J J Paskoski (six kills), Lt E L Lindsay (eight kills), Cdr T H Winters (eight kills), Lt W J Masoner (12 kills) and H J Rossi, Jr, (six kills). Kneeling, left to right, are; Lt A Seckel (six kills), Ens P O'Mara (seven kills), Lt J Wheeler (Air Combat Intelligence Officer), Ens R A Farnsworth (five kills) and Lt(jg) L D Prater (8.5 kills) (*Elvin Lindsay*)

The next day the 'Kittens' flamed 13 bandits, raising Lt Albert Seckel and Ens R A Farnsworth to acedom. Seckel got an 'Oscar', then chased an unidentified single-engined fighter to sugar-cane level where the enemy pilot bailed out. With his parachute streaming, the luckless Japanese smashed into a tree. Later it was determined that VF-19 had shot down the first Kawanishi N1K 'George' to fall to allied fire. Farnsworth made ace the hard way, taking the wing off a 'Tojo' in a mid-air collision, but another pilot was lost during the sweep – the 16th attributed to enemy action.

Lexington returned to Ulithi, expecting to head out soon, but word arrived informing Cdr Winters that Air Group 19's tour was over. The 'Kittens', with their bomber and 'torpecker' shipmates, would be home for Christmas.

By the end of the deployment, 38 VF-19 pilots were credited with 155 confirmed victories and 16 probables. The 11 aces claimed 76.5 kills, or very nearly half the squadron total. Almost 200 more enemy aircraft were thought to have been destroyed on the ground. 'Satan's Kittens' were awarded 98 combat decorations, comprising 16 Navy Crosses, nine Silver Stars, 32 DFCs, 25 Air Medals and 16 Purple Hearts.

What the well-equipped fighter ace used for transport when out of the cockpit. Lt 'Lin' Lindsay became the CO of VF-19 at just 25, following the death in combat over Manila of 'Smiley' Boles on 5 November 1944. This shot was taken early in 1945 whilst Lindsay was helping to establish the newly-formed VBF-19 in Hawaii. The aircraft is an F4U-4, as operated by his new unit, whilst the motorcycle is an Indian (*Elvin Lindsay*)

But more importantly, Winters' goal of perfection in the escort role was met – not one Air Group 19 Helldiver or Avenger was lost to Japanese fighters. In fact 'Torpedo 19' claimed two shootdowns and 'Bombing 19' an exceptional 11 – probably the highest among all SB2C units.

'Fighting 19' began the New Year by reforming at NAS Alameda, near San Francisco, in February 1945. The new commanding officer was Lt Cdr Joseph G Smith. In keeping with the revised carrier air group composition, a fighter-bomber squadron was formed from VF-19, designated VBF-19 with F4U Corsairs.

Upon moving to NAAS Santa Rosa in May, 'Satan's Kittens' became the first squadron to receive F8F-1 Bearcats. After completion of further training, VF-19 boarded the light carrier *Langley*, once more Hawaii-bound. Arriving on 8 August, the squadron set up additional training but the war was rapidly winding down. On the 15th – the squadron's second anniversary – the Japanese agreed to unconditional surrender, and VF-19's war was over.

VF-19 Aces

Lt W J Masoner, Jr	10 (+2 in F4Fs with VF-11)
Lt(jg) L D Prater	8.5
Lt E.L. Lindsay	8
Cdr T H Winters	8
Ens P O'Mara, Jr	7
Lt B W Williams	7
Ens W E Copeland	6
Lt J J Paskoski	6
Lt H J Rossi, Jr	6
Lt A Seckel, Jr	6
Ens R A Farnsworth, Jr	5

THE APPENDICES

Corsair Squadrons in which aces served

USMC
VMFs -112, -113, -121, -122, -124, -211, -212, -213, -214, -215, -221, -222, -223, -311, -312, -321, -322, -323, -351 and -451

USN
VFs -5, -10, -17, -84, -85 and VBF-83

FAA
No 47 NW and No 1836 Sqn

Aces' Corsair Carrier Deployments

HMS *Victorious*
No 1836 Sqn (July 1944-August 1945) – Sheppard
No 47 FW (July 1944-August 1945) – Hay

USS *Essex* (CV-9)
VMF-124 (January-March 1945) – Finn
VMF-213 (January-March 1945) – Thomas
VBF-83 (March-August 1945) – Godson, W H Harris, Kincaid and Reidy

USS *Intrepid* (CV-11)
VF-10 (March-August 1945) – Clarke, Farmer, Gray, Heath, Kirkwood, Lerch and Quiel

USS *Franklin* (CV-13)
VF-5 (February-March 1945) – Schiller

USS *Bunker Hill* (CV-17)
VF-84 (January-June 1945) – Chambers, Freeman, Gildea, Hedrick, Laney Marchant, Sargent and Smith
VMF-221 (February-May 1945) – Snider, Balch, Baldwin and Swett
VMF-451 (February-May 1945) – Long and Donnahue

USS *Bennington* (CV-20)
VMF-112 (January-June 1945) Hansen and Owen

USS *Shangri-La* (CV-38)
VF-85 (May-August 1945) – Robbins

USS *Cape Gloucester* (CVE-109)
VMF-351 (April-August 1945) – Yost

Corsair Aces

This comprehensive list covers only aerial victories that were officially credited. Included are aces that gained kills in other types as well as the F4U. The unit entries give the squadron in which a pilot scored the majority of his F4U kills. Credits are listed as Destroyed/Probable/Damaged, whilst the figure in brackets gives the pilot's F4U kills if he scored victories in other fighters as well. In total the aces scored 545.25 kills in the South West Pacific, compared to 240.083 in the Central Pacific.

Name	*Rank*	*Service*	*Unit*	*Kills (F4U)*
Aldrich, D N	Capt	USMC	VMF-215;	20/6/0
Alley, Jr, S C	2nd Lt	USMC	VMF-323	5/0/0
Axtell, Jr G C	Maj	USMC	VMF-323	6/0/3
Balch; D L	Capt	USMC	VMF-221	5/1/2
Baldwin, F B	Capt	USMC	VMF-221	5/1/12.5
Blackburn, J T	Lt Cdr	USN	VF-17	11/5/3
Bolt, Jnr, J F	1st Lt	USMC	VMF-214	6/0/0
Boyington,G	Maj	USMC	VMF-214	28/4/0 (22)
Braun, R L	Capt	USMC	VMF-215	5/2/1
Brown, Jr, W P	2nd Lt	USMC	VMF-311	7/0/0
Burris, H M	Lt(jg)	USN	VF-17	7.5/0/0
Carl, M E	Maj	USMC	VMF-223	18.5/0/3 (2)
Carlton,W A	Capt	USMC	VMF-212	5/2/1
Case,W N	1st Lt	USMC	VMF-214	8/1/0
Caswell, D	2nd Lt	USMC	VMF-221	7/1/0
Chambers, C J	Lt(jg)	USN	VF-84	5.333/0/1
Chandler, C	1st Lt	USMC	VMF-215	6/0/0
Chenoweth, O I	Lt	USN	VF-17	8.5/2/0 (7.5)
Clarke, W E	Lt Cdr	USN	VF-10	7/0/0 (3)
Conant, A R	Capt	USMC	VMF-215	6/3/0
Cordray, P	Lt	USN	VF-17/-10	7/1/3
Crowe, W E	Capt	USMC	VMF-124	7/1/1
Cunningham, D G	Lt(jg)	USN	VF-17	7/0/1.25
Cupp, J N	Capt	USMC	VMF-213	12.5/2/0
Davenport, M W	Lt	USN	VF-17	6.25/0/0
DeLong, P C	1st Lt	USMC	VMF-212	11.166/1/2
Dillard, J V	1st Lt	USMC	VMF-323	6.333/0/0
Dillow, E	1st Lt	USMC	VMF-221	6/2/1
Donahue, A G	Maj	USMC	VMF-112	14/1/0 (12)
Dorroh, J D	Maj	USMC	VMF-323	6/2/0
Drake, C W	2nd Lt	USMC	VMF-323	5/1/0
Durnford, D F	2nd Lt	USMC	VMF-323	6.333/0/0
Elwood, H McJ	Maj	USMC	VMF-212	5.166/2/0
Everton, L D	Maj	USMC	VMF-113	12/1/0 (2)
Farmer, C D	Lt(jg)	USN	VF-10	7.25/0/0 (4)
Farrel, W	1st Lt	USMC	VMF-312	5/1/0
Finn, H J	Capt	USMC	VMF-124	6/0/05
Fisher, D E	1st Lt	USMC	VMF-214	6/1/0
Ford, K M	Capt	USMC	VMF-121	5/1/0
Freeman, D C	Lt	USN	VF-17/-84	9/2/0
Gildea, J T	Lt(jg)	USN	VF-84	7/1/2
Gile, C D	Lt	USN	VF-17	8/0/05
Godson, L W	Lt	USN	VBF-83	5/0/0
Gray, L E	Lt(jg)	USN	VF-10	5.25/0/0 (2)

Name	Rank	Service	Unit	Kills (F4U)
Gutt, F E	Capt	USMC	VMF-223	8/0/1(4)
Hacking, Jr, A E	1st Lt	USMC	VMF-221	5/0/0
Hall, S O	1st Lt	USMC	VMF-213	6/0/0
Hansen, Jr, H	Maj	USMC	VMF-112	5.5/0/2.5
Hanson, R M	1st Lt	USMC	VMF-215/-214	25/2/0
Harris, W H	Lt	USN	VBF-83	5/0/1
Hay, R C	Lt Col	RM	No 47 NW	7/0/3 (4)
Heath, H W	Ens	USN	VF-10	7/0/0
Hedrick, R R	Lt Cdr	USN	VF-17/-84	12/0/4
Hernan, Jr, E J	1st Lt	USMC	VMF-215	8/1/0
Hood, Jr, W L	1st Lt	USMC	VMF-323	5.5/0/2
Hundley, J C	1st Lt	USMC	VMF-211	6/1/0
Ireland, J W	Maj	USMC	VMF-211	5.333/2/0
Jensen, A J	1st Lt	USMC	VMF-214/-441	7/1/0
Jones, C D	2nd Lt	USMC	VMF-222	6/1/1
Kepford, I C	Lt(jg)	USN	VF-17	16/1/1
Kincaid, R A	Lt	USN	VBF-83	5/0/0
Kirkwood, P L	Lt(jg)	USN	VF-10	12/1/0 (8)
Laney, W G	Lt	USN	VF-84	5/2/1
Lerch, A	Ens	USN	VF-10	7/0/0
Long, H H	Maj	USMC	VMF-121/-451	10/0/0 (7)
Lynch, J P	Capt	USMC	VMF-224	5.5/0/0 (2)
Maas, Jr, J B	Maj	USMC	VMF-112/-322	5.5/1/0 (2.5)
Magee, C L	1st Lt	USMC	VMF-214	9/2/0
Maberry, L A	Lt(jg)	USN	VF-84	5/0/0
March, Jr, H A	Lt	USN	VF-17	5/0/0 (4)
May, E	Lt(jg)	USN	VF-17	8.5/0/0
McCartney H A	1st Lt	USMC	VMF-121/-214	5/2.5/0 (4)
McClurg R W	1st Lt	USMC	VMF-214	7/2/0
McManus, J	1st Lt	USMC	VMF-221	6/0/0
Mims, R	Lt(jg)	USN	VF-17	6/3/0
Morgan, J L	1st Lt	USMC	VMF-213	8.5/0/0
Mullen, P A	1st Lt	USMC	VMF-214/-122/-112	6.5/1/1
O'Keefe, J J	1st Lt	USMC	VMF-323	7/0/0
Olander, E L	Capt	USMC	VMF-214	5/4/0
Overend, E F	Maj	USMC	VMF-321	8.333/0/0 (3)
Owen, D C	Capt	USMC	VMF-112	5/0/1 (2.5)
Owens, Jr, R G	Maj	USMC	VMF-215	7/4/0
Percy, J G	1st Lt	USMC	VMF-112	6/0/1 (1)

Name	Rank	Service	Unit	Kills (F4U)
Pierce, Jr, F E	Capt	USMC	VMF-121	6/1/0 (1)
Pittman Jr, J	2nd Lt	USMC	VMF-221	5/2/0 (3)
Porter, R B	Maj	USMC	VMF-121	5/1/1 (3)
Poske, G 'H'	Maj	USMC	VMF-212	5/1/0
Post, Jr, N T	Maj	USMC	VMF-221	8/0/0 (5)
Powell, E A	Capt	USMC	VMF-122	5/0/0 (4)
Quiel, N R	Ens	USN	VF-10	6/0/0
Reidy, T H	Lt	USN	VBF-83	10/0/0
Reinburg, J H	Maj	USMC	VMF-122	7/2/0 (4)
Robbins, J D	Lt	USN	VF-85	5/0/1 (3)
Ruhsam, J W	1st Lt	USMC	VMF-323	7/0/3
Sapp, D H	Maj	USMC	VMF-222	10/4/2
Sargent, J J	Lt(jg)	USN	VF-84	5.25/0/2 (1)
Scarborough, Jr, H V	1st Lt	USMC	VMF-214	5/0/0
Schiller, J E	Lt(jg)	USN	VF-5	5/1/0 (1)
See, R B	1st Lt	USMC	VMF-321	5/0/0
Segal, H E	1st Lt	USMC	VMF-221	12/1/0
Shaw, E O	1st Lt	USMC	VMF-213	14.5/1/0
Sheppard, D J	Lt	RCNVR	No 1836 Sqn	5/1/0
Shuman, P L	Capt	USMC	VMF-121	6/1/0
Sigler, W E	Capt	USMC	VMF-112/124	5.333/1/0 (4.333)
Smith, J M	Lt(jg)	USN	VF-17/-84	10/3/1
Snider, W N	1st Lt	USMC	VMF-221	11.5/1/0 (8.5)
Spears, H L	Capt	USMC	VMF-215	15/3/0
Streig, F J	Lt(jg)	USN	VF-17	5/0/2
Swett, J E	Capt	USMC	VMF-221	15.5/4/0.25 (8.5)
Synar, S T	1st Lt	USMC	VMF-112	5/0/0 (3)
Terrill, F A	1st Lt	USMC	VMF-323	6.083/0/4
Thomas, Jr, F C	1st Lt	USMC	VMF-211	9/2.5/4
Thomas, W J	Capt	USMC	VMF-213	18.5/3.333/3
Valentine, H J	Capt	USMC	VMF-312	6/1/0
Vedder, M N	1st Lt	USMC	VMF-213	6/0/0 (4)
Wade, R	1st Lt	USMC	VMF-323	7/0/3
Walsh, K A	Capt	USMC	VMF-124/-222	21/2/1
Warner, A T	Maj	USMC	VMF-215	8/2/0 (7)
Weissenberger, G J	Maj	USMC	VMF-213	5/0/0
Wells, A P	1st Lt	USMC	VMF-323	5/0/0
Williams G M H	1st Lt	USMC	VMF-215	7/2/0
Yost, D K	Lt Col	USMC	VMF-351	8/0/0 (2)
Yunck, M R	Maj	USMC	VMF-311	5/0/0 (2)

COLOUR PLATES

1
F4U-1 black 17 of 1st Lt Howard J Finn, VMF-124, Guadalcanal, February 1943

Finn was flying this aircraft on 14 February during the 'St Valentines Day Massacre'. He left formation to chase a lone Zero and was then attacked by more aircraft. He returned to the formation, taking refuge under a B-24, the gunners of which claimed the destruction of one of his pursuers. The next day AAF intelligence officers arrived at his base requesting that the 'pilot of "No 17"' verify the gunners claim. This aircraft has the early style black code under the canopy as it appeared at the start of the unit's combat operations. The two-tone paint scheme consisted of Blue Grey upper surfaces with Light Grey under surfaces, except for the folding portion of the wing where the upper surface colour was also used.

2
F4U-1 white 13/BuNo 02350 of 2nd Lt Kenneth A Walsh, VMF-124, Munda, August 1943

The aircraft wears a revised white 13 forward of the national insignia. The early style black number can still be seen under the canopy and on the cowling. When VMF–124 first received their Corsairs, the CO, Maj Gise, assigned aircraft to each of his pilots, and they were required to work on the Corsair with the crewchiefs in order to familiarise themselves with the F4U-1.

3
F4U-1 white 114 of 2nd Lt Kenneth A Walsh, VMF-124, Munda, August 1943

Walsh destroyed two *Val*s and a Zero in this machine near Vella Lavella on 15 August 1943. Although his log book shows he was flying BuNo

APPENDICES

Top-Scoring Pacific Escort Carrier F6F Units

VF-60	*Suwannee*	1943-44	25
VF-37	*Sangamon*	1943-44	20
VF-35	*Chenango*	1943-44	9
VF-40	*Suwannee*	1945	9 (+20 previously*)
VF-24	*Santee*	1945	3 (+34.5 previously*)
VF-25	*Chenango*	1945	3 (+34 previously*)

*Previous scores achieved whilst land-based or aboard light carriers

Top-Scoring Pacific CVE Hellcat Pilots

Lt(jg) K W Kenyon	VF-37	4
Lt(jg) R A Singleton	VF-60	3.25
Ens J E Donnelly	VF-37	3
Lt Cdr J C Longino	VF-40	3

Top 25 Hellcat Units 1943-1945

VF-15	*Essex*	310
VF-9	*Essex, Lexington, Yorktown*	250.75
VF-2	*Enterprise, Hornet*	248
VF-18	*Intrepid*	176.5
VF-31	*Cabot, Belleau Wood*	165.60
VF-17	*Hornet*	161
VF-30	*Belleau Wood, Monterey*	159.83
VF-80	*Ticonderoga, Hancock*	159.50
VF-20	*Enterprise, Lexington*	158.16
VF-8	*Bunker Hill*	156
VF-19	*Lexington*	155
VF-16	*Lexington, Randolph*	154.50
VF-14	*Wasp*	147
VF-83	*Essex*	137
VF-27	*Princeton, Independence*	135
VF-5	*Yorktown*	126.50
VBF-17	*Hornet*	121
VF-29	*Cabot*	113
VBF-12	*Randolph*	109
VF-11	*Hornet*	103
VF-1	*Yorktown*	101
VF-33	Solomons and *Sangamon*	90.50
VF-10	*Enterprise*	88
VF-13	*Franklin*	86
VF-82	*Bennington*	85
	Total	**3696.84**

Top Hellcat Aces

Cdr David McCampbell	VF-15	34	Twice ace in a day
Lt Eugene A Valencia	VF-9	23	6 on 17/4/45
Lt Cecil E Harris	VF-18	22	Plus 1 in F4Fs
Lt Patrick D Fleming	VF-80	19	5 on 16/2/45
Lt Cornelius Nooy	VF-31	19	5 on 21/9/44
Lt Alexander Vraciu	VF-6/-16	19	6 on 19/6/44
Lt(jg) Douglas Baker	VF-20	16.333	KIA 14/12/44
Lt Arther R Hawkins	VF-31	14	5 on 13/9/44
Lt John L Wirth	VF-31	14	
Lt Cdr George C Duncan	VF-15	13.5	
Lt(jg) Roy W Rushing	VF-15	13	6 on 24/10/44
Lt John R Strane	VF-15	13	
Lt(jg) Wendell V Twelves	VF-15	13	
Lt Daniel A Carmichael	VF-2/VBF-12	12	
Lt Cdr Hamilton McWhorter III	VF-9/-12	12	First F6F ace
Lt James A Shirley	VF-27	12	5 on 24/10/44
Lt Clement M Craig	VF-22	11.75	5 on 21/1/45
Lt(jg) George R Carr	VF-15	11.5	5 on 19/6/44
Cdr William A Dean, Jr,	VF-2	11	
Lt(jg) James B French	VF-9	11	
Lt Harvey P Picken	VF-18	11	5 on 21/9/44
Ens James V Reber, Jr,	VF-30	11	
Lt Cdr James Rigg	VF-15	11	5 on 12/9/44
Lt Cdr Marshall U Beebe	VF-17	10.5	5 on 18/3/45
Lt Carl A Brown, Jr,	VF-27	10.5	5 on 24/10/44
Lt(jg) Robert E Murray	VF-29	10.333	
Lt Cdr Leonard J Check	VF-7	10	
Lt Thaddeus T Coleman, Jr	VF-6/-83	10	
Lt(jg) Charles M Mallory	VF-18	10	5 on 21/9/44
Lt William J Masoner, Jr,	VF-19	10	Plus 2 in F4Fs
Lt(jg) Harris E Mitchell	VF-9	10	
Lt(jg) Arthur Singer, Jr	VF-15	10	
Lt Armistead B Smith, Jr,	VF-9/VBF-12	10	
Lt James Stewart	VF-31	10	
Lt Charles R Stimpson	VF-11	10	5 on 14/10/44 Plus 6 on F4Fs
Lt Robert C Coats	VF-17/-18	9.333	5 on 18/3/45
Lt(jg) Eugene D Redmond	VF-2/-10	9.25	
Lt Cdr Paul D Buie	VF-16	9	
Lt(jg) Robert B Carlson	VF-30/-40	9	
Cdr William M Collins, Jr,	VF-8	9	5 on 12/10/44
Lt Richard T Eastmond	VF-1	9	
Lt(jg) Thomas S Harris	VF-18	9	
Lt(jg) Daniel R Rehm, Jr,	VF-8/-50	9	
Lt Arthur Van Haren, Jr,	VF-2	9	
Lt(jg) Charles E Watts	VF-17/-18	8.75	
Lt Robert H Anderson	VF-80	8.5	5 on 14/12/44
Lt(jg) John L Banks	VF-2	8.5	
Ens Carl C Foster	VF-30	8.5	6 on 6/4/45
Lt(jg) Everett C Hargreaves	VF-2	8.5	5 on 24/6/44
Ens George W Pigman, Jr,	VF-15	8.5	
Ens Claude W Plant, Jr,	VF-15	8.5	
Lt(jg) Luther D Prater, Jr,	VF-19	8.5	
Ens Larry Self	VF-15	8.5	
Lt(jg) Eric A Evenson	VF-30	8.25	
Lt John F Gray	VF-5	8.25	

Bibliography

Brown, J D, *Carrier Operations in World War II. Vol. 1: The Royal Navy.* Ian Allan, London, England, 1968

Foss, J, and Simpson, W, *Flying Marine.* Zenger Publishing, 1979

Hata, I and Izawa, Y, *Japanese Naval Aces and Fighter Units.* Naval Institute Press, Annapolis, Maryland, 1989

Hess, W N, *American Fighter Aces Album.* American Fighter Aces Association, 1978

Lundstrom, J B, *The First Team.* US Naval Institute Press, 1984

Lundstrom, J B, *The First Team and the Guadalcanal campaign.* US Naval Institute Press, 1984

Millwe, T, *The Catus Air Force.* Harper and Row, 1969

Olynyk, F, *USMC Credits for Destruction of Enemy Aircraft in Air-to-air Combat, World War II.* Privately Published, 1981

Olynyk, F, *US Navy Victory Credits for Destruction of Enemy Aircraft in Aerial Combat, World War II.* Privately published, 1982

Olynyk, F, *Stars & Bars, A Tribute to the American Fighter Ace 1920–73.* Grub Street, London, England, 1995

Polmar, N, *Aircraft Carriers.* Doubleday, New York, 1969

Robertson, B, *Aircraft Camouflage and Markings 1907–1954.* Harleyford, 1964

Sherrod, R, *History of Marine Corps Aviation in World War II.* Armed Forces Press, 1952

Sturtivant, R, *British Naval Aviation: Fleet Air Arm, 1917–1990.* Naval Institute Press, Annapolis, Maryland, 1990

Sturtivant, R, and Balance, T, *The Squadrons of the Fleet Air Arm.* Air Britain Publications, 1994

Styling, M, *Corsair Aces of World War 2.* Osprey Publishing, London, England, 1996

Tillman, B, *Carrier Battle in the Philippine Sea.* Phlanx, St Paul, Minnesota, 1994

Tillman, B, *Hellcat: The FH6 in World War II.* Naval Institute Press, Annapolis, Maryland, 1979

Tillman, B, *Wildcat Aces of World War 2.* Osprey Publishing, London, England, 1995

Toliver, R, and Constable, T, *Fighter Aces.* Macmillan, New York, 1965

Winters, T H, *Skipper: Confessions of a Fighter Squadron Commander.* Champlin Fighter Museum Press, Mesa, Arizona, 1985

INDEX

References to illustrations are shown in **bold**. Colour Plates are prefixed 'pl.' and Figure Plates 'fig.pl.', with page and caption locators in brackets.